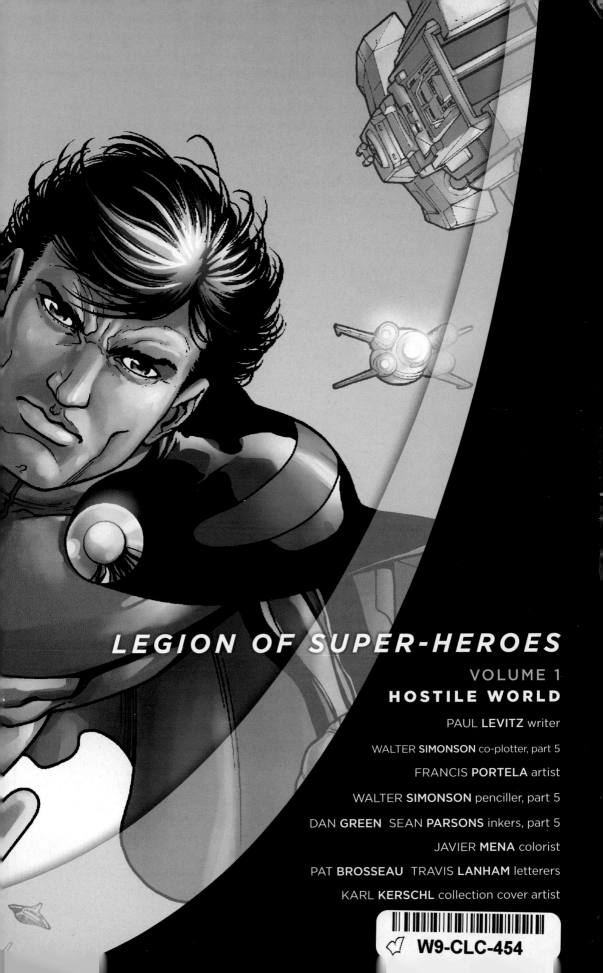

LEGION OF SUPER-HEROES

VOLUME 1
HOSTILE WORLD

PAUL **LEVITZ** writer

WALTER **SIMONSON** co-plotter, part 5

FRANCIS **PORTELA** artist

WALTER **SIMONSON** penciller, part 5

DAN **GREEN** SEAN **PARSONS** inkers, part 5

JAVIER **MENA** colorist

PAT **BROSSEAU** TRAVIS **LANHAM** letterers

KARL **KERSCHL** collection cover artist

W9-CLC-454

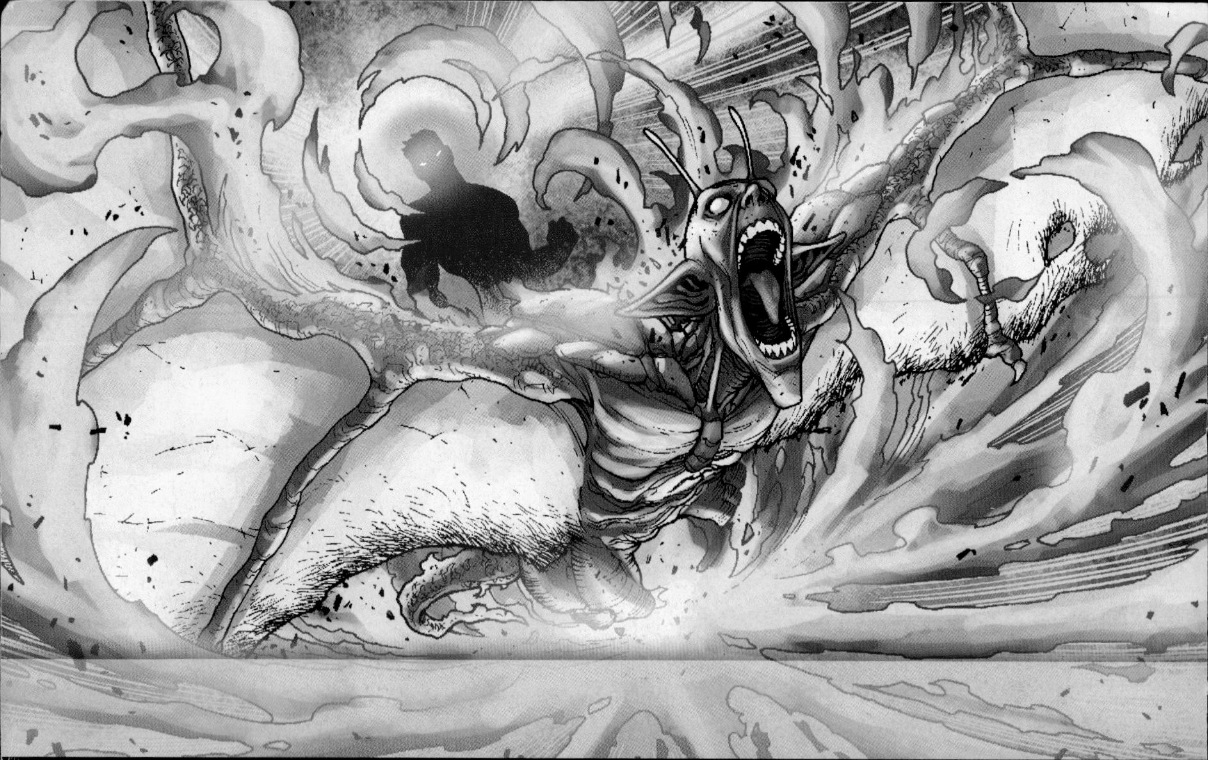

CHRIS CONROY Editor – Original Series ROWENA YOW Editor
ROBBIN BROSTERMAN Design Director – Books ROBBIE BIEDERMAN Publication Design

BOB HARRAS VP – Editor-in-Chief

DIANE NELSON President DAN DIDIO and JIM LEE Co-Publishers
GEOFF JOHNS Chief Creative Officer
JOHN ROOD Executive VP – Sales, Marketing and Business Development
AMY GENKINS Senior VP – Business and Legal Affairs NAIRI GARDINER Senior VP – Finance
JEFF BOISON VP – Publishing Operations MARK CHIARELLO VP – Art Direction and Design
JOHN CUNNINGHAM VP – Marketing TERRI CUNNINGHAM VP – Talent Relations and Services
ALISON GILL Senior VP – Manufacturing and Operations DAVID HYDE VP – Publicity
HANK KANALZ Senior VP – Digital JAY KOGAN VP – Business and Legal Affairs, Publishing
JACK MAHAN VP – Business Affairs, Talent NICK NAPOLITANO VP – Manufacturing Administration
SUE POHJA VP – Book Sales COURTNEY SIMMONS Senior VP – Publicity
BOB WAYNE Senior VP – Sales

LEGION OF SUPER-HEROES VOLUME 1: HOSTILE WORLD

cover art by KARL KERSCHL

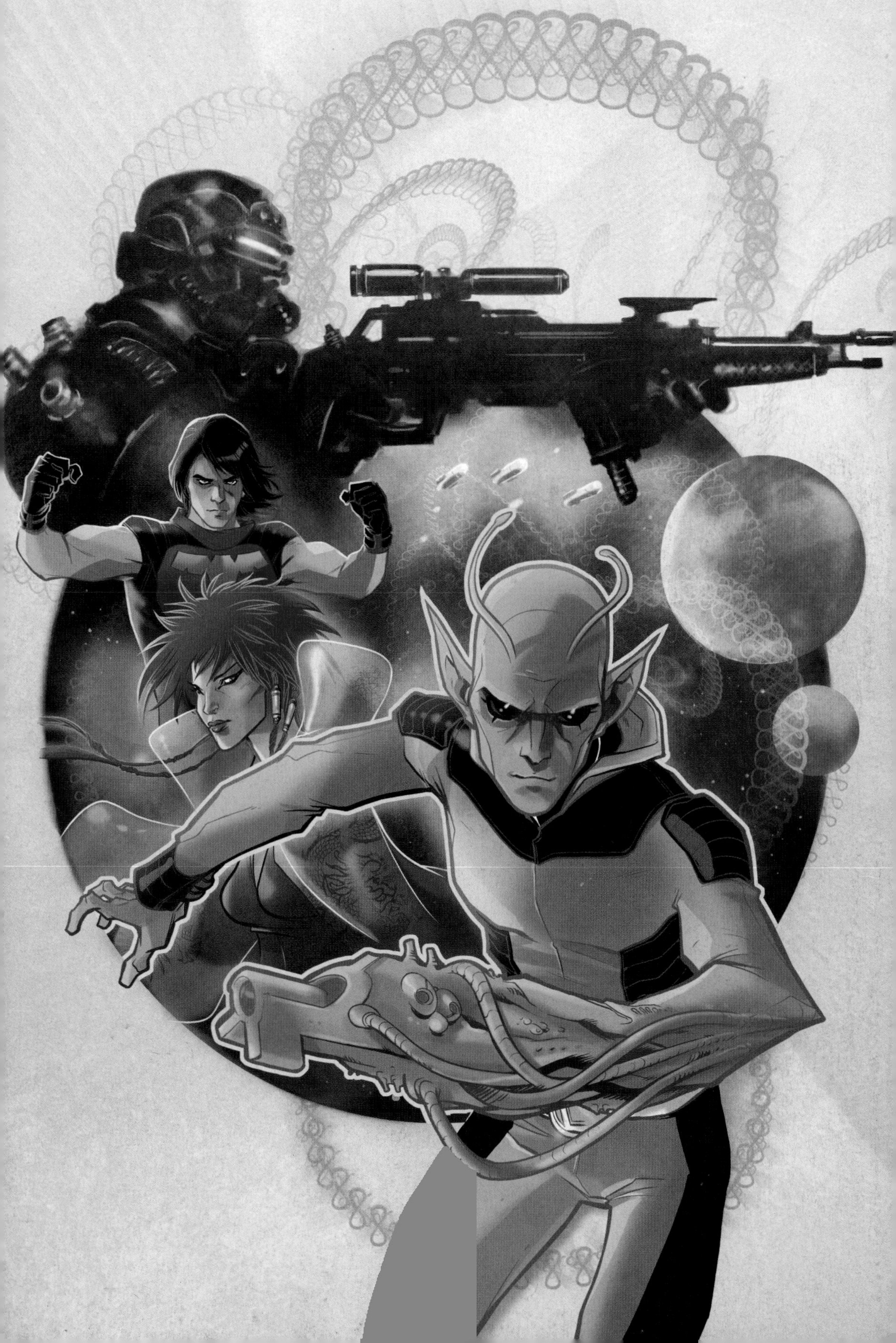

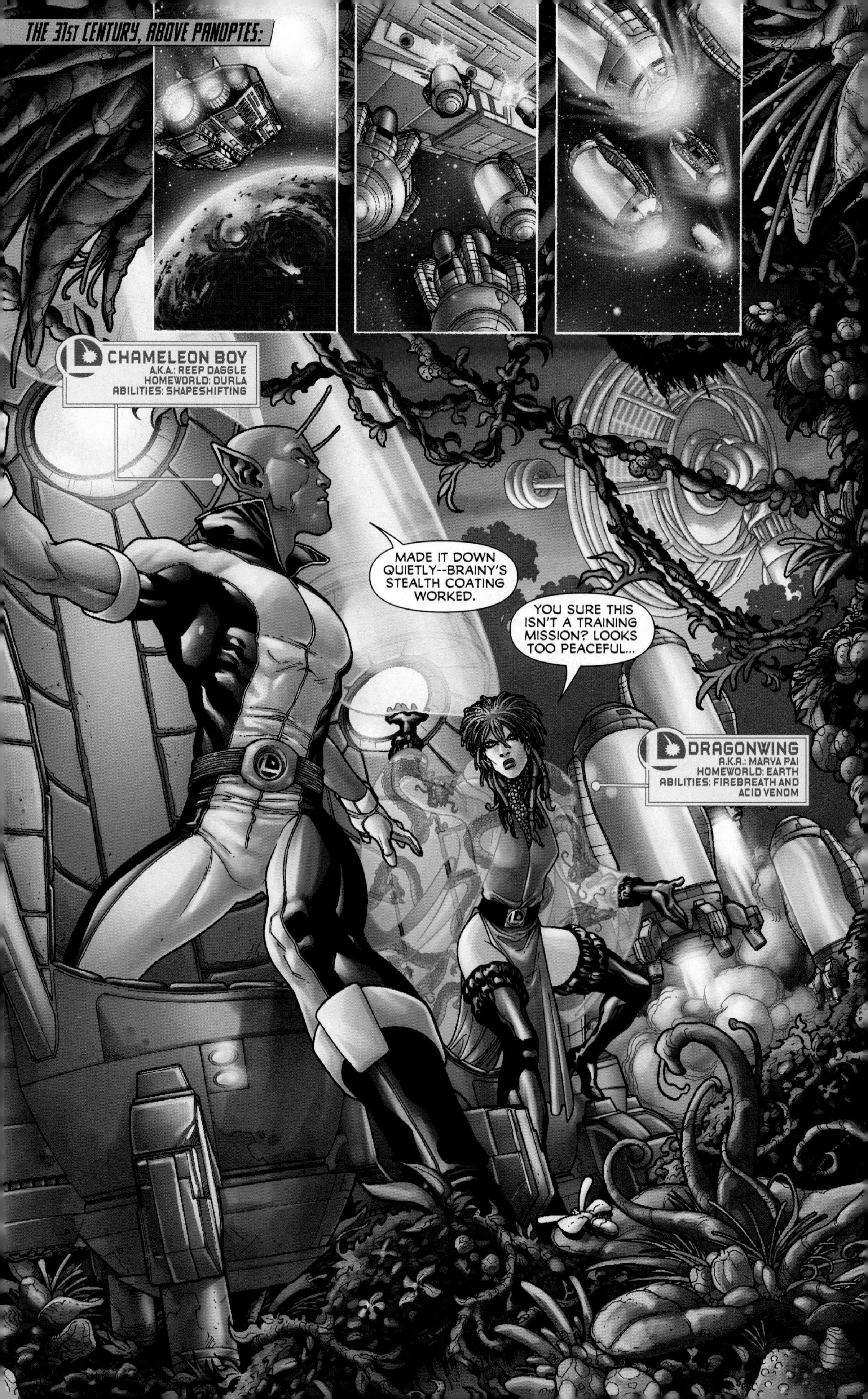
THE 31ST CENTURY, ABOVE PANOPTES:
CHAMELEON BOY
A.K.A.: REEP DAGGLE
HOMEWORLD: DURLA
ABILITIES: SHAPESHIFTING
MADE IT DOWN QUIETLY--BRAINY'S STEALTH COATING WORKED.
YOU SURE THIS ISN'T A TRAINING MISSION? LOOKS TOO PEACEFUL...
DRAGONWING
A.K.A.: MARYA PAI
HOMEWORLD: EARTH
ABILITIES: FIREBREATH AND ACID VENOM

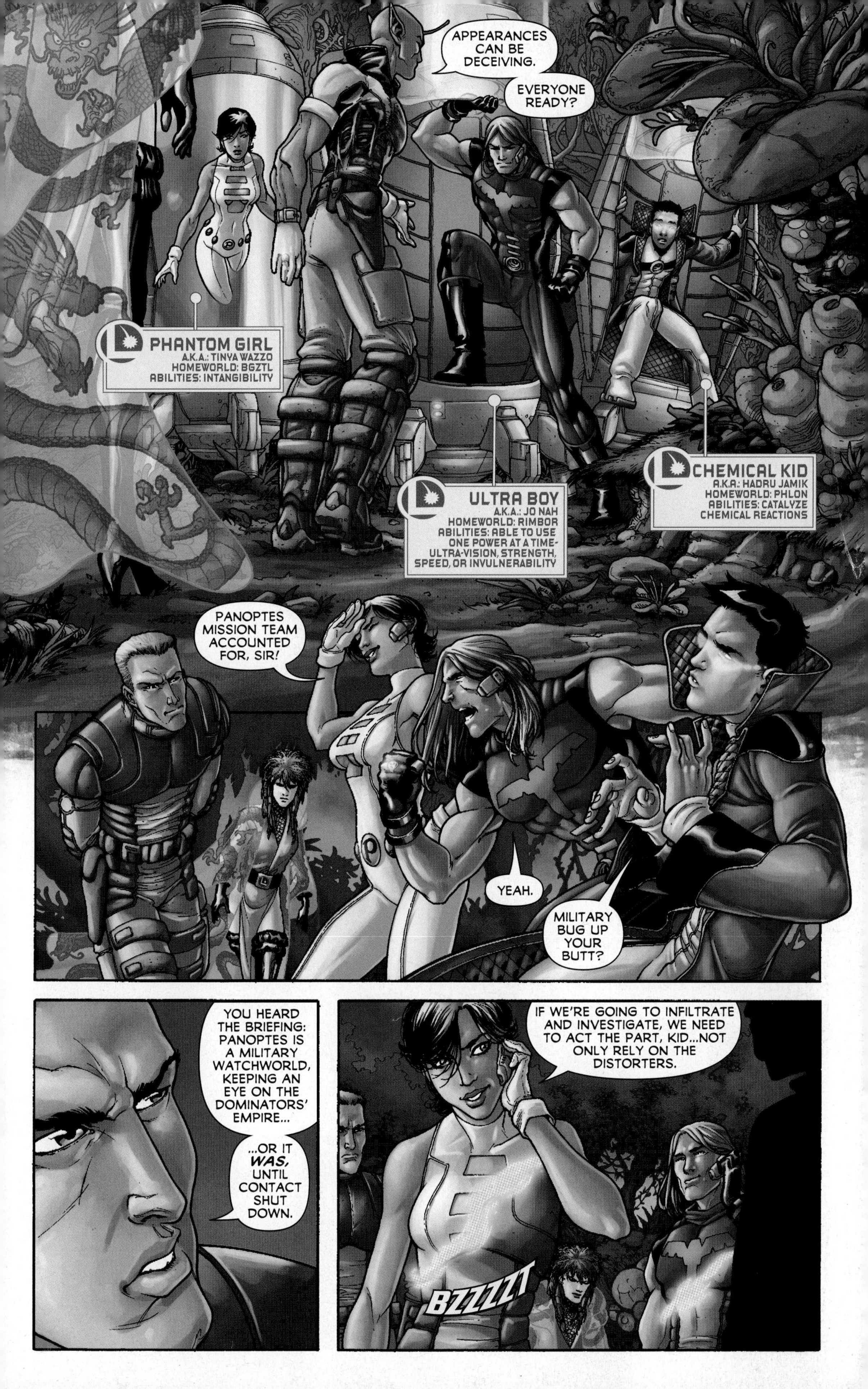
APPEARANCES CAN BE DECEIVING.
EVERYONE READY?
PHANTOM GIRL
A.K.A.: TINYA WAZZO
HOMEWORLD: BGZTL
ABILITIES: INTANGIBILITY
ULTRA BOY
A.K.A.: JO NAH
HOMEWORLD: RIMBOR
ABILITIES: ABLE TO USE ONE POWER AT A TIME-ULTRA-VISION, STRENGTH, SPEED, OR INVULNERABILITY
CHEMICAL KID
A.K.A.: HADRU JAMIK
HOMEWORLD: PHLON
ABILITIES: CATALYZE CHEMICAL REACTIONS
PANOPTES MISSION TEAM ACCOUNTED FOR, SIR!
YEAH.
MILITARY BUG UP YOUR BUTT?
YOU HEARD THE BRIEFING: PANOPTES IS A MILITARY WATCHWORLD, KEEPING AN EYE ON THE DOMINATORS' EMPIRE...
...OR IT WAS, UNTIL CONTACT SHUT DOWN.
IF WE'RE GOING TO INFILTRATE AND INVESTIGATE, WE NEED TO ACT THE PART, KID...NOT ONLY RELY ON THE DISTORTERS.
BZZZZT

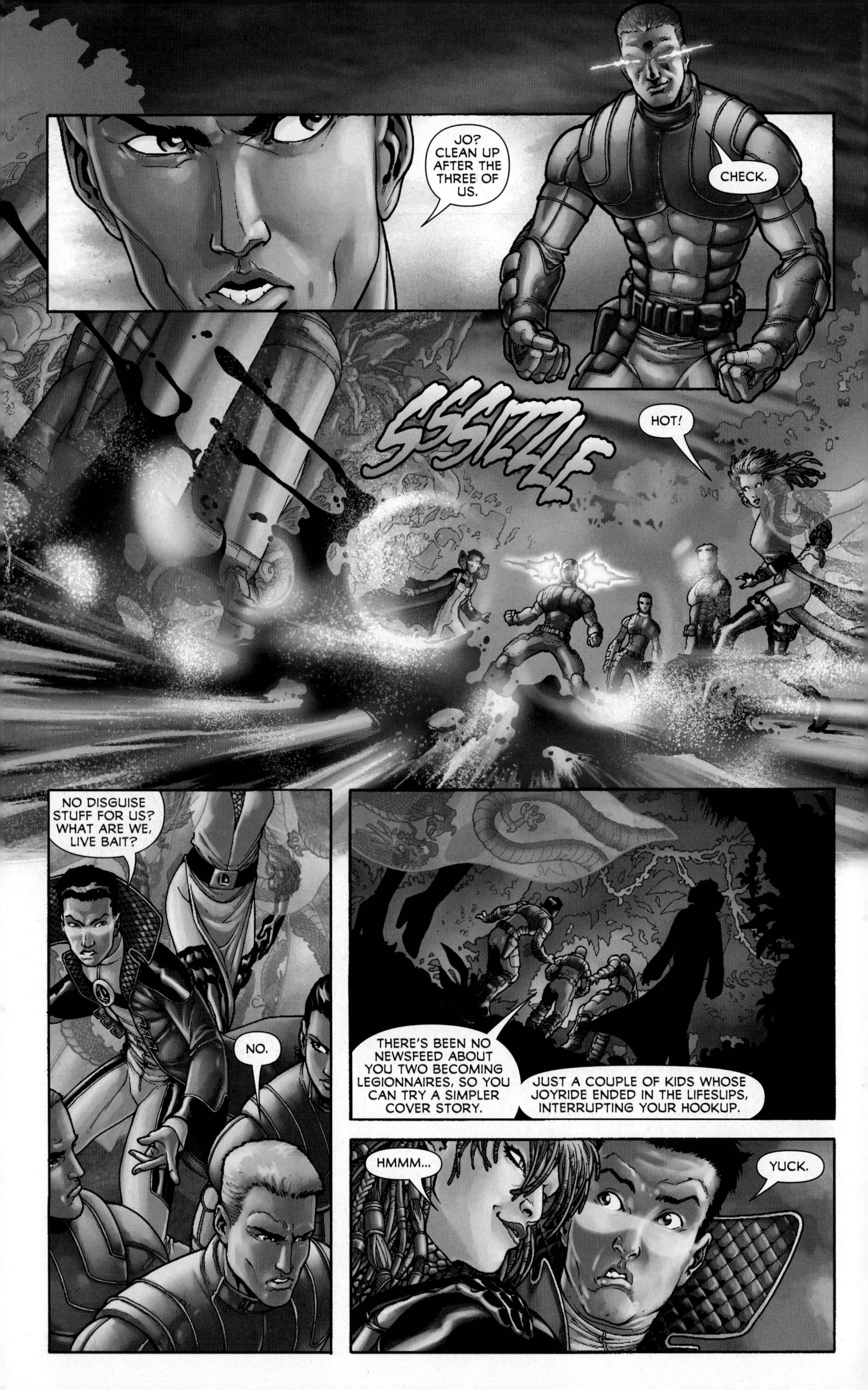
JO? CLEAN UP AFTER THE THREE OF US.
CHECK.
SSSIZZLE
HOT!
NO DISGUISE STUFF FOR US? WHAT ARE WE, LIVE BAIT?
NO.
THERE'S BEEN NO NEWSFEED ABOUT YOU TWO BECOMING LEGIONNAIRES, SO YOU CAN TRY A SIMPLER COVER STORY.
JUST A COUPLE OF KIDS WHOSE JOYRIDE ENDED IN THE LIFESLIPS, INTERRUPTING YOUR HOOKUP.
HMMM...
YUCK.

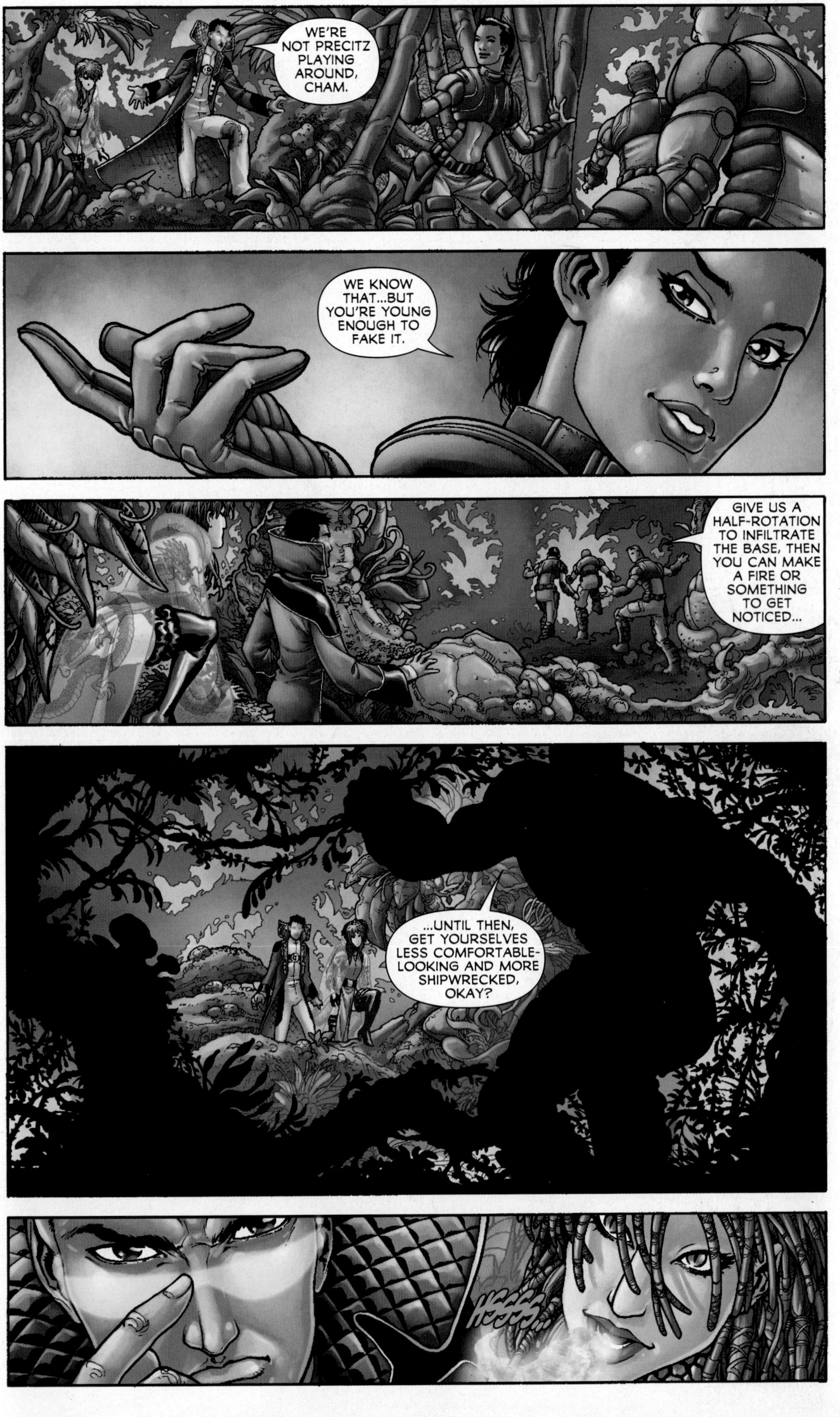
WE'RE NOT PRECITZ PLAYING AROUND, CHAM.
WE KNOW THAT...BUT YOU'RE YOUNG ENOUGH TO FAKE IT.
GIVE US A HALF-ROTATION TO INFILTRATE THE BASE, THEN YOU CAN MAKE A FIRE OR SOMETHING TO GET NOTICED...
...UNTIL THEN, GET YOURSELVES LESS COMFORTABLE-LOOKING AND MORE SHIPWRECKED, OKAY?
HSSSS...

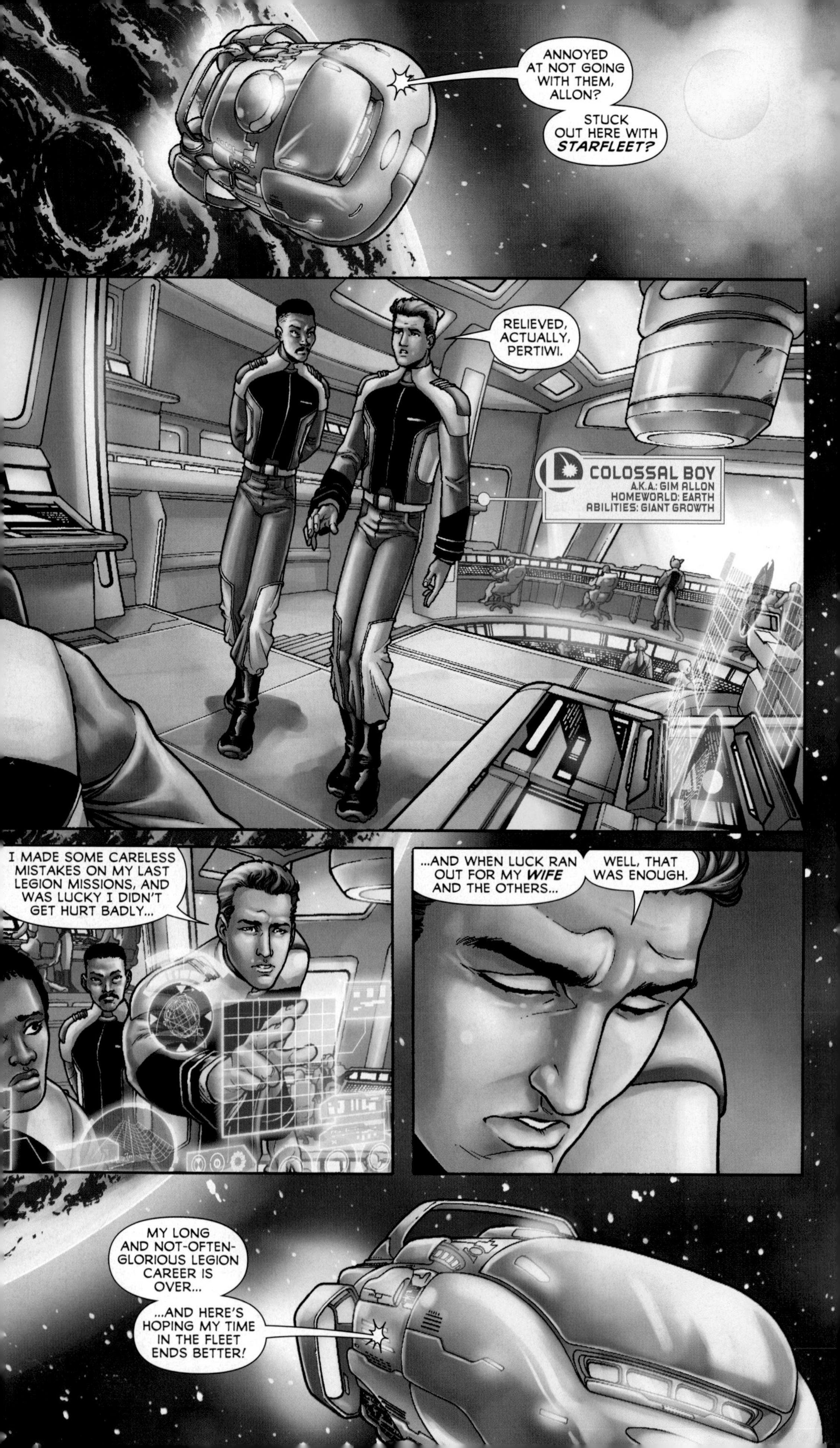
ANNOYED AT NOT GOING WITH THEM, ALLON?
STUCK OUT HERE WITH STARFLEET?
RELIEVED, ACTUALLY, PERTIWI.
COLOSSAL BOY
A.K.A.: GIM ALLON
HOMEWORLD: EARTH
ABILITIES: GIANT GROWTH
I MADE SOME CARELESS MISTAKES ON MY LAST LEGION MISSIONS, AND WAS LUCKY I DIDN'T GET HURT BADLY...
...AND WHEN LUCK RAN OUT FOR MY WIFE AND THE OTHERS...
WELL, THAT WAS ENOUGH.
MY LONG AND NOT-OFTEN-GLORIOUS LEGION CAREER IS OVER...
...AND HERE'S HOPING MY TIME IN THE FLEET ENDS BETTER!

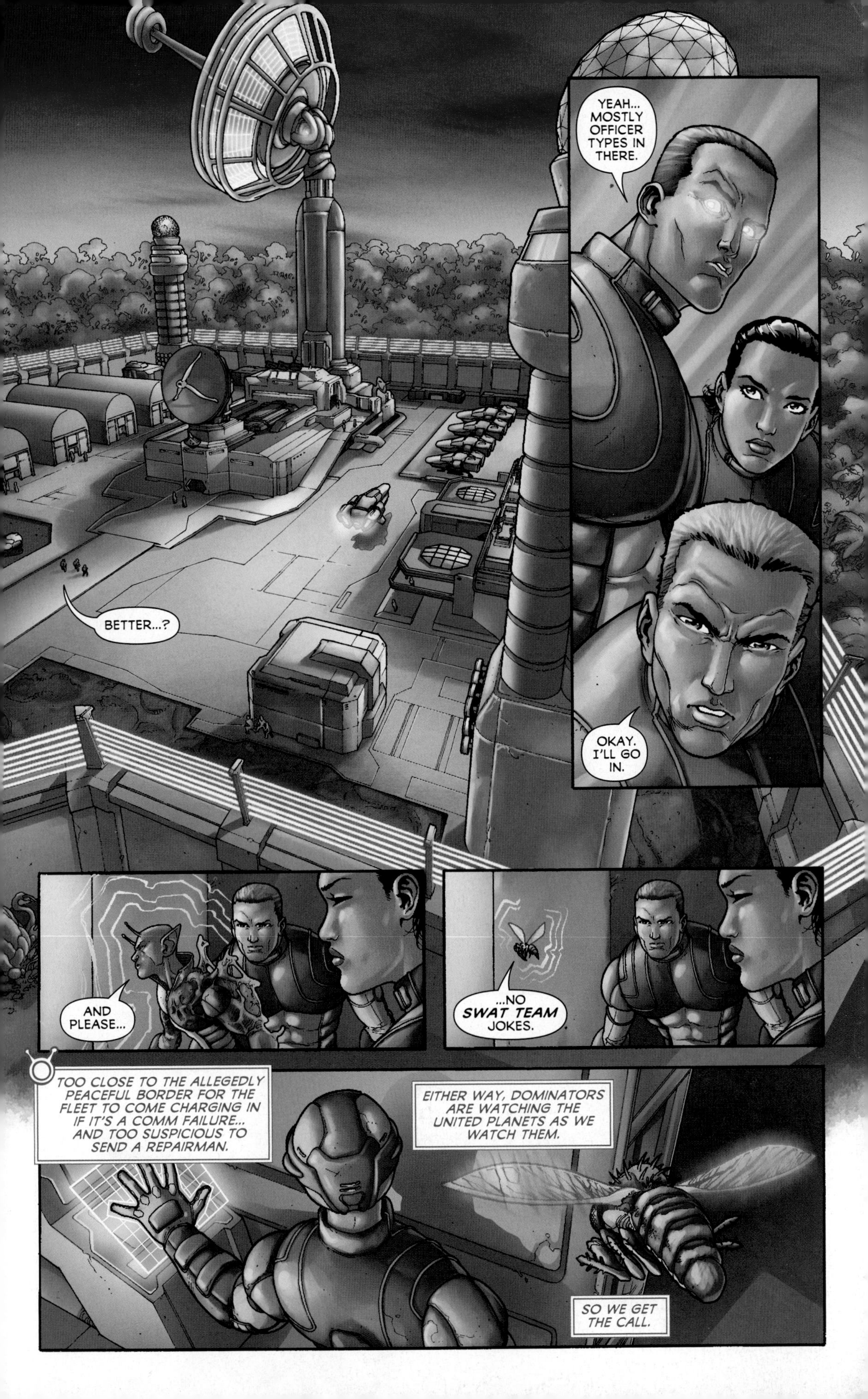
YEAH... MOSTLY OFFICER TYPES IN THERE.
BETTER...?
OKAY. I'LL GO IN.
AND PLEASE...
...NO SWAT TEAM JOKES.
TOO CLOSE TO THE ALLEGEDLY PEACEFUL BORDER FOR THE FLEET TO COME CHARGING IN IF IT'S A COMM FAILURE... AND TOO SUSPICIOUS TO SEND A REPAIRMAN.
EITHER WAY, DOMINATORS ARE WATCHING THE UNITED PLANETS AS WE WATCH THEM.
SO WE GET THE CALL.

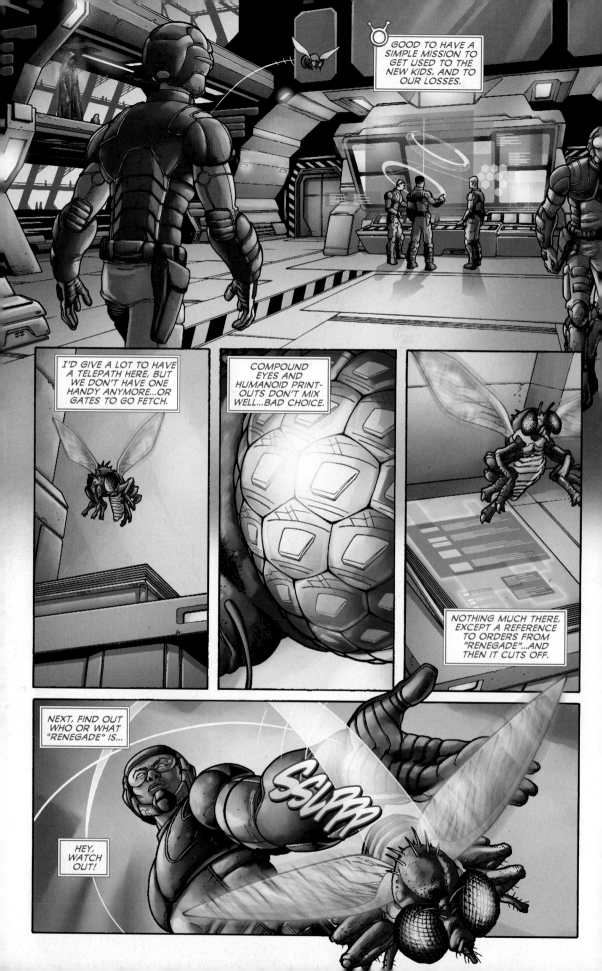

GOOD TO HAVE A SIMPLE MISSION TO GET USED TO THE NEW KIDS, AND TO OUR LOSSES.

I'D GIVE A LOT TO HAVE A TELEPATH HERE, BUT WE DON'T HAVE ONE HANDY ANYMORE...OR GATES TO GO FETCH.

COMPOUND EYES AND HUMANOID PRINT-OUTS DON'T MIX WELL...BAD CHOICE.

NOTHING MUCH THERE, EXCEPT A REFERENCE TO ORDERS FROM "RENEGADE"...AND THEN IT CUTS OFF.

NEXT, FIND OUT WHO OR WHAT "RENEGADE" IS...

SSLFFF

HEY, WATCH OUT!

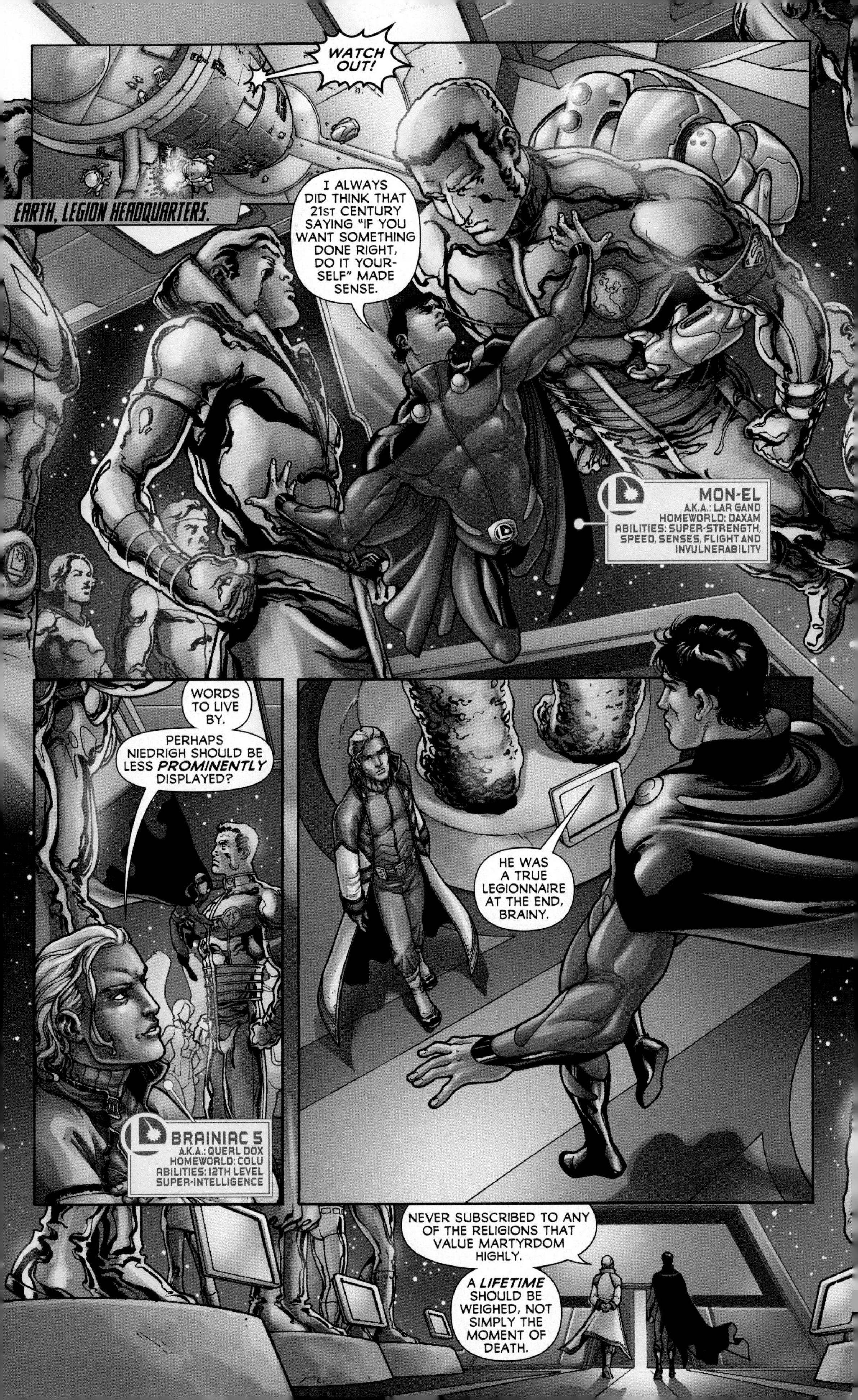

WATCH OUT!
EARTH, LEGION HEADQUARTERS.
I ALWAYS DID THINK THAT 21ST CENTURY SAYING "IF YOU WANT SOMETHING DONE RIGHT, DO IT YOURSELF" MADE SENSE.
MON-EL
A.K.A.: LAR GAND
HOMEWORLD: DAXAM
ABILITIES: SUPER-STRENGTH, SPEED, SENSES, FLIGHT AND INVULNERABILITY
WORDS TO LIVE BY.
PERHAPS NIEDRIGH SHOULD BE LESS *PROMINENTLY* DISPLAYED?
BRAINIAC 5
A.K.A.: QUERL DOX
HOMEWORLD: COLU
ABILITIES: 12TH LEVEL SUPER-INTELLIGENCE
HE WAS A TRUE LEGIONNAIRE AT THE END, BRAINY.
NEVER SUBSCRIBED TO ANY OF THE RELIGIONS THAT VALUE MARTYRDOM HIGHLY.
A *LIFETIME* SHOULD BE WEIGHED, NOT SIMPLY THE MOMENT OF DEATH.

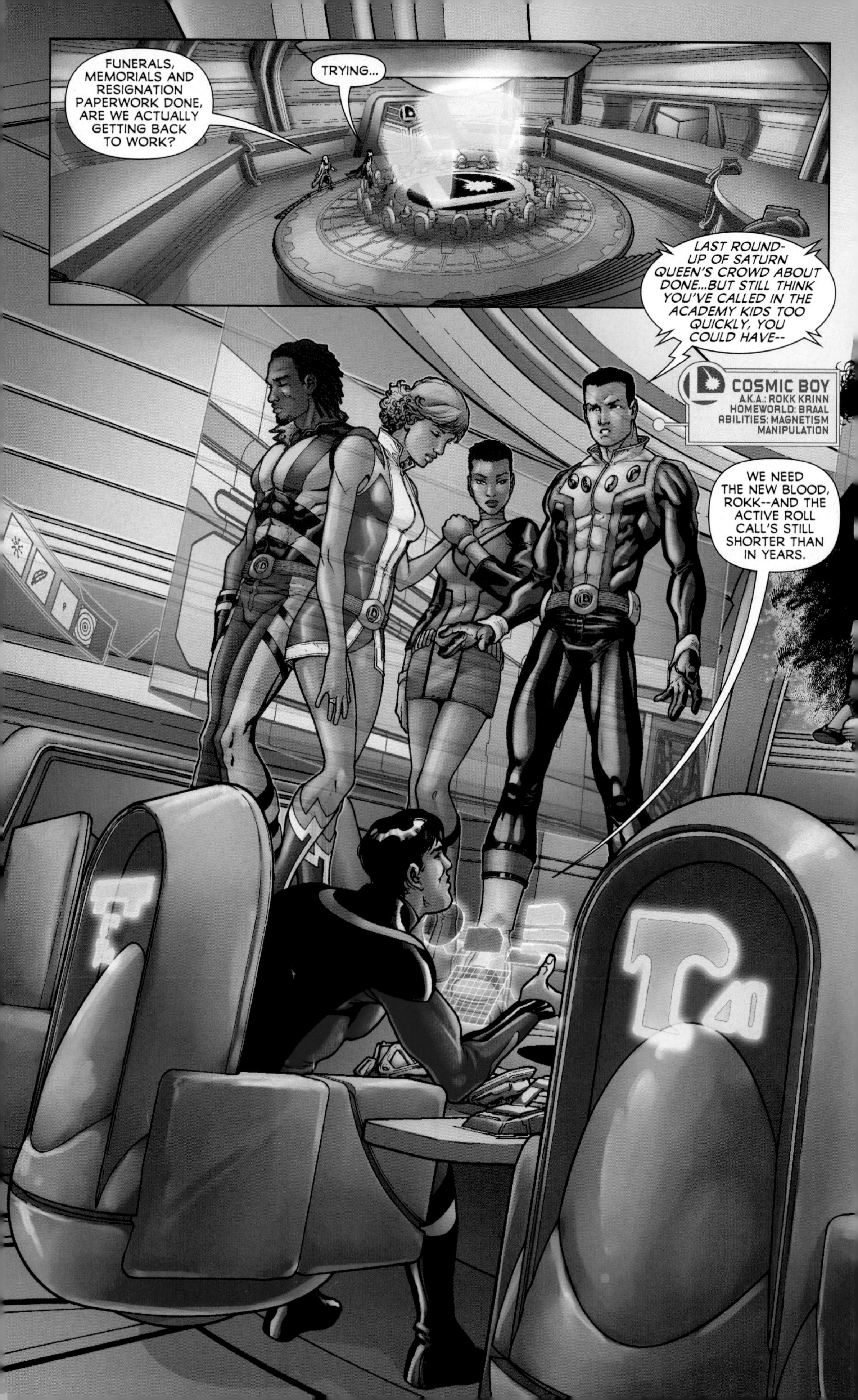
FUNERALS, MEMORIALS AND RESIGNATION PAPERWORK DONE, ARE WE ACTUALLY GETTING BACK TO WORK?
TRYING...
LAST ROUND-UP OF SATURN QUEEN'S CROWD ABOUT DONE...BUT STILL THINK YOU'VE CALLED IN THE ACADEMY KIDS TOO QUICKLY, YOU COULD HAVE--
COSMIC BOY
A.K.A.: ROKK KRINN
HOMEWORLD: BRAAL
ABILITIES: MAGNETISM MANIPULATION
WE NEED THE NEW BLOOD, ROKK--AND THE ACTIVE ROLL CALL'S STILL SHORTER THAN IN YEARS.

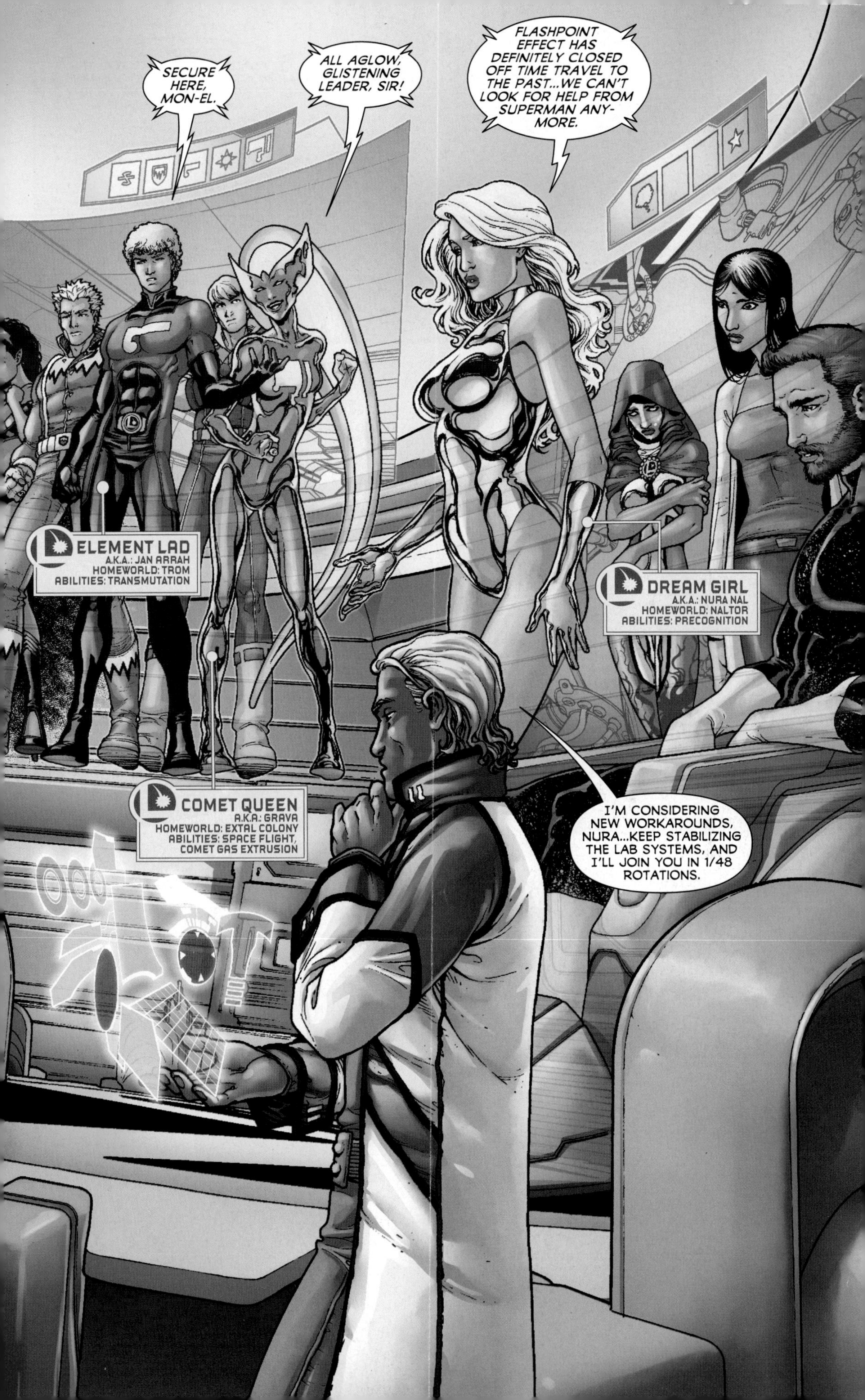
SECURE HERE, MON-EL.
ALL AGLOW, GLISTENING LEADER, SIR!
FLASHPOINT EFFECT HAS DEFINITELY CLOSED OFF TIME TRAVEL TO THE PAST...WE CAN'T LOOK FOR HELP FROM SUPERMAN ANY-MORE.
ELEMENT LAD A.K.A.: JAN ARRAH HOMEWORLD: TROM ABILITIES: TRANSMUTATION
DREAM GIRL A.K.A.: NURA NAL HOMEWORLD: NALTOR ABILITIES: PRECOGNITION
COMET QUEEN A.K.A.: GRAVA HOMEWORLD: EXTAL COLONY ABILITIES: SPACE FLIGHT, COMET GAS EXTRUSION
I'M CONSIDERING NEW WORKAROUNDS, NURA...KEEP STABILIZING THE LAB SYSTEMS, AND I'LL JOIN YOU IN 1/48 ROTATIONS.

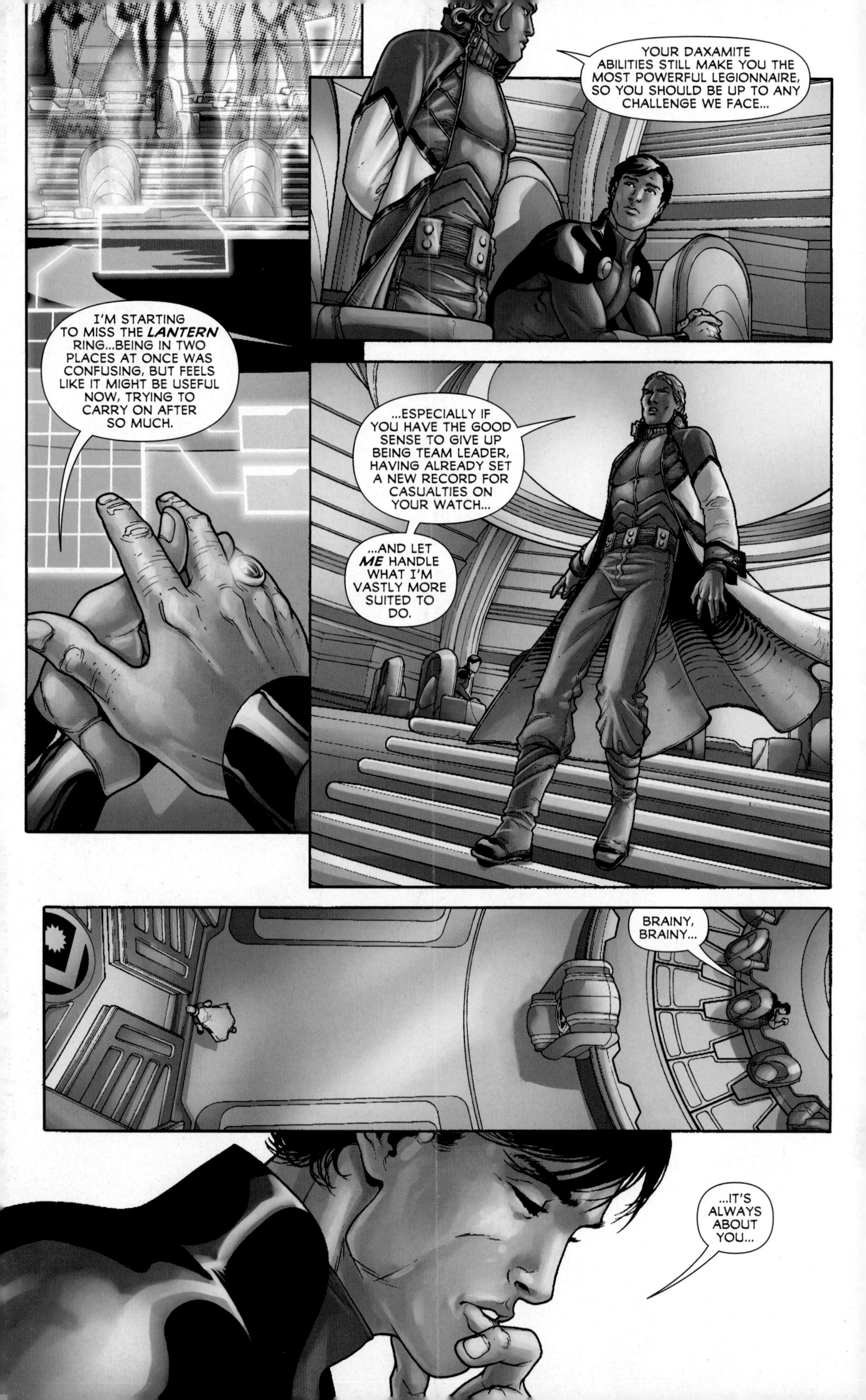
YOUR DAXAMITE ABILITIES STILL MAKE YOU THE MOST POWERFUL LEGIONNAIRE, SO YOU SHOULD BE UP TO ANY CHALLENGE WE FACE...
I'M STARTING TO MISS THE *LANTERN* RING...BEING IN TWO PLACES AT ONCE WAS CONFUSING, BUT FEELS LIKE IT MIGHT BE USEFUL NOW, TRYING TO CARRY ON AFTER SO MUCH.
...ESPECIALLY IF YOU HAVE THE GOOD SENSE TO GIVE UP BEING TEAM LEADER, HAVING ALREADY SET A NEW RECORD FOR CASUALTIES ON YOUR WATCH...
...AND LET *ME* HANDLE WHAT I'M VASTLY MORE SUITED TO DO.
BRAINY, BRAINY...
...IT'S ALWAYS ABOUT YOU...

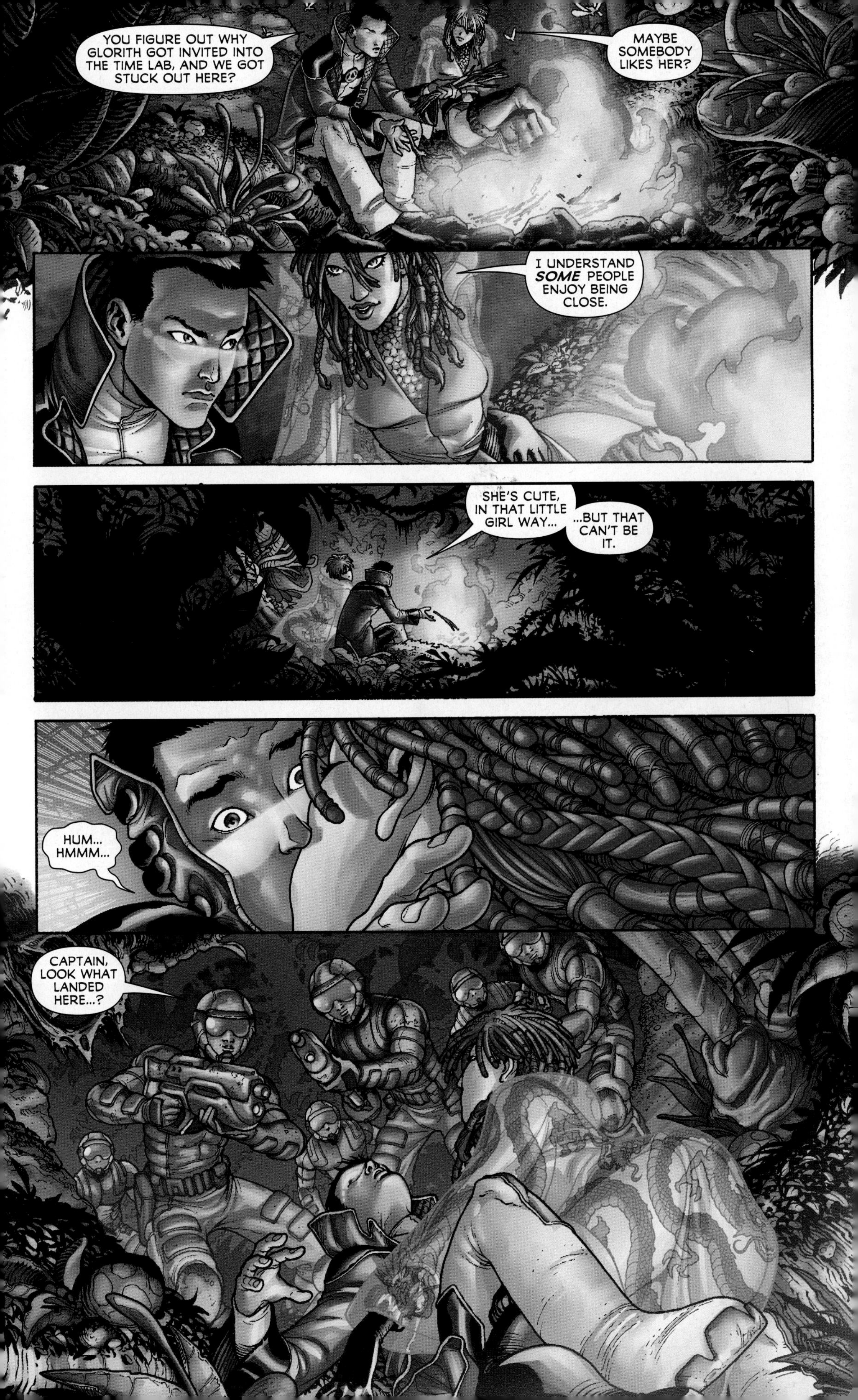
YOU FIGURE OUT WHY GLORITH GOT INVITED INTO THE TIME LAB, AND WE GOT STUCK OUT HERE?
MAYBE SOMEBODY LIKES HER?
I UNDERSTAND SOME PEOPLE ENJOY BEING CLOSE.
SHE'S CUTE, IN THAT LITTLE GIRL WAY...
...BUT THAT CAN'T BE IT.
HUM... HMMM...
CAPTAIN, LOOK WHAT LANDED HERE...?

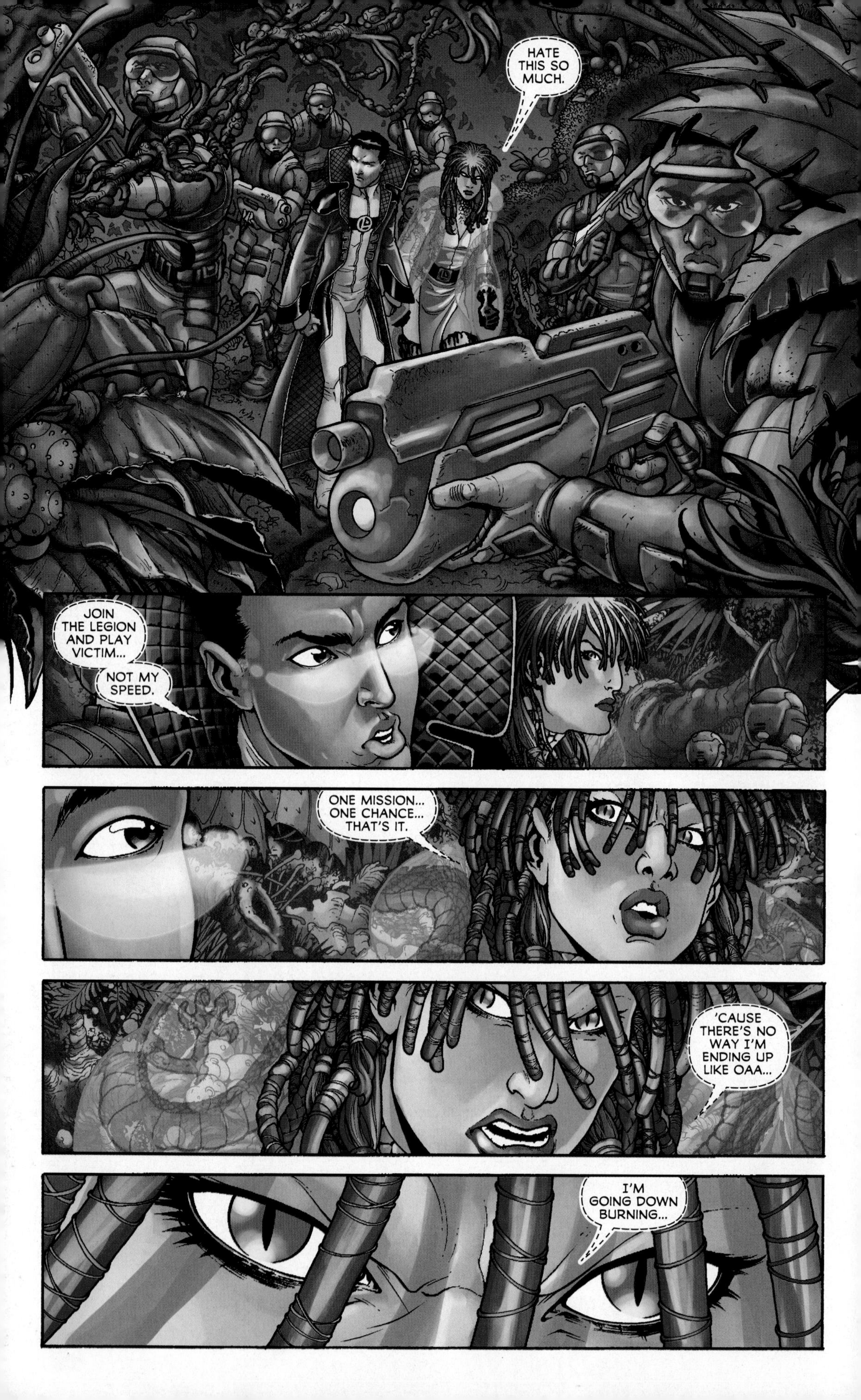
HATE THIS SO MUCH.
JOIN THE LEGION AND PLAY VICTIM...
NOT MY SPEED.
ONE MISSION... ONE CHANCE... THAT'S IT.
'CAUSE THERE'S NO WAY I'M ENDING UP LIKE OAA...
I'M GOING DOWN BURNING...

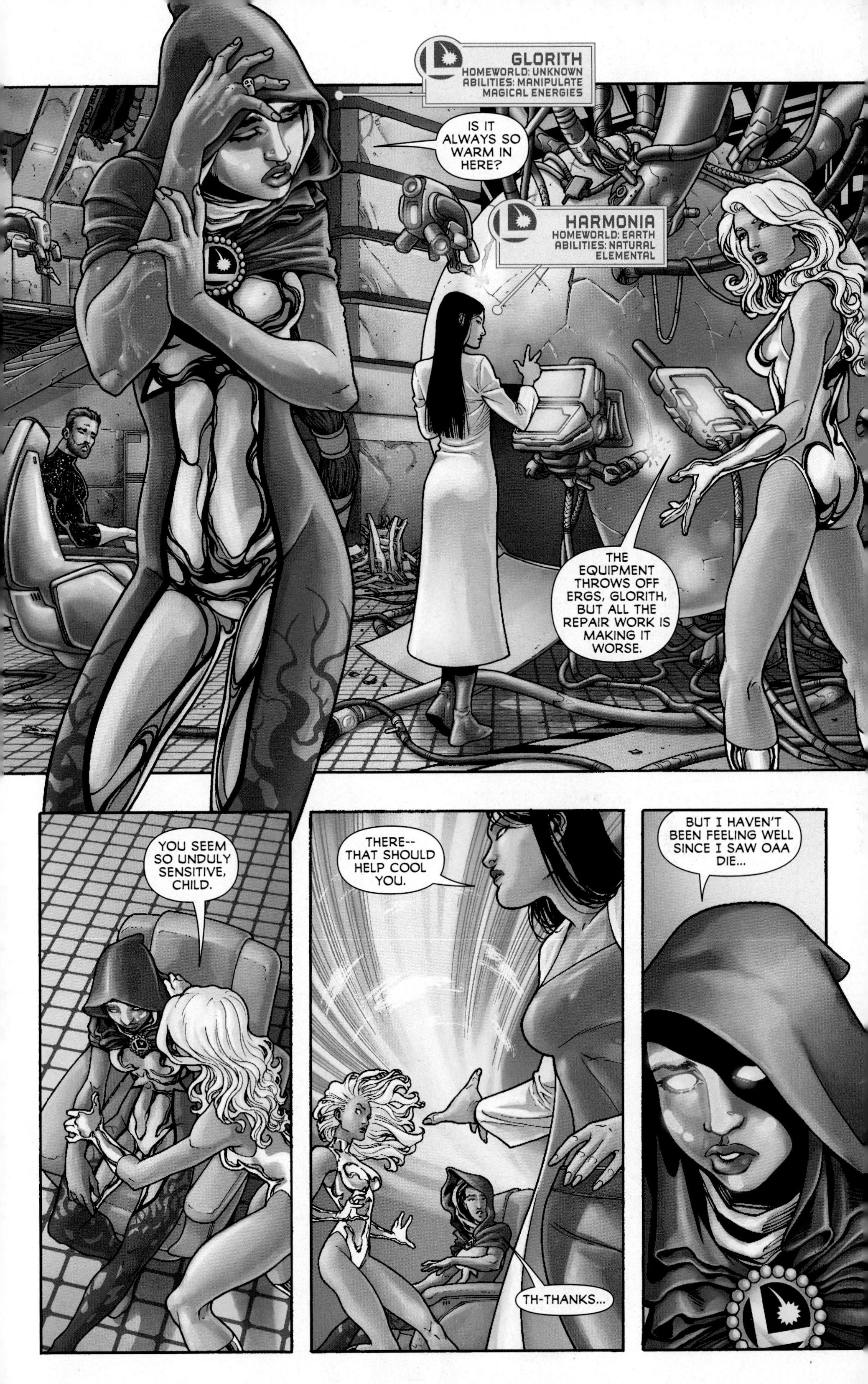
GLORITH
HOMEWORLD: UNKNOWN
ABILITIES: MANIPULATE MAGICAL ENERGIES
IS IT ALWAYS SO WARM IN HERE?
HARMONIA
HOMEWORLD: EARTH
ABILITIES: NATURAL ELEMENTAL
THE EQUIPMENT THROWS OFF ERGS, GLORITH, BUT ALL THE REPAIR WORK IS MAKING IT WORSE.
YOU SEEM SO UNDULY SENSITIVE, CHILD.
THERE-- THAT SHOULD HELP COOL YOU.
TH-THANKS...
BUT I HAVEN'T BEEN FEELING WELL SINCE I SAW OAA DIE...

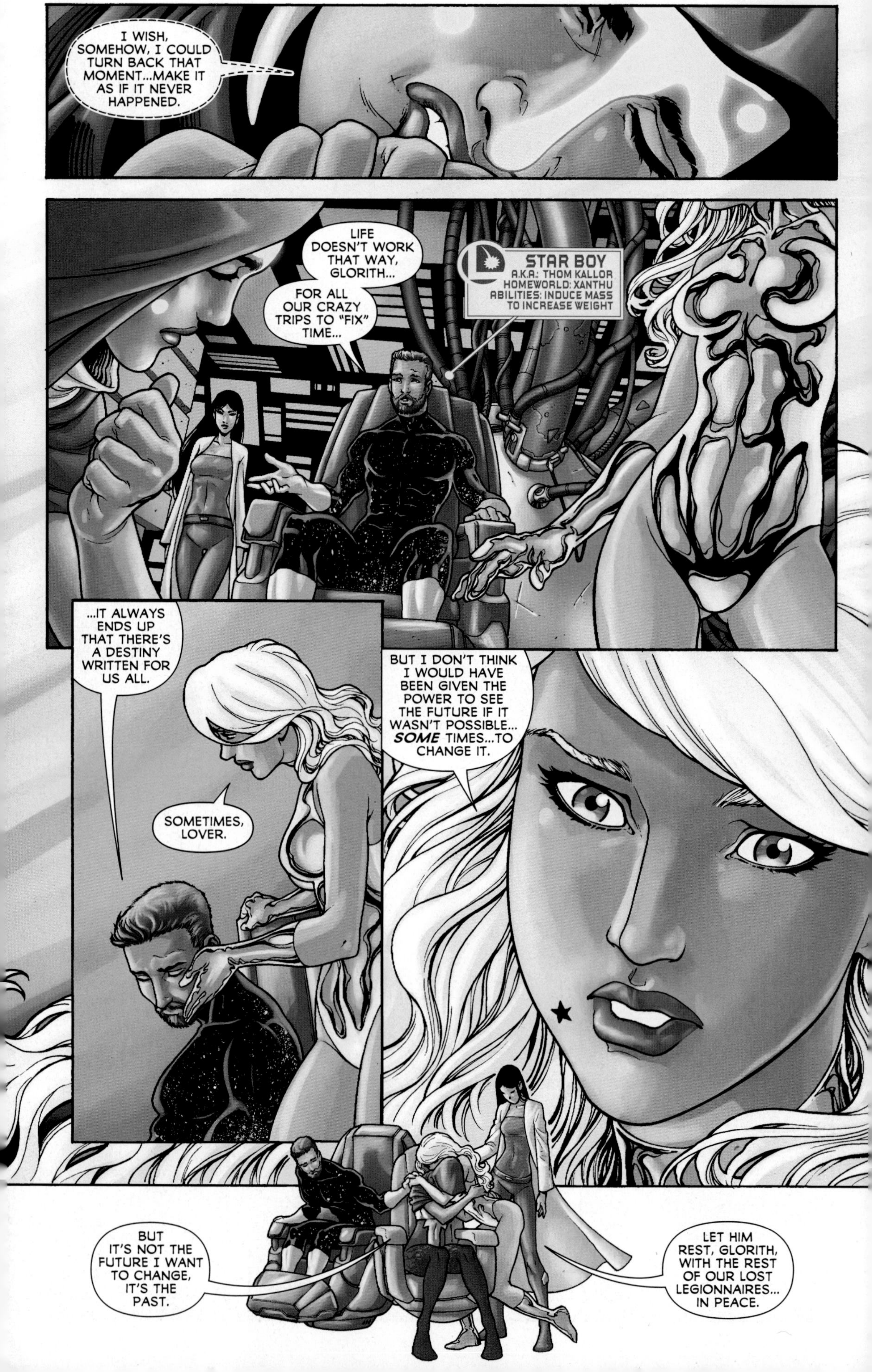
I WISH, SOMEHOW, I COULD TURN BACK THAT MOMENT...MAKE IT AS IF IT NEVER HAPPENED.
LIFE DOESN'T WORK THAT WAY, GLORITH...
FOR ALL OUR CRAZY TRIPS TO "FIX" TIME...
STAR BOY
A.K.A.: THOM KALLOR
HOMEWORLD: XANTHU
ABILITIES: INDUCE MASS TO INCREASE WEIGHT
...IT ALWAYS ENDS UP THAT THERE'S A DESTINY WRITTEN FOR US ALL.
SOMETIMES, LOVER.
BUT I DON'T THINK I WOULD HAVE BEEN GIVEN THE POWER TO SEE THE FUTURE IF IT WASN'T POSSIBLE... SOME TIMES...TO CHANGE IT.
BUT IT'S NOT THE FUTURE I WANT TO CHANGE, IT'S THE PAST.
LET HIM REST, GLORITH, WITH THE REST OF OUR LOST LEGIONNAIRES... IN PEACE.

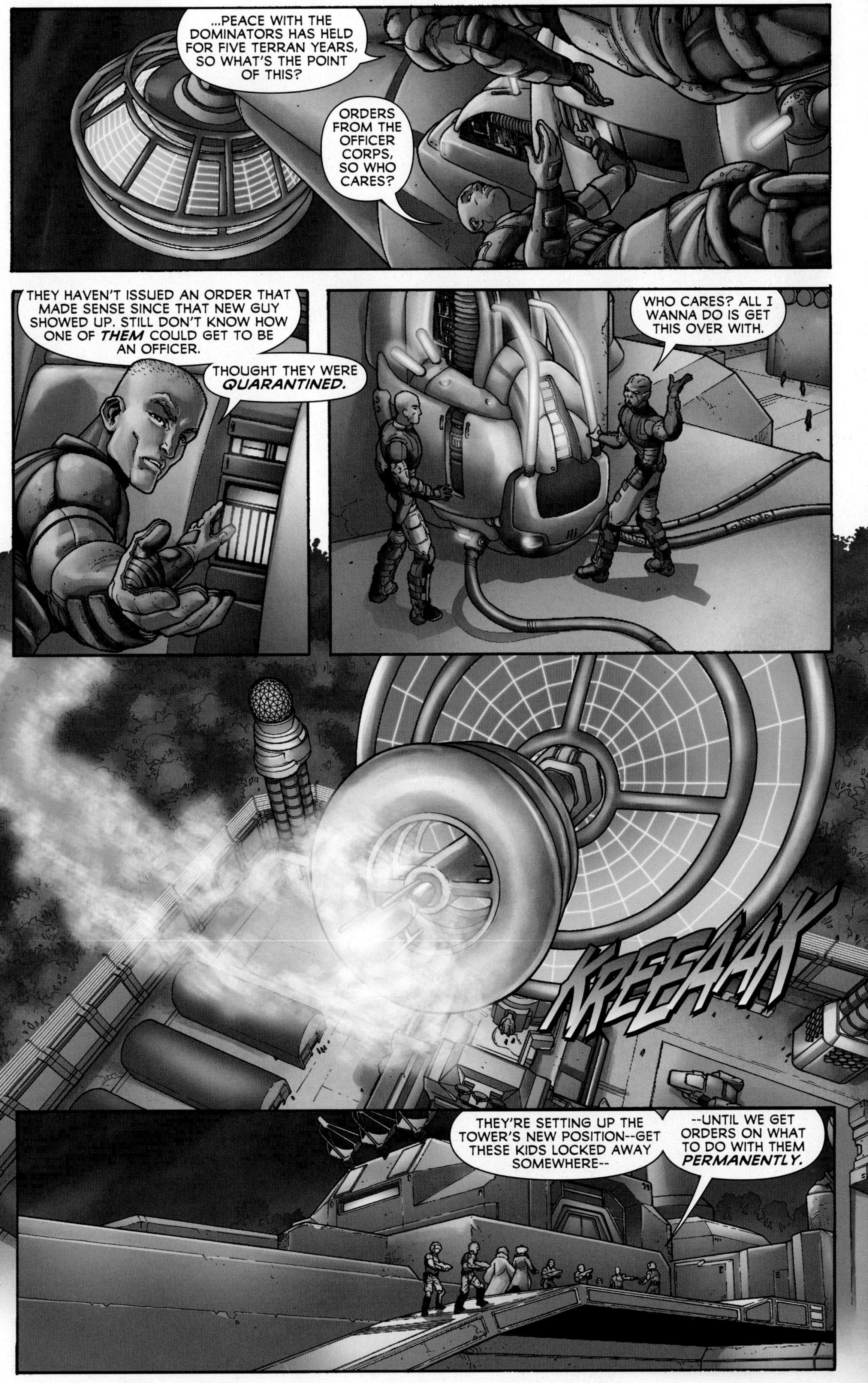
...PEACE WITH THE DOMINATORS HAS HELD FOR FIVE TERRAN YEARS, SO WHAT'S THE POINT OF THIS?
ORDERS FROM THE OFFICER CORPS, SO WHO CARES?
THEY HAVEN'T ISSUED AN ORDER THAT MADE SENSE SINCE THAT NEW GUY SHOWED UP. STILL DON'T KNOW HOW ONE OF *THEM* COULD GET TO BE AN OFFICER.
THOUGHT THEY WERE ***QUARANTINED.***
WHO CARES? ALL I WANNA DO IS GET THIS OVER WITH.
KREEAAK
THEY'RE SETTING UP THE TOWER'S NEW POSITION--GET THESE KIDS LOCKED AWAY SOMEWHERE--
--UNTIL WE GET ORDERS ON WHAT TO DO WITH THEM ***PERMANENTLY.***

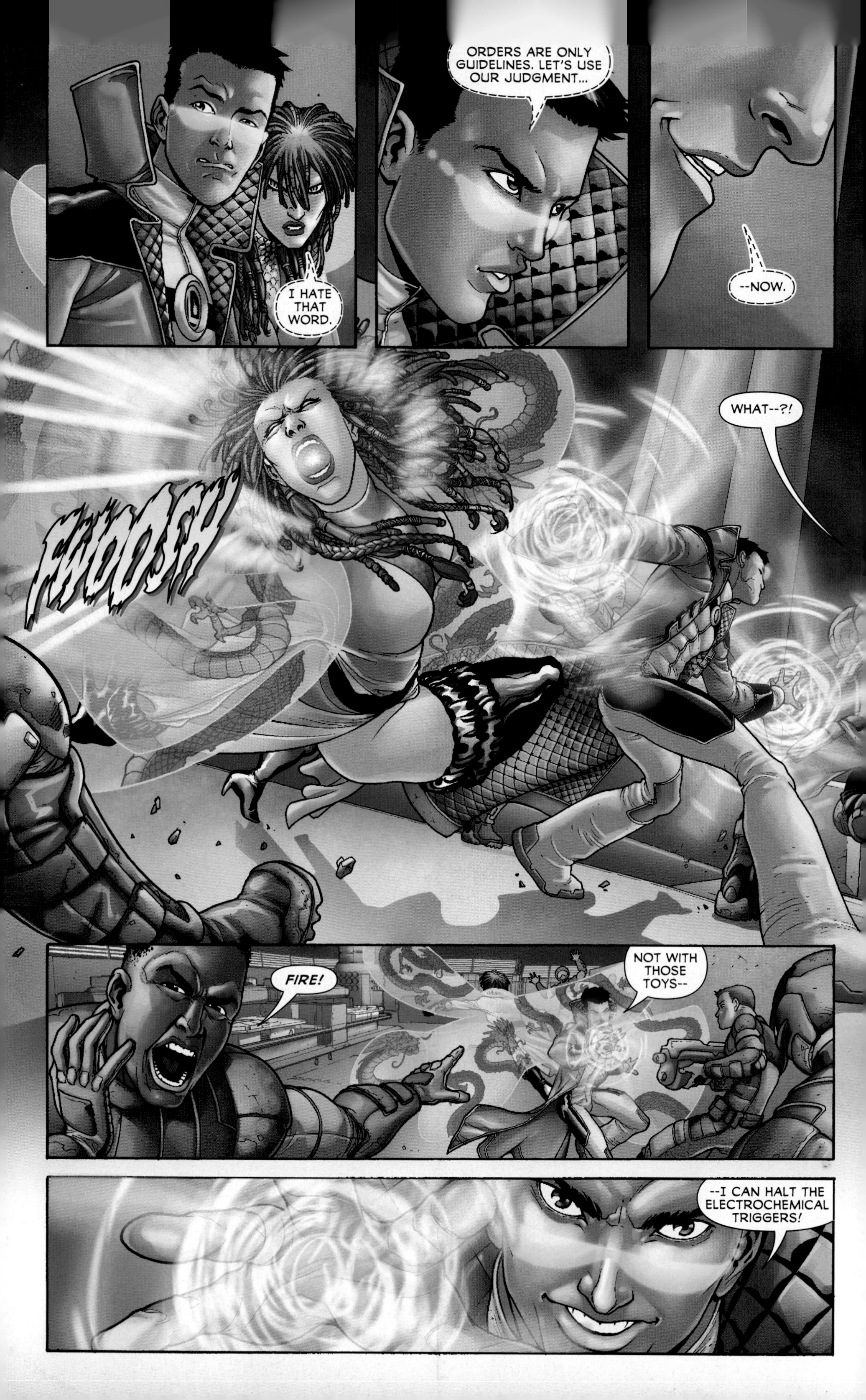
I HATE THAT WORD.
ORDERS ARE ONLY GUIDELINES. LET'S USE OUR JUDGMENT...
--NOW.
FWOOSH
WHAT--?!
FIRE!
NOT WITH THOSE TOYS--
--I CAN HALT THE ELECTROCHEMICAL TRIGGERS!

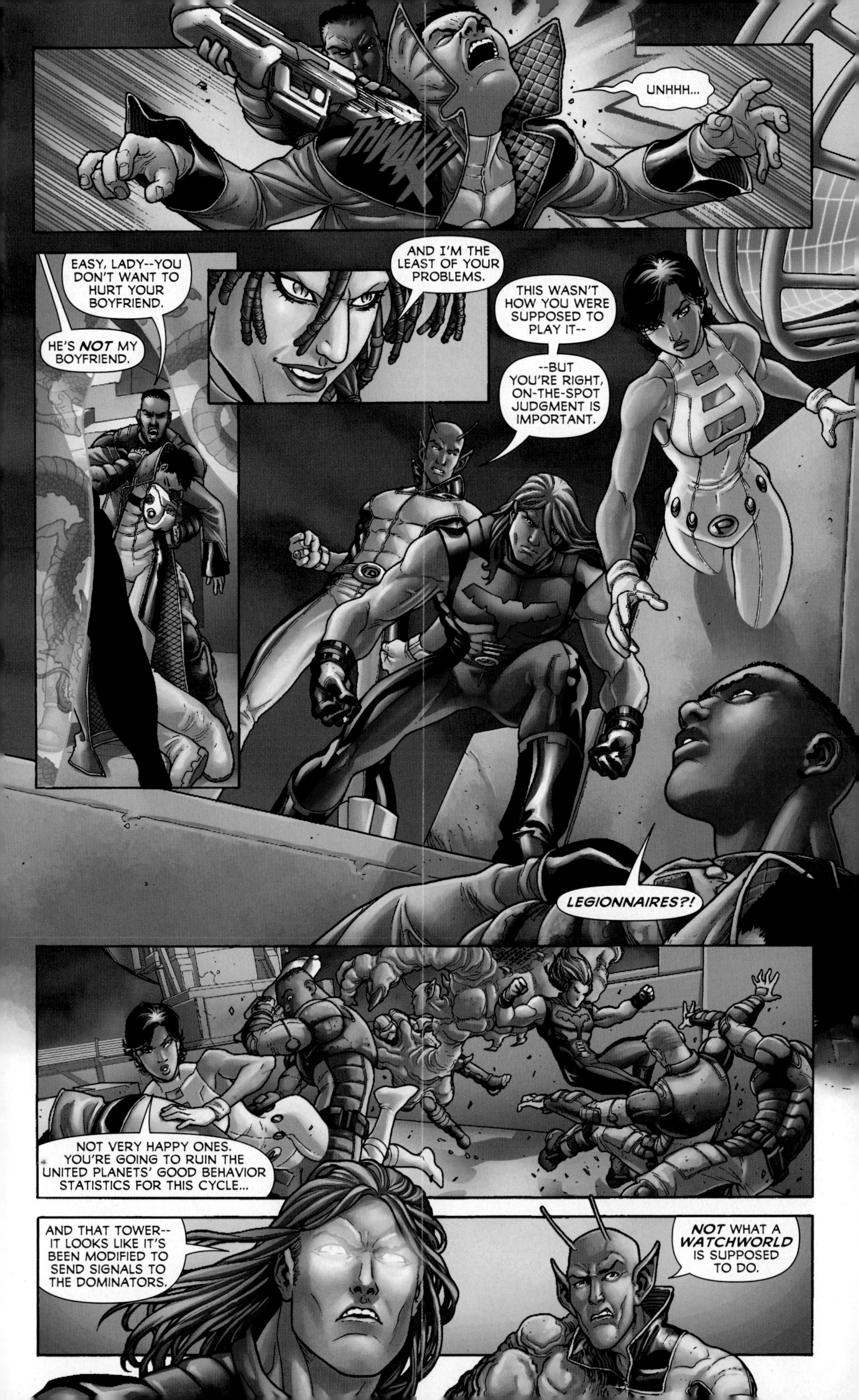
THWAK!
UNHHH...
EASY, LADY--YOU DON'T WANT TO HURT YOUR BOYFRIEND.
HE'S NOT MY BOYFRIEND.
AND I'M THE LEAST OF YOUR PROBLEMS.
THIS WASN'T HOW YOU WERE SUPPOSED TO PLAY IT--
--BUT YOU'RE RIGHT, ON-THE-SPOT JUDGMENT IS IMPORTANT.
LEGIONNAIRES?!
NOT VERY HAPPY ONES. YOU'RE GOING TO RUIN THE UNITED PLANETS' GOOD BEHAVIOR STATISTICS FOR THIS CYCLE...
AND THAT TOWER-- IT LOOKS LIKE IT'S BEEN MODIFIED TO SEND SIGNALS TO THE DOMINATORS.
NOT WHAT A WATCHWORLD IS SUPPOSED TO DO.

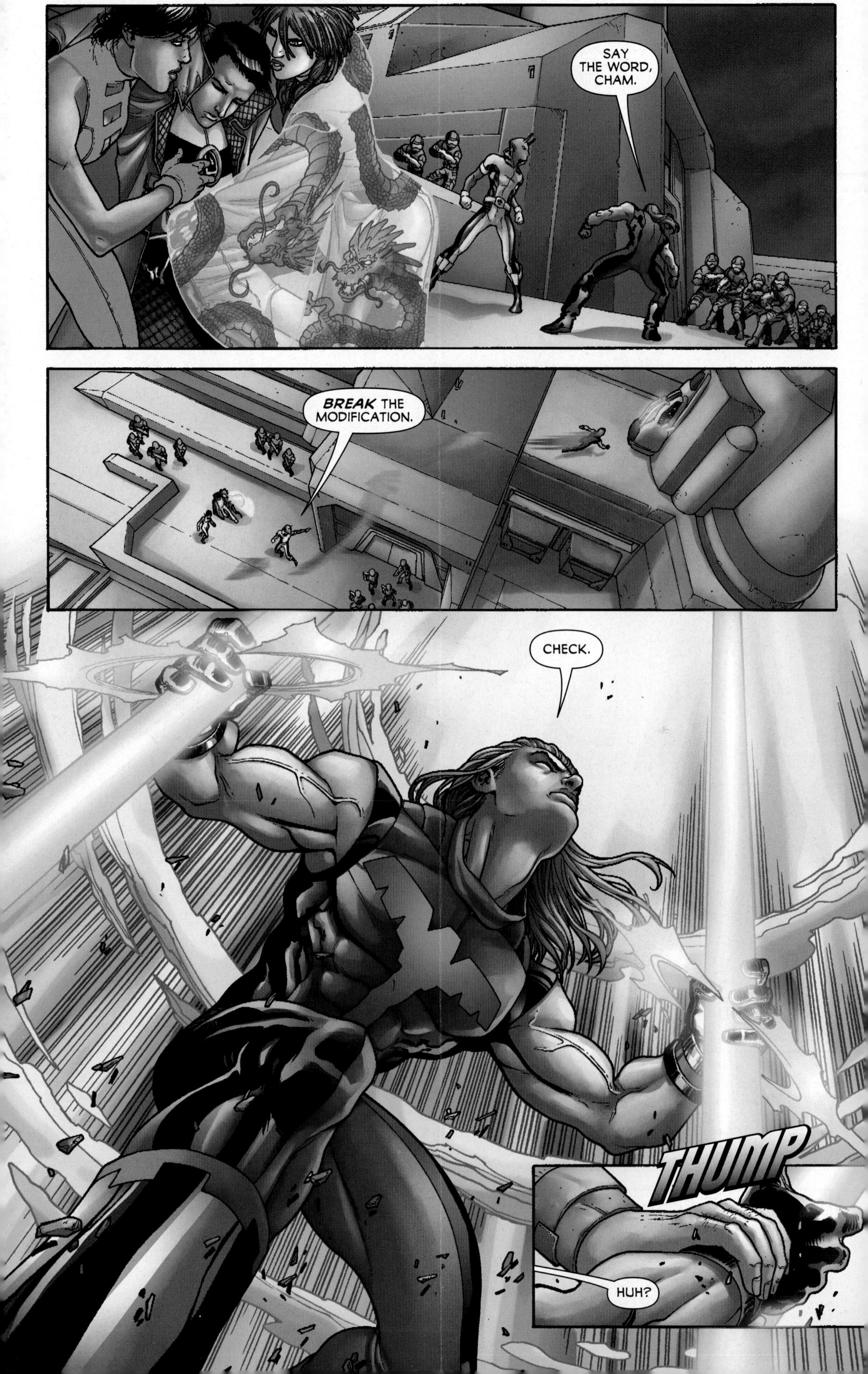
SAY THE WORD, CHAM.
BREAK THE MODIFICATION.
CHECK.
THUMP
HUH?

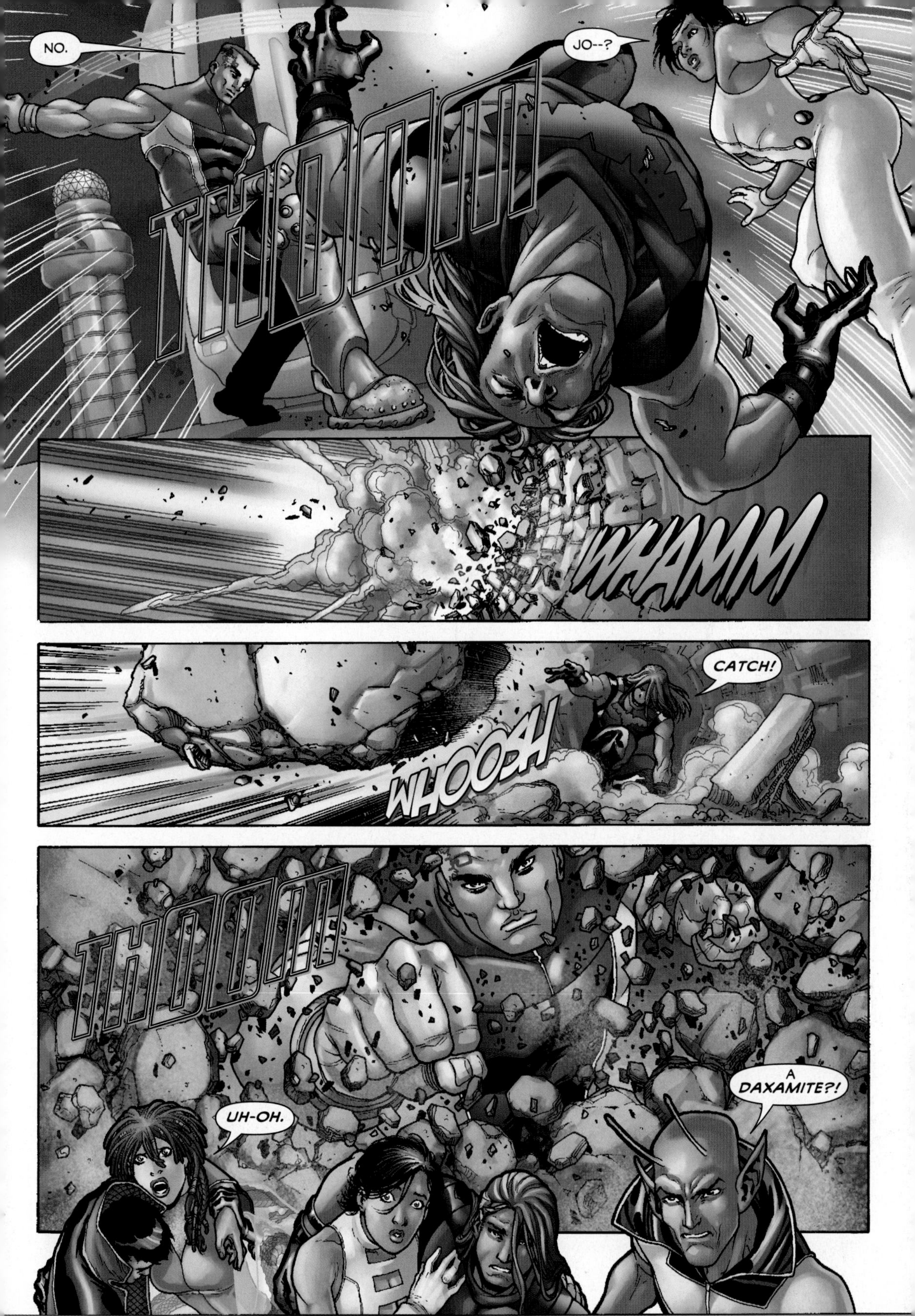
NO.
JO--?
THOOOM
WHAMM
CATCH!
WHOOSH
THOOM
UH-OH.
A DAXAMITE?!

cover art by
CHRIS SPROUSE, KARL STORY & GUY MAJOR

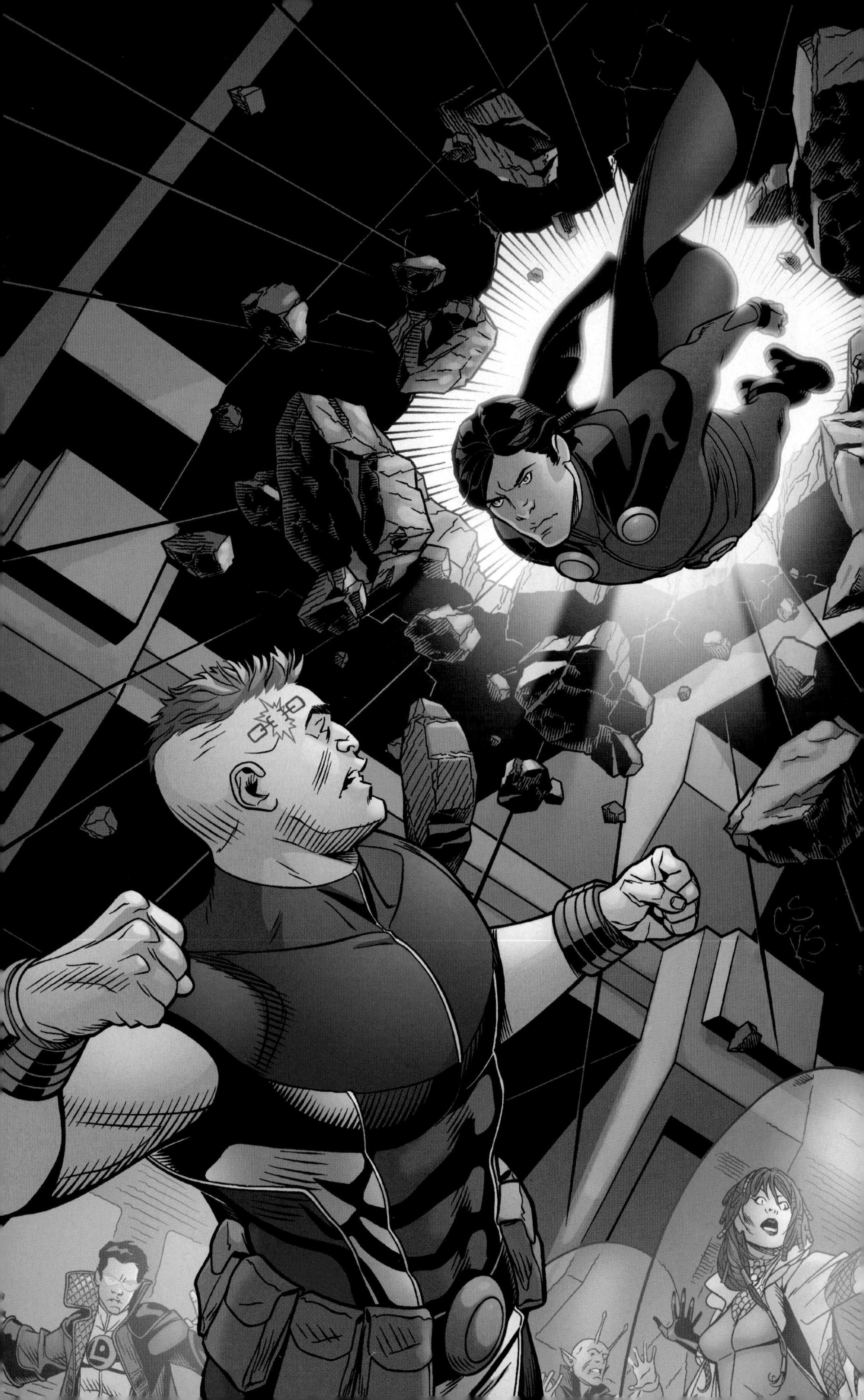

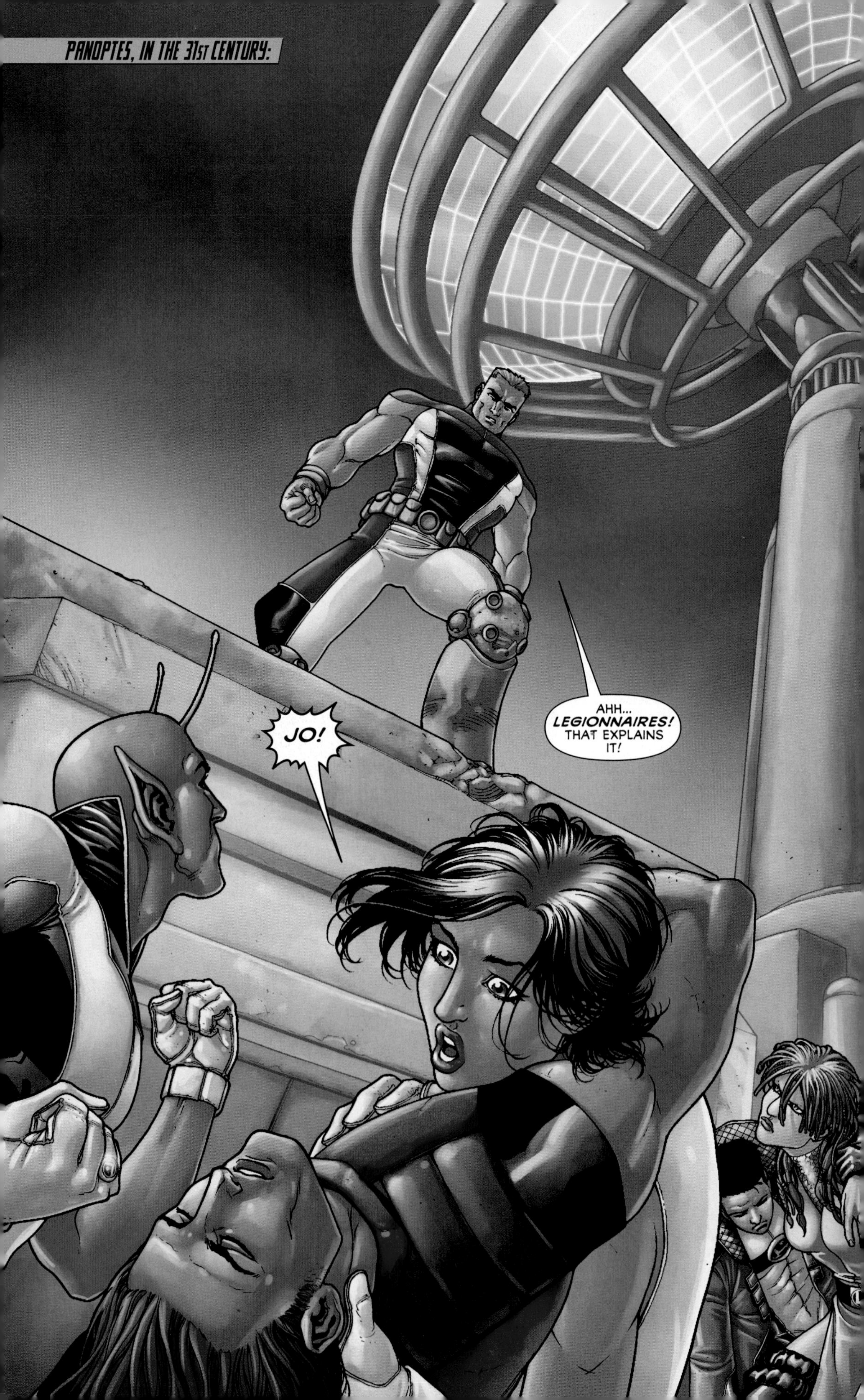
PANOPTES, IN THE 31st CENTURY:
AHH... LEGIONNAIRES! THAT EXPLAINS IT!
JO!

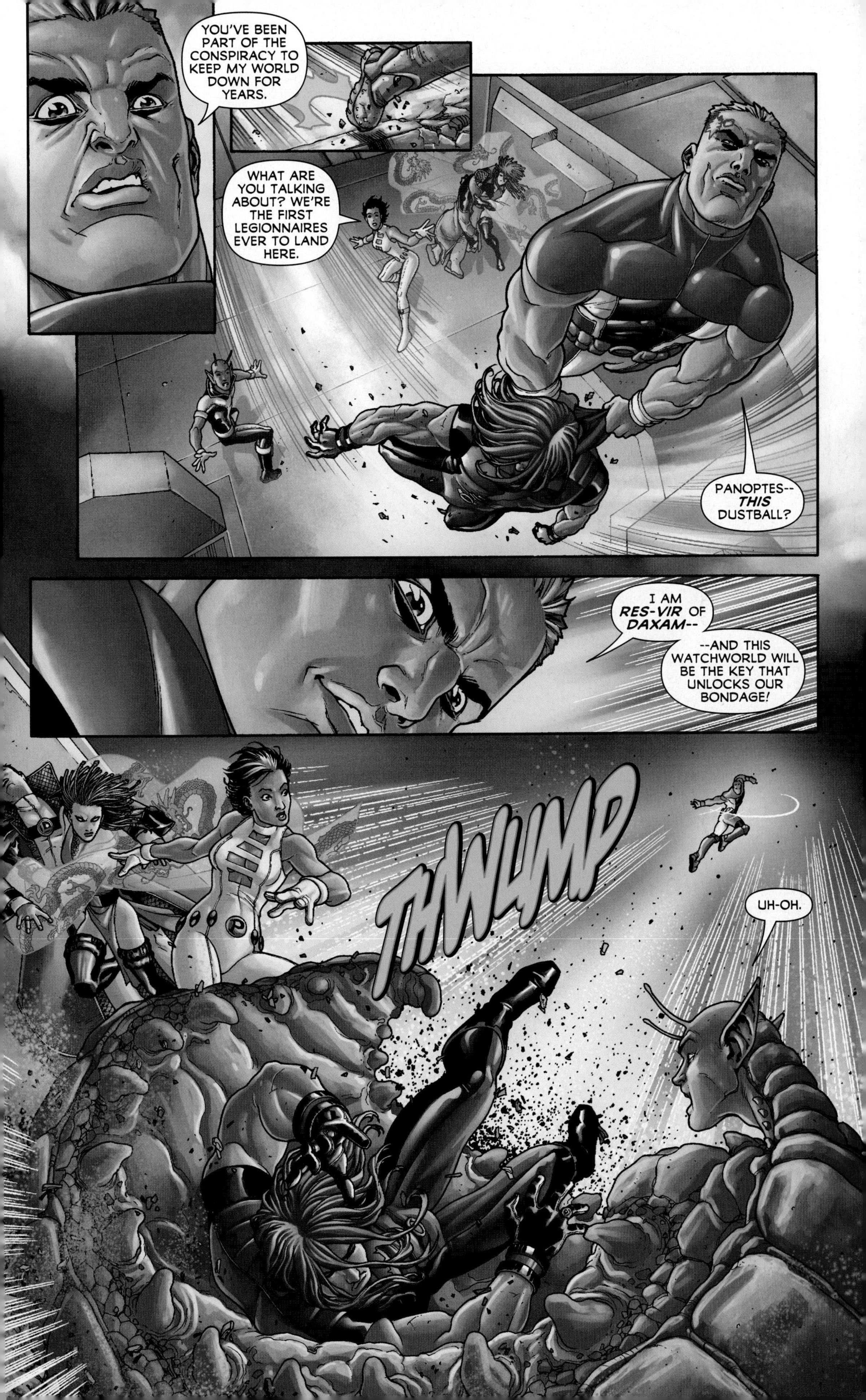

YOU'VE BEEN PART OF THE CONSPIRACY TO KEEP MY WORLD DOWN FOR YEARS.
WHAT ARE YOU TALKING ABOUT? WE'RE THE FIRST LEGIONNAIRES EVER TO LAND HERE.
PANOPTES-- *THIS* DUSTBALL?
I AM *RES-VIR* OF *DAXAM*--
--AND THIS WATCHWORLD WILL BE THE KEY THAT UNLOCKS OUR BONDAGE!
THWUMP
UH-OH.

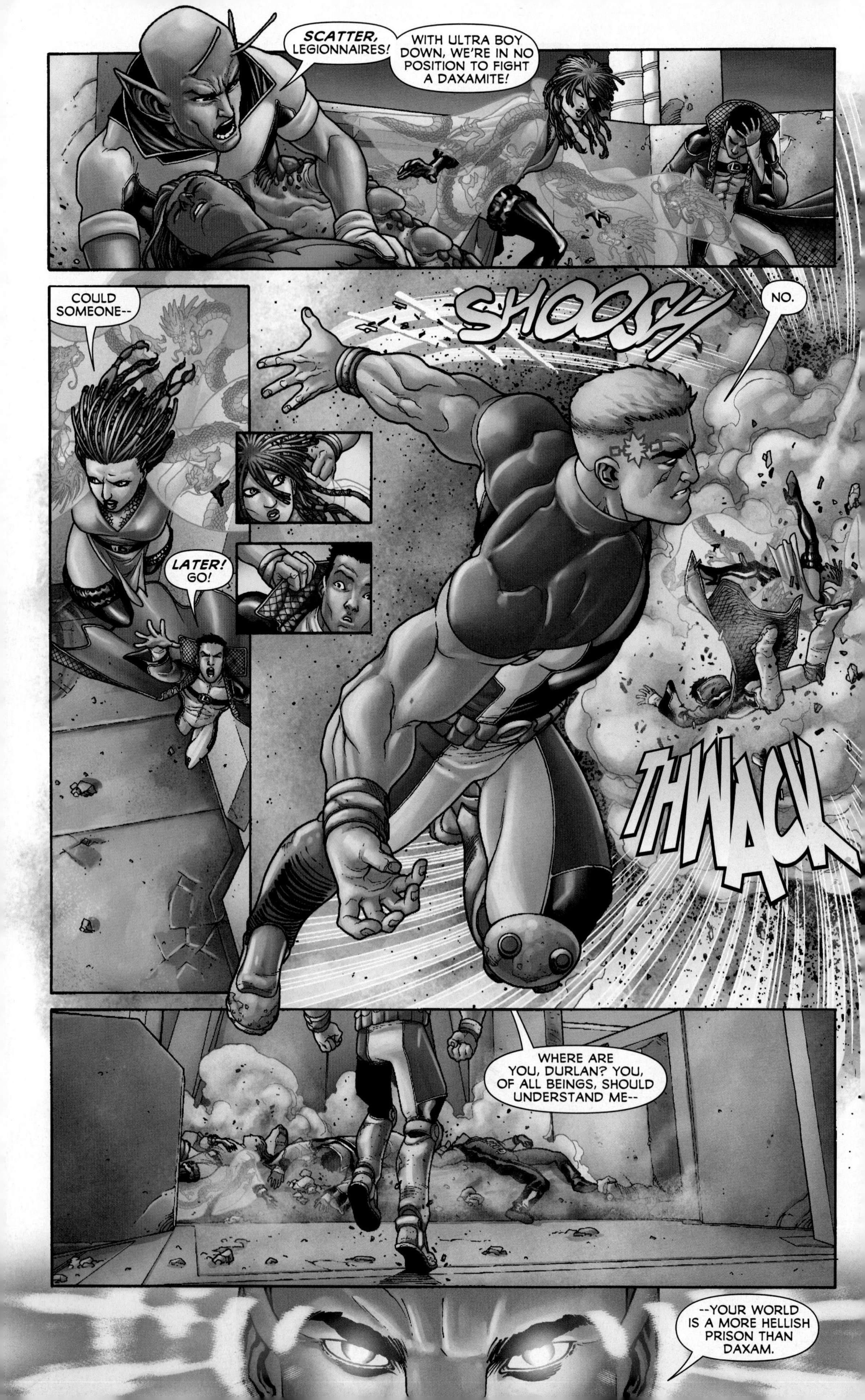
SCATTER, LEGIONNAIRES!
WITH ULTRA BOY DOWN, WE'RE IN NO POSITION TO FIGHT A DAXAMITE!
COULD SOMEONE--
SHOOSH
NO.
LATER! GO!
THWACK
WHERE ARE YOU, DURLAN? YOU, OF ALL BEINGS, SHOULD UNDERSTAND ME--
--YOUR WORLD IS A MORE HELLISH PRISON THAN DAXAM.

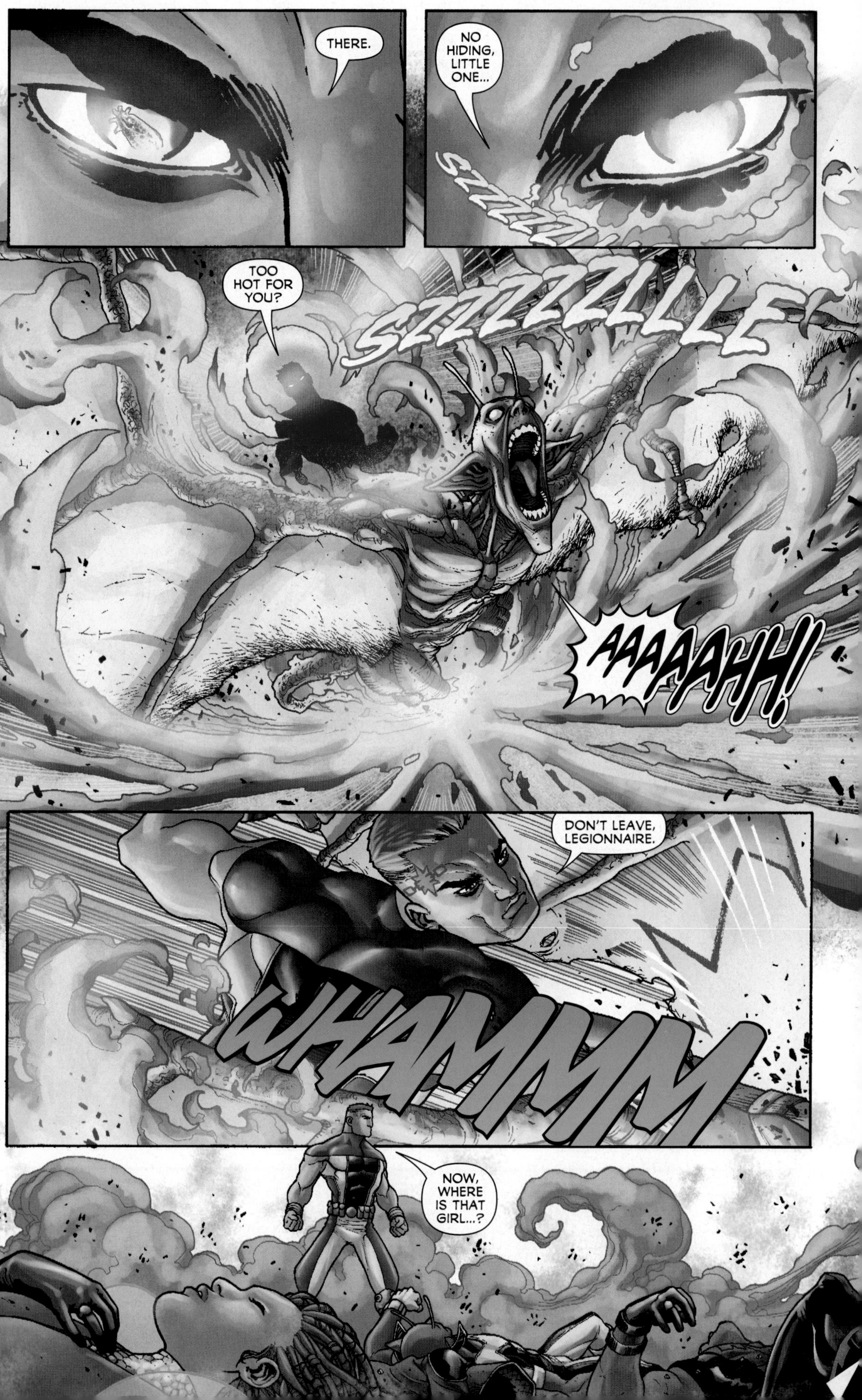

THERE.
NO HIDING, LITTLE ONE...
SZZZZZZ
TOO HOT FOR YOU?
SZZZZZZLLLE
AAAAAHH!
DON'T LEAVE, LEGIONNAIRE.
WHAMMM
NOW, WHERE IS THAT GIRL...?

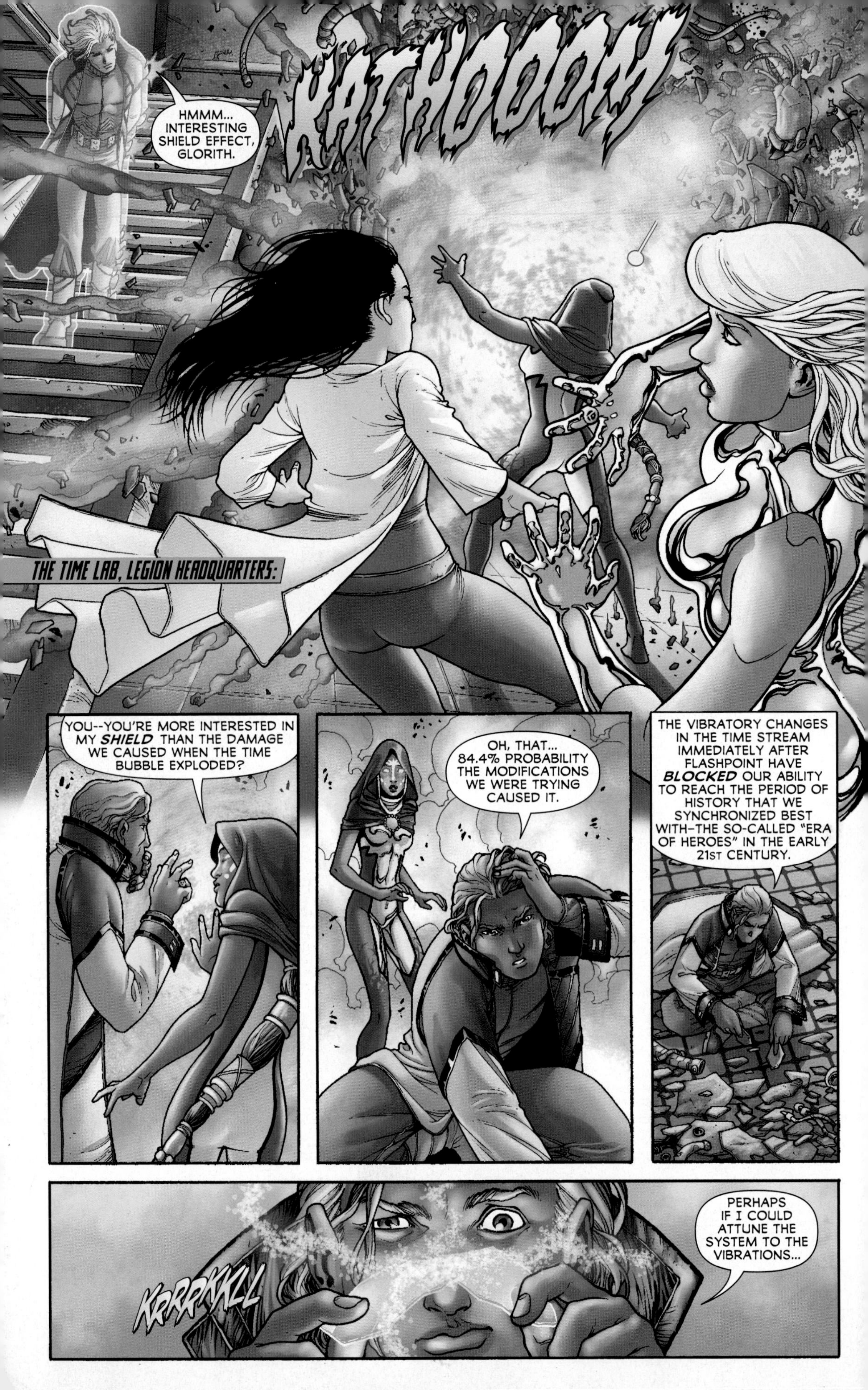
KATHOOOM
HMMM... INTERESTING SHIELD EFFECT, GLORITH.
THE TIME LAB, LEGION HEADQUARTERS:
YOU--YOU'RE MORE INTERESTED IN MY SHIELD THAN THE DAMAGE WE CAUSED WHEN THE TIME BUBBLE EXPLODED?
OH, THAT... 84.4% PROBABILITY THE MODIFICATIONS WE WERE TRYING CAUSED IT.
THE VIBRATORY CHANGES IN THE TIME STREAM IMMEDIATELY AFTER FLASHPOINT HAVE BLOCKED OUR ABILITY TO REACH THE PERIOD OF HISTORY THAT WE SYNCHRONIZED BEST WITH--THE SO-CALLED "ERA OF HEROES" IN THE EARLY 21ST CENTURY.
KRRRKKLL
PERHAPS IF I COULD ATTUNE THE SYSTEM TO THE VIBRATIONS...

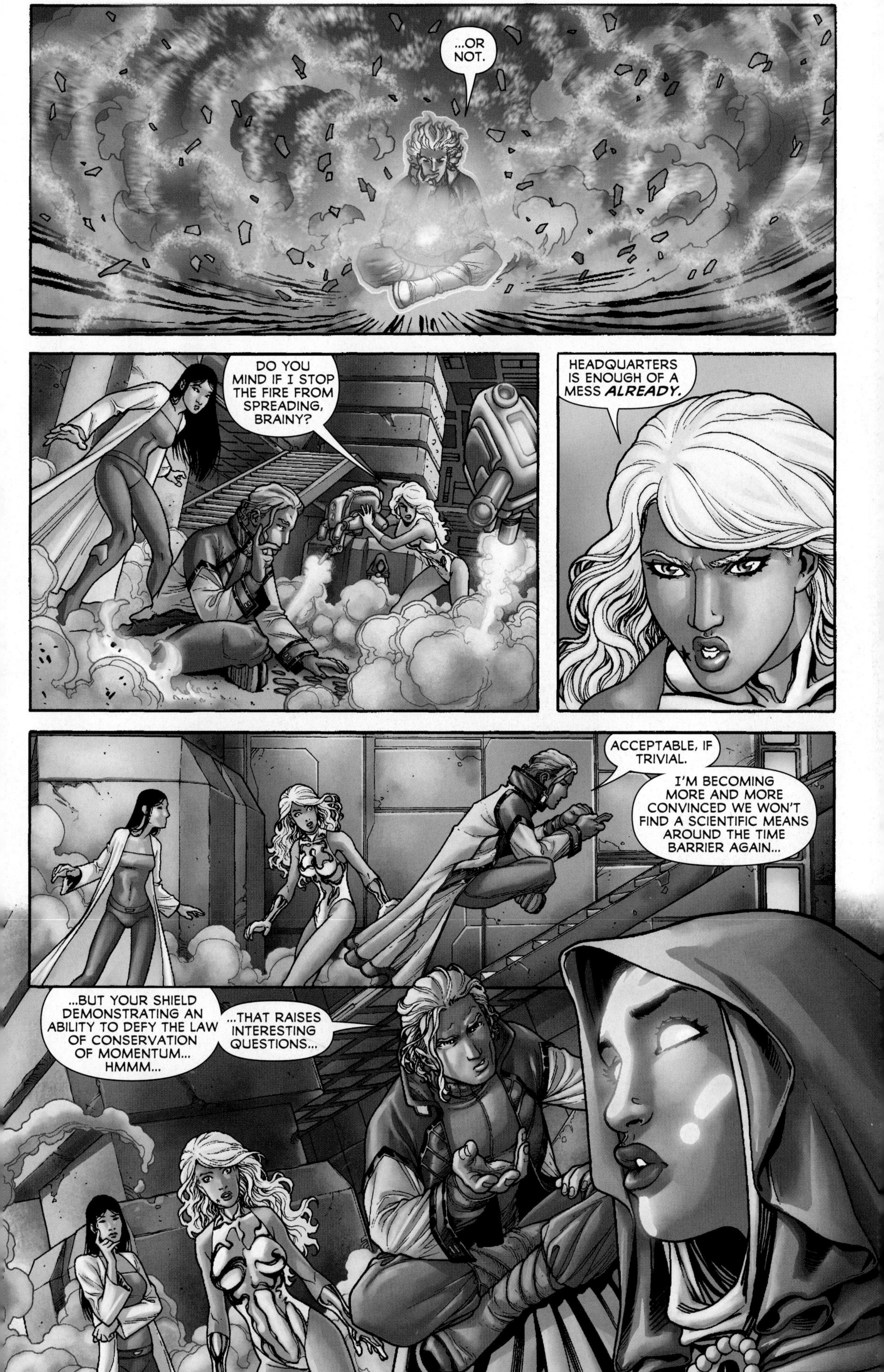

...OR NOT.
DO YOU MIND IF I STOP THE FIRE FROM SPREADING, BRAINY?
HEADQUARTERS IS ENOUGH OF A MESS ALREADY.
ACCEPTABLE, IF TRIVIAL.
I'M BECOMING MORE AND MORE CONVINCED WE WON'T FIND A SCIENTIFIC MEANS AROUND THE TIME BARRIER AGAIN...
...BUT YOUR SHIELD DEMONSTRATING AN ABILITY TO DEFY THE LAW OF CONSERVATION OF MOMENTUM... HMMM...
...THAT RAISES INTERESTING QUESTIONS...

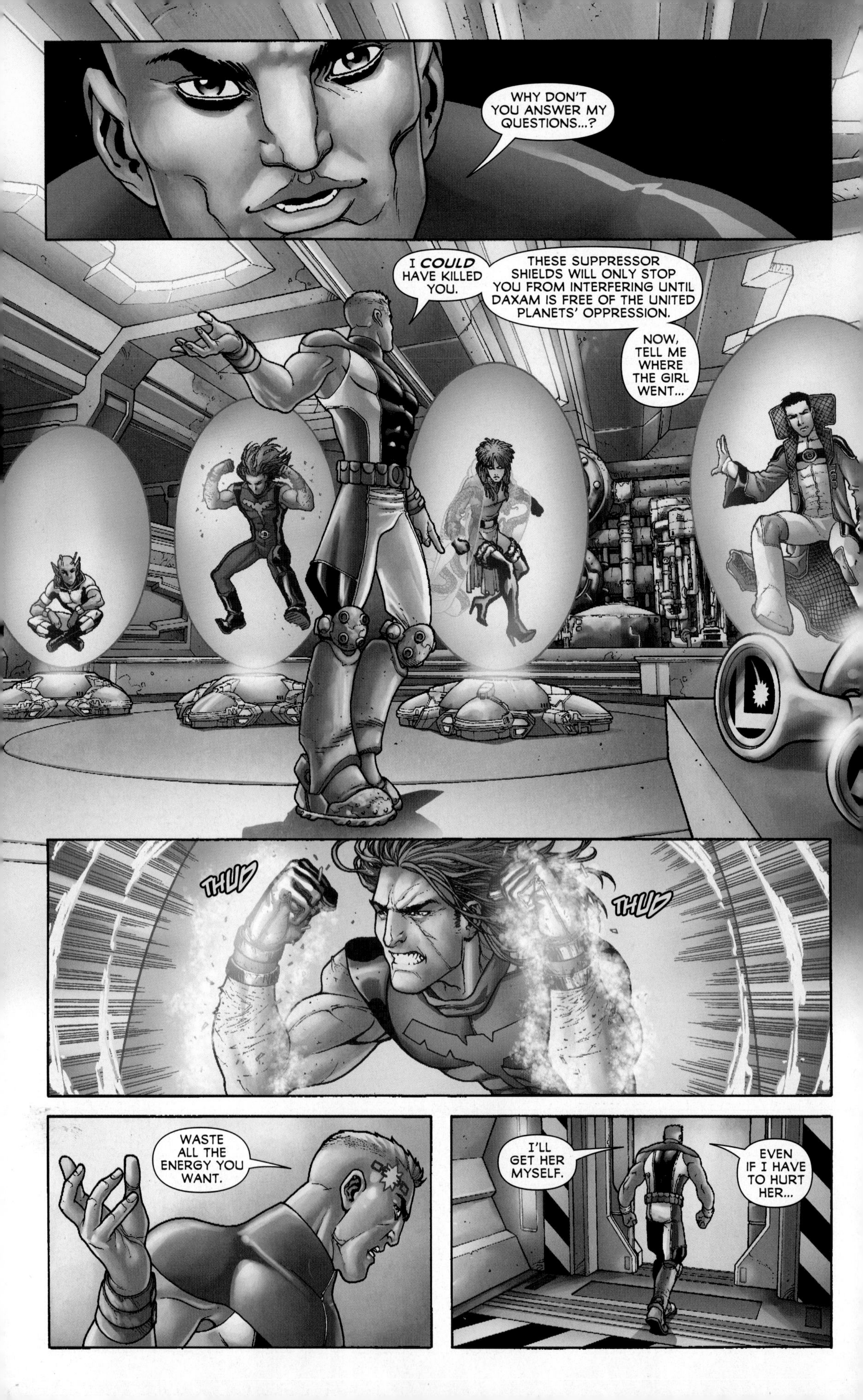
WHY DON'T YOU ANSWER MY QUESTIONS...?
I *COULD* HAVE KILLED YOU.
THESE SUPPRESSOR SHIELDS WILL ONLY STOP YOU FROM INTERFERING UNTIL DAXAM IS FREE OF THE UNITED PLANETS' OPPRESSION.
NOW, TELL ME WHERE THE GIRL WENT...
THUD
THUD
WASTE ALL THE ENERGY YOU WANT.
I'LL GET HER MYSELF.
EVEN IF I HAVE TO HURT HER...

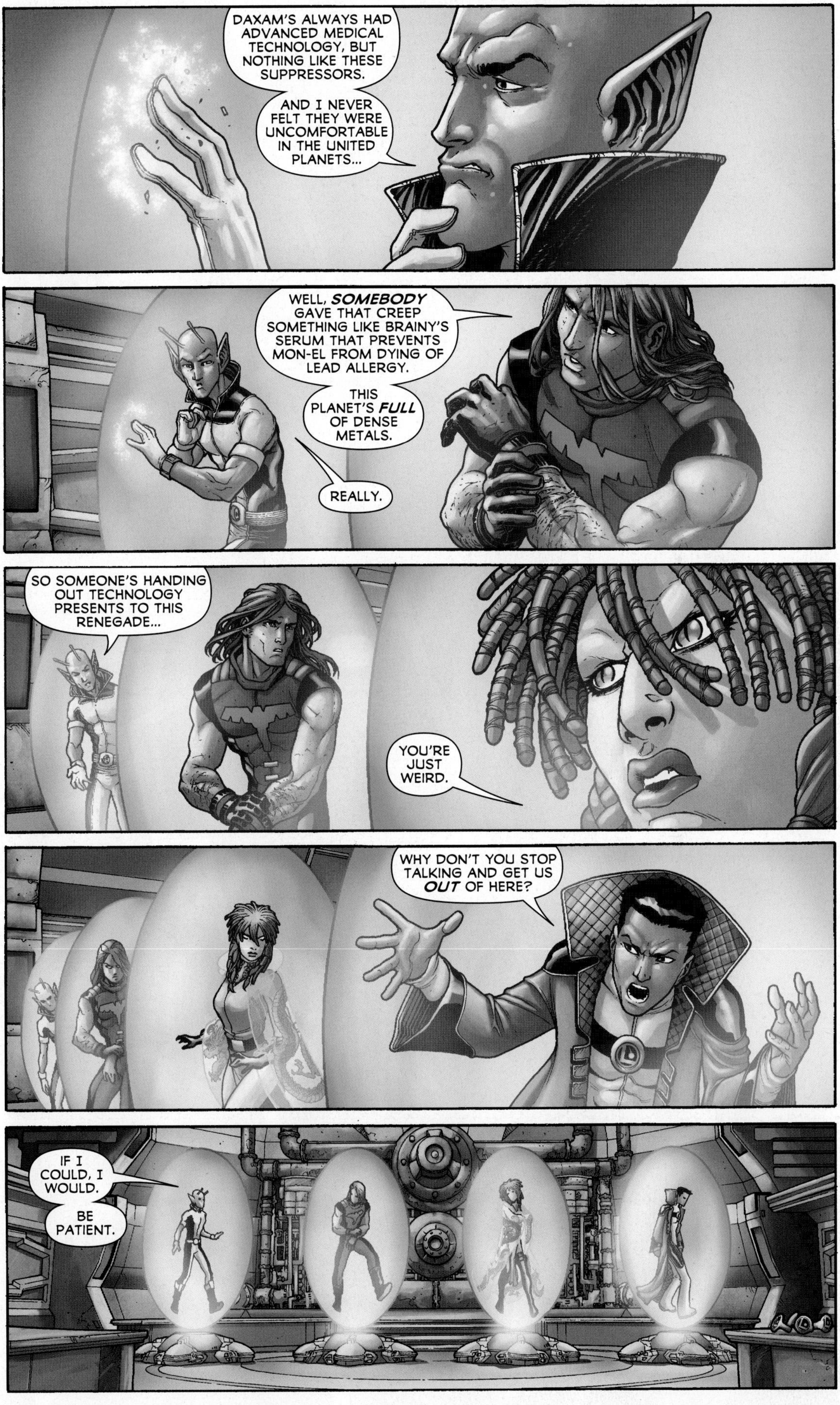
DAXAM'S ALWAYS HAD ADVANCED MEDICAL TECHNOLOGY, BUT NOTHING LIKE THESE SUPPRESSORS.
AND I NEVER FELT THEY WERE UNCOMFORTABLE IN THE UNITED PLANETS...
WELL, SOMEBODY GAVE THAT CREEP SOMETHING LIKE BRAINY'S SERUM THAT PREVENTS MON-EL FROM DYING OF LEAD ALLERGY.
THIS PLANET'S FULL OF DENSE METALS.
REALLY.
SO SOMEONE'S HANDING OUT TECHNOLOGY PRESENTS TO THIS RENEGADE...
YOU'RE JUST WEIRD.
WHY DON'T YOU STOP TALKING AND GET US OUT OF HERE?
IF I COULD, I WOULD.
BE PATIENT.

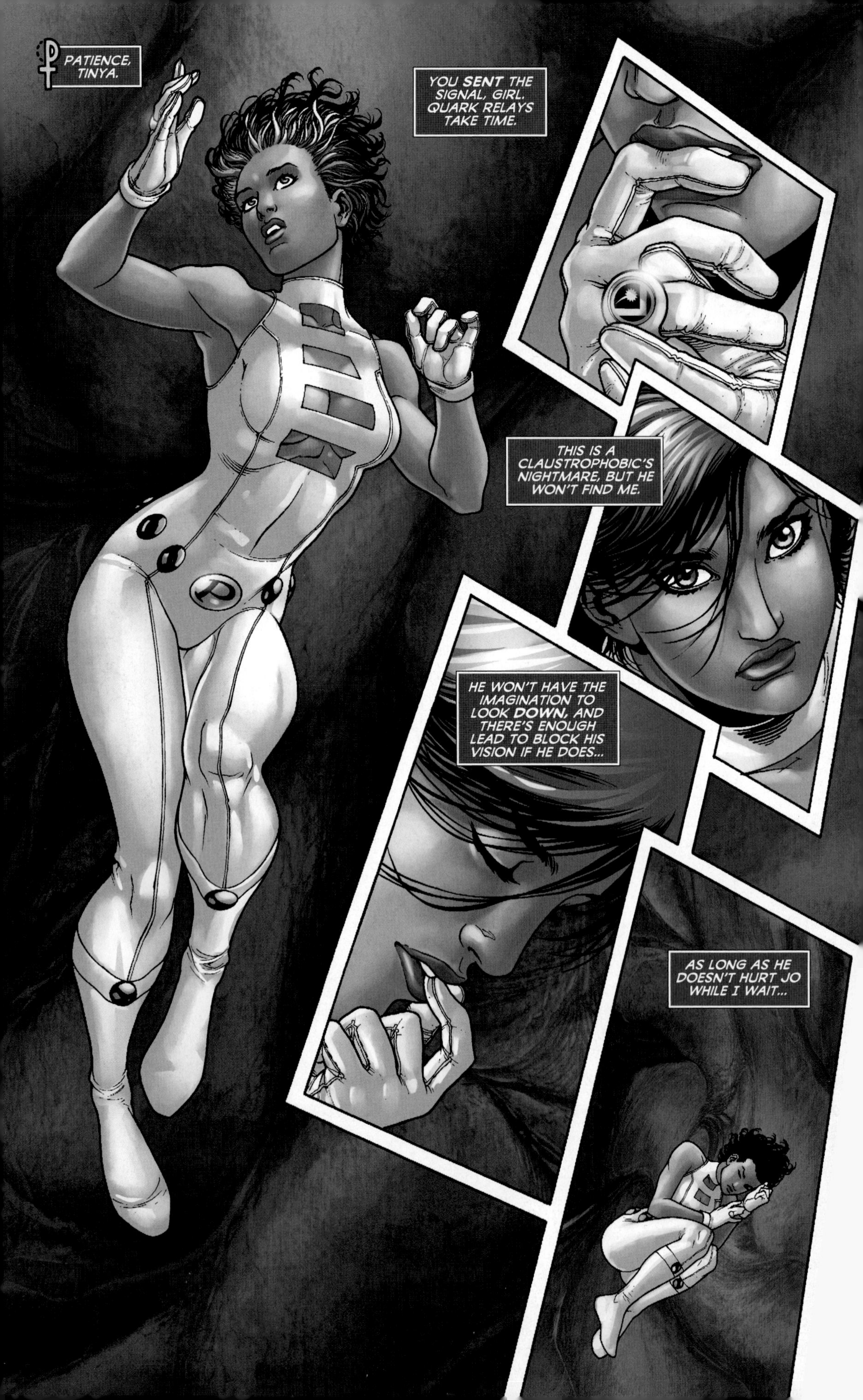
PATIENCE, TINYA.
YOU SENT THE SIGNAL, GIRL. QUARK RELAYS TAKE TIME.
THIS IS A CLAUSTROPHOBIC'S NIGHTMARE, BUT HE WON'T FIND ME.
HE WON'T HAVE THE IMAGINATION TO LOOK DOWN, AND THERE'S ENOUGH LEAD TO BLOCK HIS VISION IF HE DOES...
AS LONG AS HE DOESN'T HURT JO WHILE I WAIT...

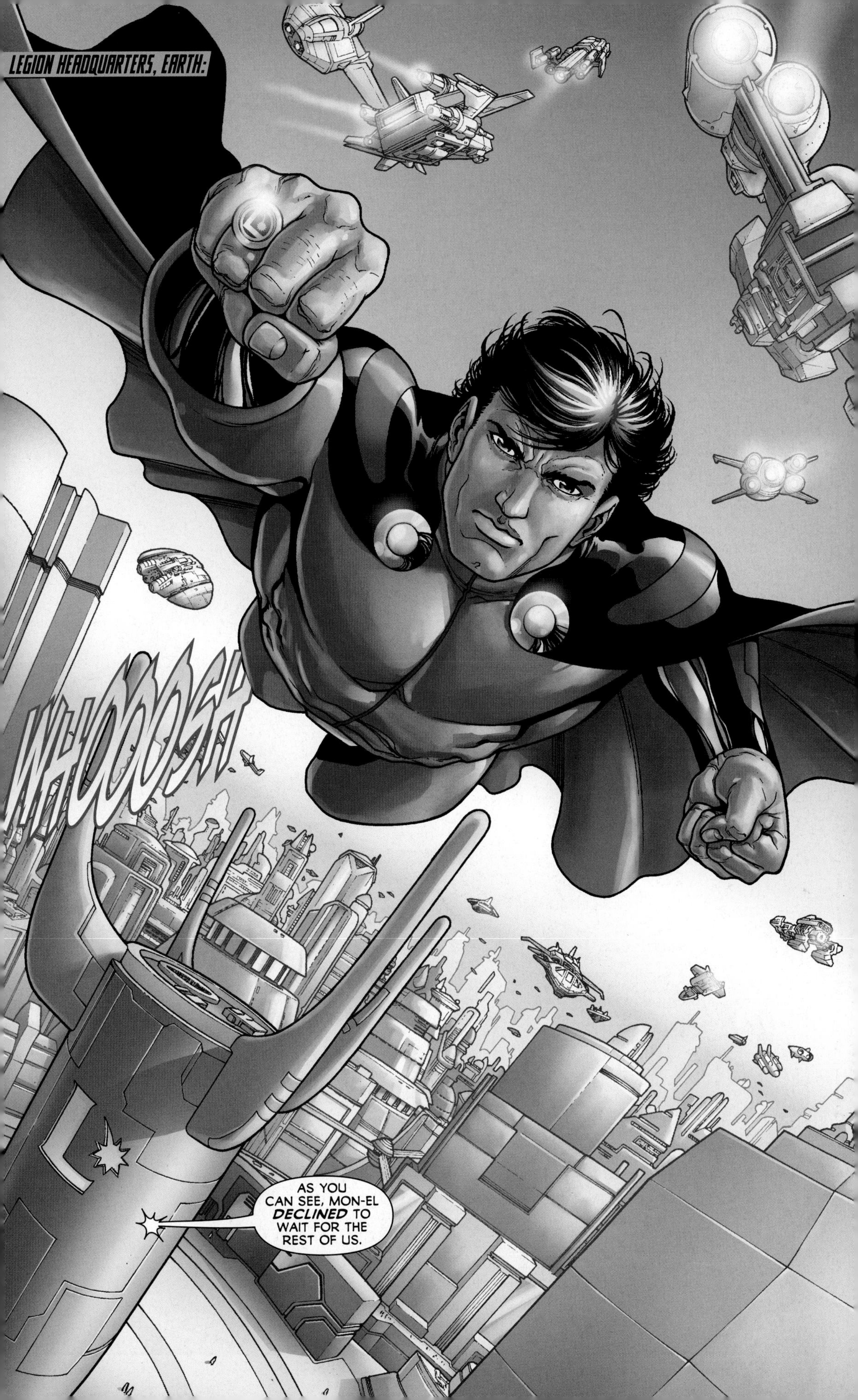
LEGION HEADQUARTERS, EARTH:
WHOOOSH
AS YOU CAN SEE, MON-EL *DECLINED* TO WAIT FOR THE REST OF US.

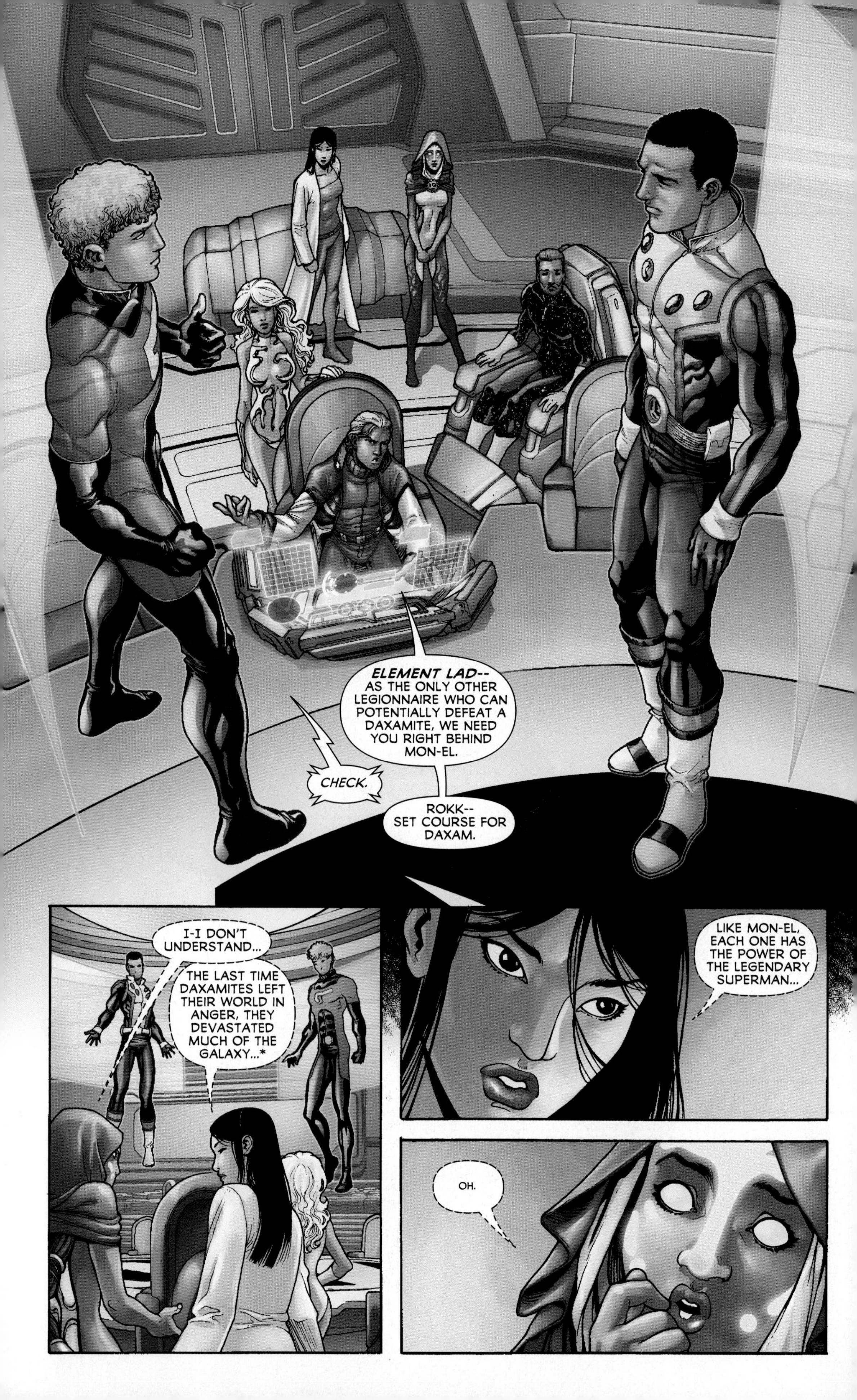
ELEMENT LAD-- AS THE ONLY OTHER LEGIONNAIRE WHO CAN POTENTIALLY DEFEAT A DAXAMITE, WE NEED YOU RIGHT BEHIND MON-EL.
CHECK.
ROKK-- SET COURSE FOR DAXAM.
I-I DON'T UNDERSTAND...
THE LAST TIME DAXAMITES LEFT THEIR WORLD IN ANGER, THEY DEVASTATED MUCH OF THE GALAXY...*
LIKE MON-EL, EACH ONE HAS THE POWER OF THE LEGENDARY SUPERMAN...
OH.

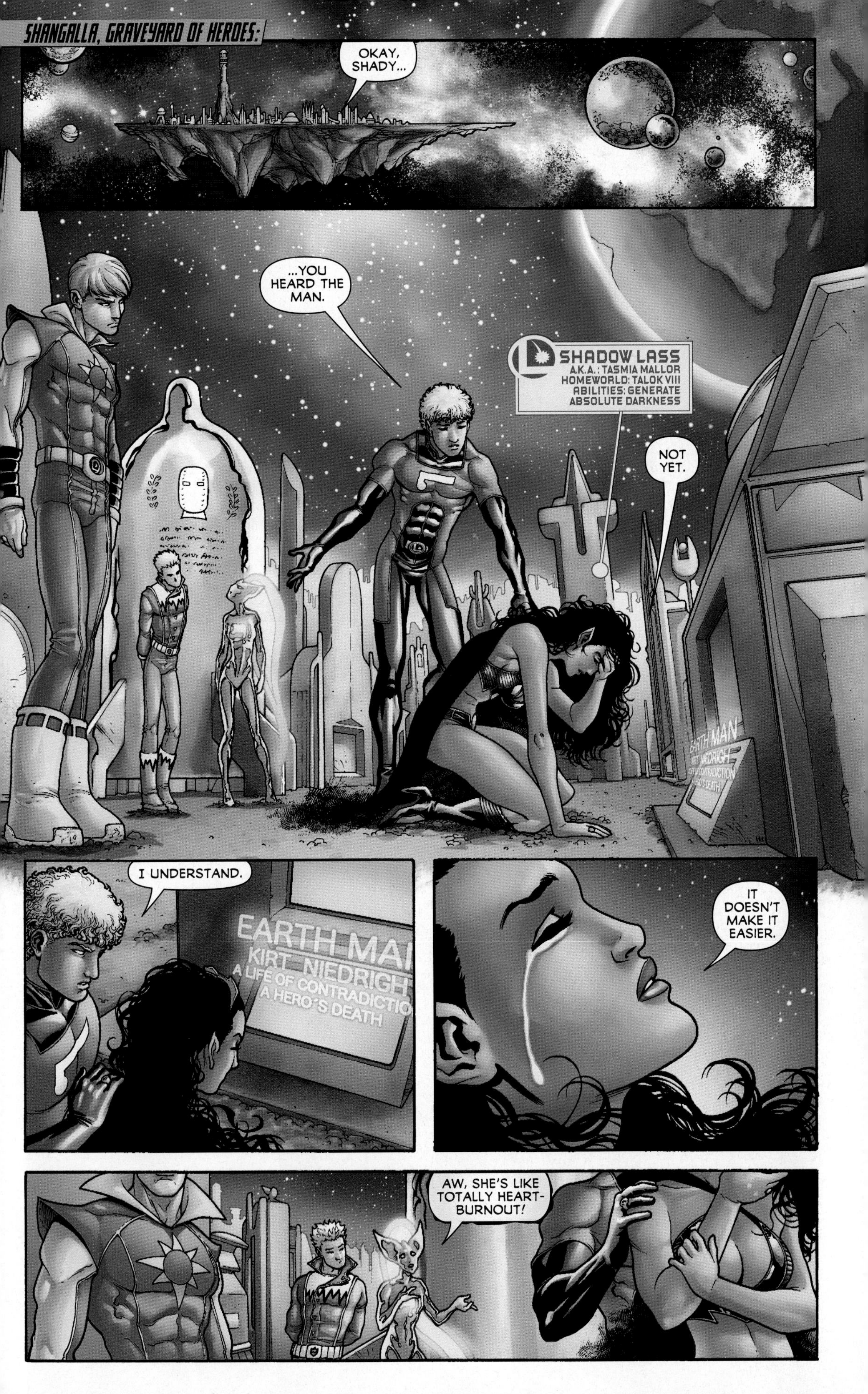
SHANGALLA, GRAVEYARD OF HEROES:
OKAY, SHADY...
...YOU HEARD THE MAN.
SHADOW LASS
A.K.A.: TASMIA MALLOR
HOMEWORLD: TALOK VIII
ABILITIES: GENERATE ABSOLUTE DARKNESS
NOT YET.
EARTH MAN
I UNDERSTAND.
EARTH MA
KIRT NIEDRIGH
A LIFE OF CONTRADICTIO
A HERO'S DEATH
IT DOESN'T MAKE IT EASIER.
AW, SHE'S LIKE TOTALLY HEART-BURNOUT!

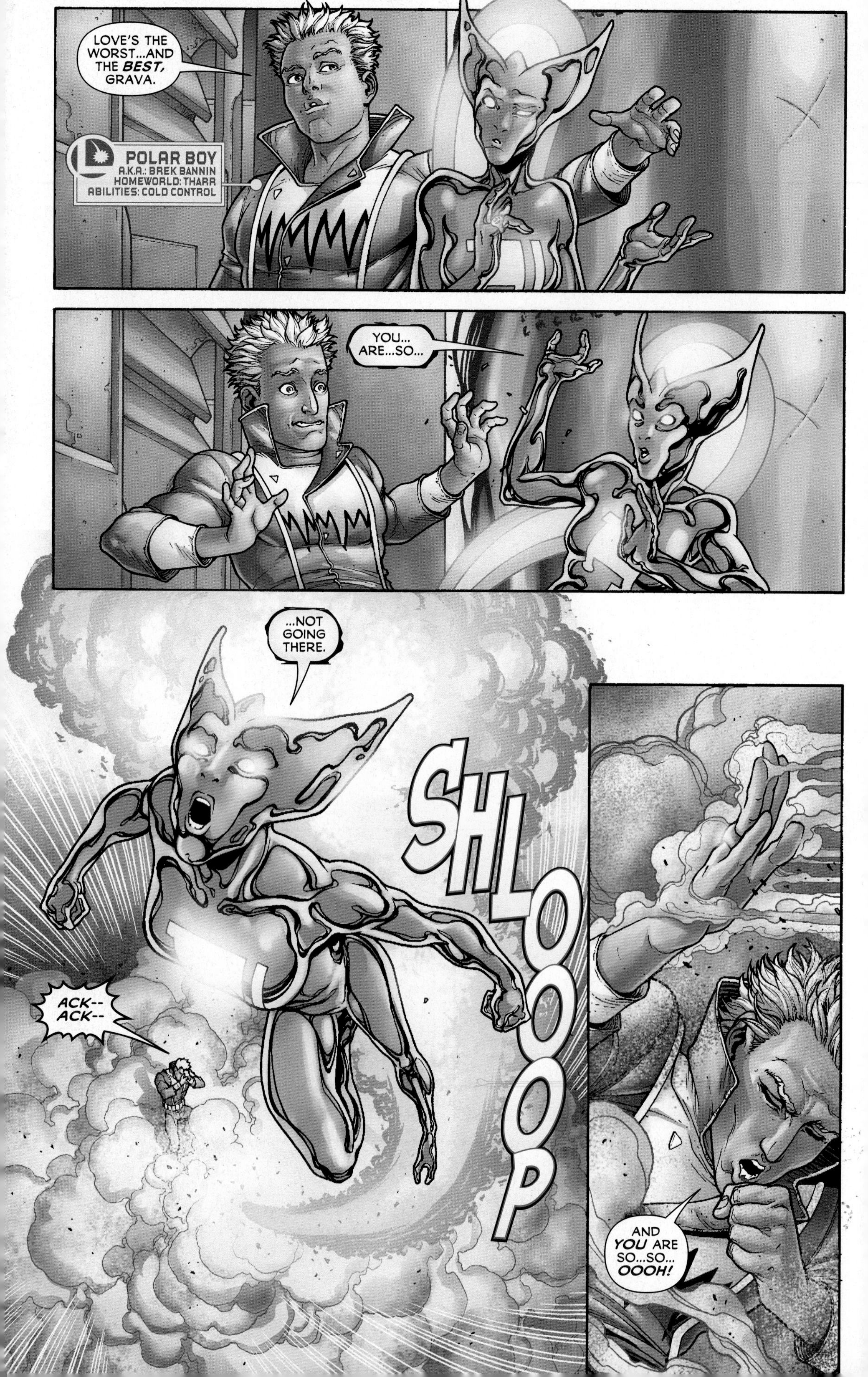
LOVE'S THE WORST...AND THE *BEST,* GRAVA.
POLAR BOY
A.K.A.: BREK BANNIN
HOMEWORLD: THARR
ABILITIES: COLD CONTROL
YOU... ARE...SO...
...NOT GOING THERE.
SHLOOOOP
ACK-- ACK--
AND *YOU* ARE SO...SO... *OOOH!*

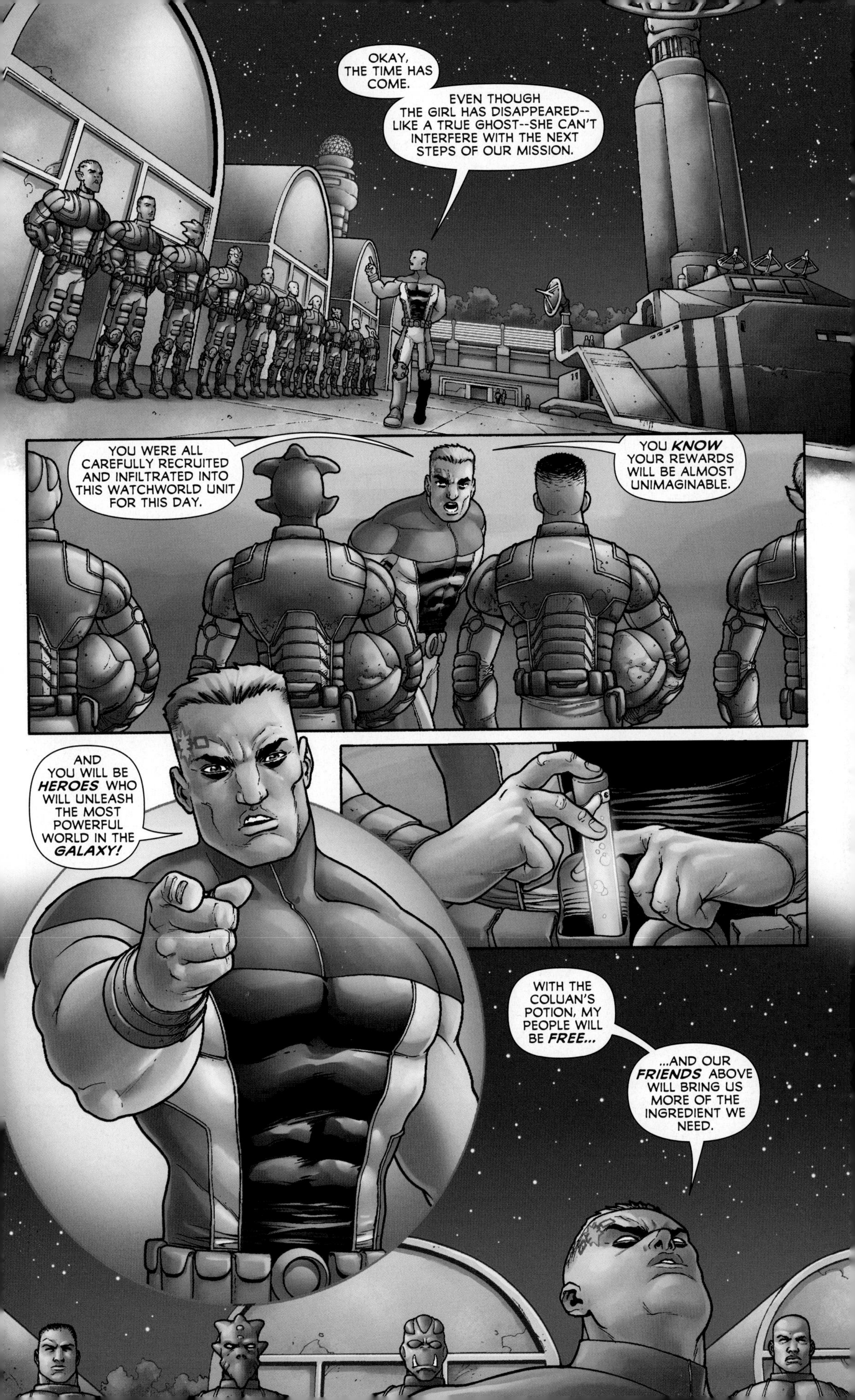
OKAY, THE TIME HAS COME.
EVEN THOUGH THE GIRL HAS DISAPPEARED-- LIKE A TRUE GHOST--SHE CAN'T INTERFERE WITH THE NEXT STEPS OF OUR MISSION.
YOU WERE ALL CAREFULLY RECRUITED AND INFILTRATED INTO THIS WATCHWORLD UNIT FOR THIS DAY.
YOU *KNOW* YOUR REWARDS WILL BE ALMOST UNIMAGINABLE.
AND YOU WILL BE *HEROES* WHO WILL UNLEASH THE MOST POWERFUL WORLD IN THE *GALAXY!*
WITH THE COLUAN'S POTION, MY PEOPLE WILL BE *FREE...*
...AND OUR *FRIENDS* ABOVE WILL BRING US MORE OF THE INGREDIENT WE NEED.

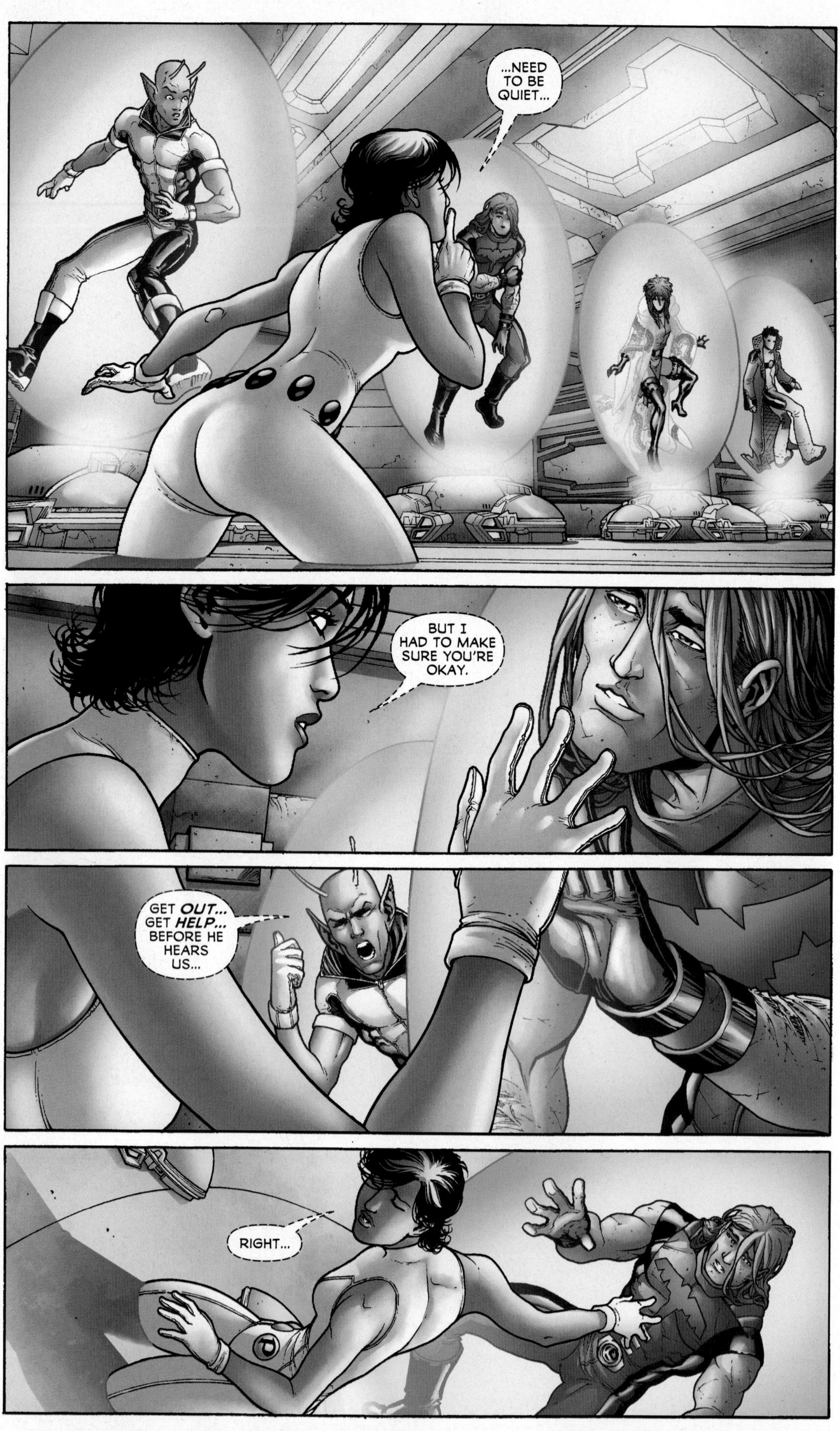
...NEED TO BE QUIET...
BUT I HAD TO MAKE SURE YOU'RE OKAY.
GET *OUT*... GET *HELP*... BEFORE HE HEARS US...
RIGHT...

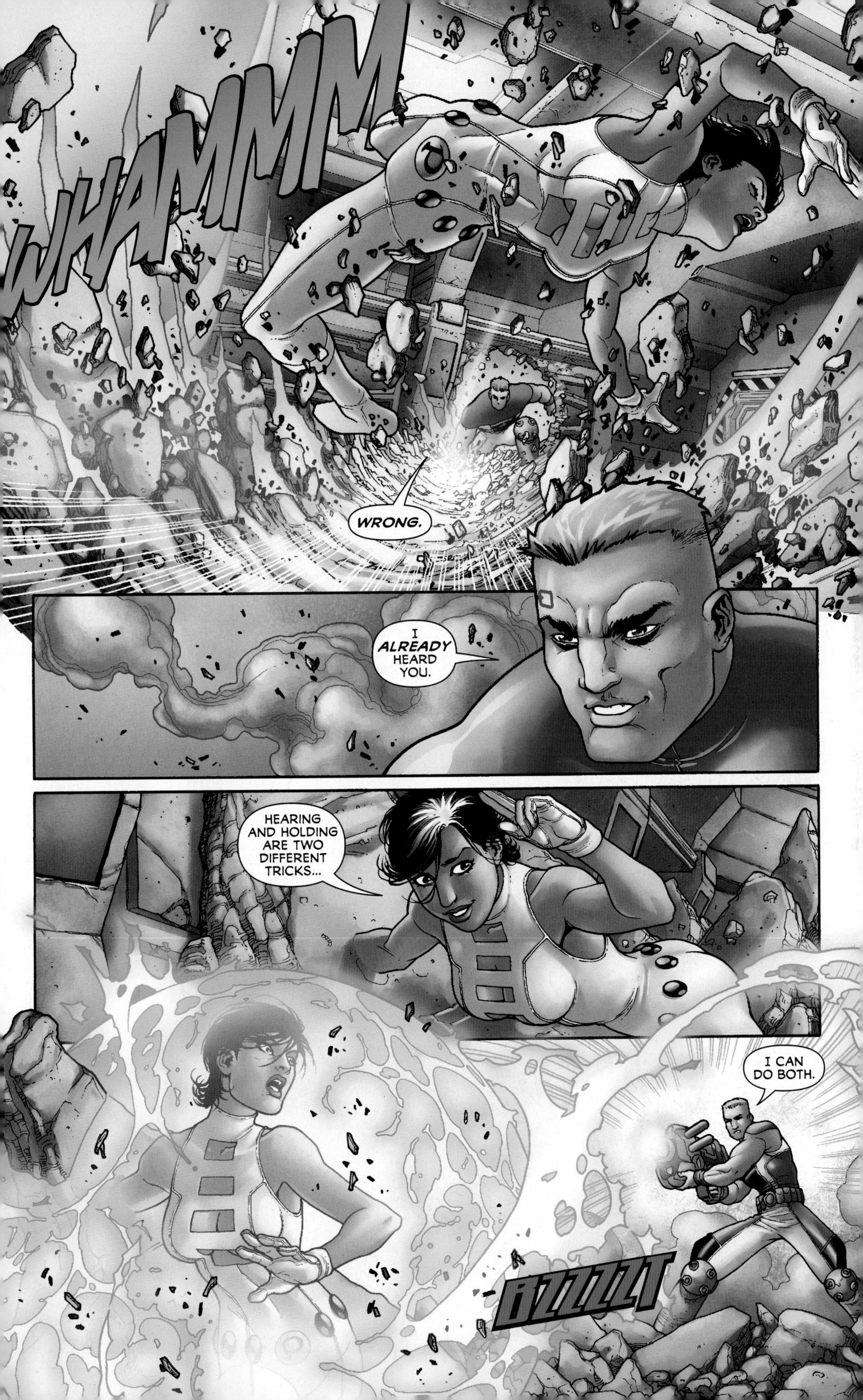
WHAMMMM
WRONG.
I ALREADY HEARD YOU.
HEARING AND HOLDING ARE TWO DIFFERENT TRICKS...
I CAN DO BOTH.
BZZZZT

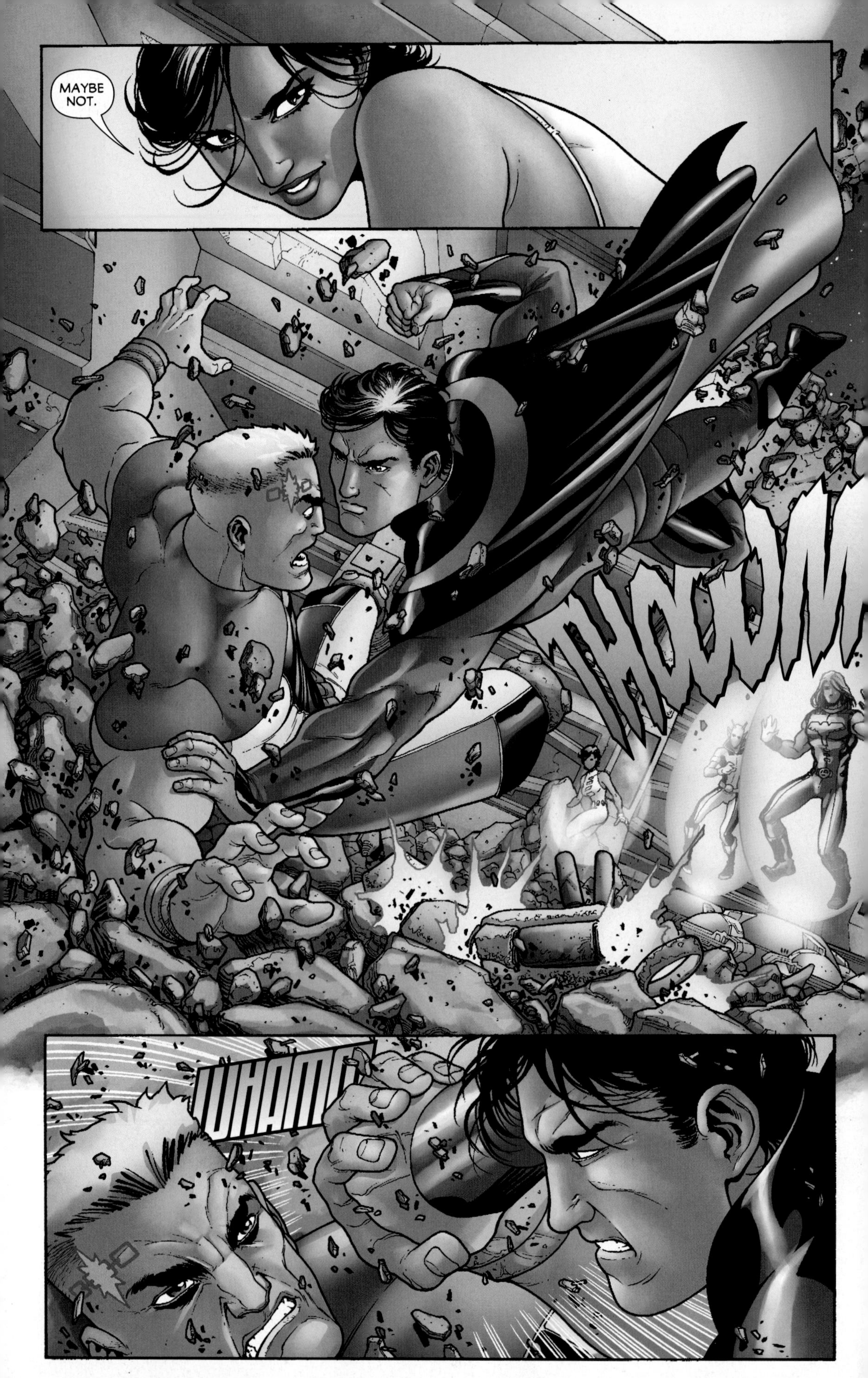
MAYBE NOT.
WHOOOM
WHAMM

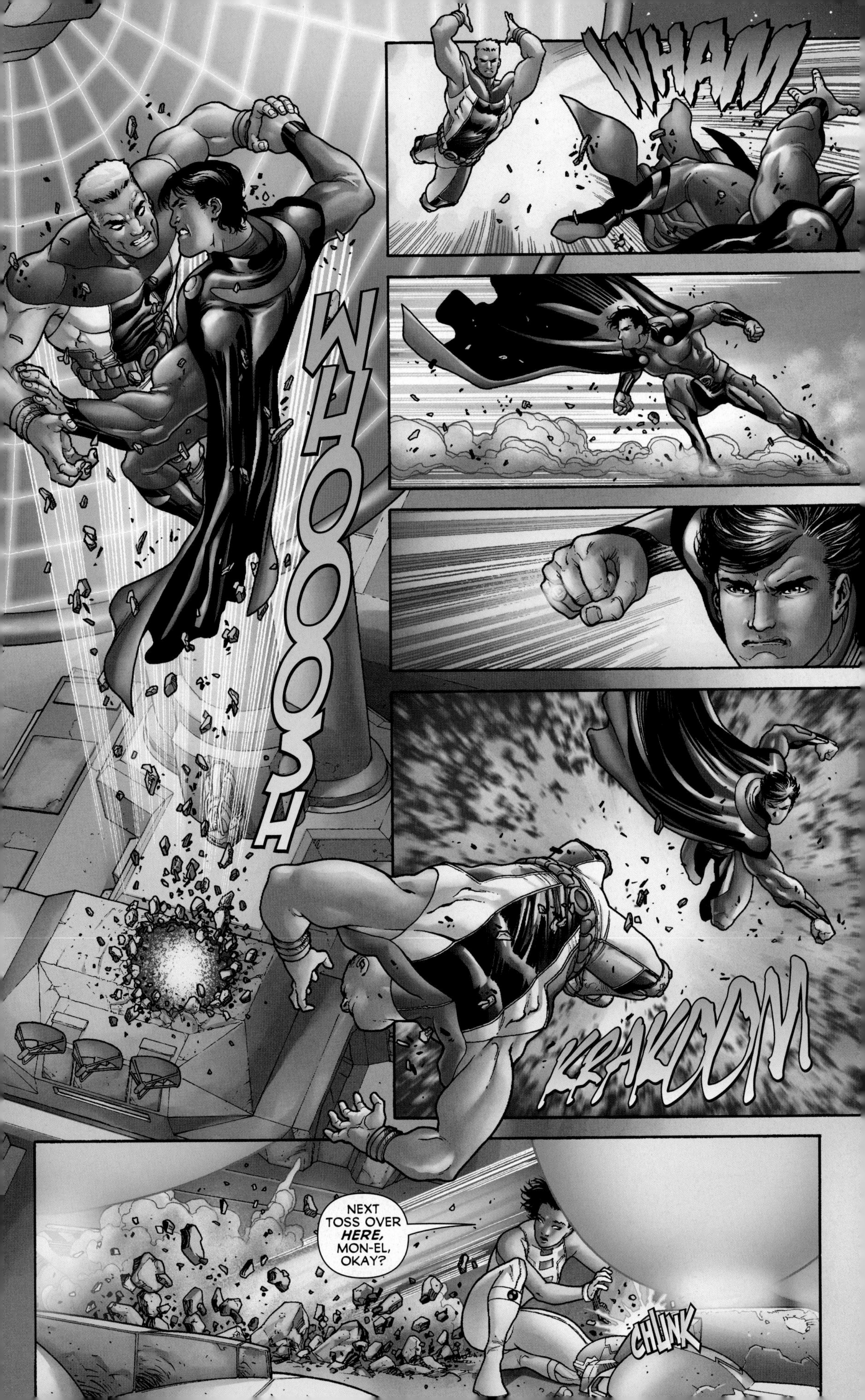
WHAM
WHOOOOSH
KRAKOOM
NEXT TOSS OVER *HERE,* MON-EL, OKAY?
CHUNK

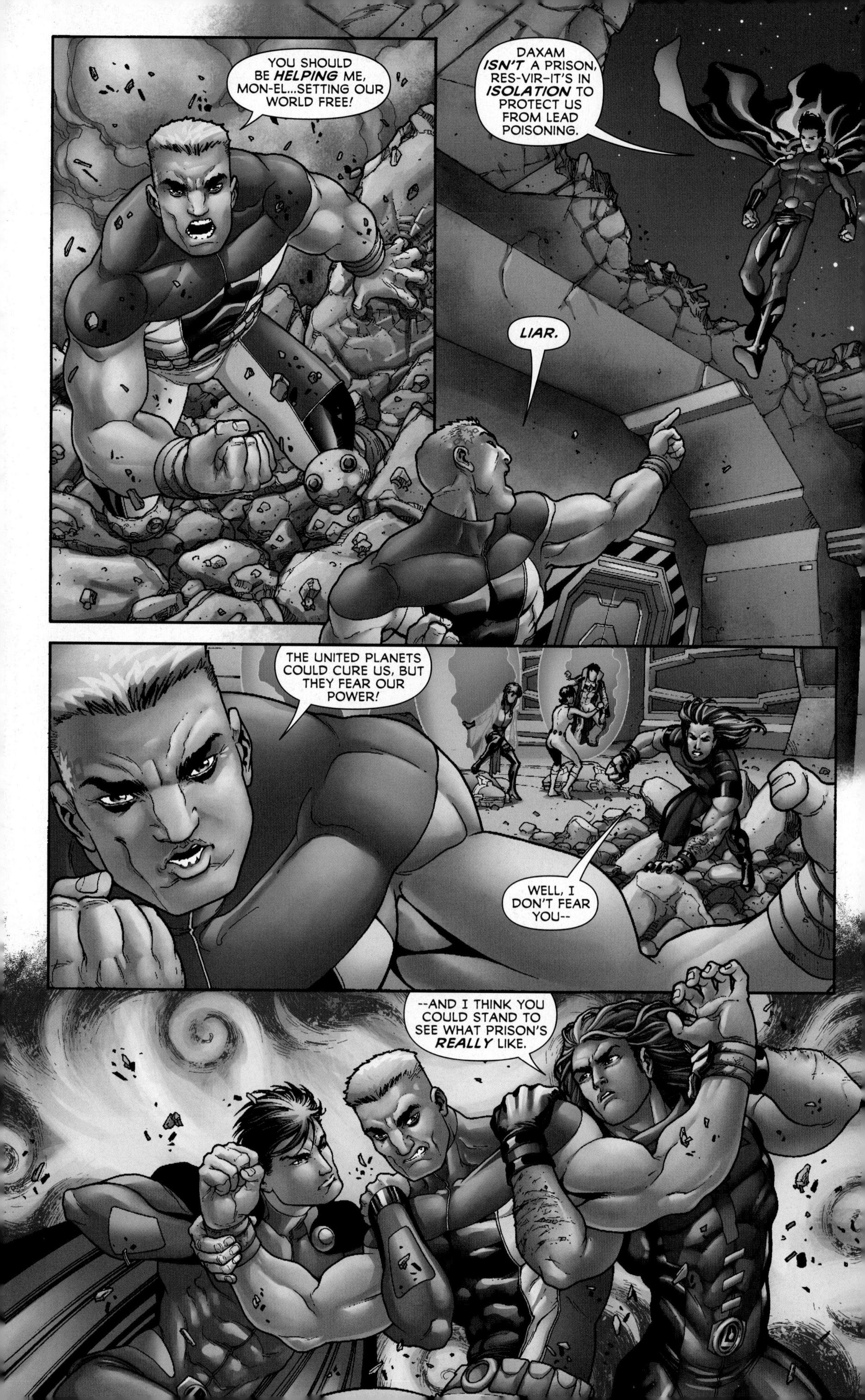

YOU SHOULD BE *HELPING* ME, MON-EL...SETTING OUR WORLD FREE!
DAXAM *ISN'T* A PRISON, RES-VIR--IT'S IN *ISOLATION* TO PROTECT US FROM LEAD POISONING.
LIAR.
THE UNITED PLANETS COULD CURE US, BUT THEY FEAR OUR POWER!
WELL, I DON'T FEAR YOU--
--AND I THINK YOU COULD STAND TO SEE WHAT PRISON'S *REALLY* LIKE.

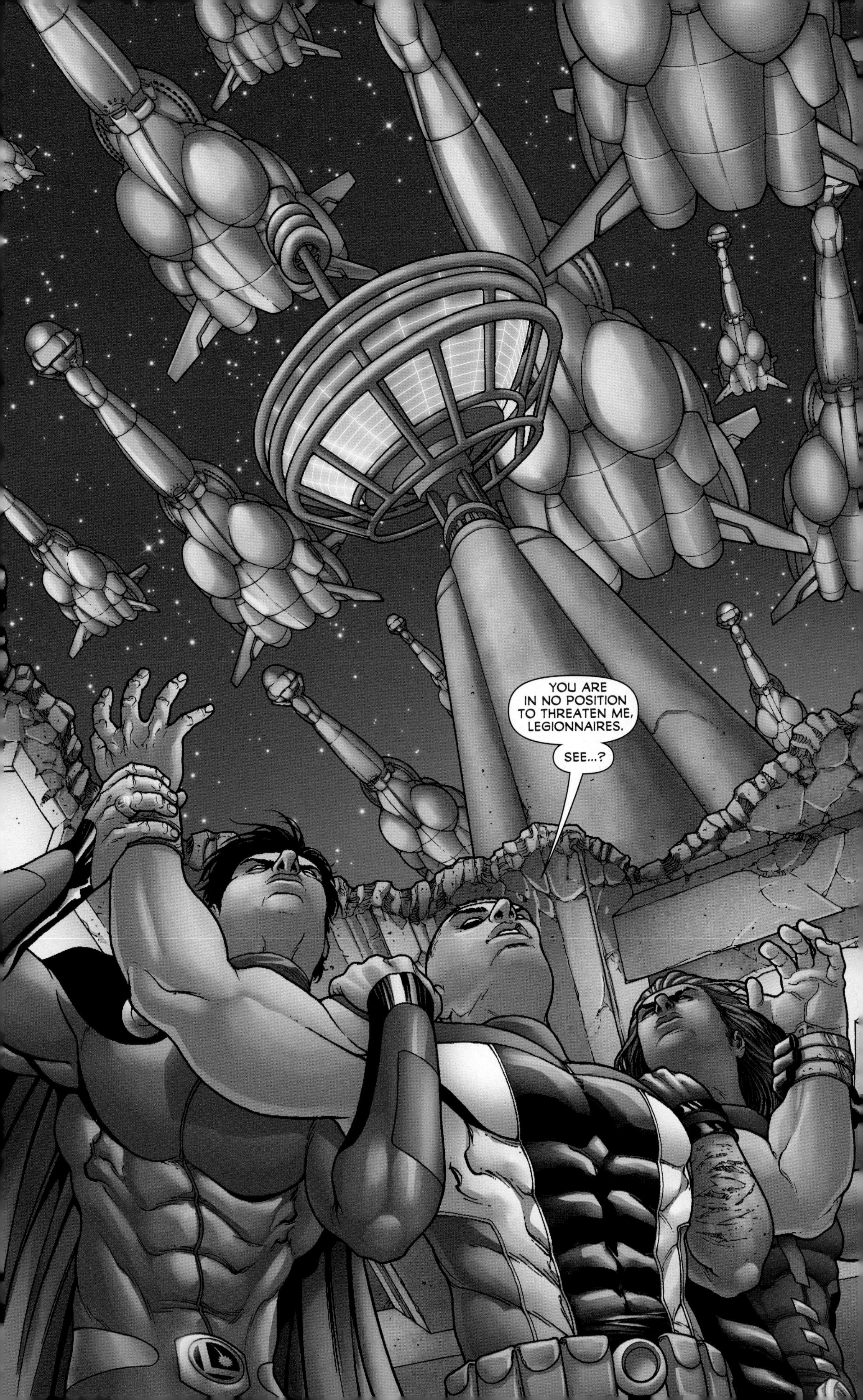
YOU ARE IN NO POSITION TO THREATEN ME, LEGIONNAIRES.
SEE...?

cover art by
CHRIS SPROUSE, KARL STORY & GUY MAJOR

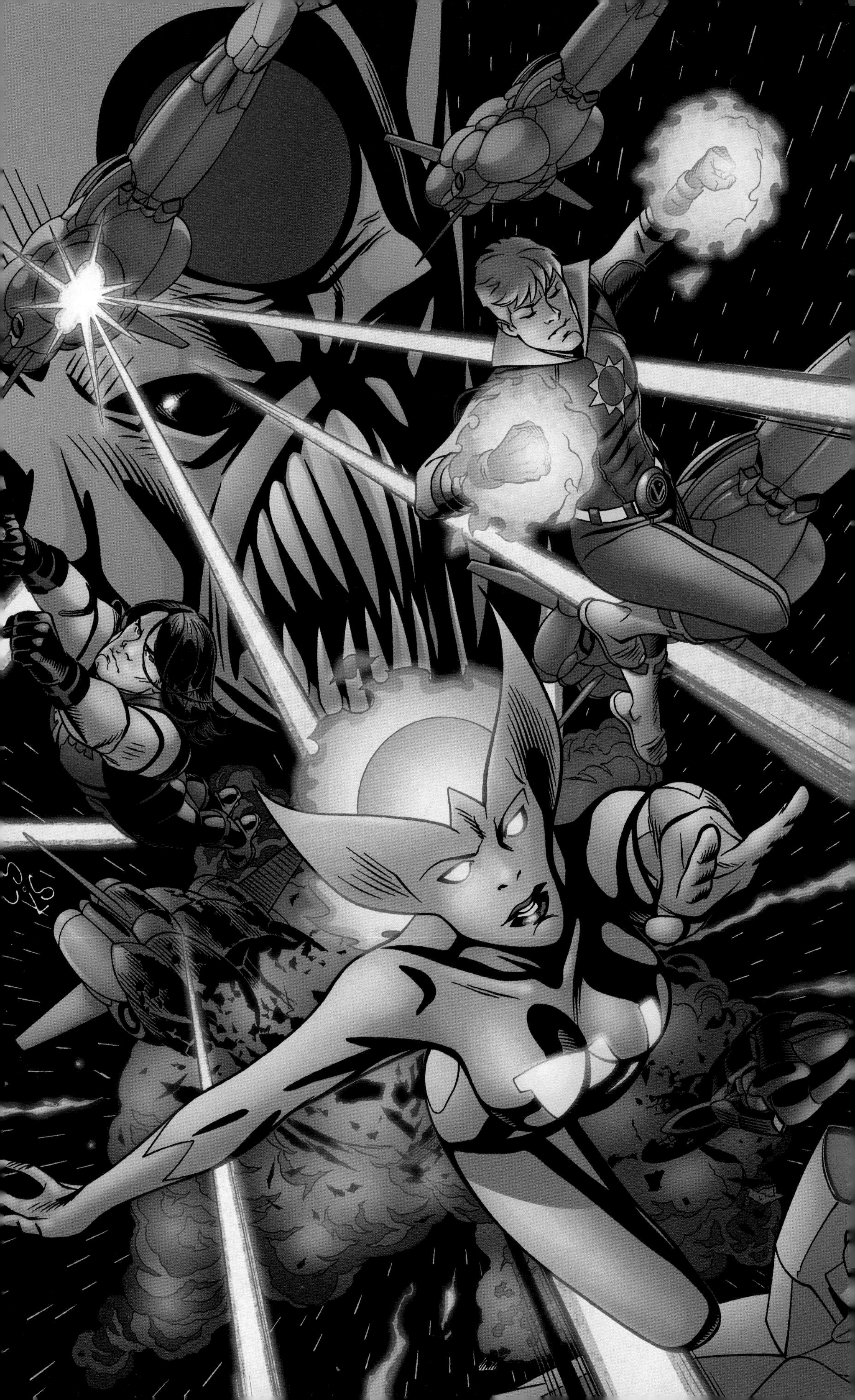

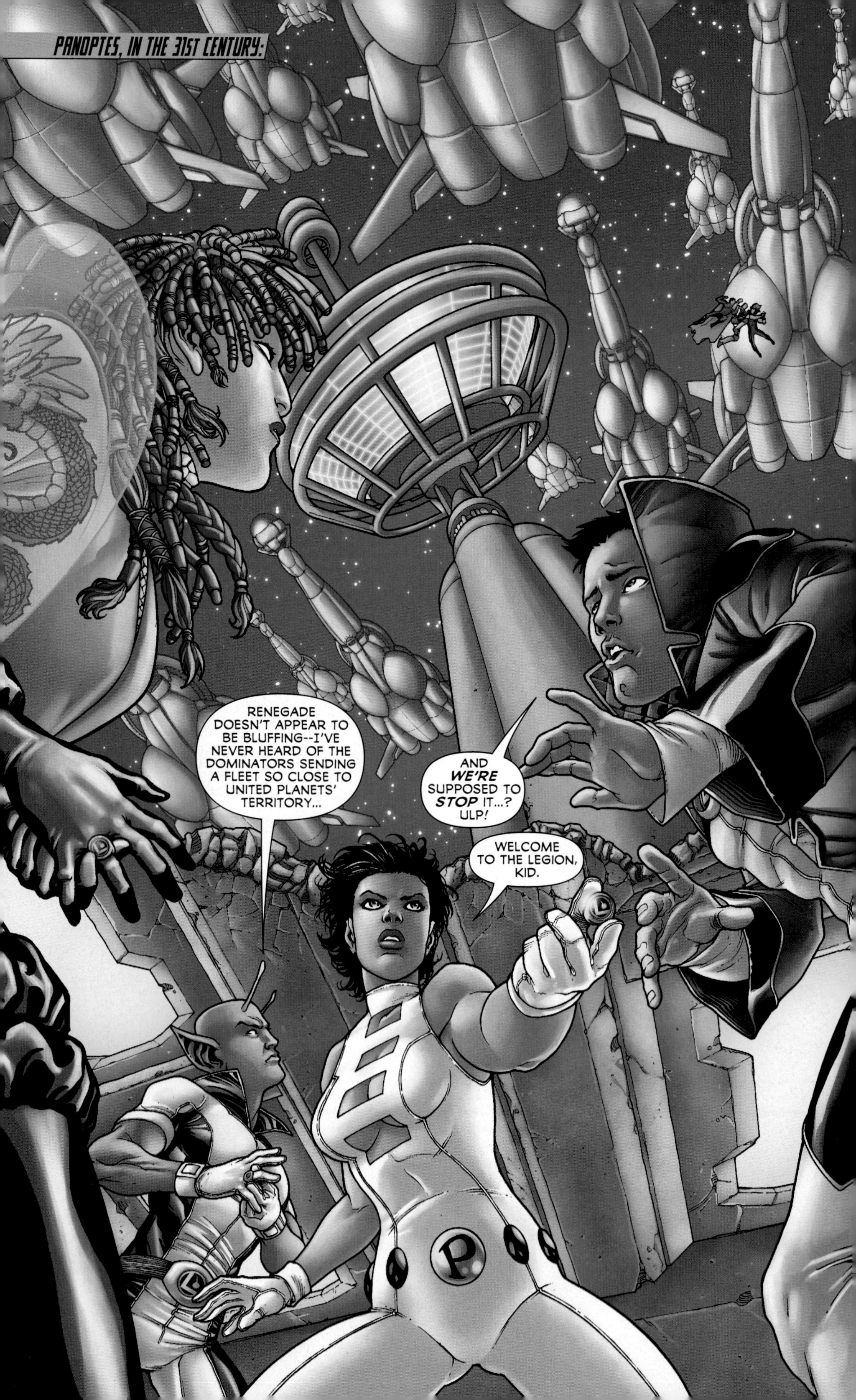
PANOPTES, IN THE 31ST CENTURY:
RENEGADE DOESN'T APPEAR TO BE BLUFFING--I'VE NEVER HEARD OF THE DOMINATORS SENDING A FLEET SO CLOSE TO UNITED PLANETS' TERRITORY...
AND WE'RE SUPPOSED TO STOP IT...? ULP!
WELCOME TO THE LEGION, KID.

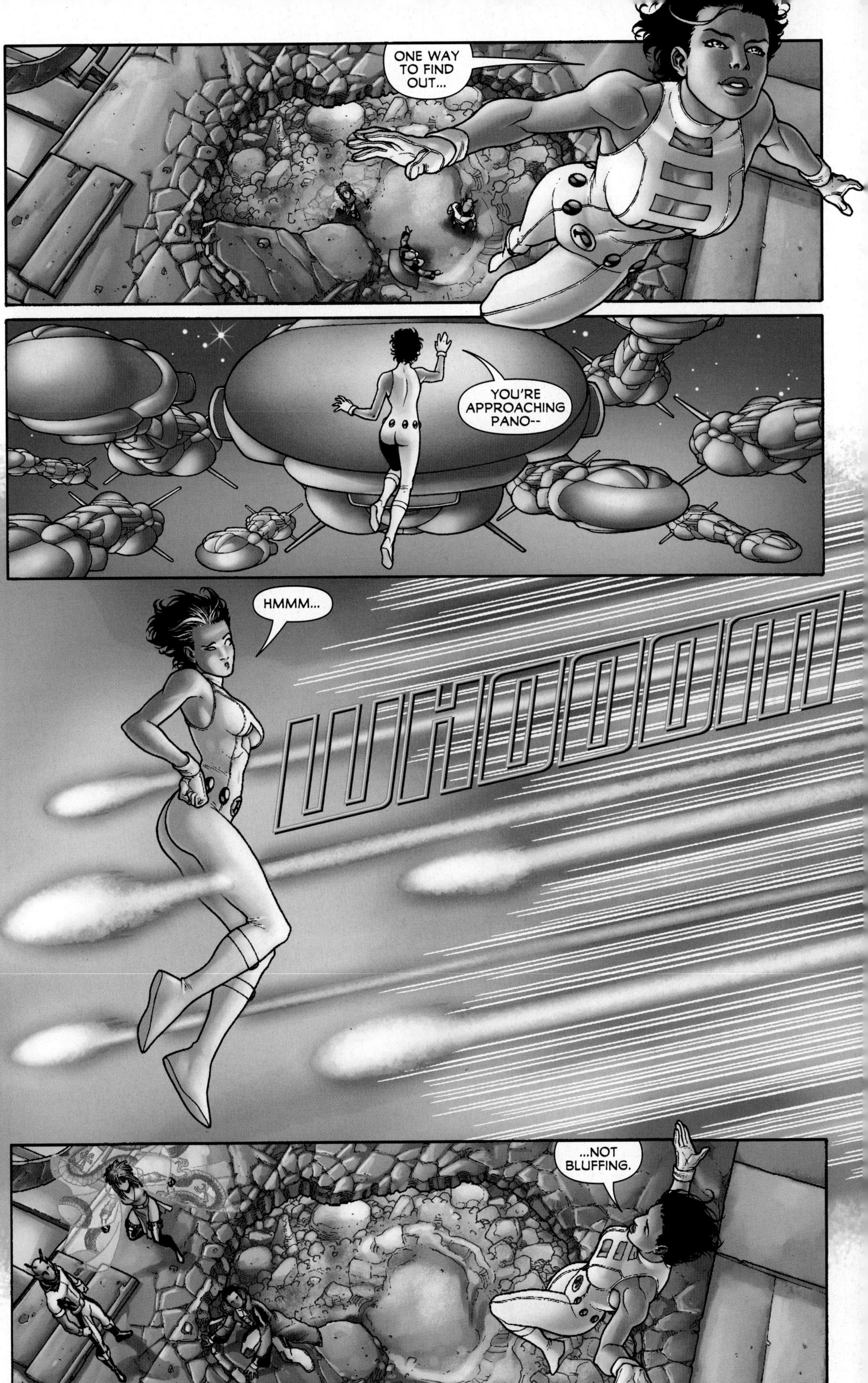
ONE WAY TO FIND OUT...
YOU'RE APPROACHING PANO--
HMMM...
WHOOOOM
...NOT BLUFFING.

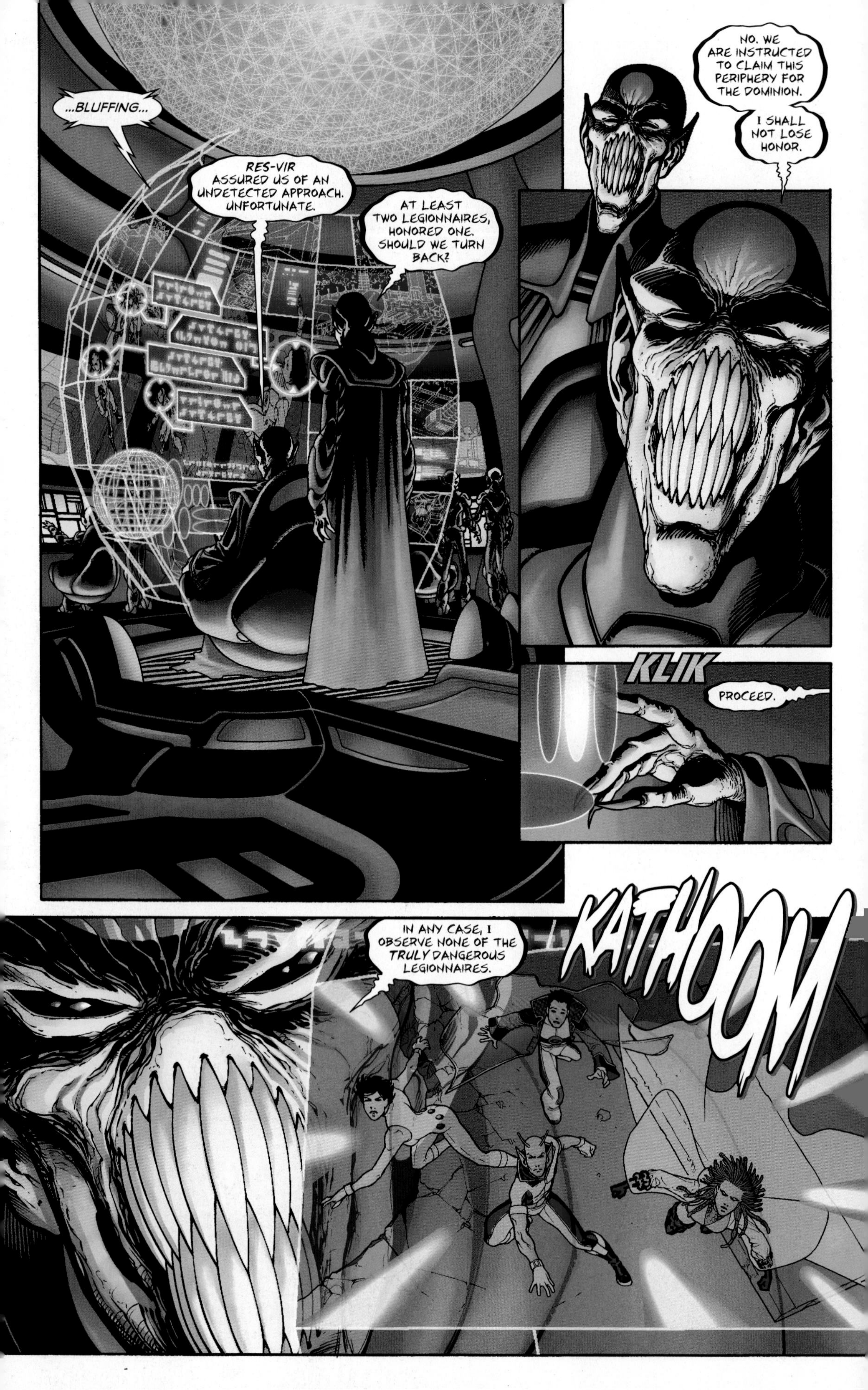
...BLUFFING...
RES-VIR ASSURED US OF AN UNDETECTED APPROACH. UNFORTUNATE.
AT LEAST TWO LEGIONNAIRES, HONORED ONE. SHOULD WE TURN BACK?
NO. WE ARE INSTRUCTED TO CLAIM THIS PERIPHERY FOR THE DOMINION.
I SHALL NOT LOSE HONOR.
KLIK
PROCEED.
KATHOOM
IN ANY CASE, I OBSERVE NONE OF THE TRULY DANGEROUS LEGIONNAIRES.

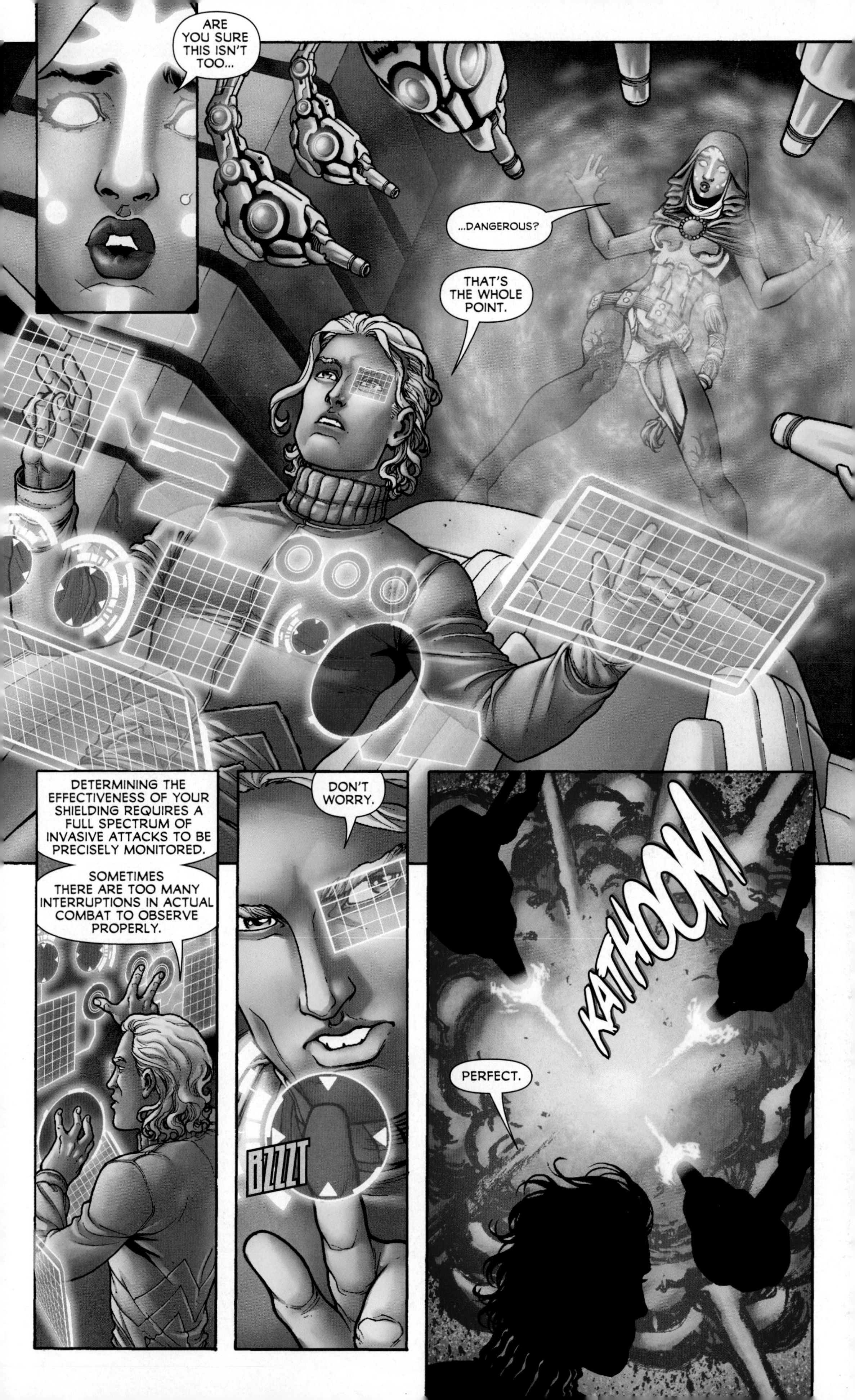
ARE YOU SURE THIS ISN'T TOO...
...DANGEROUS?
THAT'S THE WHOLE POINT.
DETERMINING THE EFFECTIVENESS OF YOUR SHIELDING REQUIRES A FULL SPECTRUM OF INVASIVE ATTACKS TO BE PRECISELY MONITORED.
SOMETIMES THERE ARE TOO MANY INTERRUPTIONS IN ACTUAL COMBAT TO OBSERVE PROPERLY.
DON'T WORRY.
BZZZT
KATHOOM
PERFECT.

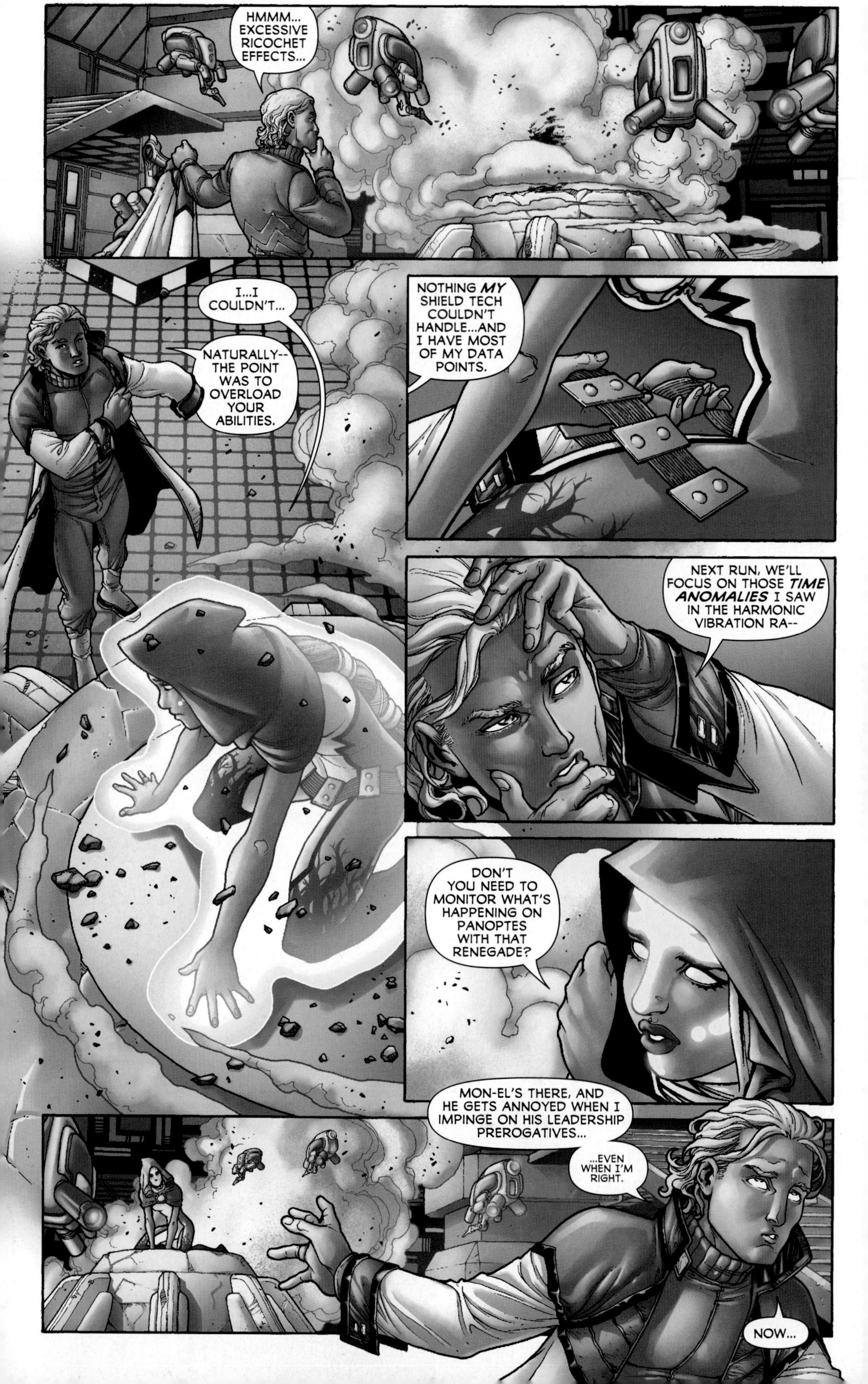
HMMM... EXCESSIVE RICOCHET EFFECTS...
I...I COULDN'T...
NATURALLY-- THE POINT WAS TO OVERLOAD YOUR ABILITIES.
NOTHING MY SHIELD TECH COULDN'T HANDLE...AND I HAVE MOST OF MY DATA POINTS.
NEXT RUN, WE'LL FOCUS ON THOSE TIME ANOMALIES I SAW IN THE HARMONIC VIBRATION RA--
DON'T YOU NEED TO MONITOR WHAT'S HAPPENING ON PANOPTES WITH THAT RENEGADE?
MON-EL'S THERE, AND HE GETS ANNOYED WHEN I IMPINGE ON HIS LEADERSHIP PREROGATIVES...
...EVEN WHEN I'M RIGHT.
NOW...

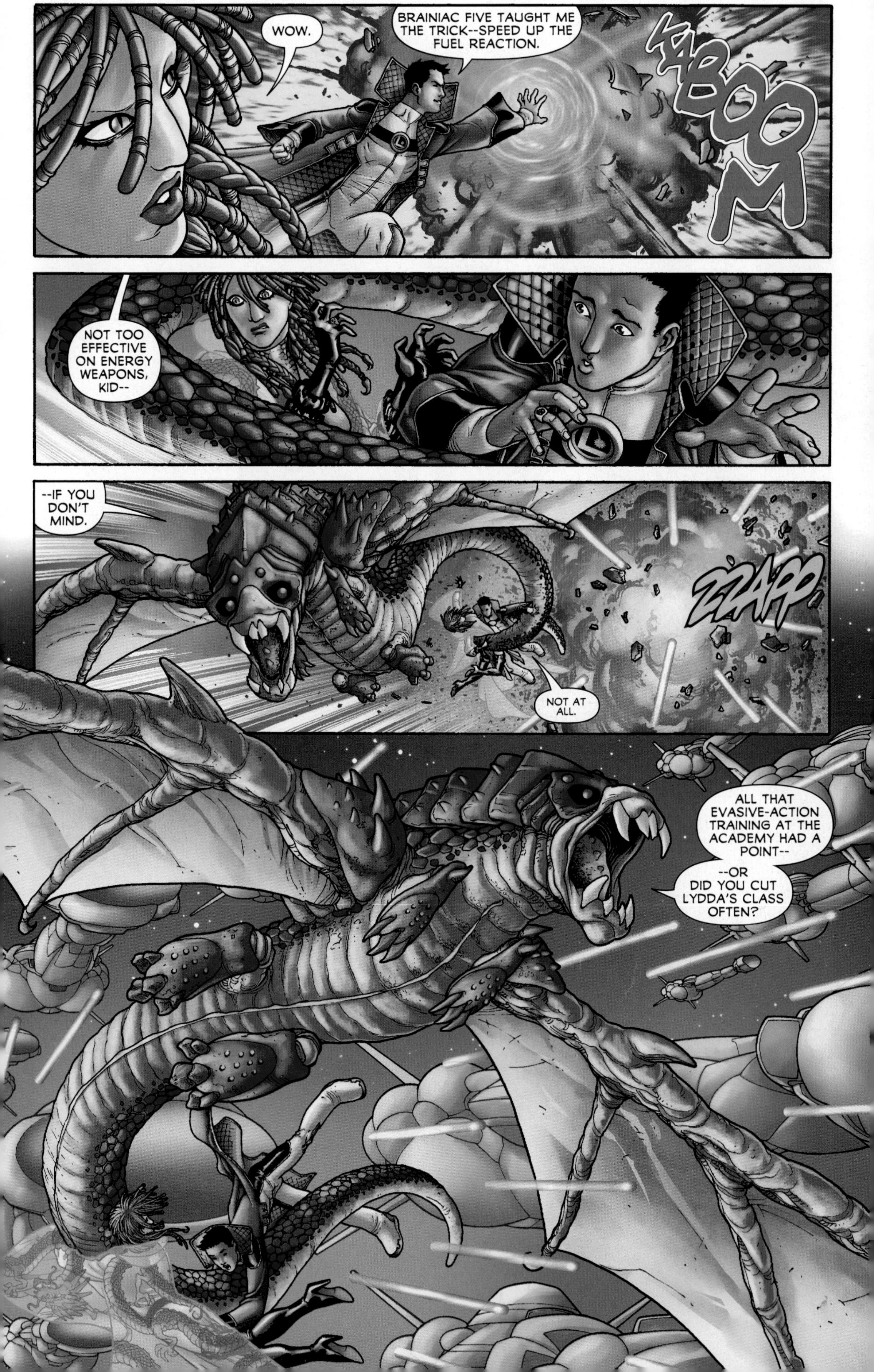
WOW.
BRAINIAC FIVE TAUGHT ME THE TRICK--SPEED UP THE FUEL REACTION.
KABOOM
NOT TOO EFFECTIVE ON ENERGY WEAPONS, KID--
--IF YOU DON'T MIND.
ZZAPP
NOT AT ALL.
ALL THAT EVASIVE-ACTION TRAINING AT THE ACADEMY HAD A POINT--
--OR DID YOU CUT LYDDA'S CLASS OFTEN?

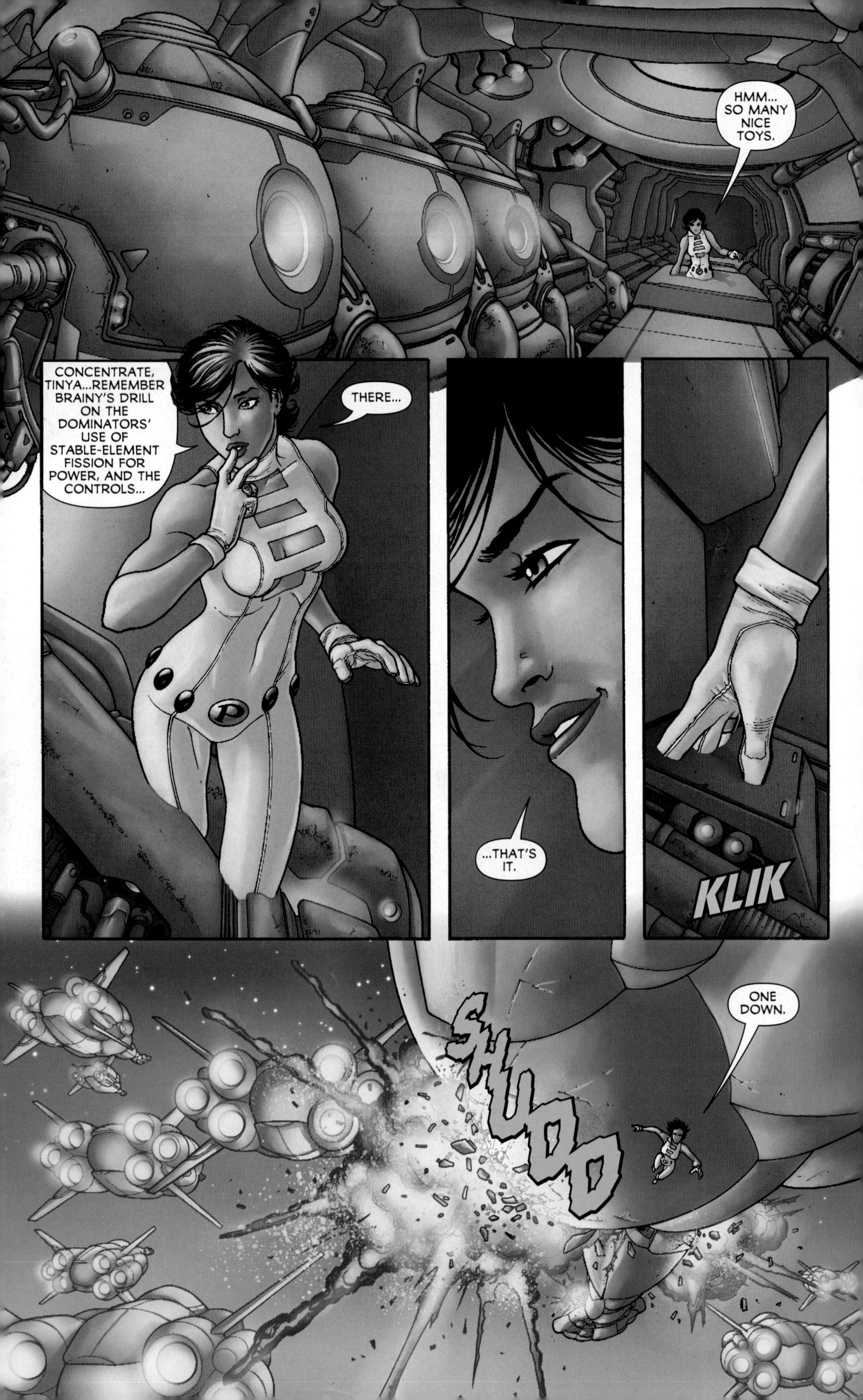
HMM... SO MANY NICE TOYS.
CONCENTRATE, TINYA...REMEMBER BRAINY'S DRILL ON THE DOMINATORS' USE OF STABLE-ELEMENT FISSION FOR POWER, AND THE CONTROLS...
THERE...
...THAT'S IT.
KLIK
SHUDD
ONE DOWN.

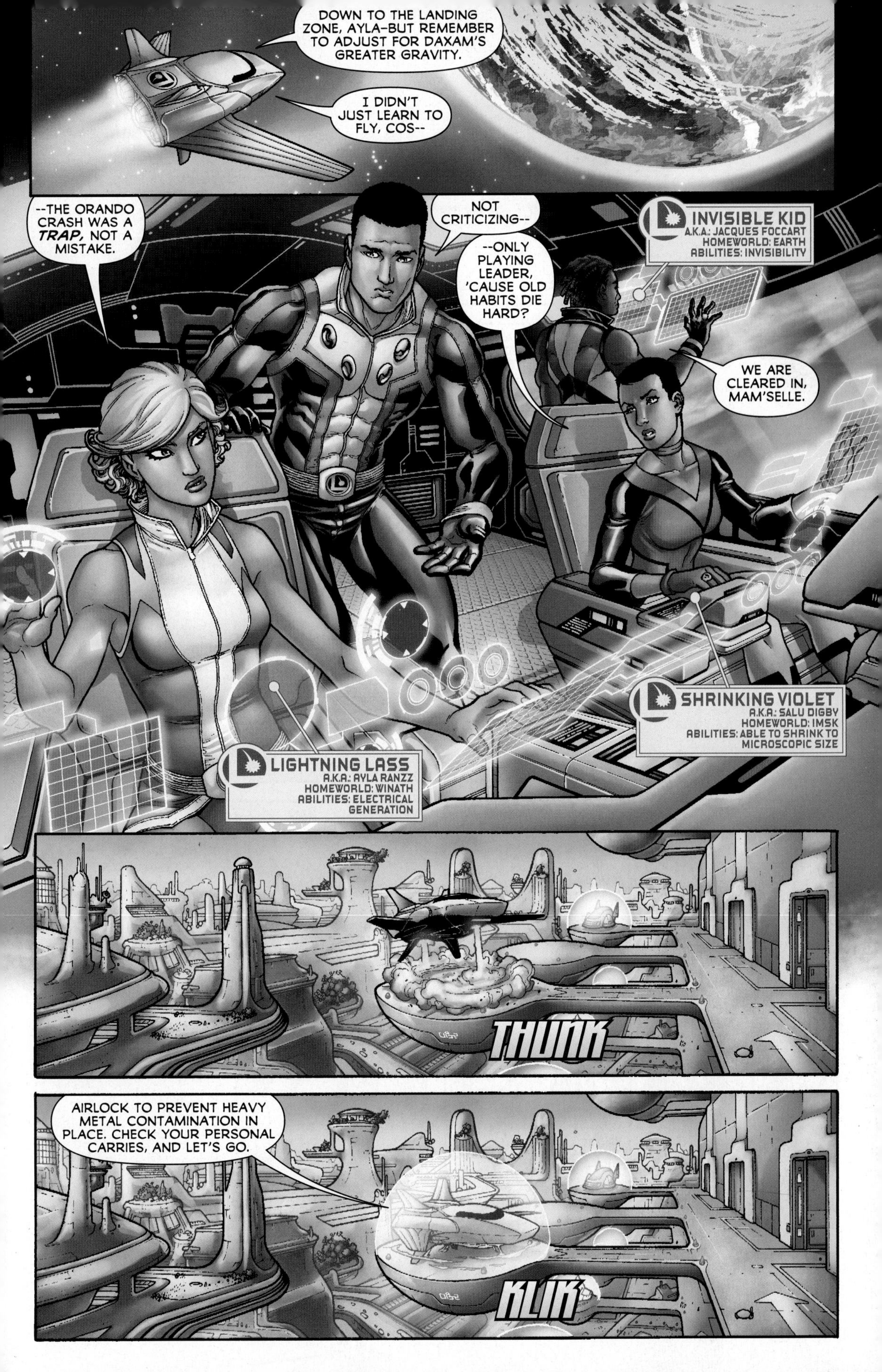

DOWN TO THE LANDING ZONE, AYLA–BUT REMEMBER TO ADJUST FOR DAXAM'S GREATER GRAVITY.
I DIDN'T JUST LEARN TO FLY, COS--
--THE ORANDO CRASH WAS A *TRAP,* NOT A MISTAKE.
NOT CRITICIZING--
--ONLY PLAYING LEADER, 'CAUSE OLD HABITS DIE HARD?
INVISIBLE KID
A.K.A.: JACQUES FOCCART
HOMEWORLD: EARTH
ABILITIES: INVISIBILITY
WE ARE CLEARED IN, MAM'SELLE.
SHRINKING VIOLET
A.K.A.: SALU DIGBY
HOMEWORLD: IMSK
ABILITIES: ABLE TO SHRINK TO MICROSCOPIC SIZE
LIGHTNING LASS
A.K.A.: AYLA RANZZ
HOMEWORLD: WINATH
ABILITIES: ELECTRICAL GENERATION
THUNK
AIRLOCK TO PREVENT HEAVY METAL CONTAMINATION IN PLACE. CHECK YOUR PERSONAL CARRIES, AND LET'S GO.
KLIK

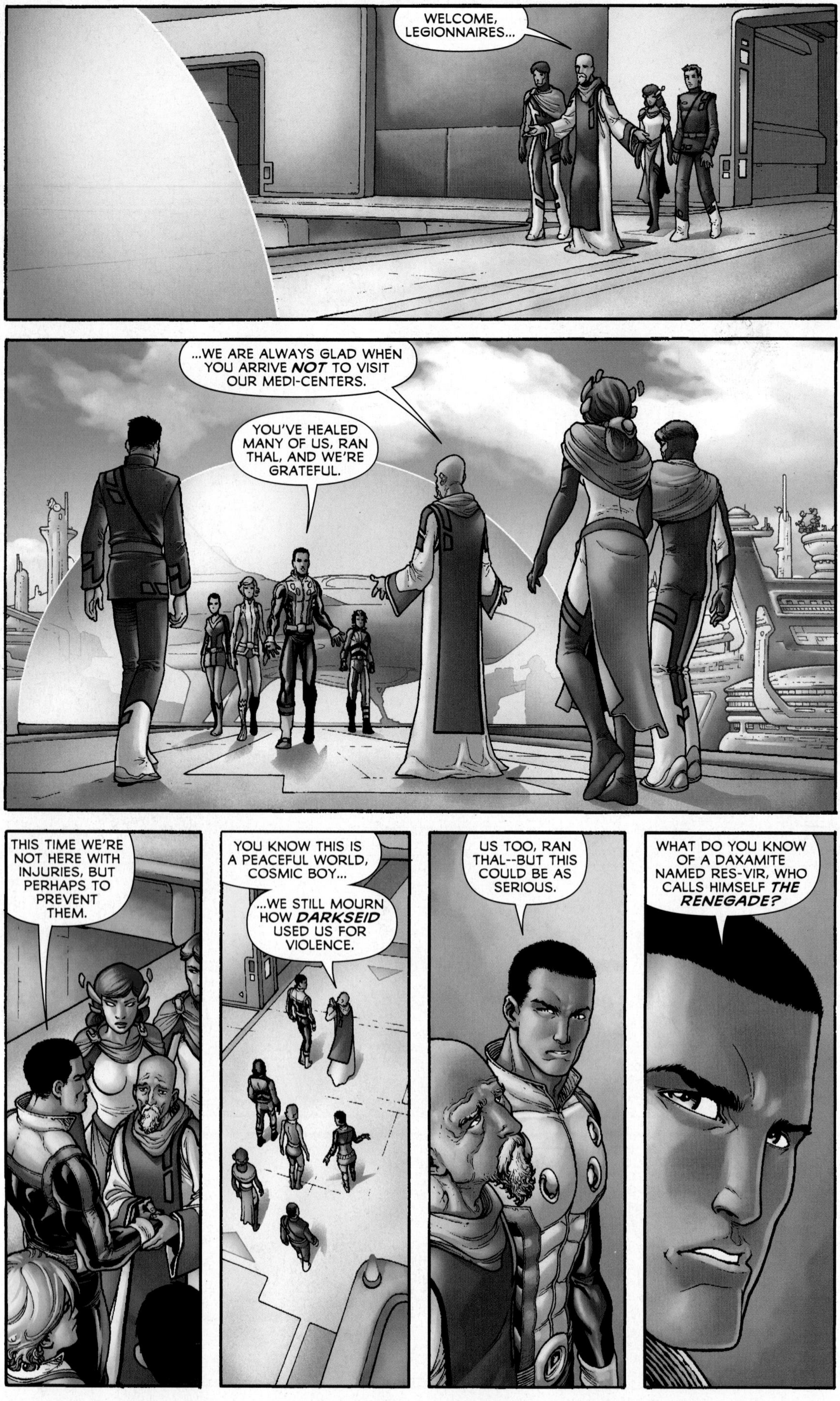
WELCOME, LEGIONNAIRES...
...WE ARE ALWAYS GLAD WHEN YOU ARRIVE *NOT* TO VISIT OUR MEDI-CENTERS.
YOU'VE HEALED MANY OF US, RAN THAL, AND WE'RE GRATEFUL.
THIS TIME WE'RE NOT HERE WITH INJURIES, BUT PERHAPS TO PREVENT THEM.
YOU KNOW THIS IS A PEACEFUL WORLD, COSMIC BOY...
...WE STILL MOURN HOW *DARKSEID* USED US FOR VIOLENCE.
US TOO, RAN THAL--BUT THIS COULD BE AS SERIOUS.
WHAT DO YOU KNOW OF A DAXAMITE NAMED RES-VIR, WHO CALLS HIMSELF *THE RENEGADE?*

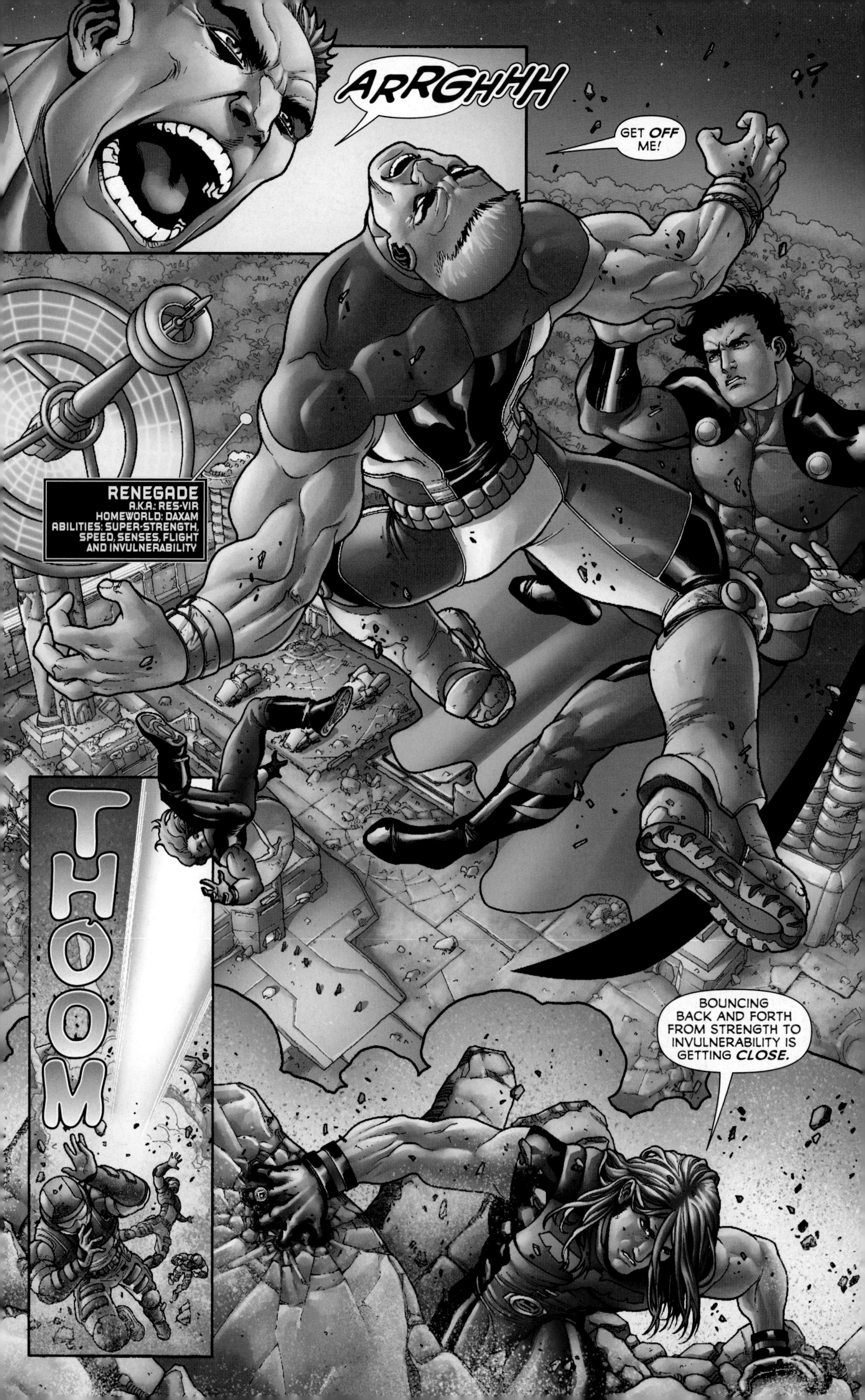

ARRGHHH
GET OFF ME!
RENEGADE
A.K.A.: RES-VIR
HOMEWORLD: DAXAM
ABILITIES: SUPER-STRENGTH, SPEED, SENSES, FLIGHT AND INVULNERABILITY
THOOM
BOUNCING BACK AND FORTH FROM STRENGTH TO INVULNERABILITY IS GETTING CLOSE.

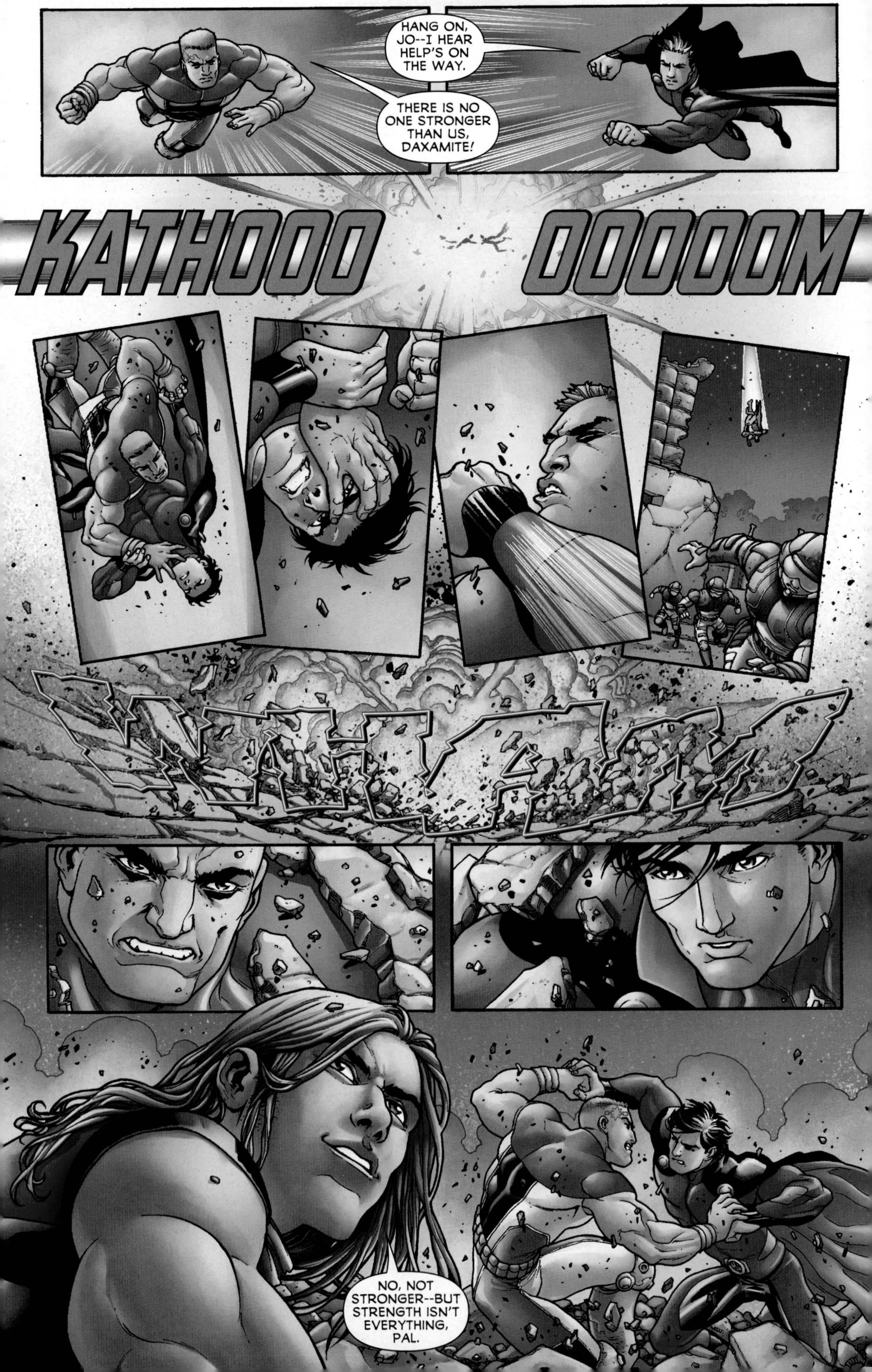
HANG ON, JO--I HEAR HELP'S ON THE WAY.
THERE IS NO ONE STRONGER THAN US, DAXAMITE!
KATHOOO OOOOOM
NO, NOT STRONGER--BUT STRENGTH ISN'T EVERYTHING, PAL.

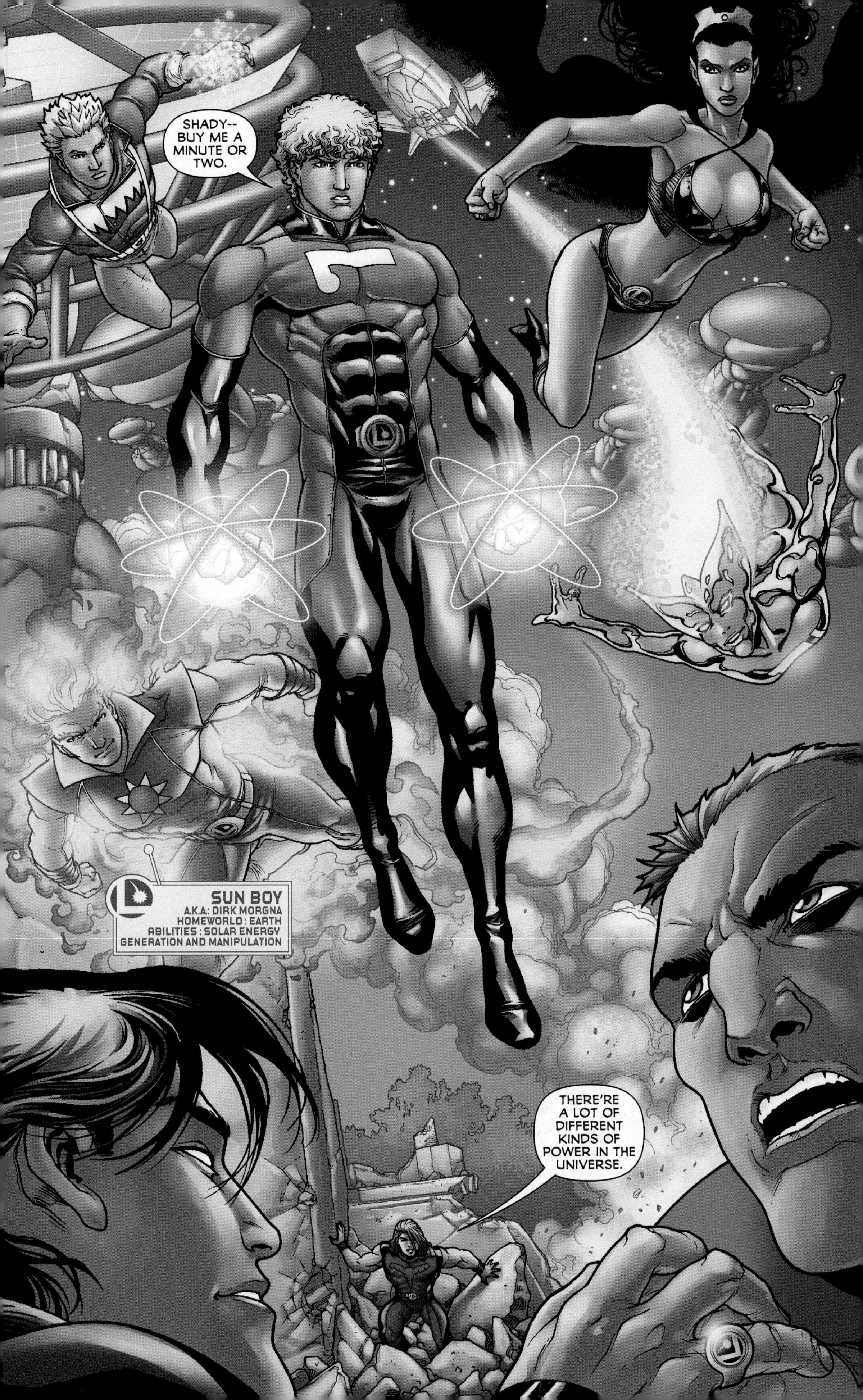

SHADY--
BUY ME A
MINUTE OR
TWO.
SUN BOY
A.K.A.: DIRK MORGNA
HOMEWORLD: EARTH
ABILITIES: SOLAR ENERGY
GENERATION AND MANIPULATION
THERE'RE
A LOT OF
DIFFERENT
KINDS OF
POWER IN THE
UNIVERSE.

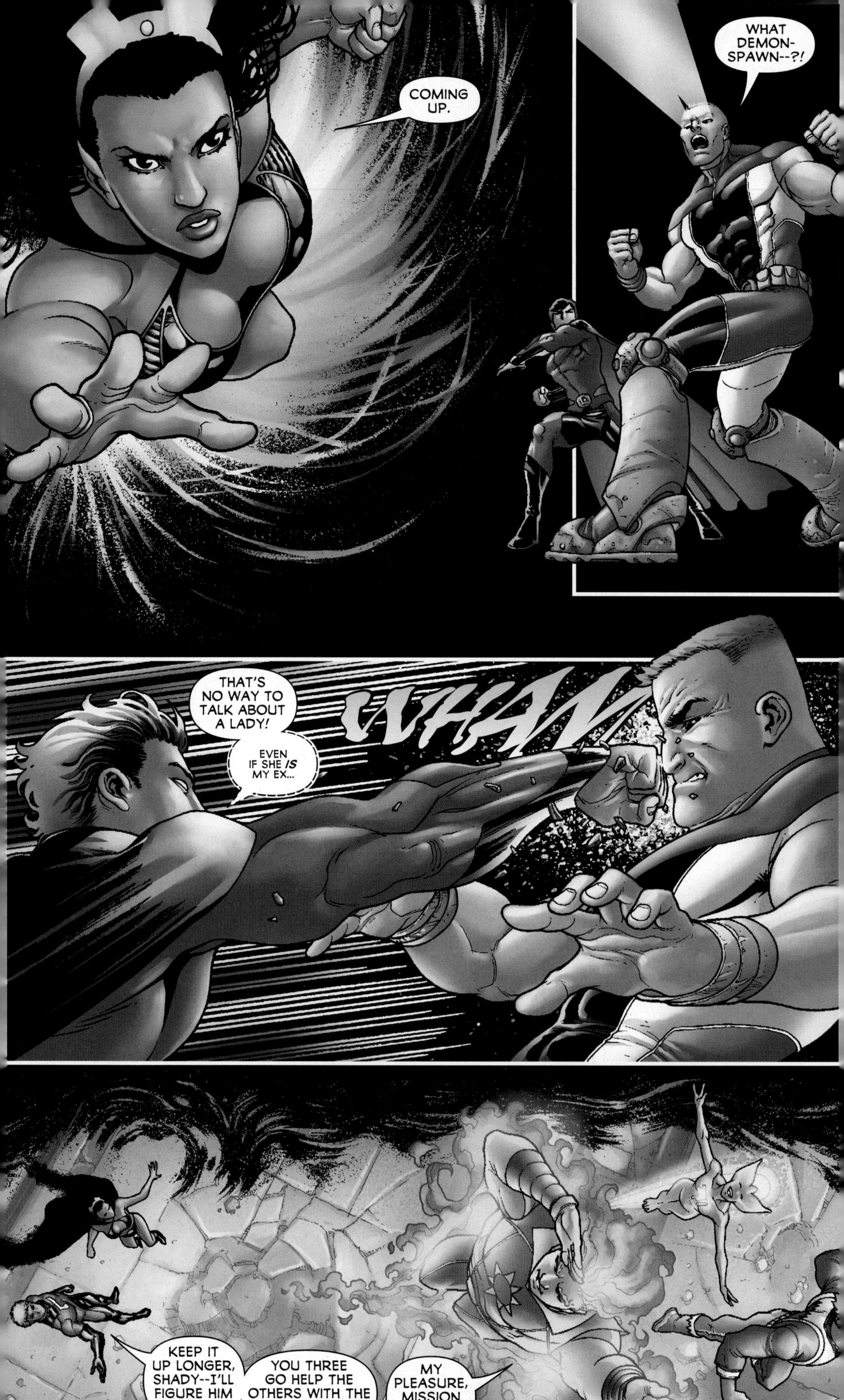
COMING UP.
WHAT DEMON-SPAWN--?!
THAT'S NO WAY TO TALK ABOUT A LADY!
EVEN IF SHE *IS* MY EX...
WHAM
KEEP IT UP LONGER, SHADY--I'LL FIGURE HIM OUT.
YOU THREE GO HELP THE OTHERS WITH THE DOMINATORS' SHIPS.
MY PLEASURE, MISSION LEADER, SIR!

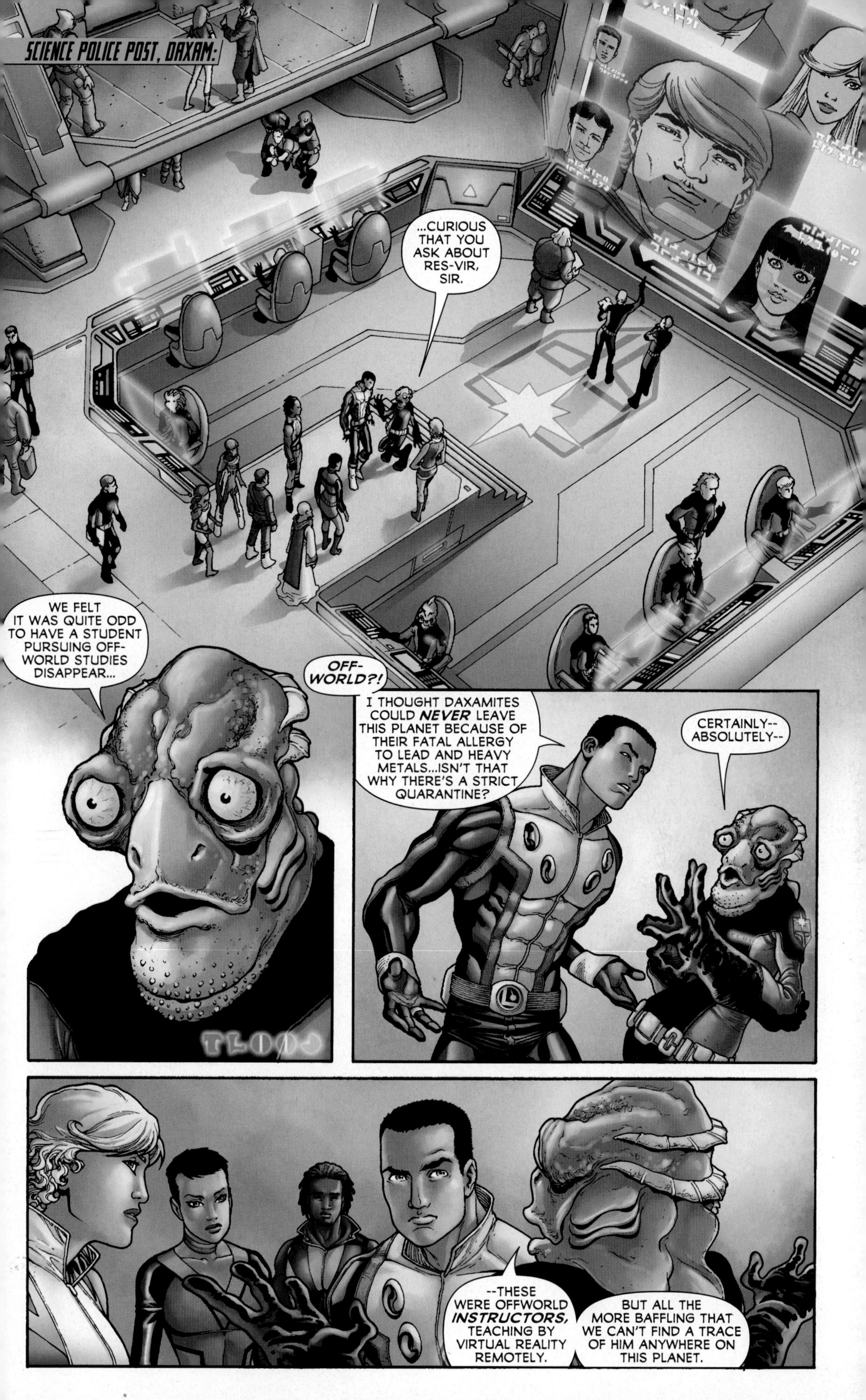
SCIENCE POLICE POST, DAXAM:
...CURIOUS THAT YOU ASK ABOUT RES-VIR, SIR.
WE FELT IT WAS QUITE ODD TO HAVE A STUDENT PURSUING OFF-WORLD STUDIES DISAPPEAR...
OFF-WORLD?!
I THOUGHT DAXAMITES COULD NEVER LEAVE THIS PLANET BECAUSE OF THEIR FATAL ALLERGY TO LEAD AND HEAVY METALS...ISN'T THAT WHY THERE'S A STRICT QUARANTINE?
CERTAINLY--ABSOLUTELY--
--THESE WERE OFFWORLD INSTRUCTORS, TEACHING BY VIRTUAL REALITY REMOTELY.
BUT ALL THE MORE BAFFLING THAT WE CAN'T FIND A TRACE OF HIM ANYWHERE ON THIS PLANET.

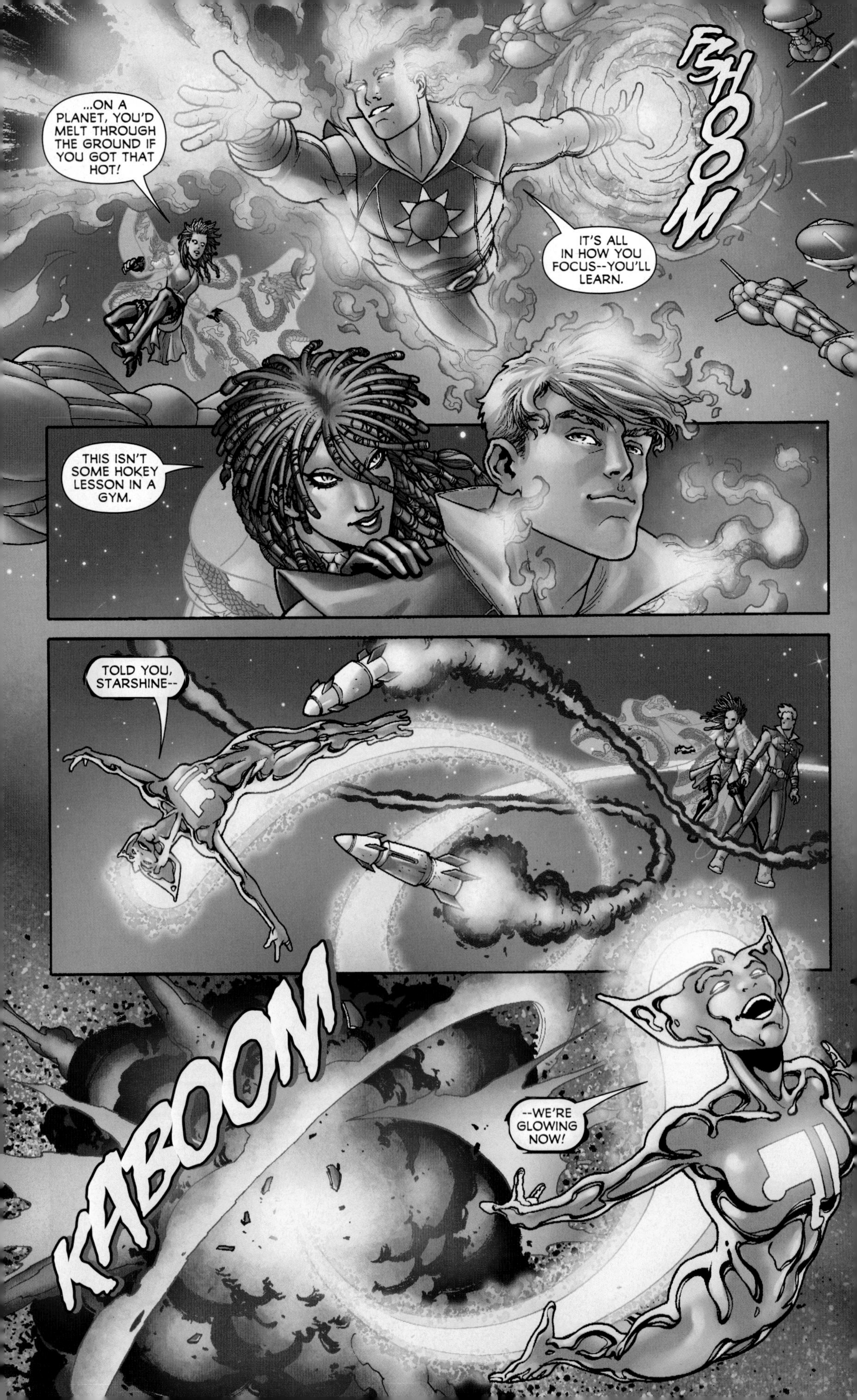
FSHOOOM
...ON A PLANET, YOU'D MELT THROUGH THE GROUND IF YOU GOT THAT HOT!
IT'S ALL IN HOW YOU FOCUS--YOU'LL LEARN.
THIS ISN'T SOME HOKEY LESSON IN A GYM.
TOLD YOU, STARSHINE--
KABOOM
--WE'RE GLOWING NOW!

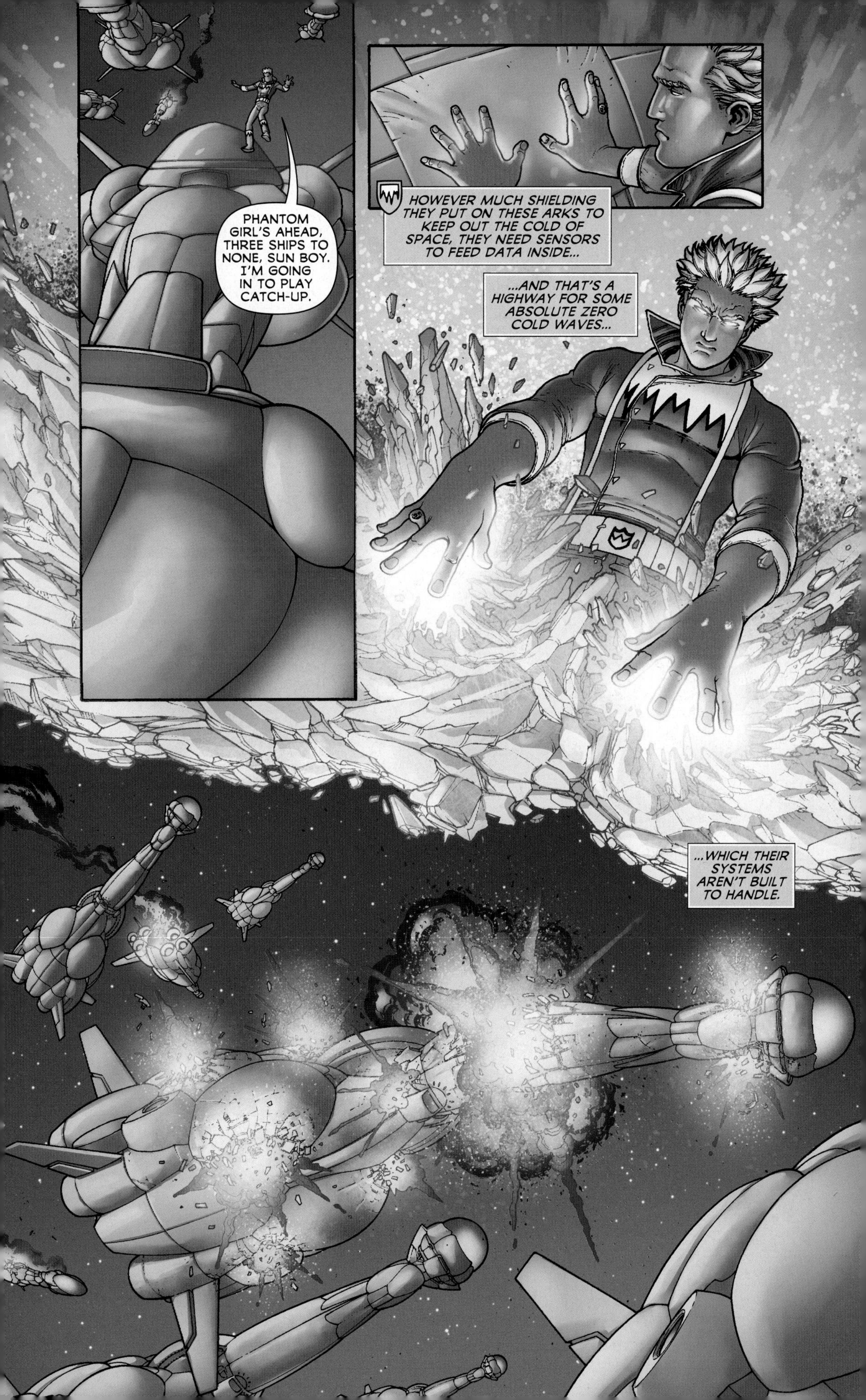
PHANTOM GIRL'S AHEAD, THREE SHIPS TO NONE, SUN BOY. I'M GOING IN TO PLAY CATCH-UP.
HOWEVER MUCH SHIELDING THEY PUT ON THESE ARKS TO KEEP OUT THE COLD OF SPACE, THEY NEED SENSORS TO FEED DATA INSIDE...
...AND THAT'S A HIGHWAY FOR SOME ABSOLUTE ZERO COLD WAVES...
...WHICH THEIR SYSTEMS AREN'T BUILT TO HANDLE.

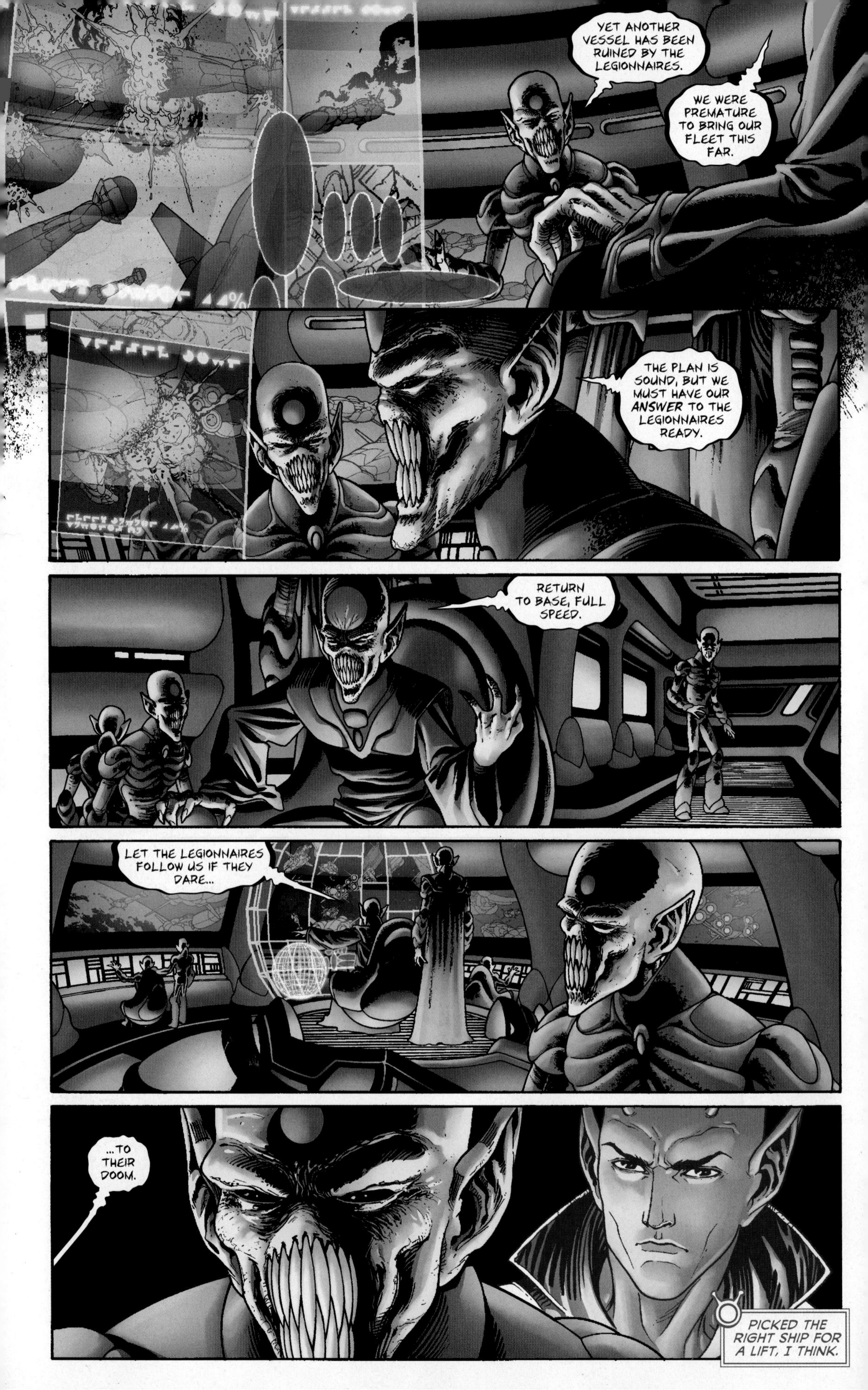
YET ANOTHER VESSEL HAS BEEN RUINED BY THE LEGIONNAIRES.
WE WERE PREMATURE TO BRING OUR FLEET THIS FAR.
THE PLAN IS SOUND, BUT WE MUST HAVE OUR ANSWER TO THE LEGIONNAIRES READY.
RETURN TO BASE, FULL SPEED.
LET THE LEGIONNAIRES FOLLOW US IF THEY DARE...
...TO THEIR DOOM.
PICKED THE RIGHT SHIP FOR A LIFT, I THINK.

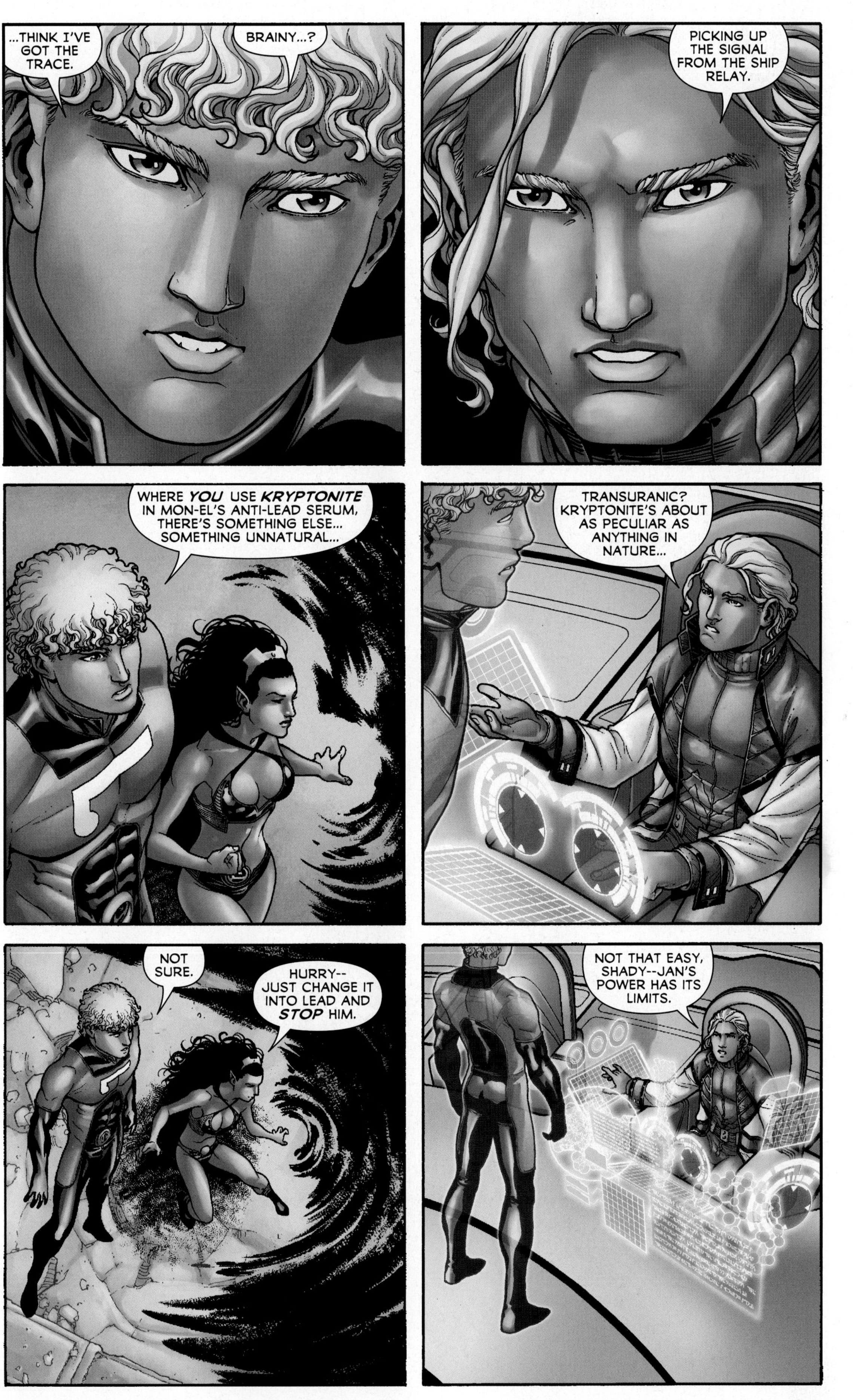
...THINK I'VE GOT THE TRACE.
BRAINY...?
PICKING UP THE SIGNAL FROM THE SHIP RELAY.
WHERE YOU USE KRYPTONITE IN MON-EL'S ANTI-LEAD SERUM, THERE'S SOMETHING ELSE... SOMETHING UNNATURAL...
TRANSURANIC? KRYPTONITE'S ABOUT AS PECULIAR AS ANYTHING IN NATURE...
NOT SURE.
HURRY-- JUST CHANGE IT INTO LEAD AND STOP HIM.
NOT THAT EASY, SHADY--JAN'S POWER HAS ITS LIMITS.

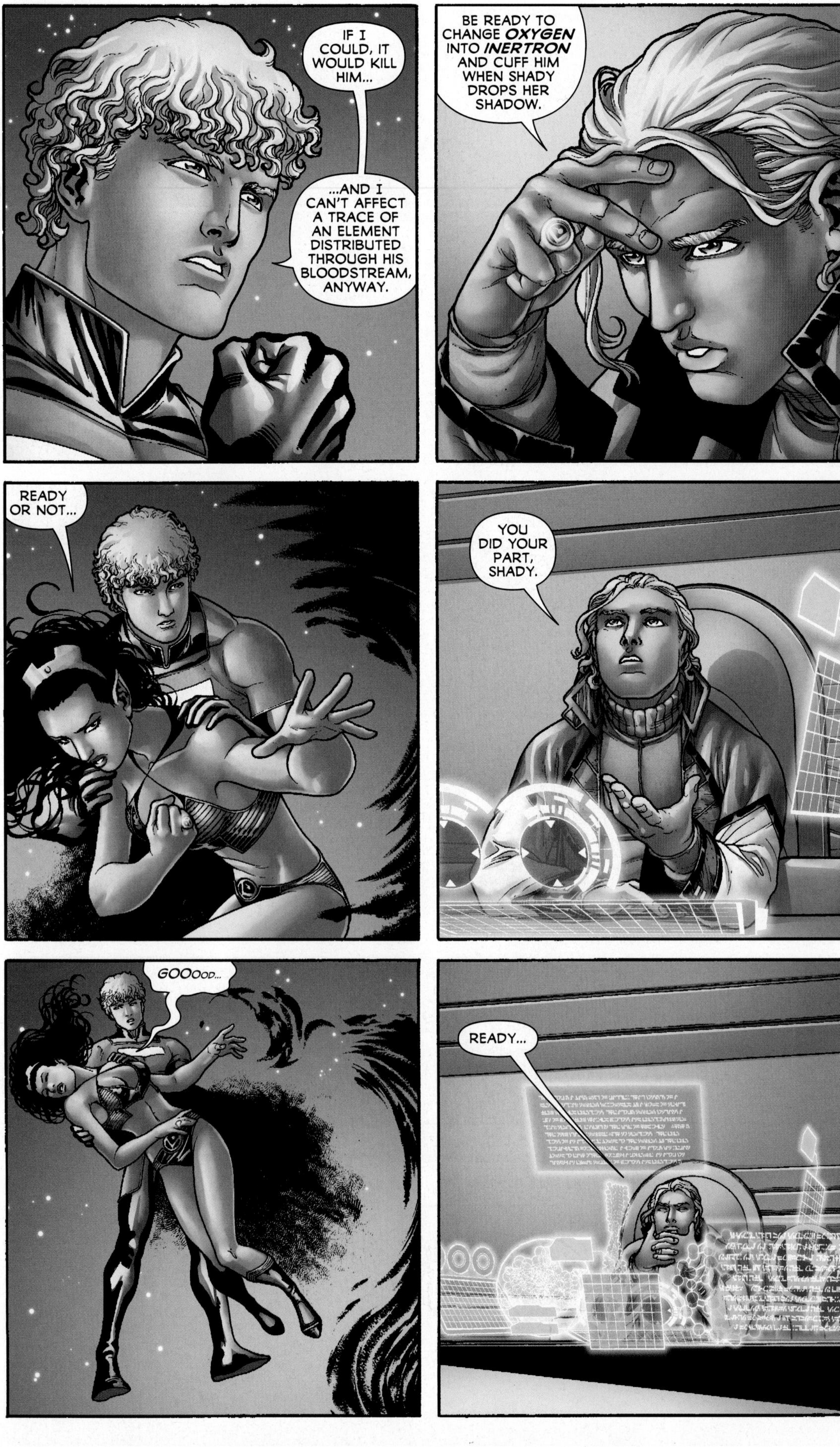
IF I COULD, IT WOULD KILL HIM...
...AND I CAN'T AFFECT A TRACE OF AN ELEMENT DISTRIBUTED THROUGH HIS BLOODSTREAM, ANYWAY.
BE READY TO CHANGE *OXYGEN* INTO *INERTRON* AND CUFF HIM WHEN SHADY DROPS HER SHADOW.
READY OR NOT...
YOU DID YOUR PART, SHADY.
GOOood...
READY...

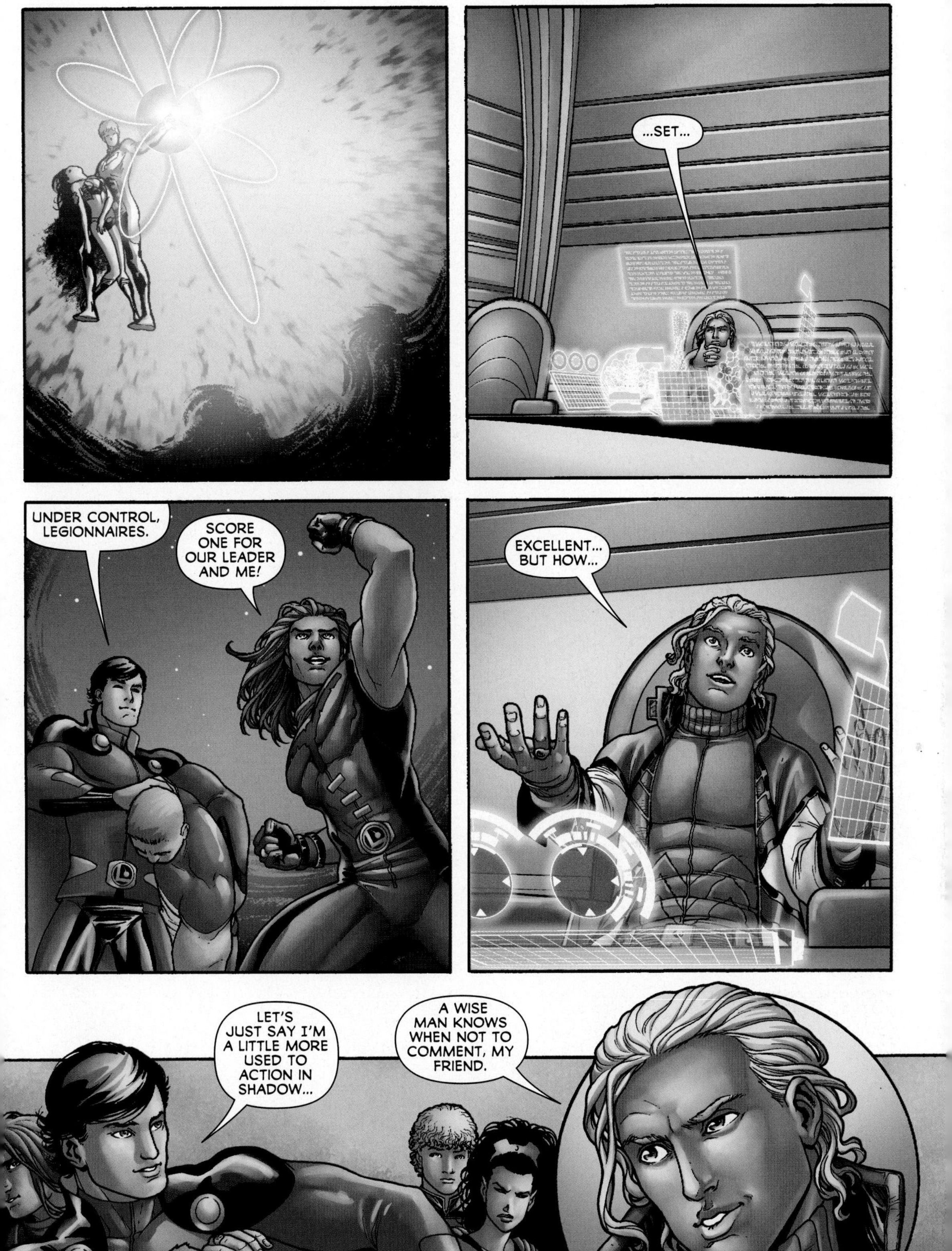
...SET...
UNDER CONTROL, LEGIONNAIRES.
SCORE ONE FOR OUR LEADER AND ME!
EXCELLENT... BUT HOW...
LET'S JUST SAY I'M A LITTLE MORE USED TO ACTION IN SHADOW...
A WISE MAN KNOWS WHEN NOT TO COMMENT, MY FRIEND.

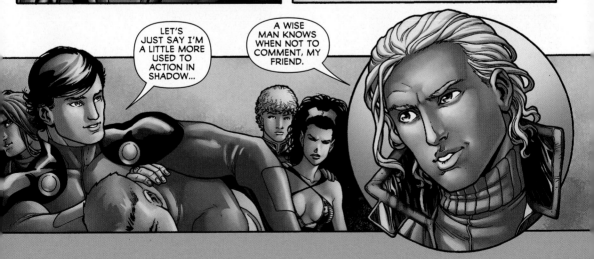

cover art by
CHRIS SPROUSE, KARL STORY & GUY MAJOR

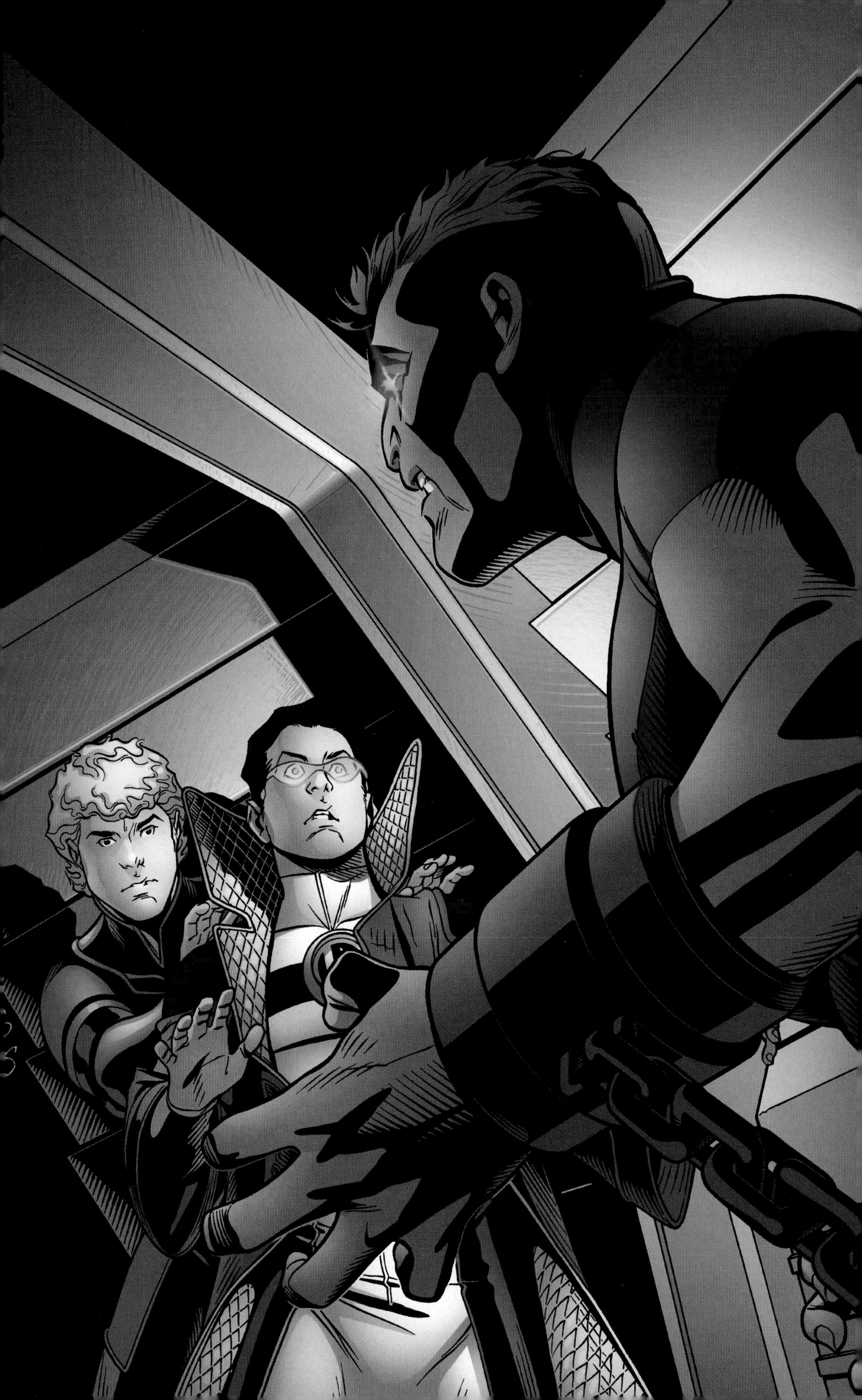

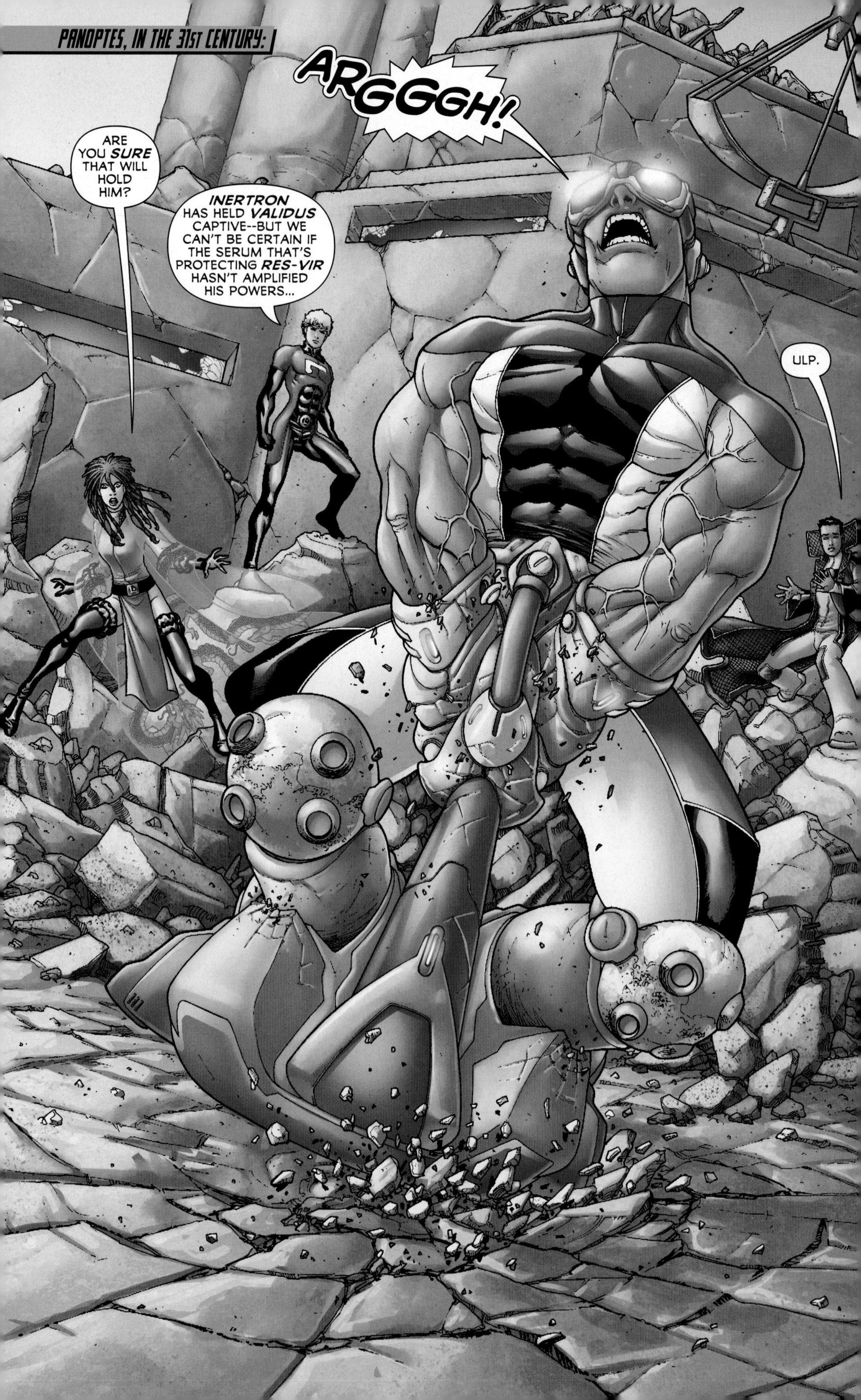
PANOPTES, IN THE 31ST CENTURY:
ARGGGH!
ARE YOU SURE THAT WILL HOLD HIM?
INERTRON HAS HELD VALIDUS CAPTIVE--BUT WE CAN'T BE CERTAIN IF THE SERUM THAT'S PROTECTING RES-VIR HASN'T AMPLIFIED HIS POWERS...
ULP.

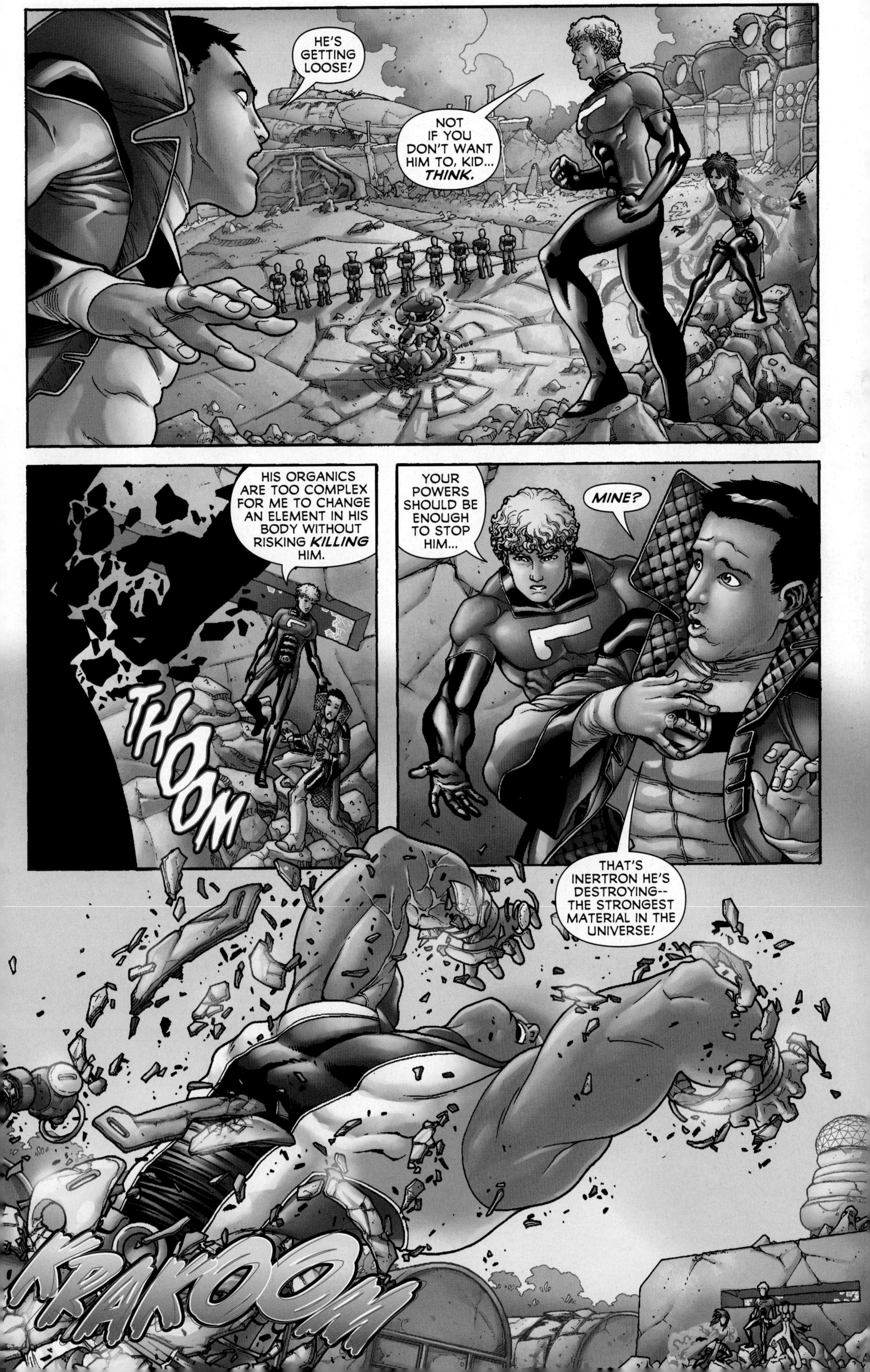
HE'S GETTING LOOSE!
NOT IF YOU DON'T WANT HIM TO, KID... THINK.
HIS ORGANICS ARE TOO COMPLEX FOR ME TO CHANGE AN ELEMENT IN HIS BODY WITHOUT RISKING KILLING HIM.
THOOM
YOUR POWERS SHOULD BE ENOUGH TO STOP HIM...
MINE?
THAT'S INERTRON HE'S DESTROYING-- THE STRONGEST MATERIAL IN THE UNIVERSE!
KRAKOOM

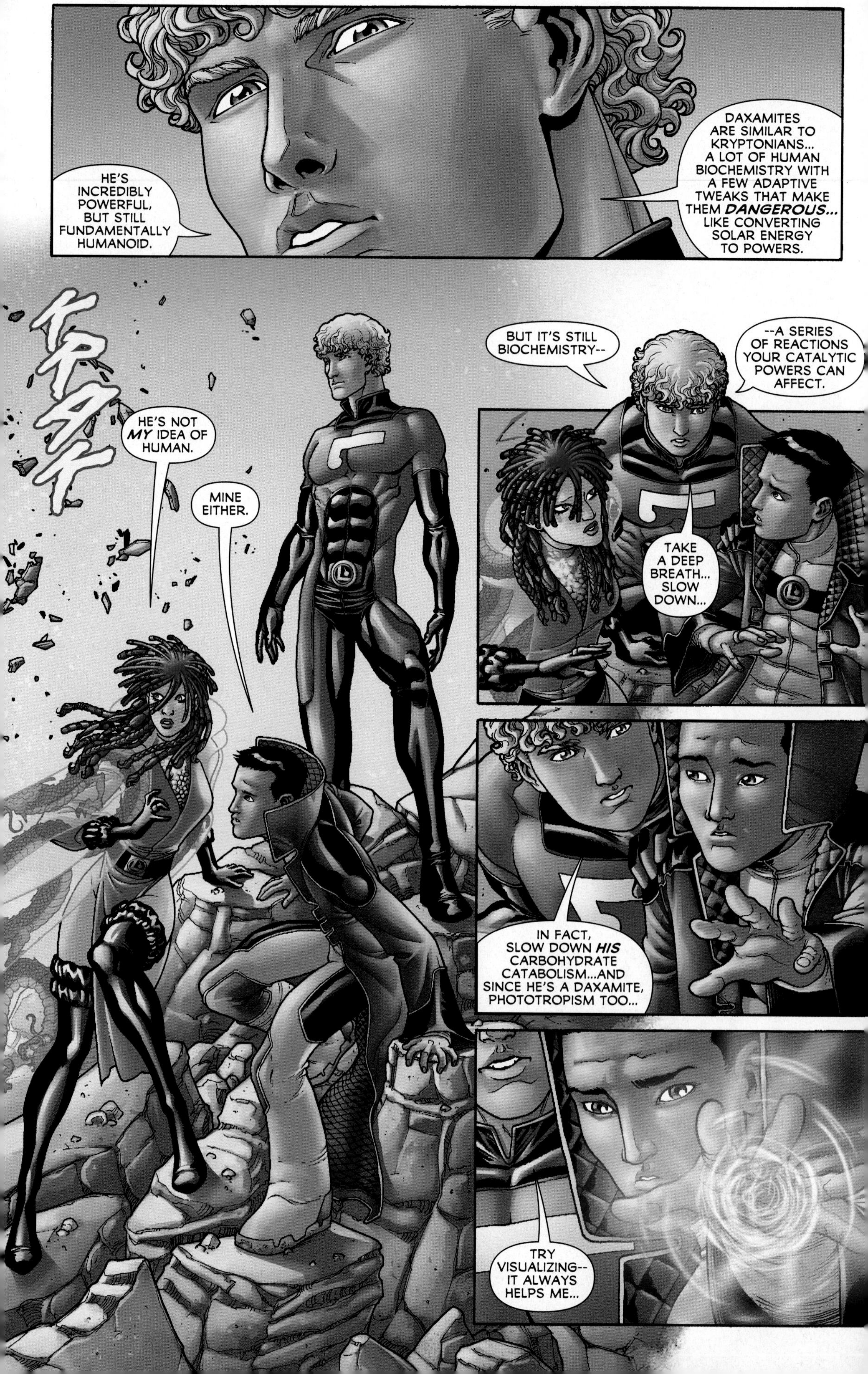
HE'S INCREDIBLY POWERFUL, BUT STILL FUNDAMENTALLY HUMANOID.
DAXAMITES ARE SIMILAR TO KRYPTONIANS... A LOT OF HUMAN BIOCHEMISTRY WITH A FEW ADAPTIVE TWEAKS THAT MAKE THEM *DANGEROUS...* LIKE CONVERTING SOLAR ENERGY TO POWERS.
KRAK
HE'S NOT *MY* IDEA OF HUMAN.
MINE EITHER.
BUT IT'S STILL BIOCHEMISTRY--
--A SERIES OF REACTIONS YOUR CATALYTIC POWERS CAN AFFECT.
TAKE A DEEP BREATH... SLOW DOWN...
IN FACT, SLOW DOWN *HIS* CARBOHYDRATE CATABOLISM...AND SINCE HE'S A DAXAMITE, PHOTOTROPISM TOO...
TRY VISUALIZING-- IT ALWAYS HELPS ME...

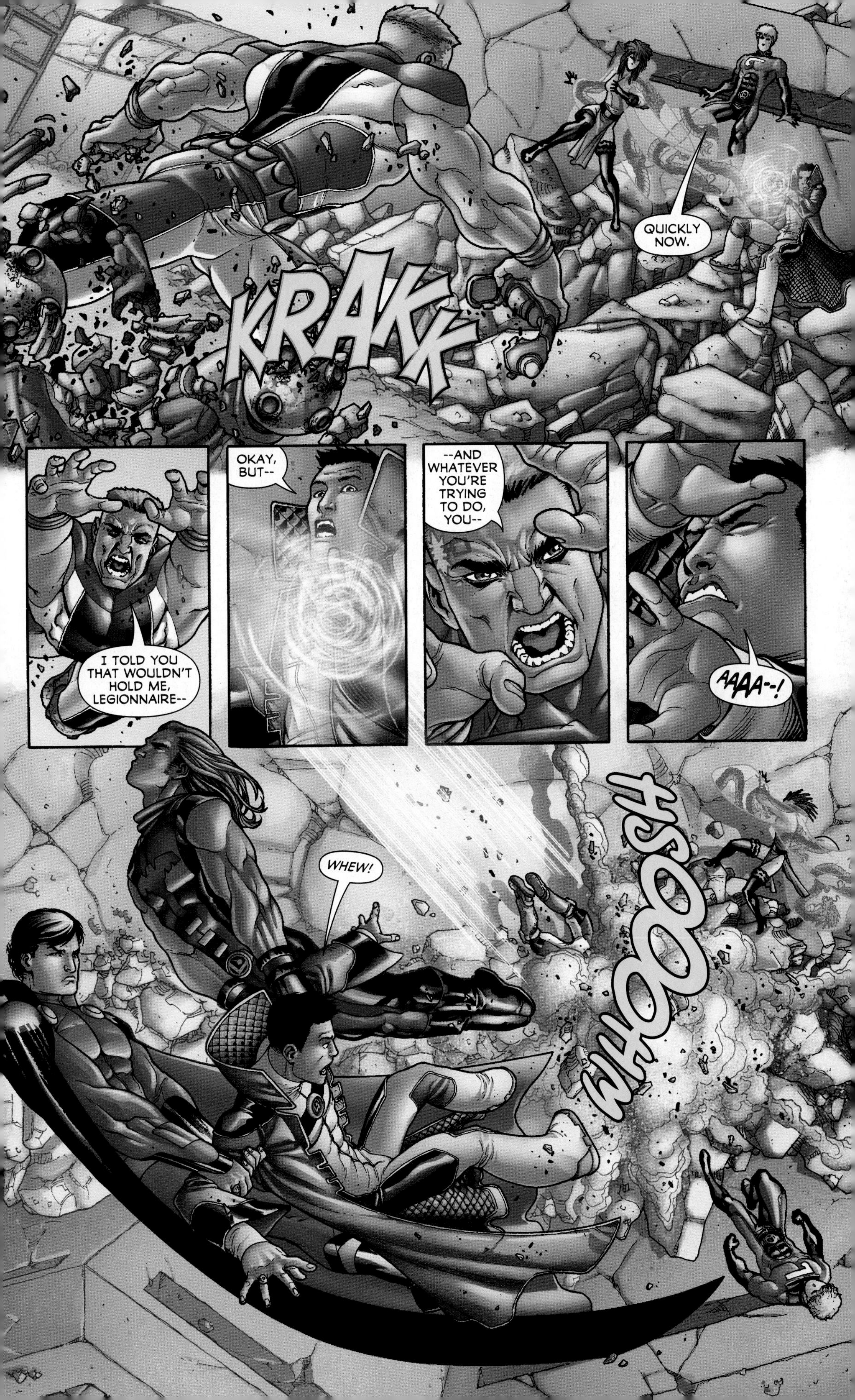
QUICKLY NOW.
KRAKK
I TOLD YOU THAT WOULDN'T HOLD ME, LEGIONNAIRE--
OKAY, BUT--
--AND WHATEVER YOU'RE TRYING TO DO, YOU--
AAAA--!
WHEW!
WHOOOSH

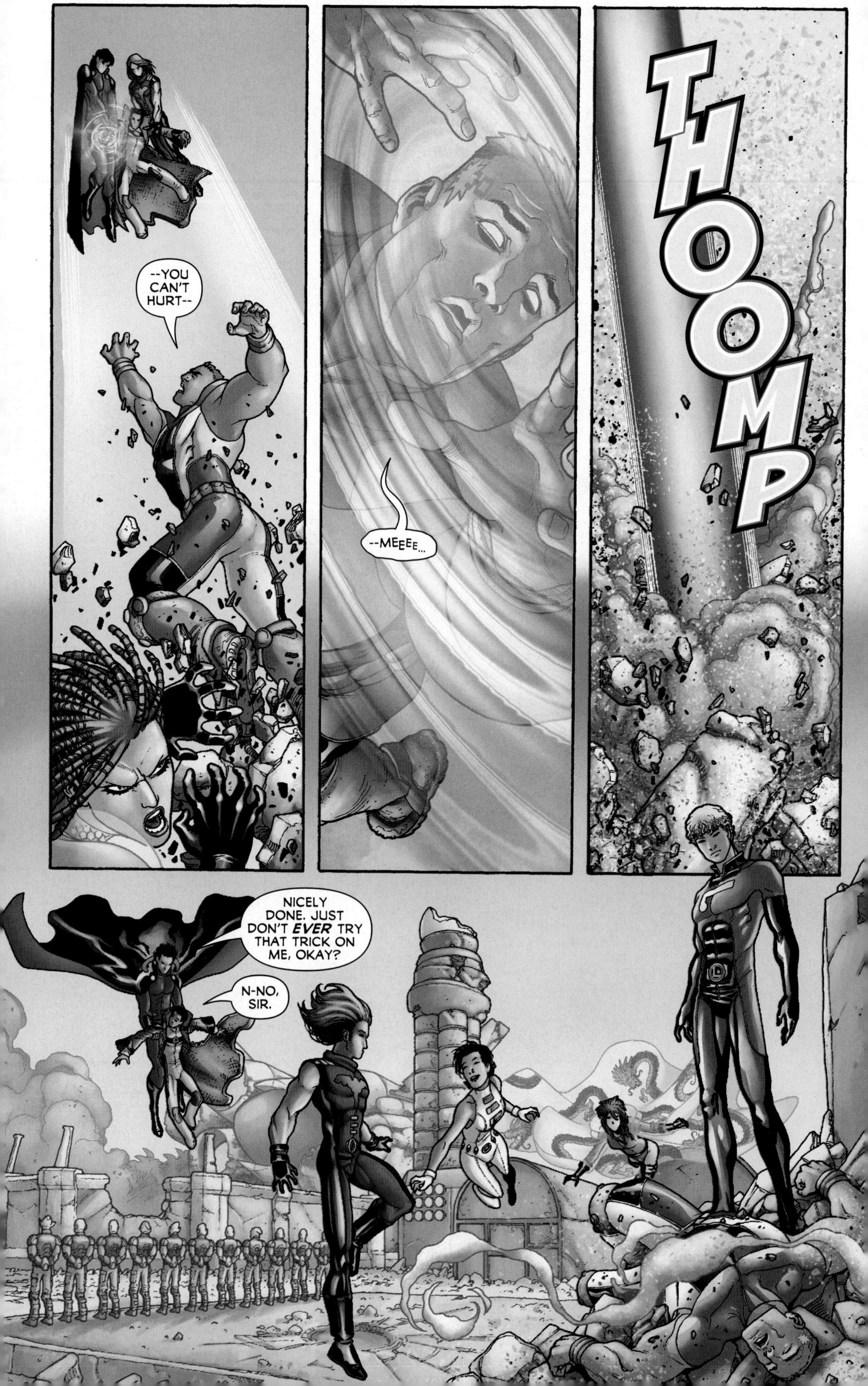
--YOU CAN'T HURT--
--MEEEE...
THOOMP
NICELY DONE. JUST DON'T *EVER* TRY THAT TRICK ON ME, OKAY?
N-NO, SIR.

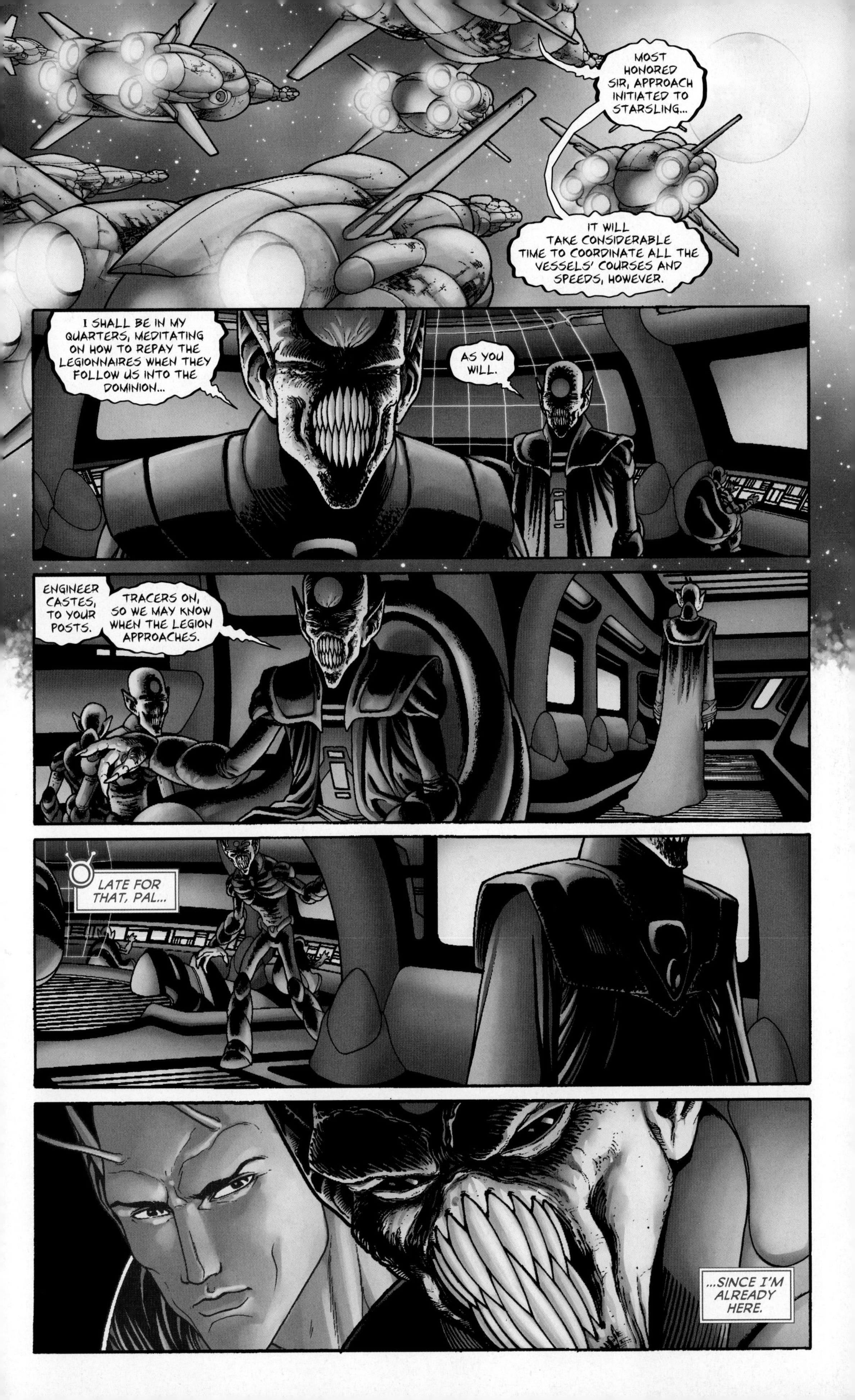
MOST HONORED SIR, APPROACH INITIATED TO STARSLING...
IT WILL TAKE CONSIDERABLE TIME TO COORDINATE ALL THE VESSELS' COURSES AND SPEEDS, HOWEVER.
I SHALL BE IN MY QUARTERS, MEDITATING ON HOW TO REPAY THE LEGIONNAIRES WHEN THEY FOLLOW US INTO THE DOMINION...
AS YOU WILL.
ENGINEER CASTES, TO YOUR POSTS.
TRACERS ON, SO WE MAY KNOW WHEN THE LEGION APPROACHES.
LATE FOR THAT, PAL...
...SINCE I'M ALREADY HERE.

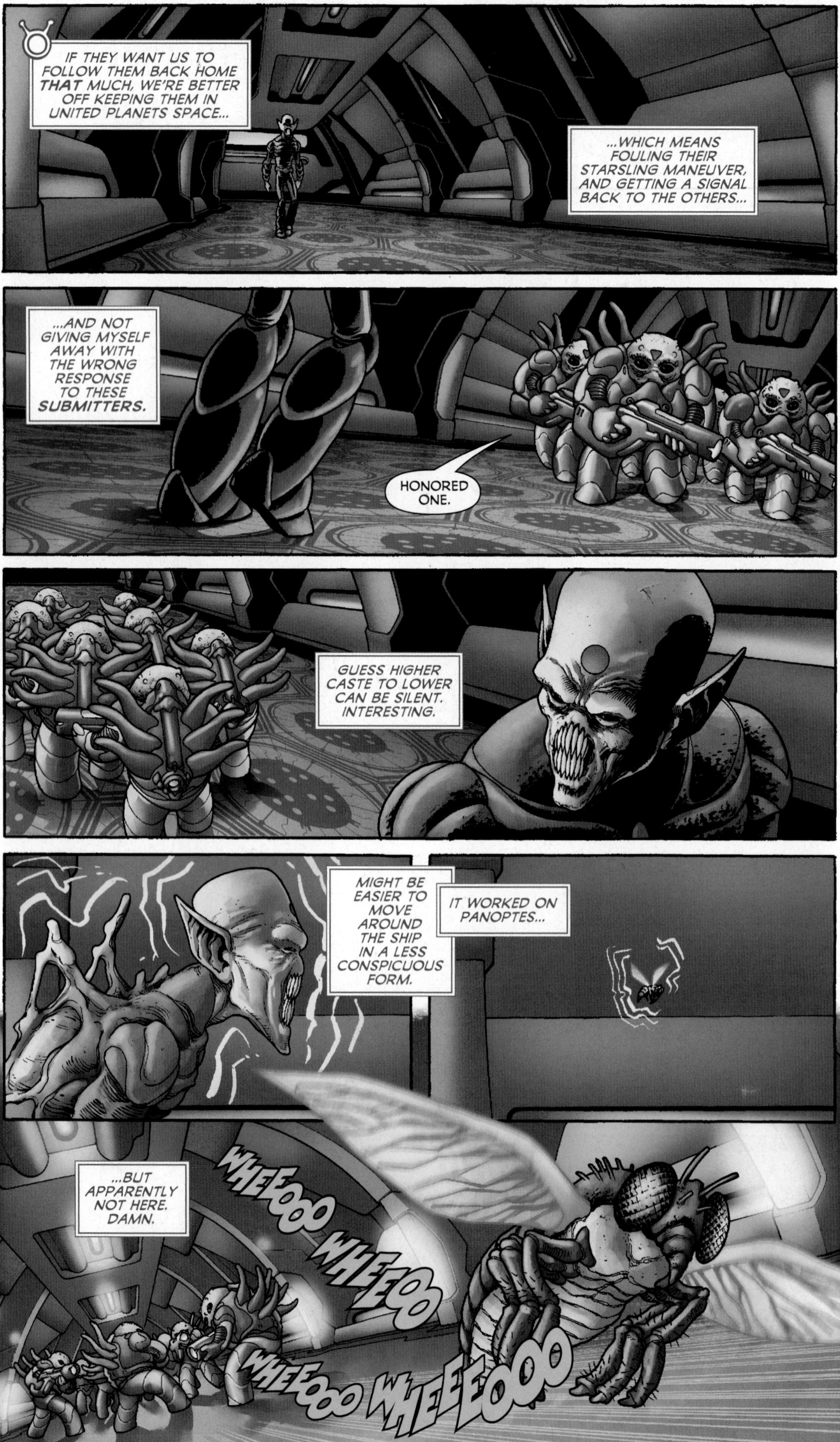
IF THEY WANT US TO FOLLOW THEM BACK HOME THAT MUCH, WE'RE BETTER OFF KEEPING THEM IN UNITED PLANETS SPACE...
...WHICH MEANS FOULING THEIR STARSLING MANEUVER, AND GETTING A SIGNAL BACK TO THE OTHERS...
...AND NOT GIVING MYSELF AWAY WITH THE WRONG RESPONSE TO THESE SUBMITTERS.
HONORED ONE.
GUESS HIGHER CASTE TO LOWER CAN BE SILENT. INTERESTING.
MIGHT BE EASIER TO MOVE AROUND THE SHIP IN A LESS CONSPICUOUS FORM.
IT WORKED ON PANOPTES...
...BUT APPARENTLY NOT HERE. DAMN.
WHEEOOO WHEEOO WHEEOOO WHEEEOOO

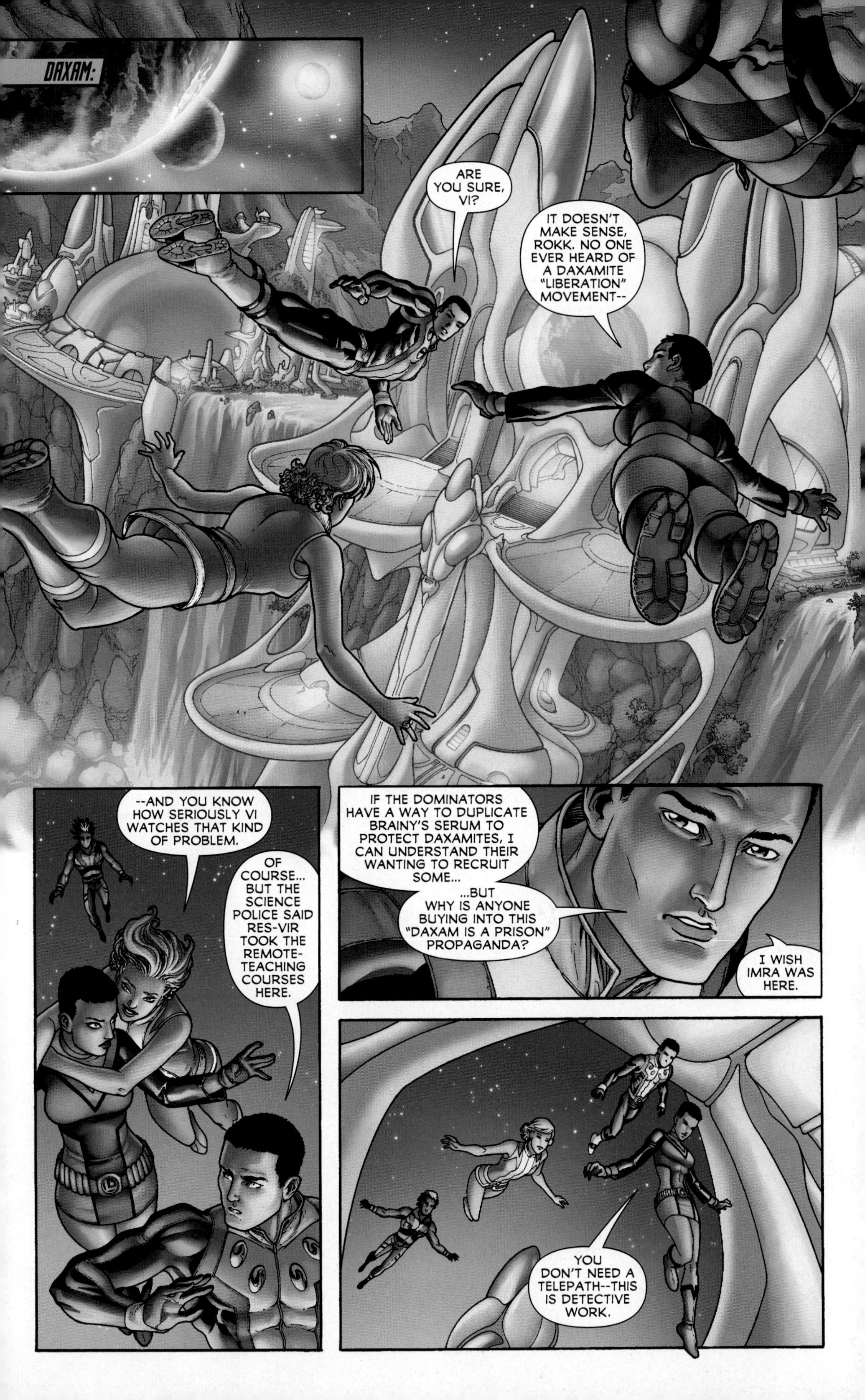
DAXAM:
ARE YOU SURE, VI?
IT DOESN'T MAKE SENSE, ROKK. NO ONE EVER HEARD OF A DAXAMITE "LIBERATION" MOVEMENT--
--AND YOU KNOW HOW SERIOUSLY VI WATCHES THAT KIND OF PROBLEM.
OF COURSE... BUT THE SCIENCE POLICE SAID RES-VIR TOOK THE REMOTE-TEACHING COURSES HERE.
IF THE DOMINATORS HAVE A WAY TO DUPLICATE BRAINY'S SERUM TO PROTECT DAXAMITES, I CAN UNDERSTAND THEIR WANTING TO RECRUIT SOME...
...BUT WHY IS ANYONE BUYING INTO THIS "DAXAM IS A PRISON" PROPAGANDA?
I WISH IMRA WAS HERE.
YOU DON'T NEED A TELEPATH--THIS IS DETECTIVE WORK.

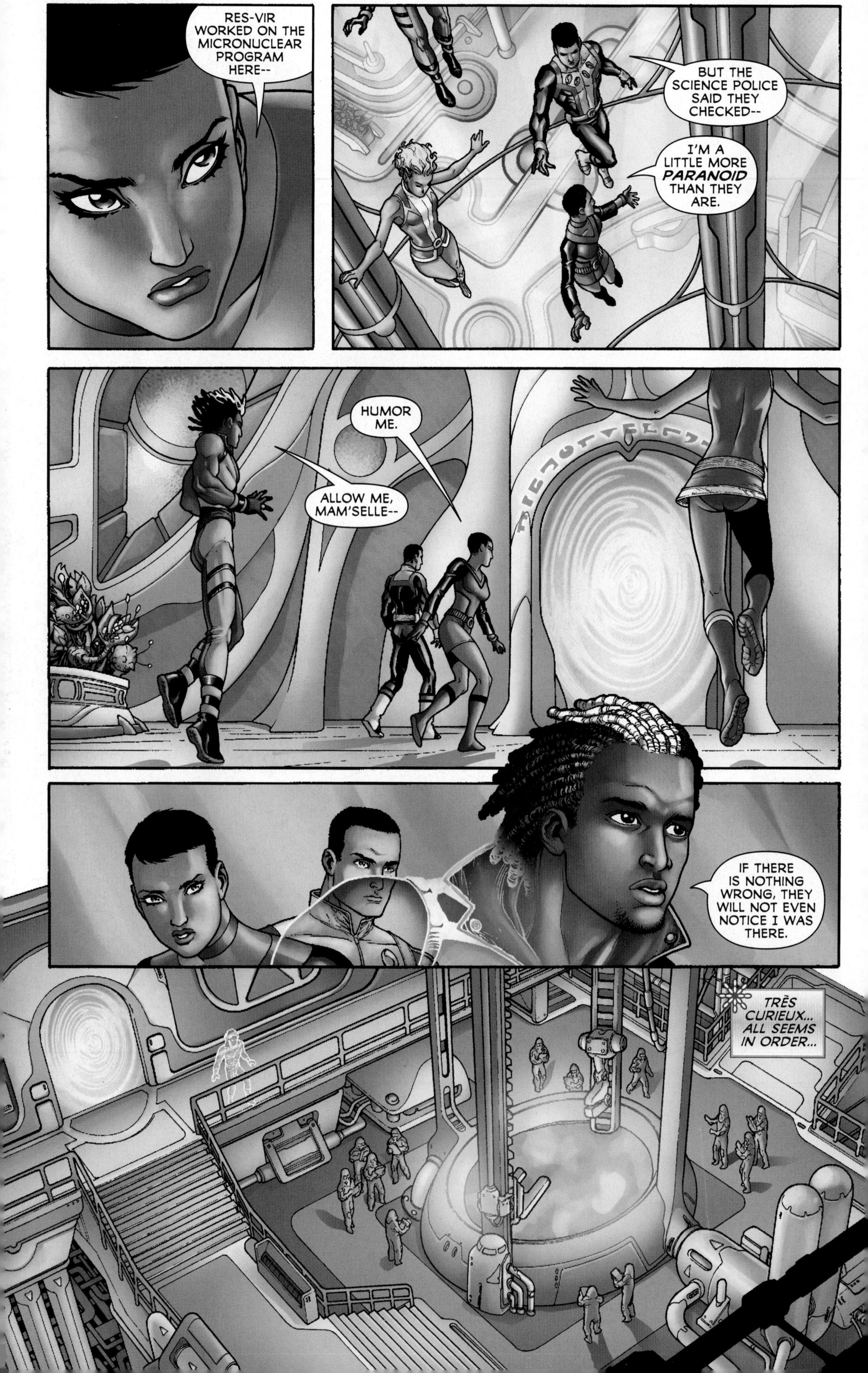
RES-VIR WORKED ON THE MICRONUCLEAR PROGRAM HERE--
BUT THE SCIENCE POLICE SAID THEY CHECKED--
I'M A LITTLE MORE *PARANOID* THAN THEY ARE.
HUMOR ME.
ALLOW ME, MAM'SELLE--
IF THERE IS NOTHING WRONG, THEY WILL NOT EVEN NOTICE I WAS THERE.
TRÈS CURIEUX... ALL SEEMS IN ORDER...

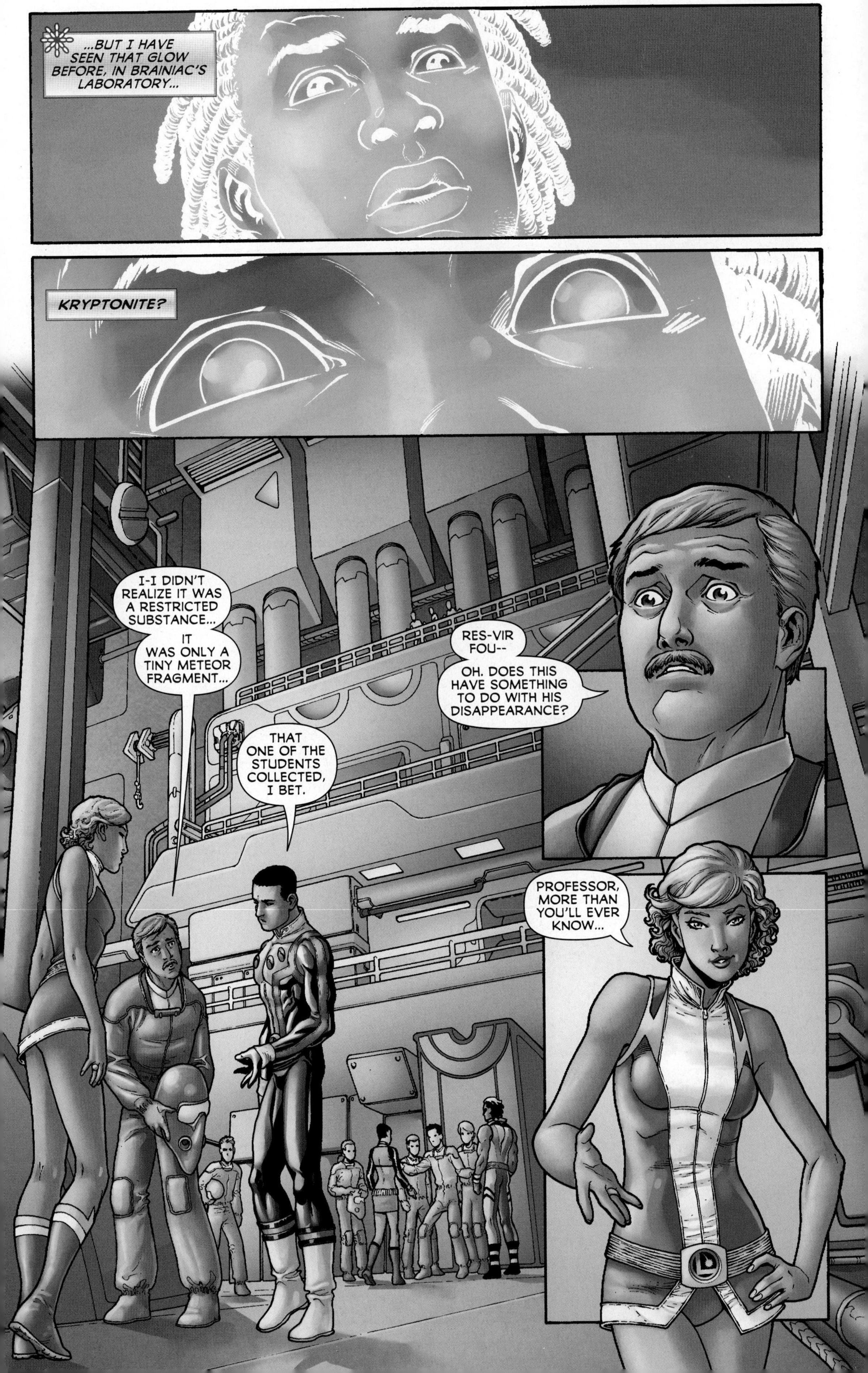
...BUT I HAVE SEEN THAT GLOW BEFORE, IN BRAINIAC'S LABORATORY...
KRYPTONITE?
I-I DIDN'T REALIZE IT WAS A RESTRICTED SUBSTANCE...
IT WAS ONLY A TINY METEOR FRAGMENT...
THAT ONE OF THE STUDENTS COLLECTED, I BET.
RES-VIR FOU--
OH. DOES THIS HAVE SOMETHING TO DO WITH HIS DISAPPEARANCE?
PROFESSOR, MORE THAN YOU'LL EVER KNOW...

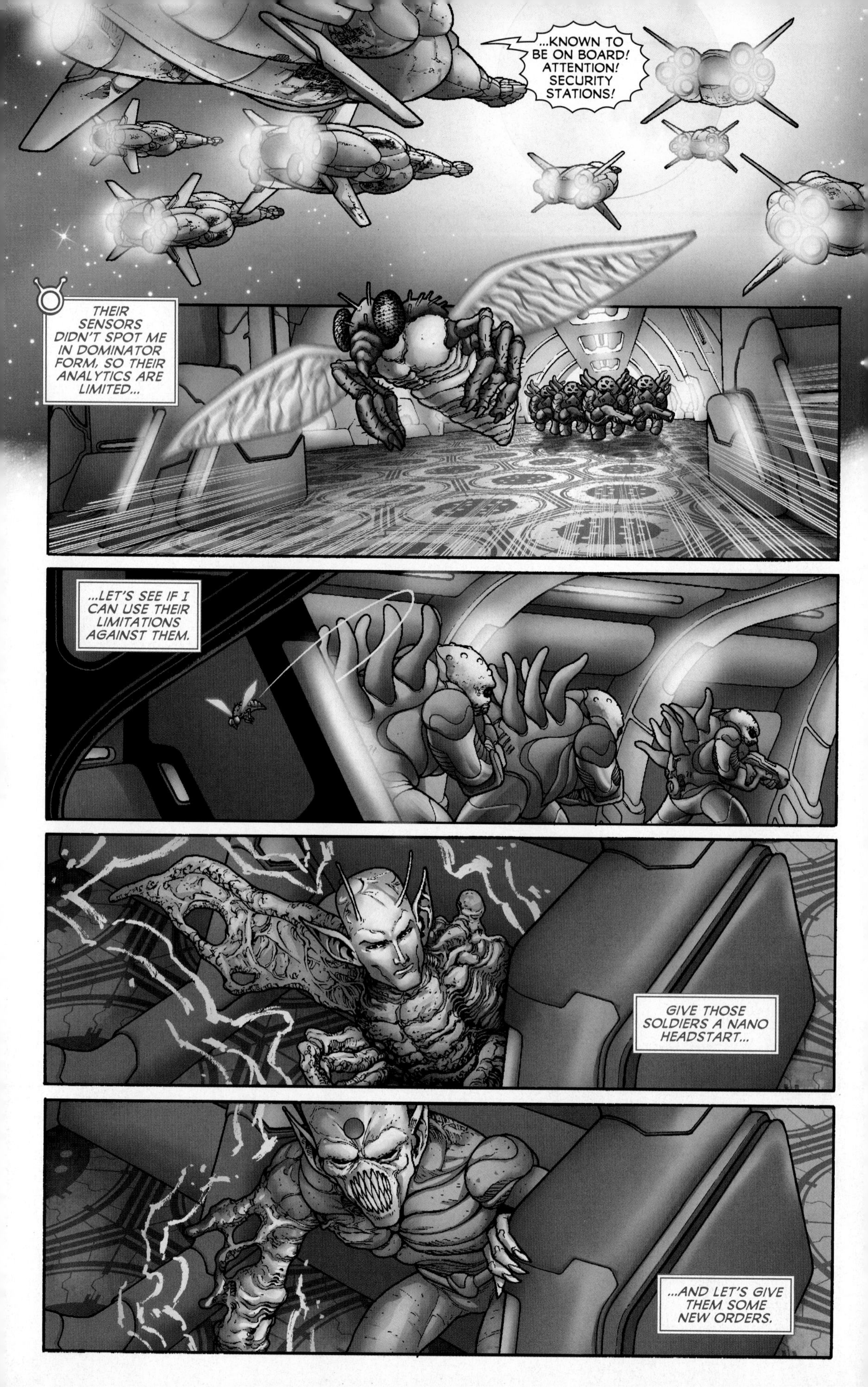
...KNOWN TO BE ON BOARD! ATTENTION! SECURITY STATIONS!
THEIR SENSORS DIDN'T SPOT ME IN DOMINATOR FORM, SO THEIR ANALYTICS ARE LIMITED...
...LET'S SEE IF I CAN USE THEIR LIMITATIONS AGAINST THEM.
GIVE THOSE SOLDIERS A NANO HEADSTART...
...AND LET'S GIVE THEM SOME NEW ORDERS.

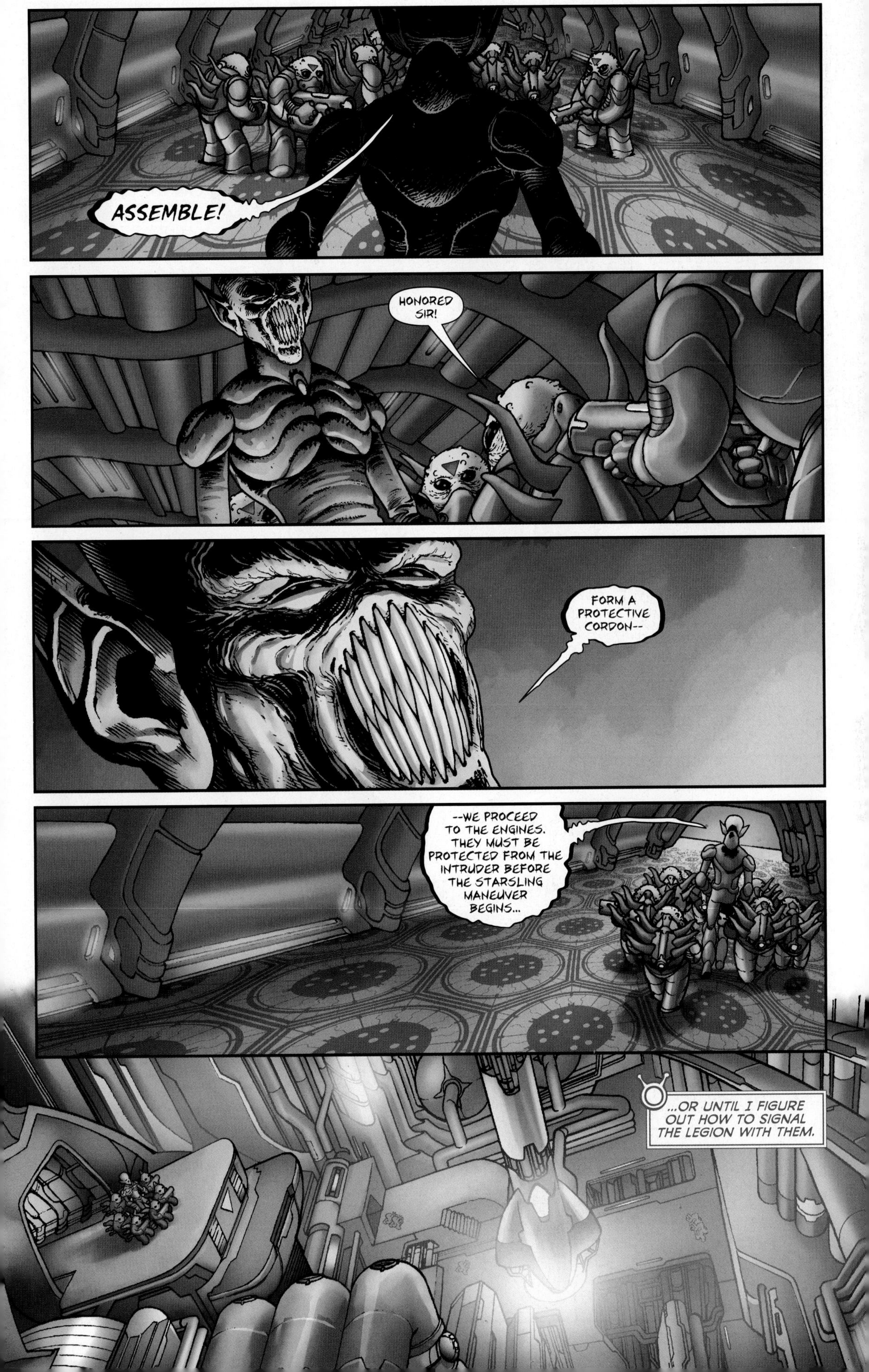
ASSEMBLE!
HONORED SIR!
FORM A PROTECTIVE CORDON--
--WE PROCEED TO THE ENGINES. THEY MUST BE PROTECTED FROM THE INTRUDER BEFORE THE STARSLING MANEUVER BEGINS...
...OR UNTIL I FIGURE OUT HOW TO SIGNAL THE LEGION WITH THEM.

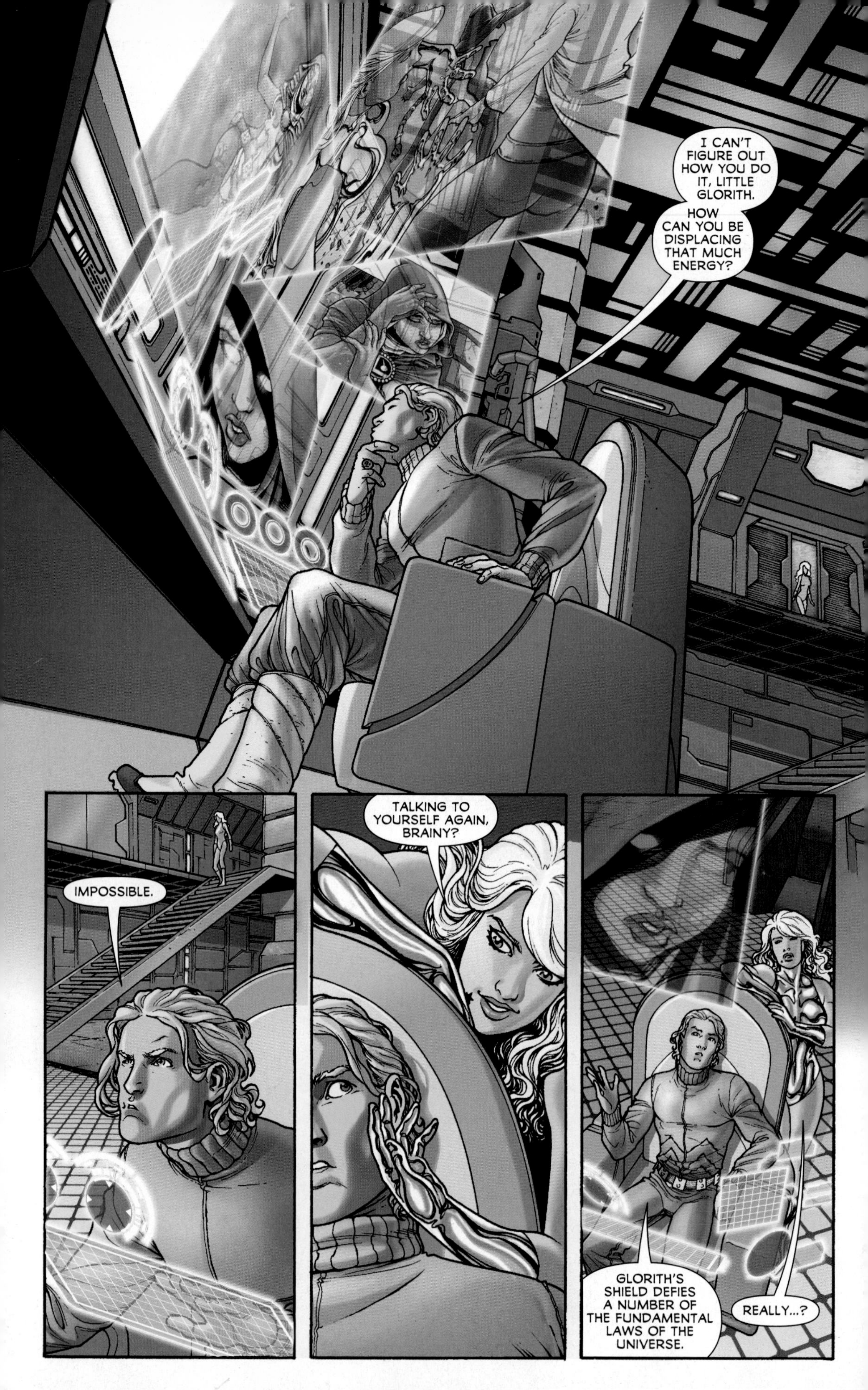
I CAN'T FIGURE OUT HOW YOU DO IT, LITTLE GLORITH.
HOW CAN YOU BE DISPLACING THAT MUCH ENERGY?
IMPOSSIBLE.
TALKING TO YOURSELF AGAIN, BRAINY?
GLORITH'S SHIELD DEFIES A NUMBER OF THE FUNDAMENTAL LAWS OF THE UNIVERSE.
REALLY...?

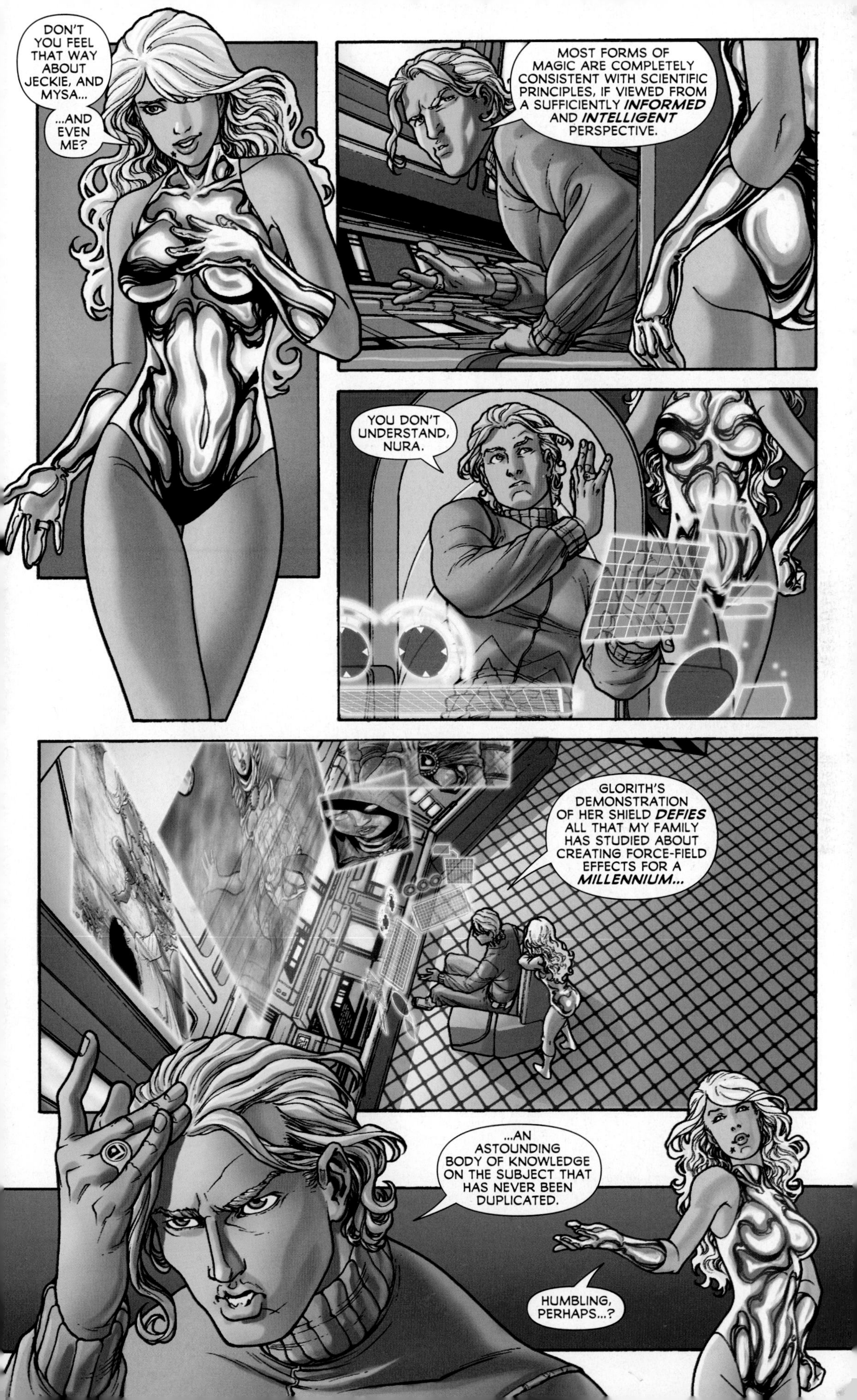
DON'T YOU FEEL THAT WAY ABOUT JECKIE, AND MYSA...
...AND EVEN ME?
MOST FORMS OF MAGIC ARE COMPLETELY CONSISTENT WITH SCIENTIFIC PRINCIPLES, IF VIEWED FROM A SUFFICIENTLY *INFORMED* AND *INTELLIGENT* PERSPECTIVE.
YOU DON'T UNDERSTAND, NURA.
GLORITH'S DEMONSTRATION OF HER SHIELD *DEFIES* ALL THAT MY FAMILY HAS STUDIED ABOUT CREATING FORCE-FIELD EFFECTS FOR A *MILLENNIUM...*
...AN ASTOUNDING BODY OF KNOWLEDGE ON THE SUBJECT THAT HAS NEVER BEEN DUPLICATED.
HUMBLING, PERHAPS...?

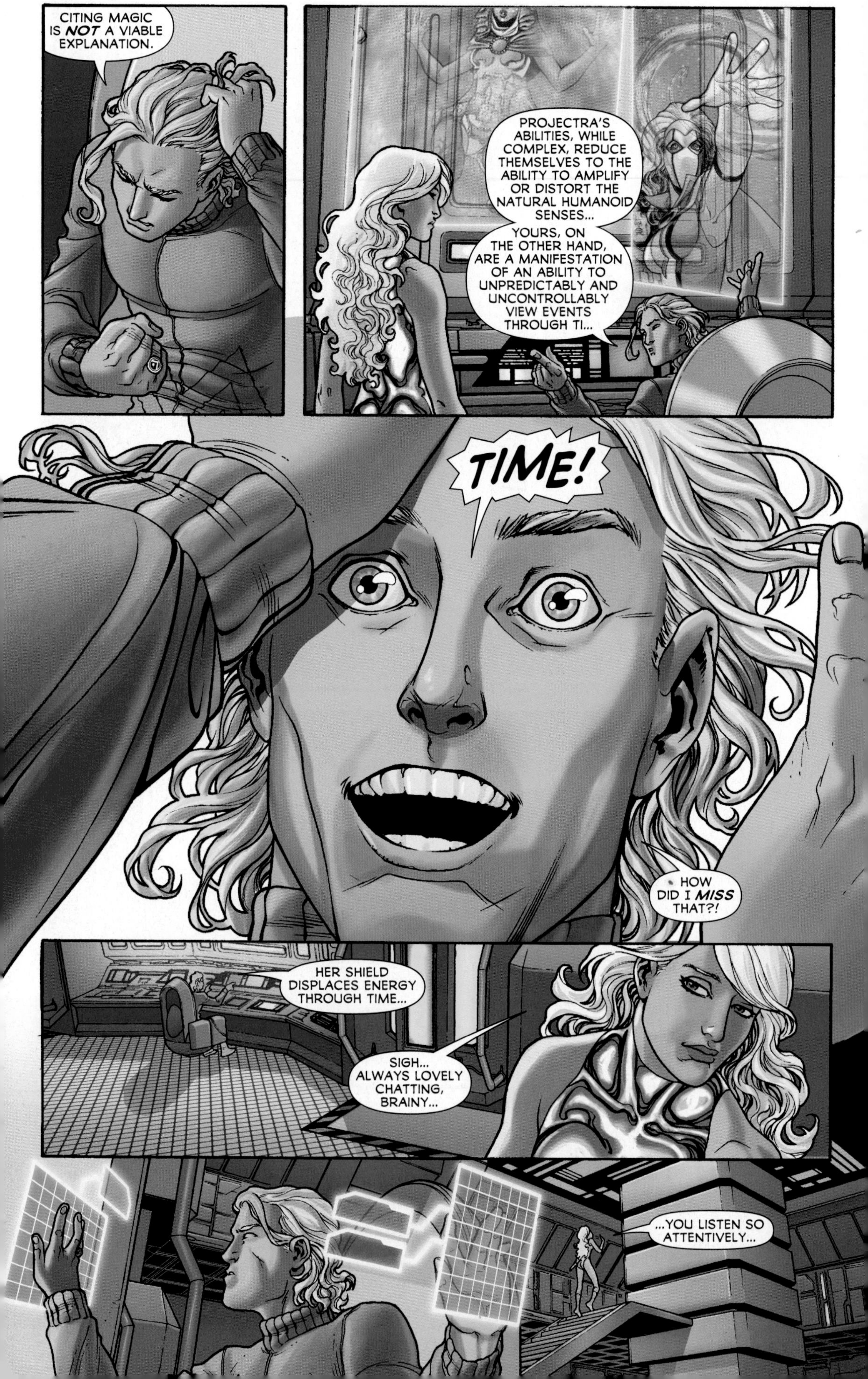
CITING MAGIC IS NOT A VIABLE EXPLANATION.
PROJECTRA'S ABILITIES, WHILE COMPLEX, REDUCE THEMSELVES TO THE ABILITY TO AMPLIFY OR DISTORT THE NATURAL HUMANOID SENSES...
YOURS, ON THE OTHER HAND, ARE A MANIFESTATION OF AN ABILITY TO UNPREDICTABLY AND UNCONTROLLABLY VIEW EVENTS THROUGH TI...
TIME!
HOW DID I MISS THAT?!
HER SHIELD DISPLACES ENERGY THROUGH TIME...
SIGH... ALWAYS LOVELY CHATTING, BRAINY...
...YOU LISTEN SO ATTENTIVELY...

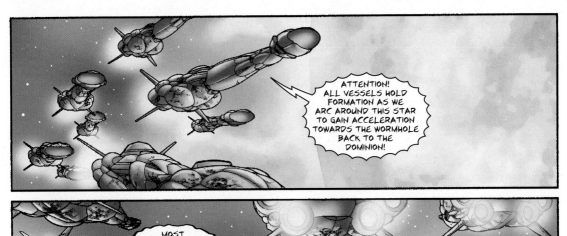

ATTENTION! ALL VESSELS HOLD FORMATION AS WE ARC AROUND THIS STAR TO GAIN ACCELERATION TOWARDS THE WORMHOLE BACK TO THE DOMINION!

MOST HONORED SIR-- ANOTHER STARSHIP IS INTERCEPTING OUR COURSE!

IT IS A SMALL CRUISER. SMASH IT OUT OF OUR PATH.

MOST HONORED SIR... WE HAVE A PROBLEM.

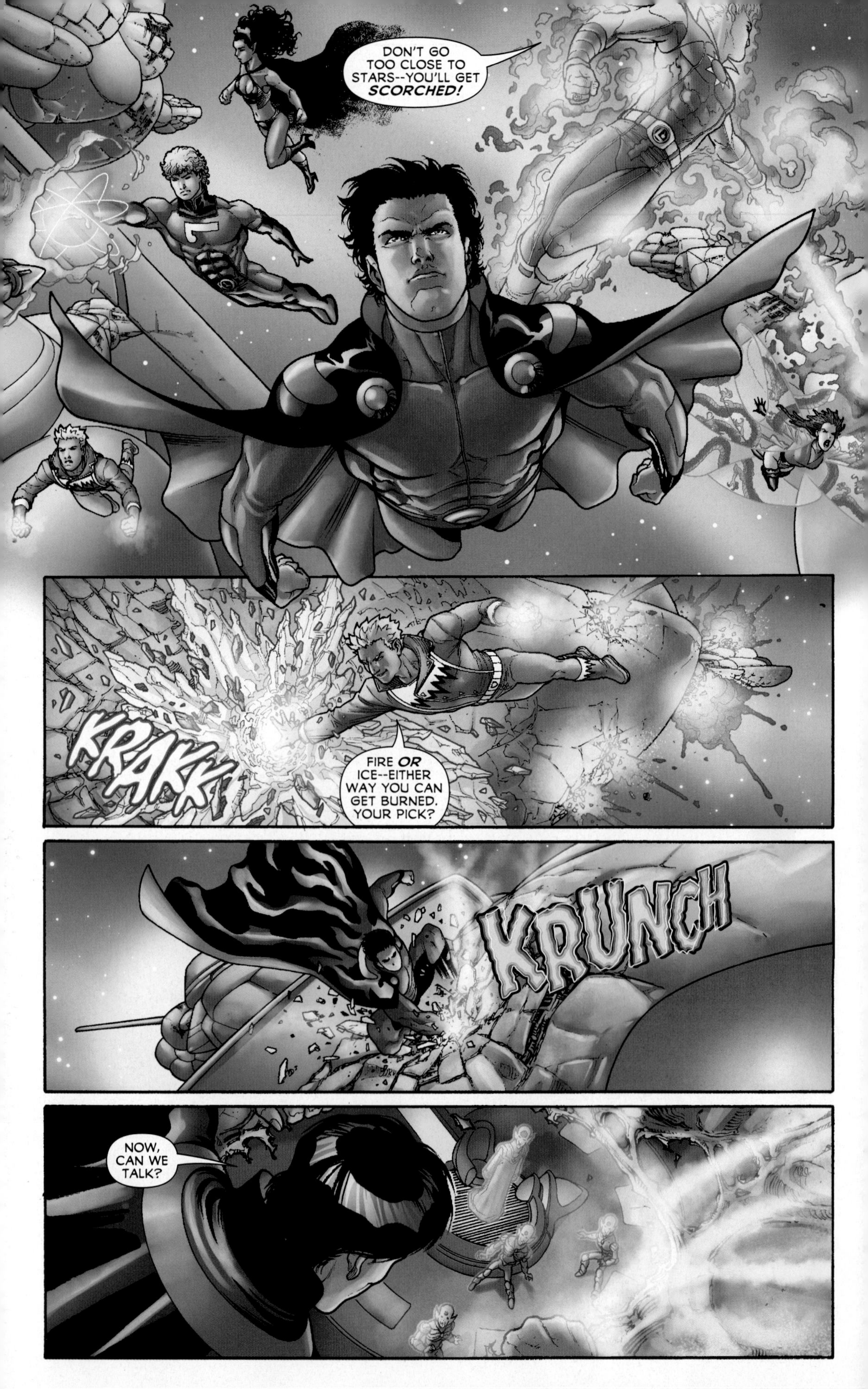
DON'T GO TOO CLOSE TO STARS--YOU'LL GET *SCORCHED!*
KRAKK
FIRE *OR* ICE--EITHER WAY YOU CAN GET BURNED. YOUR PICK?
KRUNCH
NOW, CAN WE TALK?

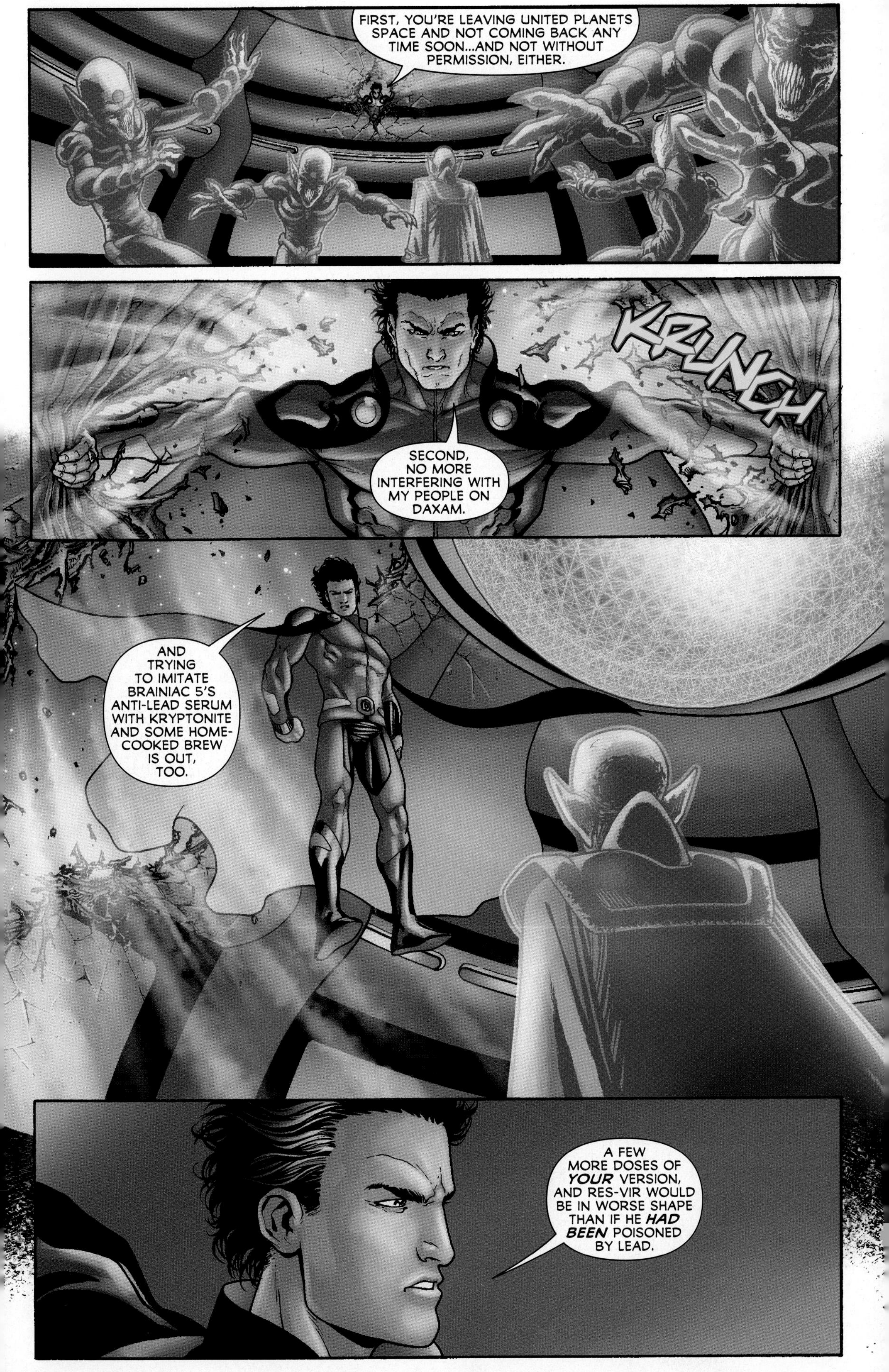

FIRST, YOU'RE LEAVING UNITED PLANETS SPACE AND NOT COMING BACK ANY TIME SOON...AND NOT WITHOUT PERMISSION, EITHER.
KRUNCH
SECOND, NO MORE INTERFERING WITH MY PEOPLE ON DAXAM.
AND TRYING TO IMITATE BRAINIAC 5'S ANTI-LEAD SERUM WITH KRYPTONITE AND SOME HOME-COOKED BREW IS OUT, TOO.
A FEW MORE DOSES OF *YOUR* VERSION, AND RES-VIR WOULD BE IN WORSE SHAPE THAN IF HE *HAD BEEN* POISONED BY LEAD.

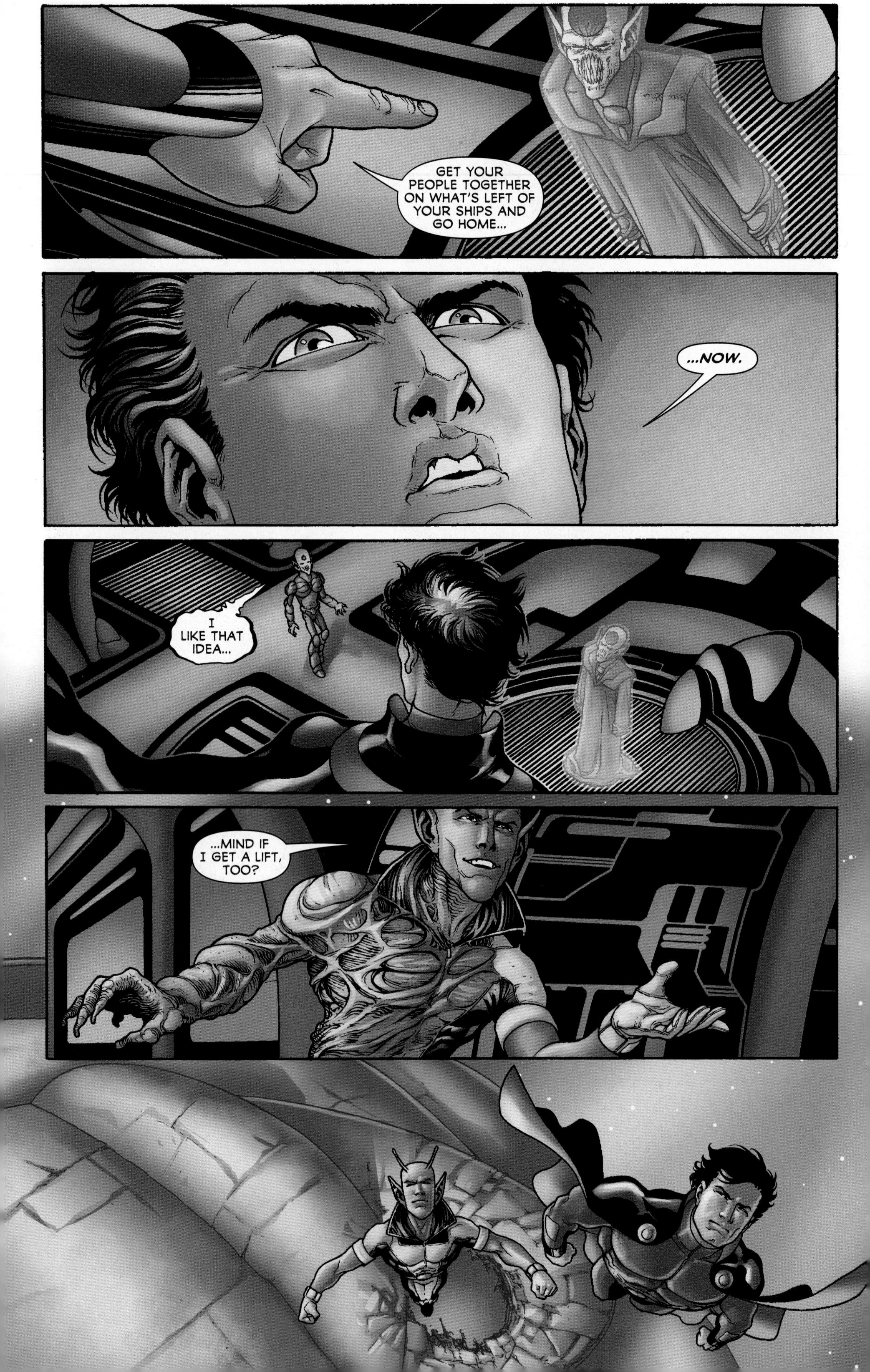
GET YOUR PEOPLE TOGETHER ON WHAT'S LEFT OF YOUR SHIPS AND GO HOME...
...NOW.
I LIKE THAT IDEA...
...MIND IF I GET A LIFT, TOO?

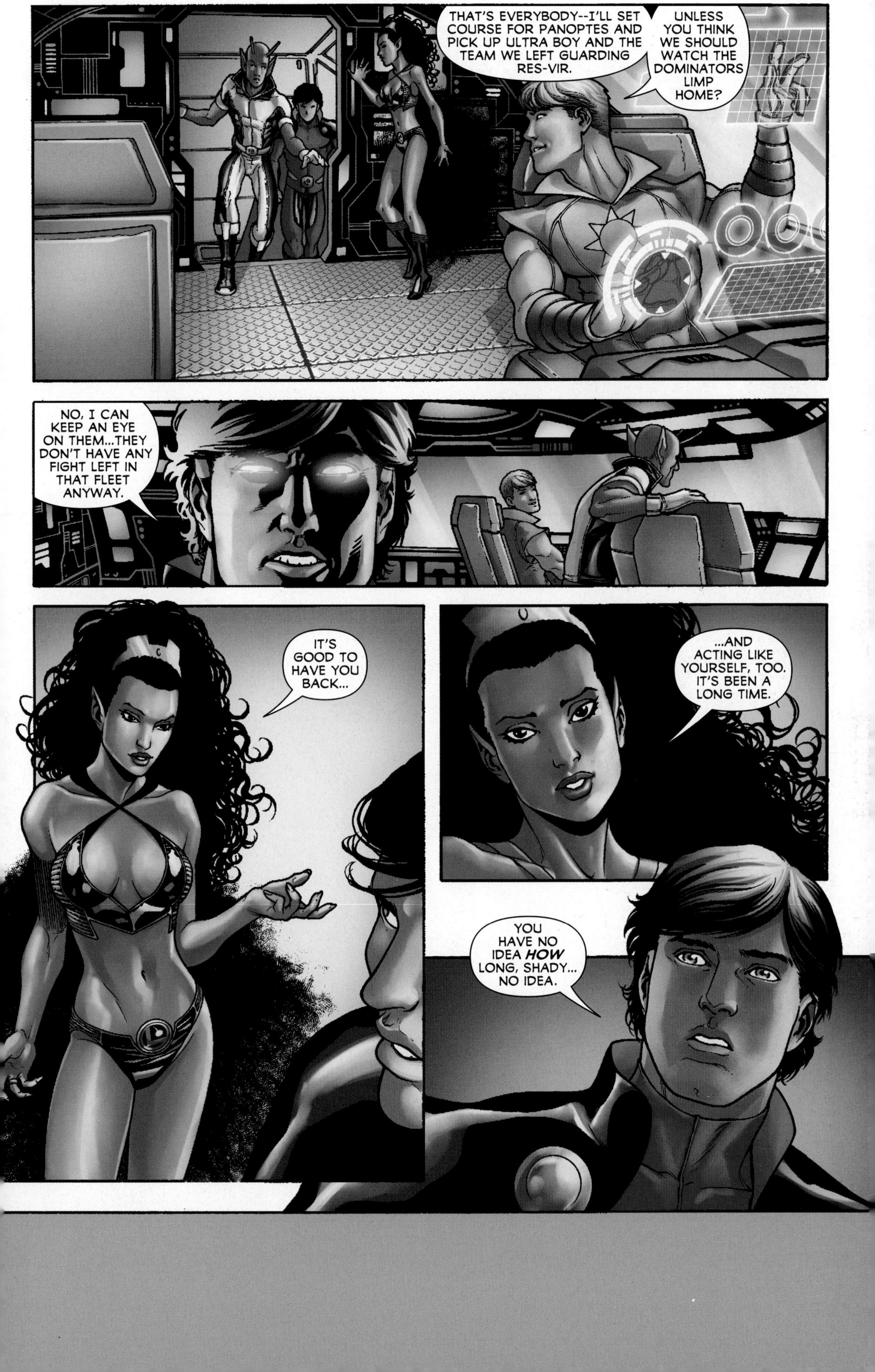
THAT'S EVERYBODY--I'LL SET COURSE FOR PANOPTES AND PICK UP ULTRA BOY AND THE TEAM WE LEFT GUARDING RES-VIR.
UNLESS YOU THINK WE SHOULD WATCH THE DOMINATORS LIMP HOME?
NO, I CAN KEEP AN EYE ON THEM...THEY DON'T HAVE ANY FIGHT LEFT IN THAT FLEET ANYWAY.
IT'S GOOD TO HAVE YOU BACK...
...AND ACTING LIKE YOURSELF, TOO. IT'S BEEN A LONG TIME.
YOU HAVE NO IDEA *HOW* LONG, SHADY... NO IDEA.

cover art by
WALTER SIMONSON & GUY MAJOR

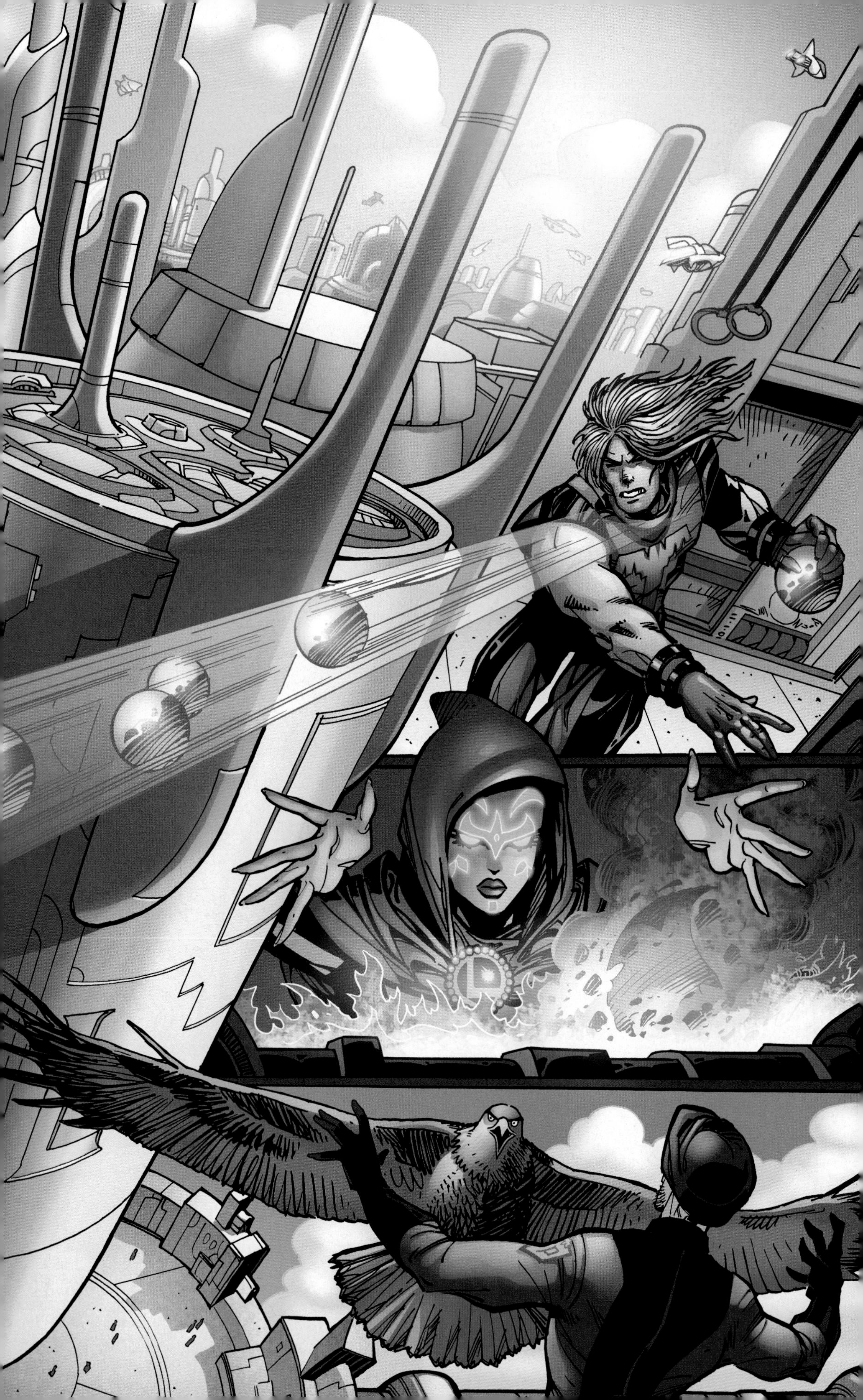

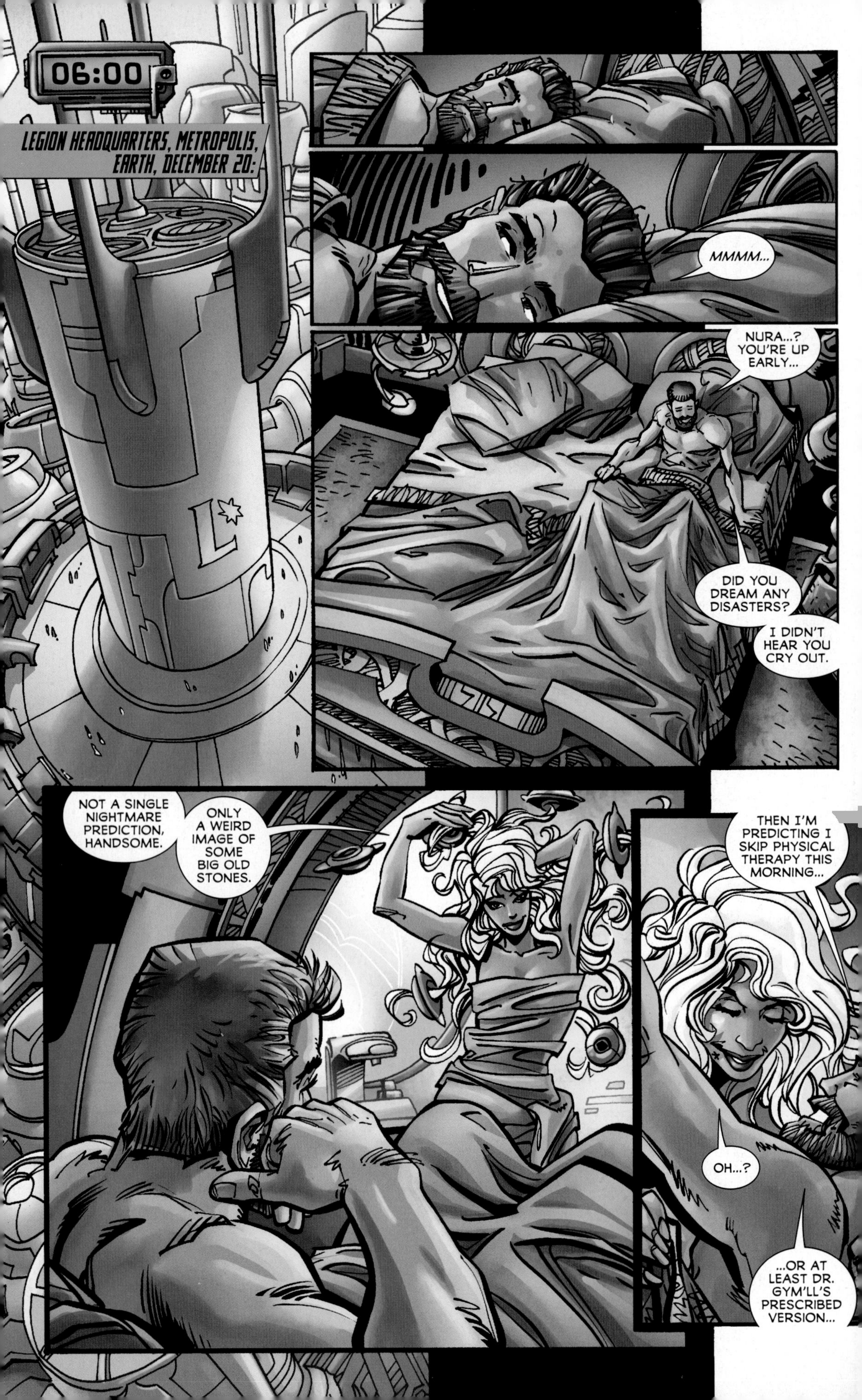
06:00
LEGION HEADQUARTERS, METROPOLIS, EARTH, DECEMBER 20:
MMMM...
NURA...? YOU'RE UP EARLY...
DID YOU DREAM ANY DISASTERS?
I DIDN'T HEAR YOU CRY OUT.
NOT A SINGLE NIGHTMARE PREDICTION, HANDSOME.
ONLY A WEIRD IMAGE OF SOME BIG OLD STONES.
THEN I'M PREDICTING I SKIP PHYSICAL THERAPY THIS MORNING...
OH...?
...OR AT LEAST DR. GYM'LL'S PRESCRIBED VERSION...

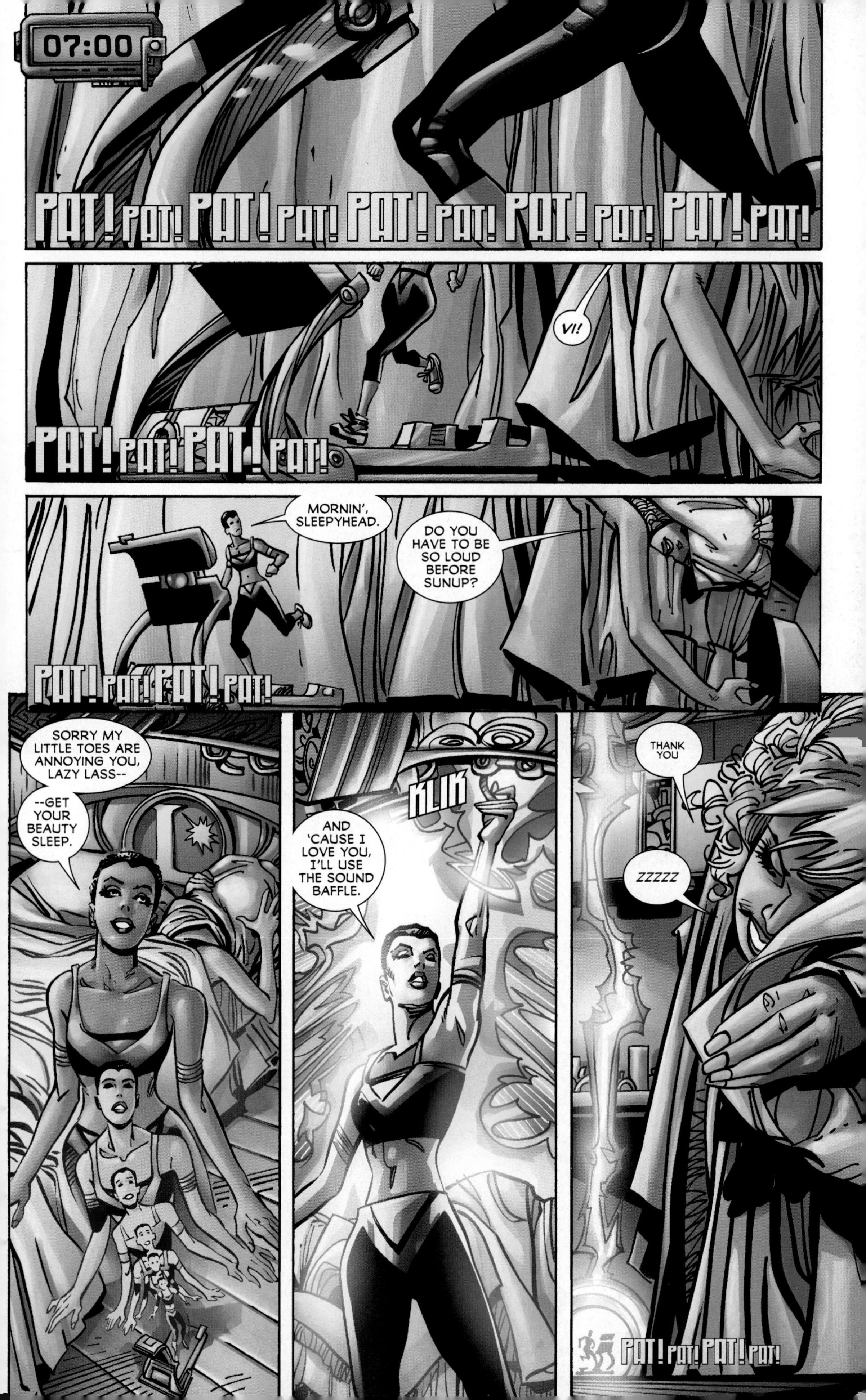
07:00
PAT! PAT! PAT! PAT! PAT! PAT! PAT! PAT! PAT! PAT!
VI!
PAT! PAT! PAT! PAT!
MORNIN', SLEEPYHEAD.
DO YOU HAVE TO BE SO LOUD BEFORE SUNUP?
PAT! PAT! PAT! PAT!
SORRY MY LITTLE TOES ARE ANNOYING YOU, LAZY LASS--
--GET YOUR BEAUTY SLEEP.
KLIK
AND 'CAUSE I LOVE YOU, I'LL USE THE SOUND BAFFLE.
THANK YOU
ZZZZZ
PAT! PAT! PAT! PAT!

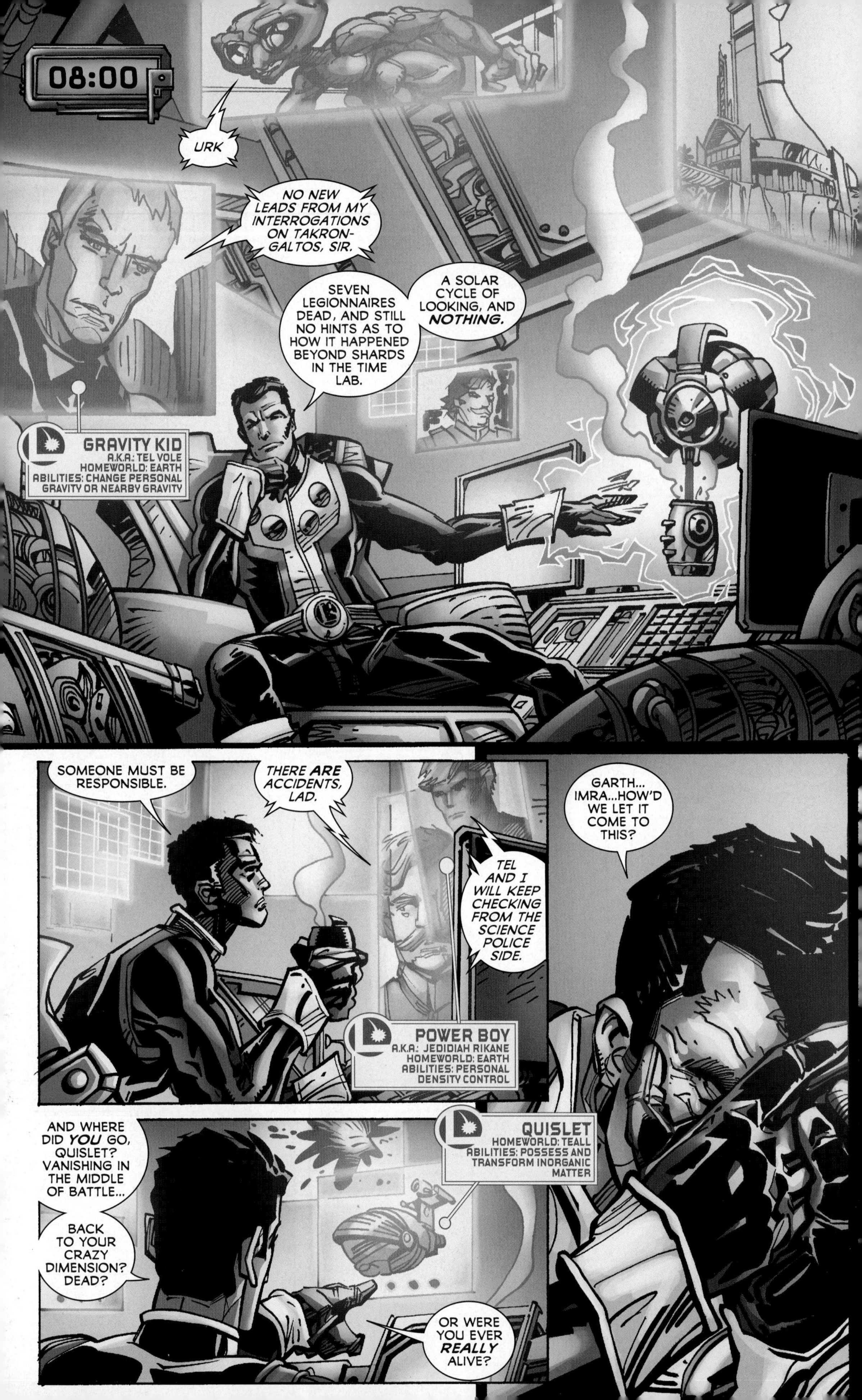
08:00
URK
NO NEW LEADS FROM MY INTERROGATIONS ON TAKRON-GALTOS, SIR.
SEVEN LEGIONNAIRES DEAD, AND STILL NO HINTS AS TO HOW IT HAPPENED BEYOND SHARDS IN THE TIME LAB.
A SOLAR CYCLE OF LOOKING, AND NOTHING.
GRAVITY KID
A.K.A.: TEL VOLE
HOMEWORLD: EARTH
ABILITIES: CHANGE PERSONAL GRAVITY OR NEARBY GRAVITY
SOMEONE MUST BE RESPONSIBLE.
THERE ARE ACCIDENTS, LAD.
TEL AND I WILL KEEP CHECKING FROM THE SCIENCE POLICE SIDE.
POWER BOY
A.K.A.: JEDIDIAH RIKANE
HOMEWORLD: EARTH
ABILITIES: PERSONAL DENSITY CONTROL
GARTH... IMRA...HOW'D WE LET IT COME TO THIS?
AND WHERE DID YOU GO, QUISLET? VANISHING IN THE MIDDLE OF BATTLE...
QUISLET
HOMEWORLD: TEALL
ABILITIES: POSSESS AND TRANSFORM INORGANIC MATTER
BACK TO YOUR CRAZY DIMENSION? DEAD?
OR WERE YOU EVER REALLY ALIVE?

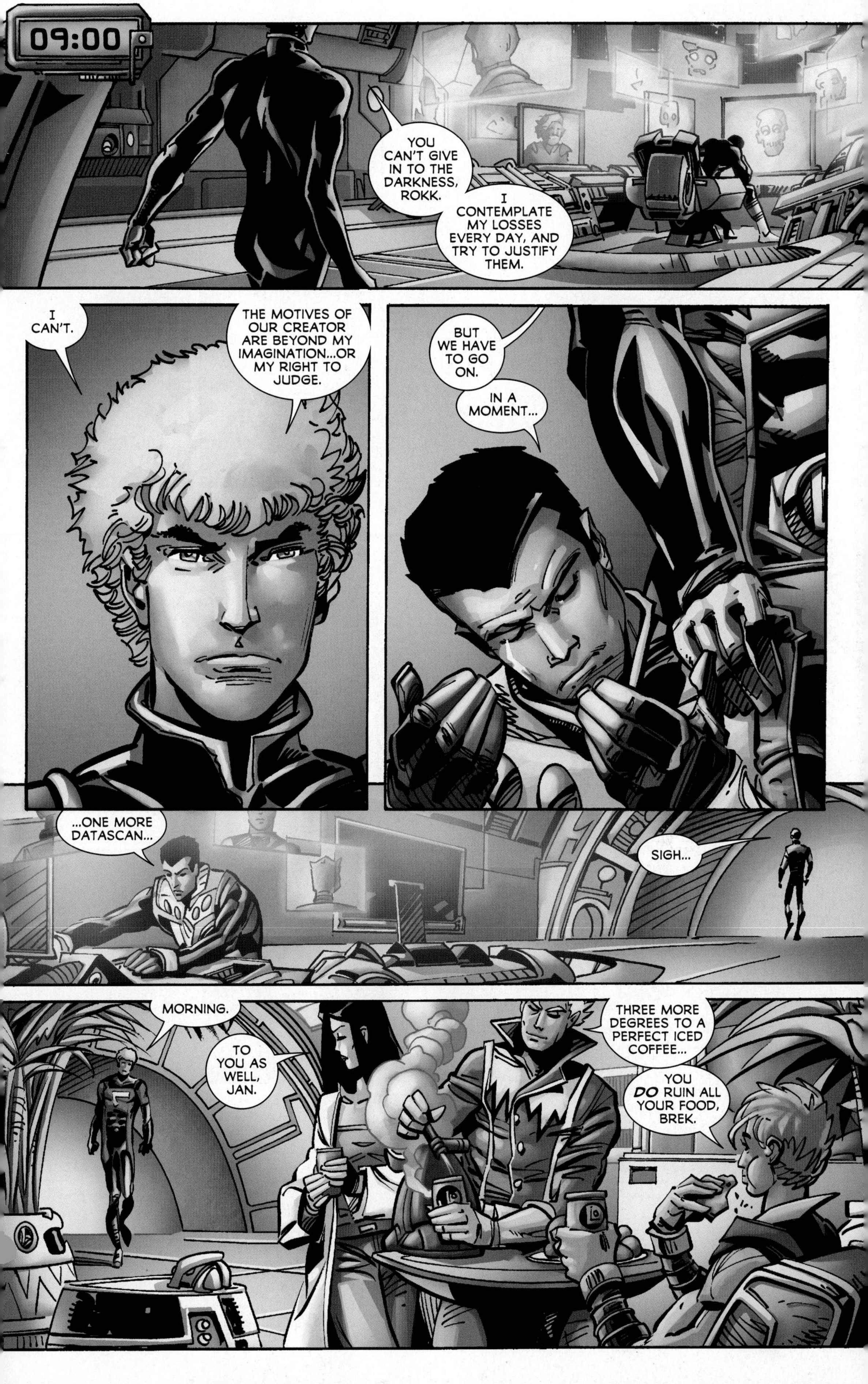
09:00
YOU CAN'T GIVE IN TO THE DARKNESS, ROKK.
I CONTEMPLATE MY LOSSES EVERY DAY, AND TRY TO JUSTIFY THEM.
I CAN'T.
THE MOTIVES OF OUR CREATOR ARE BEYOND MY IMAGINATION...OR MY RIGHT TO JUDGE.
BUT WE HAVE TO GO ON.
IN A MOMENT...
...ONE MORE DATASCAN...
SIGH...
MORNING.
TO YOU AS WELL, JAN.
THREE MORE DEGREES TO A PERFECT ICED COFFEE...
YOU DO RUIN ALL YOUR FOOD, BREK.

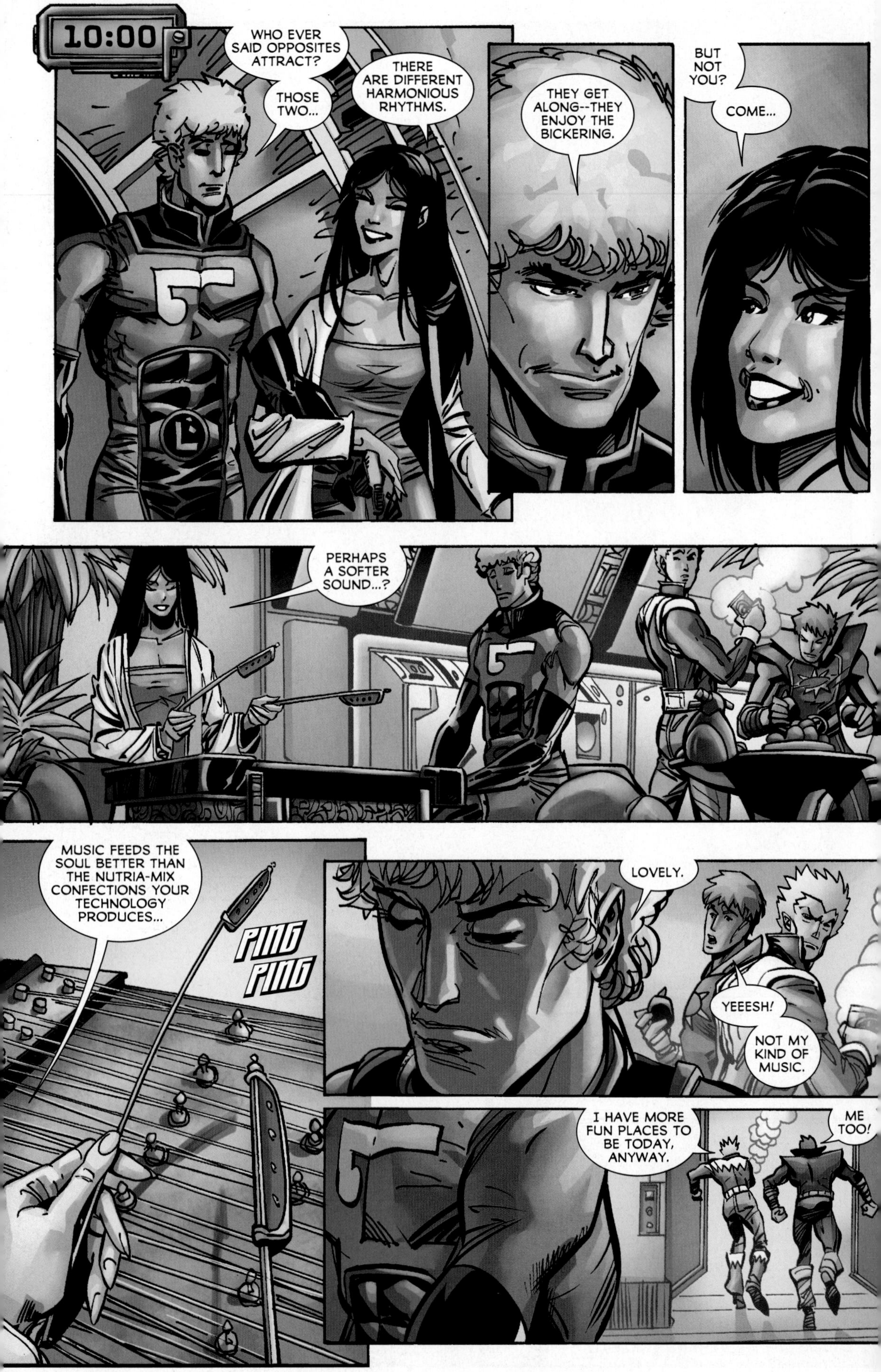
10:00
WHO EVER SAID OPPOSITES ATTRACT?
THOSE TWO...
THERE ARE DIFFERENT HARMONIOUS RHYTHMS.
THEY GET ALONG--THEY ENJOY THE BICKERING.
BUT NOT YOU?
COME...
PERHAPS A SOFTER SOUND...?
MUSIC FEEDS THE SOUL BETTER THAN THE NUTRIA-MIX CONFECTIONS YOUR TECHNOLOGY PRODUCES...
PING PING
LOVELY.
YEEESH!
NOT MY KIND OF MUSIC.
I HAVE MORE FUN PLACES TO BE TODAY, ANYWAY.
ME TOO!

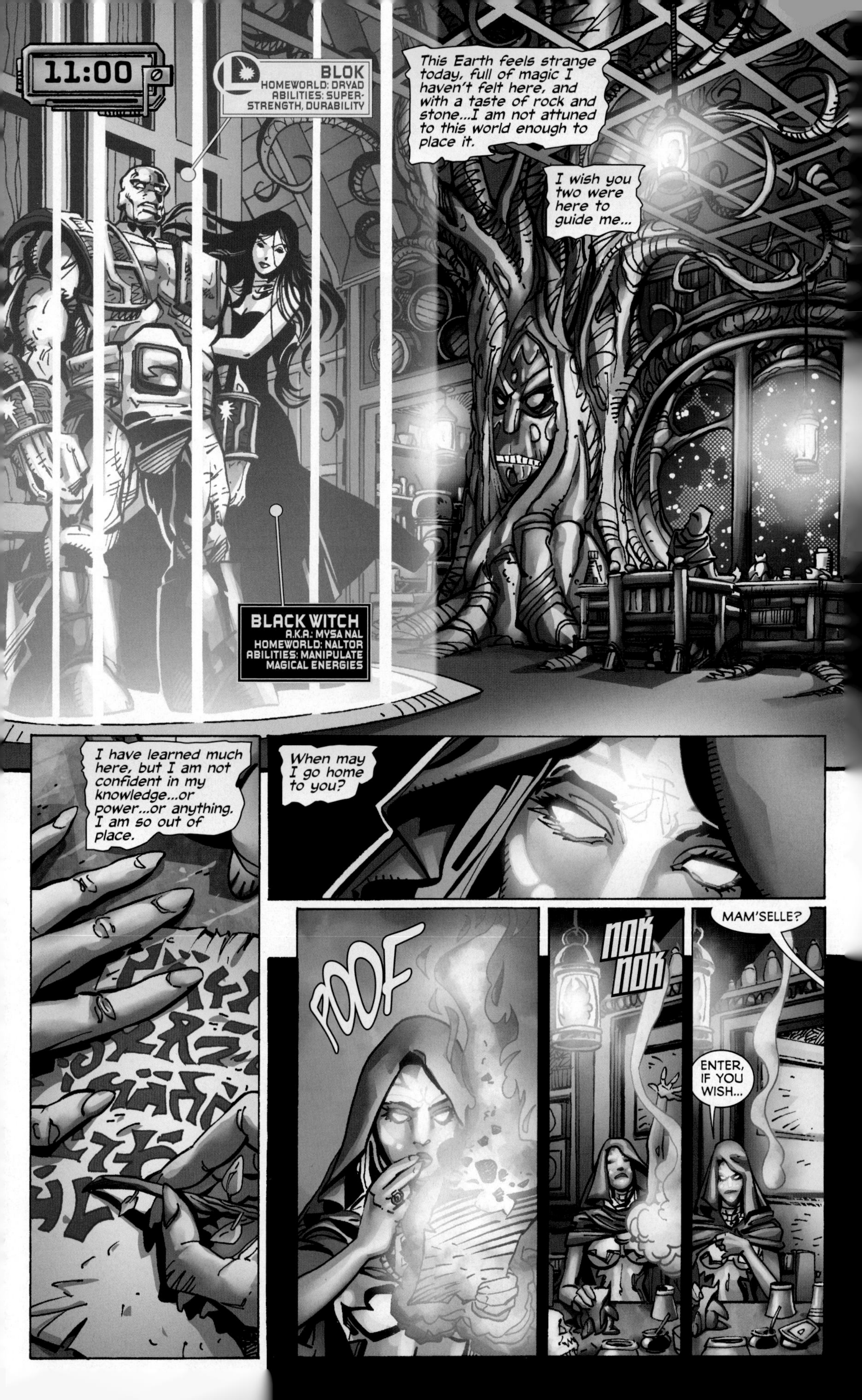
11:00
BLOK
HOMEWORLD: DRYAD
ABILITIES: SUPER-STRENGTH, DURABILITY
BLACK WITCH
A.K.A.: MYSA NAL
HOMEWORLD: NALTOR
ABILITIES: MANIPULATE MAGICAL ENERGIES
This Earth feels strange today, full of magic I haven't felt here, and with a taste of rock and stone...I am not attuned to this world enough to place it.
I wish you two were here to guide me...
I have learned much here, but I am not confident in my knowledge...or power...or anything. I am so out of place.
When may I go home to you?
POOF
NOK NOK
MAM'SELLE?
ENTER, IF YOU WISH...

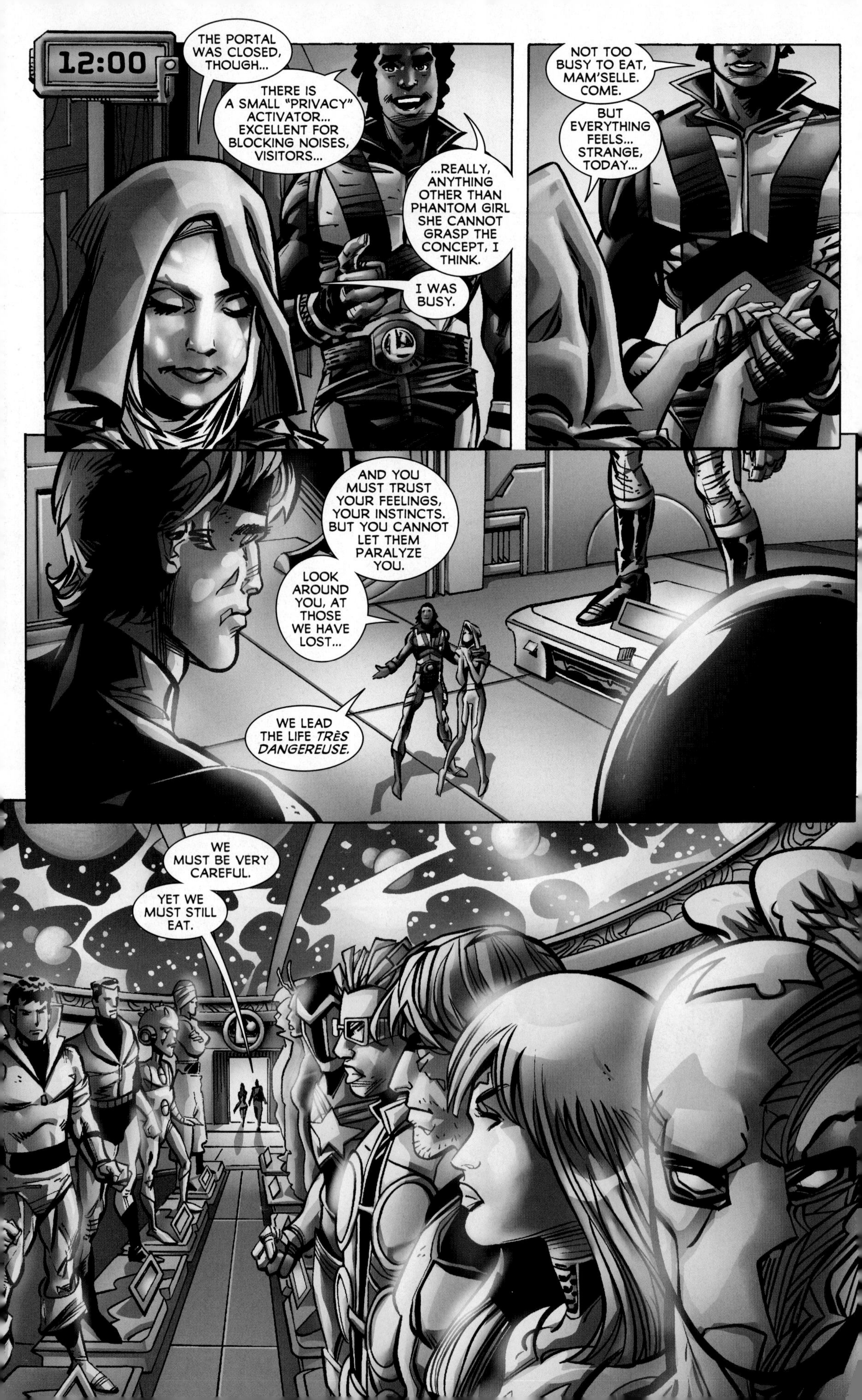
12:00
THE PORTAL WAS CLOSED, THOUGH...
THERE IS A SMALL "PRIVACY" ACTIVATOR... EXCELLENT FOR BLOCKING NOISES, VISITORS...
...REALLY, ANYTHING OTHER THAN PHANTOM GIRL SHE CANNOT GRASP THE CONCEPT, I THINK.
I WAS BUSY.
NOT TOO BUSY TO EAT, MAM'SELLE. COME.
BUT EVERYTHING FEELS... STRANGE, TODAY...
AND YOU MUST TRUST YOUR FEELINGS, YOUR INSTINCTS. BUT YOU CANNOT LET THEM PARALYZE YOU.
LOOK AROUND YOU, AT THOSE WE HAVE LOST...
WE LEAD THE LIFE *TRÈS DANGEREUSE.*
WE MUST BE VERY CAREFUL.
YET WE MUST STILL EAT.

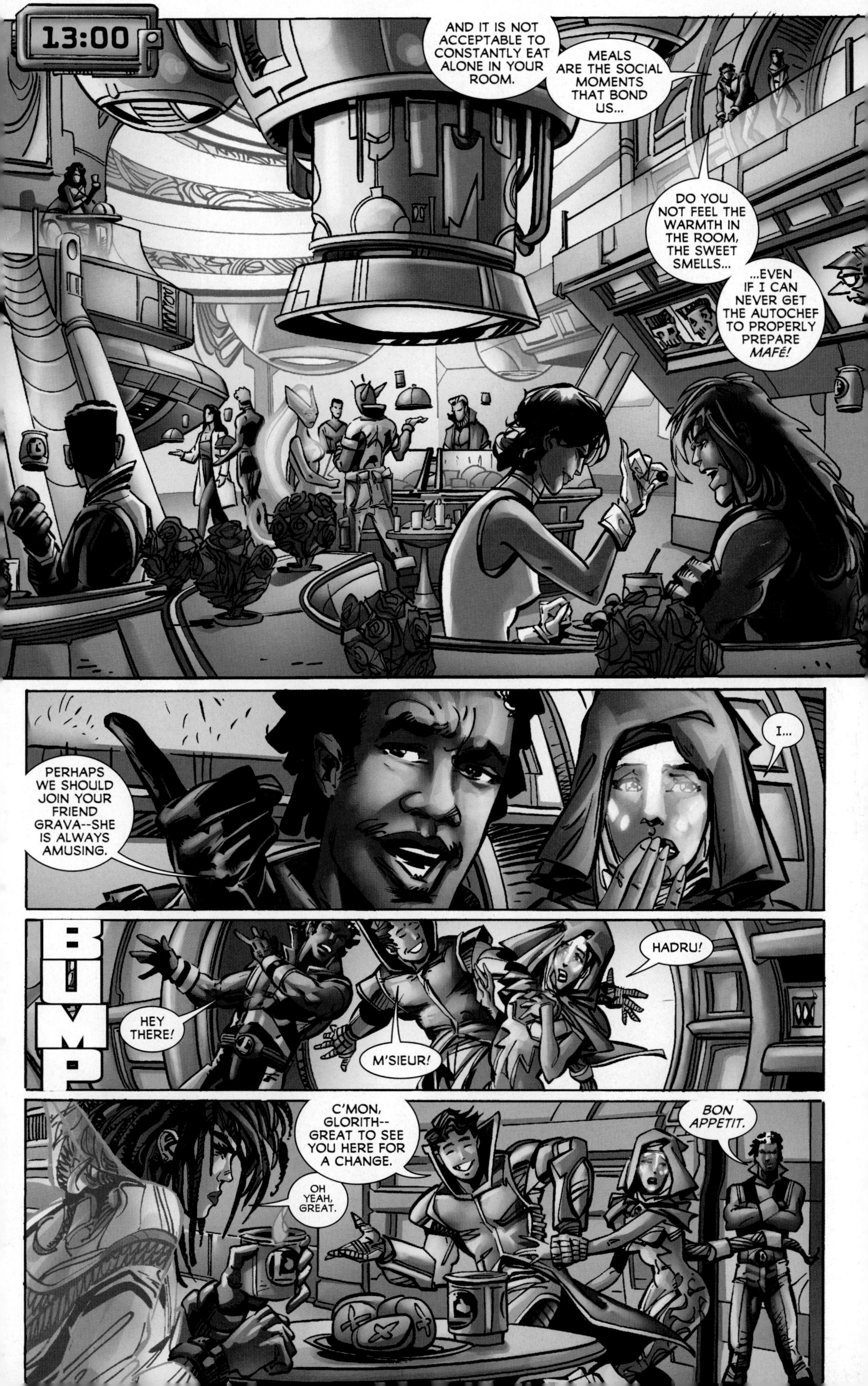
13:00
AND IT IS NOT ACCEPTABLE TO CONSTANTLY EAT ALONE IN YOUR ROOM.
MEALS ARE THE SOCIAL MOMENTS THAT BOND US...
DO YOU NOT FEEL THE WARMTH IN THE ROOM, THE SWEET SMELLS...
...EVEN IF I CAN NEVER GET THE AUTOCHEF TO PROPERLY PREPARE *MAFÉ!*
PERHAPS WE SHOULD JOIN YOUR FRIEND GRAVA--SHE IS ALWAYS AMUSING.
I...
BUMP
HADRU!
HEY THERE!
M'SIEUR!
C'MON, GLORITH-- GREAT TO SEE YOU HERE FOR A CHANGE.
OH YEAH, GREAT.
BON APPETIT.

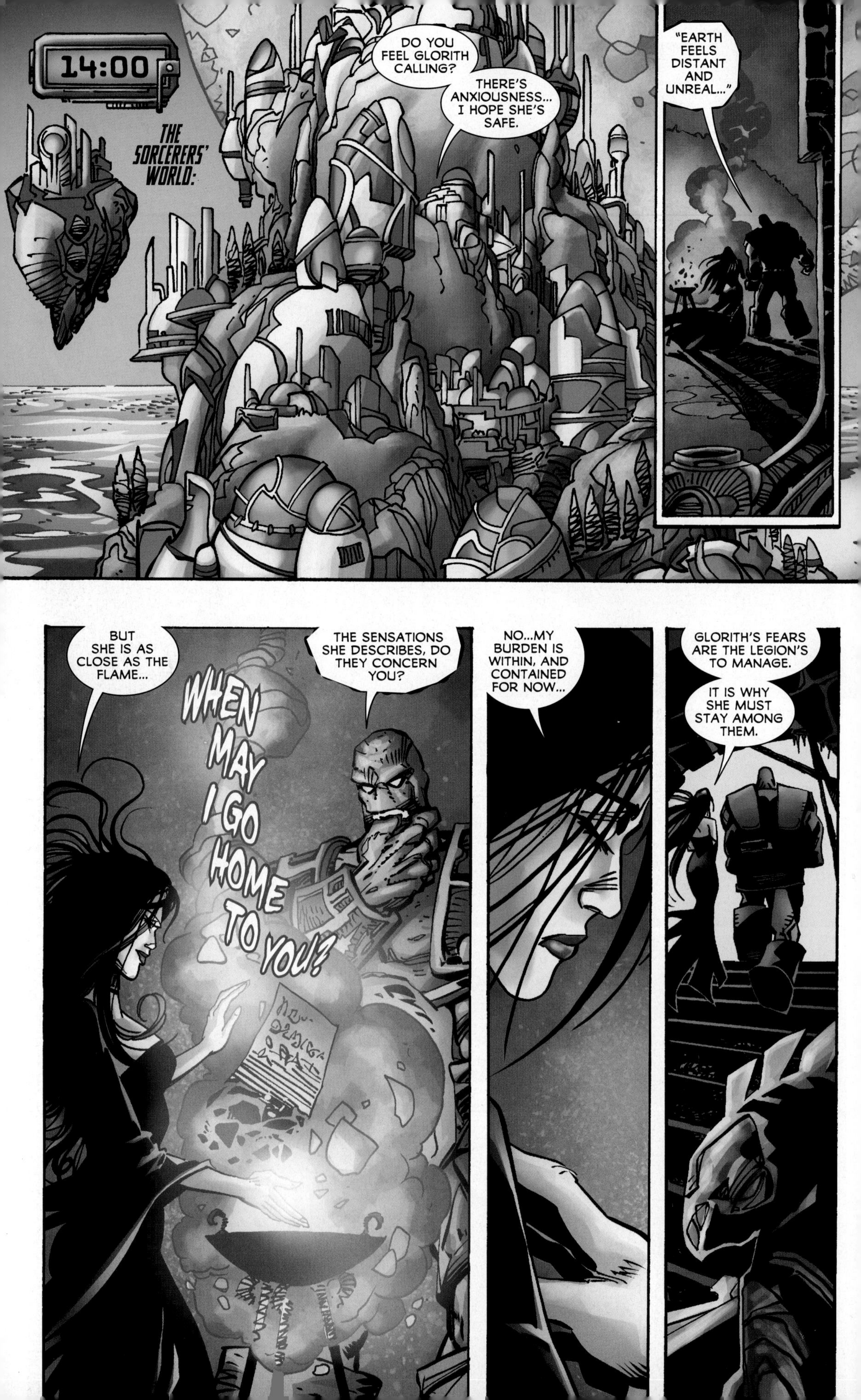
14:00
THE SORCERERS' WORLD:
DO YOU FEEL GLORITH CALLING?
THERE'S ANXIOUSNESS... I HOPE SHE'S SAFE.
"EARTH FEELS DISTANT AND UNREAL..."
BUT SHE IS AS CLOSE AS THE FLAME...
WHEN MAY I GO HOME TO YOU!?
THE SENSATIONS SHE DESCRIBES, DO THEY CONCERN YOU?
NO...MY BURDEN IS WITHIN, AND CONTAINED FOR NOW...
GLORITH'S FEARS ARE THE LEGION'S TO MANAGE.
IT IS WHY SHE MUST STAY AMONG THEM.

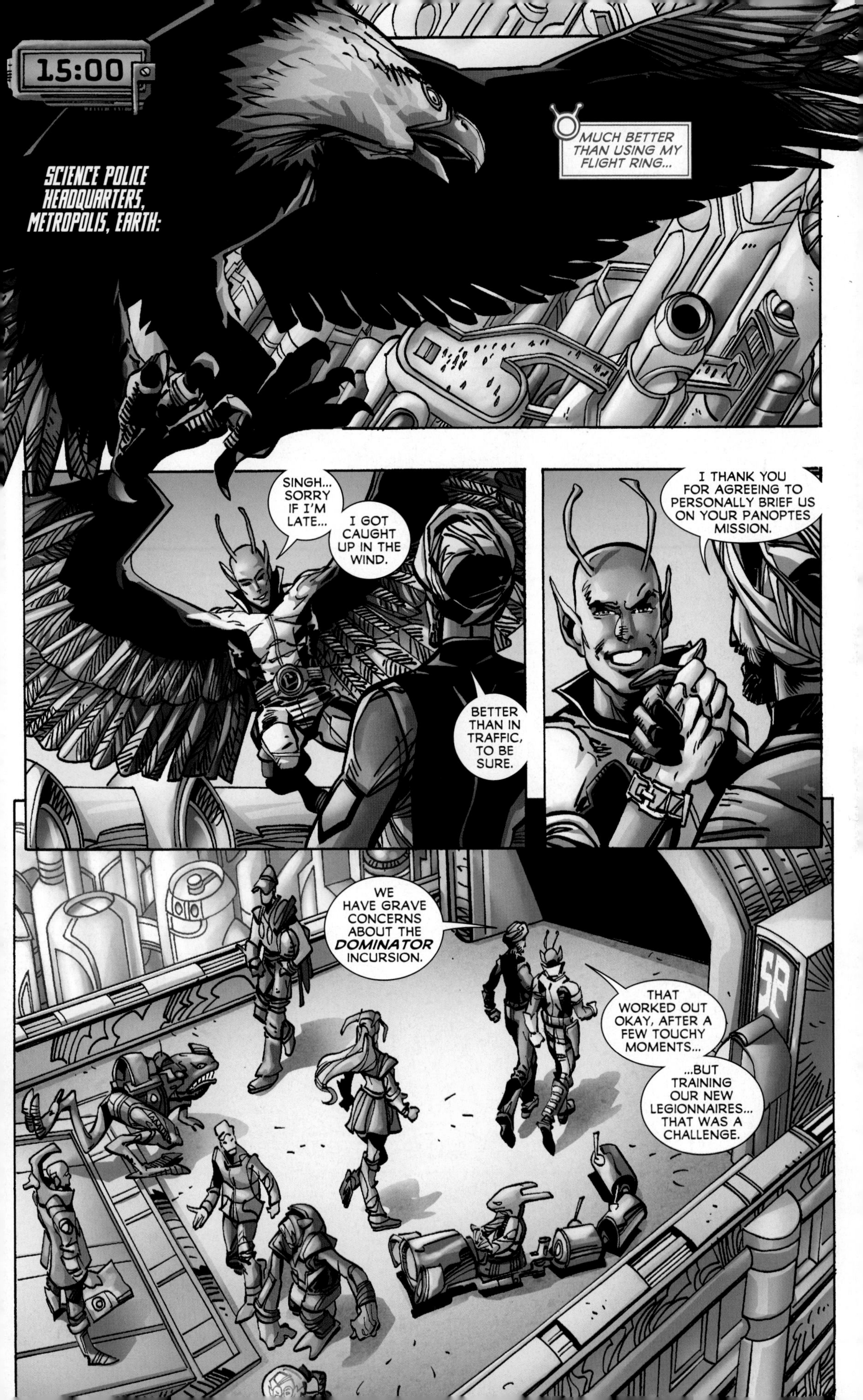
15:00
SCIENCE POLICE HEADQUARTERS, METROPOLIS, EARTH:
MUCH BETTER THAN USING MY FLIGHT RING...
SINGH... SORRY IF I'M LATE...
I GOT CAUGHT UP IN THE WIND.
BETTER THAN IN TRAFFIC, TO BE SURE.
I THANK YOU FOR AGREEING TO PERSONALLY BRIEF US ON YOUR PANOPTES MISSION.
WE HAVE GRAVE CONCERNS ABOUT THE DOMINATOR INCURSION.
THAT WORKED OUT OKAY, AFTER A FEW TOUCHY MOMENTS...
...BUT TRAINING OUR NEW LEGIONNAIRES... THAT WAS A CHALLENGE.
SP

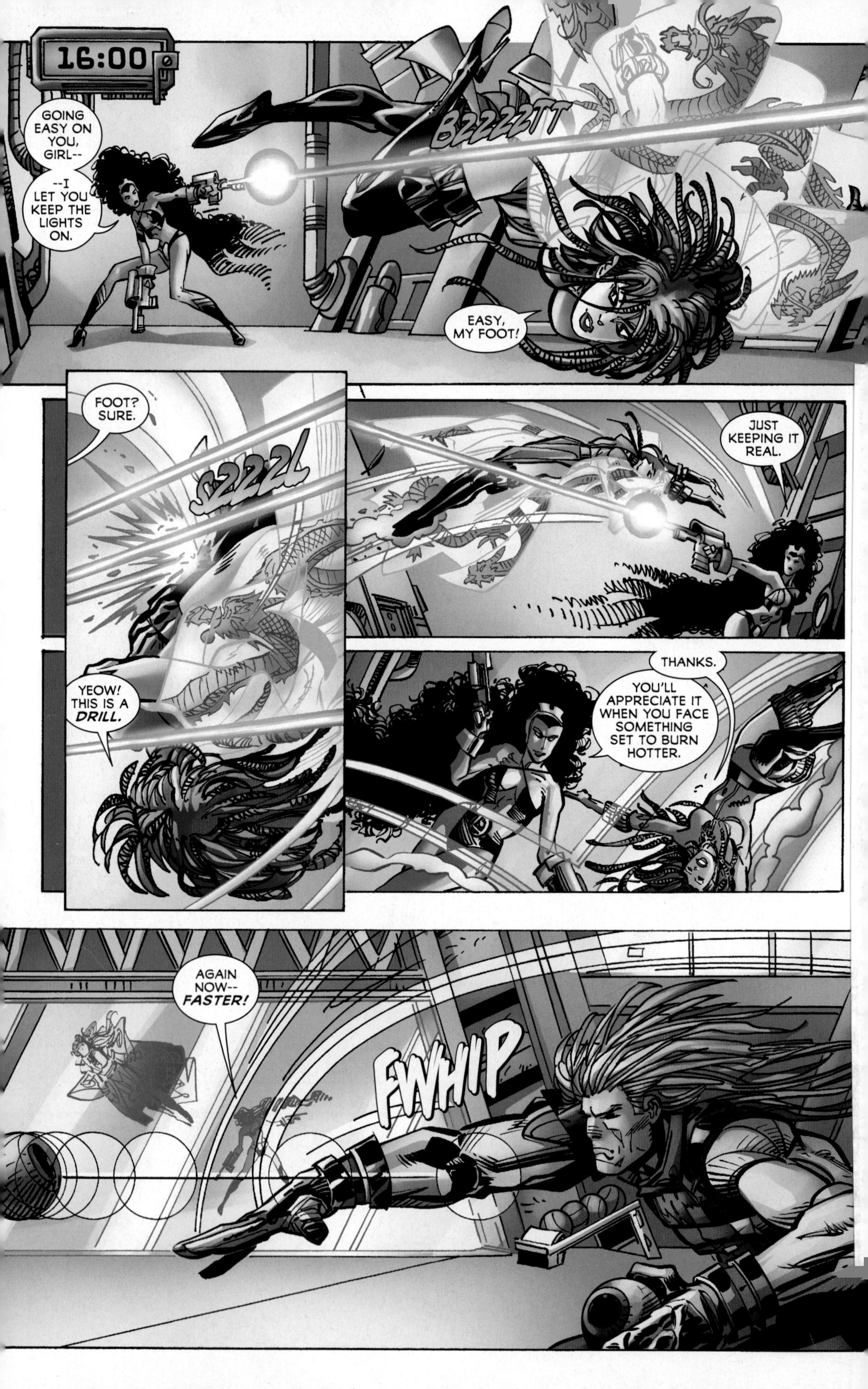
16:00
GOING EASY ON YOU, GIRL--
--I LET YOU KEEP THE LIGHTS ON.
BZZZZZTT
EASY, MY FOOT!
FOOT? SURE.
SZZZL
JUST KEEPING IT REAL.
YEOW! THIS IS A *DRILL.*
THANKS.
YOU'LL APPRECIATE IT WHEN YOU FACE SOMETHING SET TO BURN HOTTER.
AGAIN NOW-- *FASTER!*
FWHIP

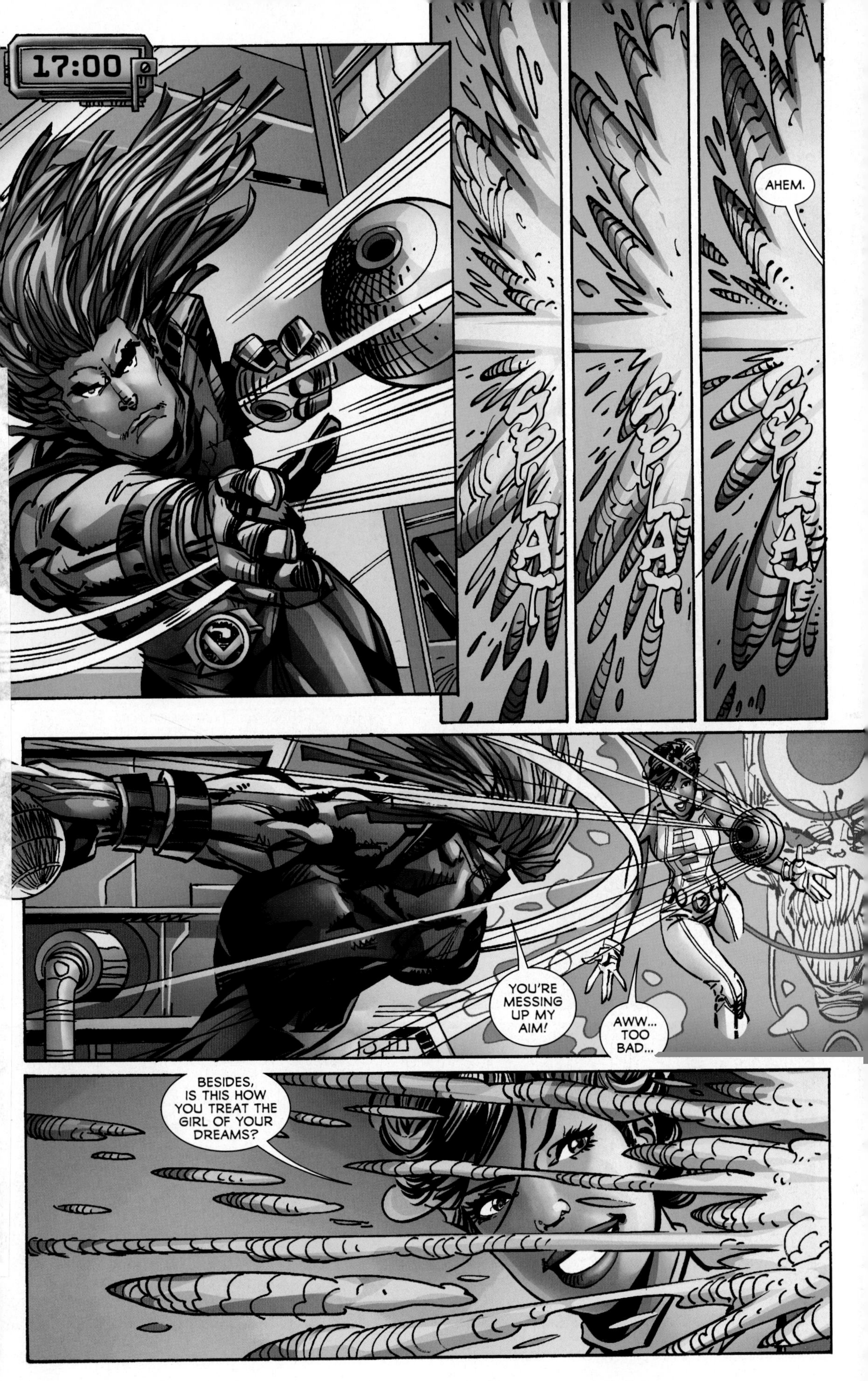
17:00
SPLAT
SPLAT
AHEM.
SPLAT
YOU'RE MESSING UP MY AIM!
AWW... TOO BAD...
BESIDES, IS THIS HOW YOU TREAT THE GIRL OF YOUR DREAMS?

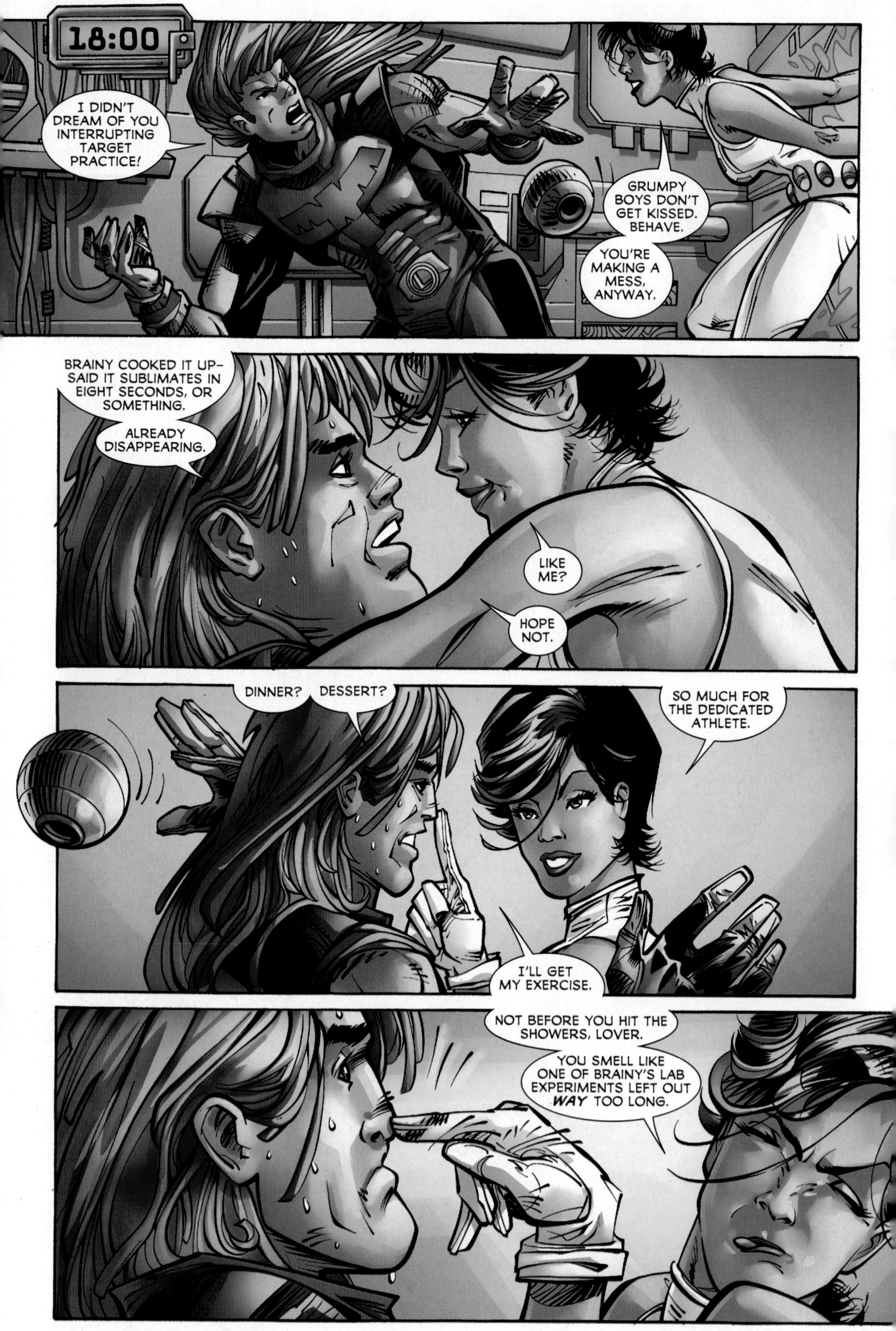
18:00
I DIDN'T DREAM OF YOU INTERRUPTING TARGET PRACTICE!
GRUMPY BOYS DON'T GET KISSED. BEHAVE.
YOU'RE MAKING A MESS, ANYWAY.
BRAINY COOKED IT UP-- SAID IT SUBLIMATES IN EIGHT SECONDS, OR SOMETHING.
ALREADY DISAPPEARING.
LIKE ME?
HOPE NOT.
DINNER?
DESSERT?
SO MUCH FOR THE DEDICATED ATHLETE.
I'LL GET MY EXERCISE.
NOT BEFORE YOU HIT THE SHOWERS, LOVER.
YOU SMELL LIKE ONE OF BRAINY'S LAB EXPERIMENTS LEFT OUT *WAY* TOO LONG.

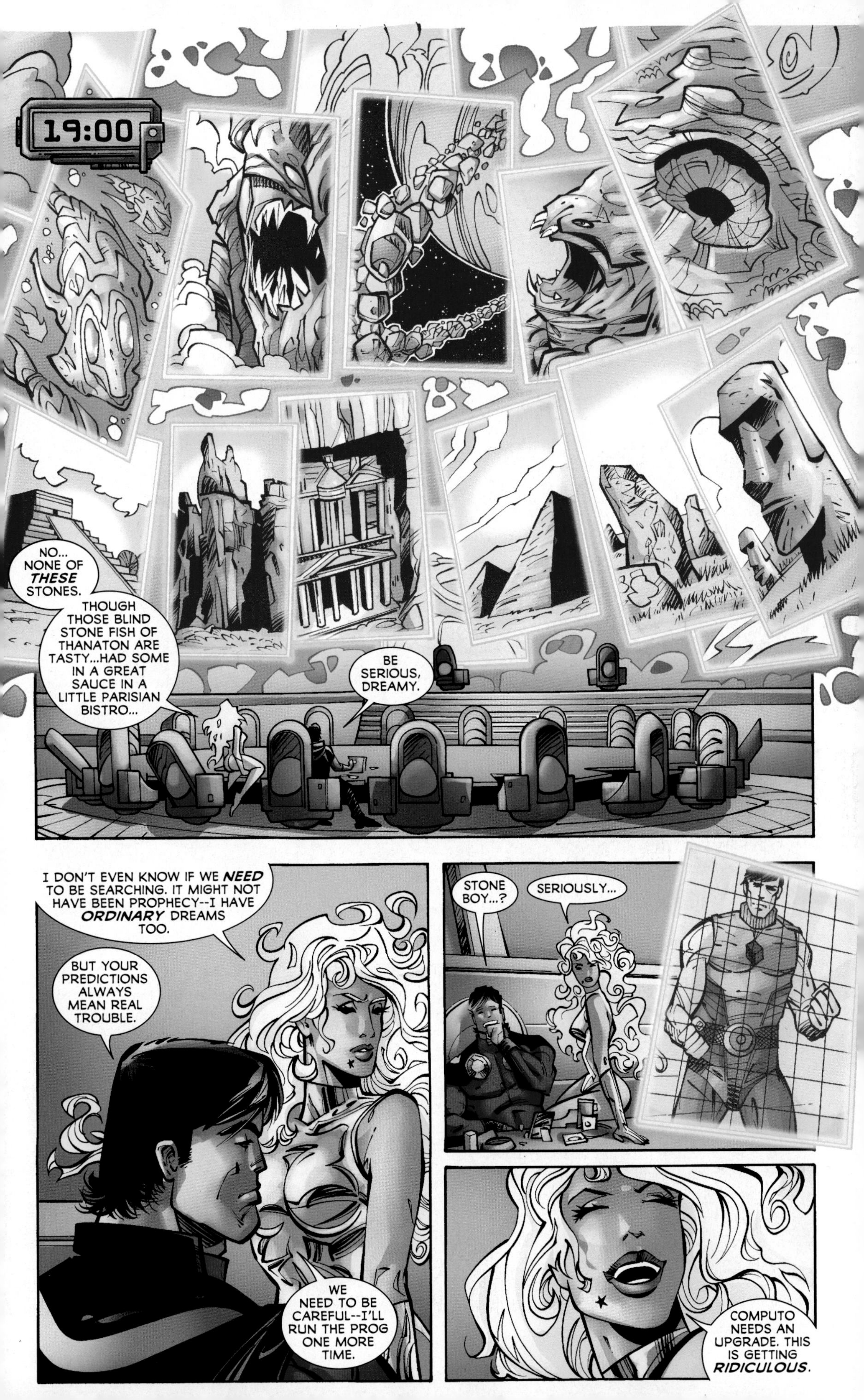
19:00
NO... NONE OF THESE STONES.
THOUGH THOSE BLIND STONE FISH OF THANATON ARE TASTY...HAD SOME IN A GREAT SAUCE IN A LITTLE PARISIAN BISTRO...
BE SERIOUS, DREAMY.
I DON'T EVEN KNOW IF WE NEED TO BE SEARCHING. IT MIGHT NOT HAVE BEEN PROPHECY--I HAVE ORDINARY DREAMS TOO.
BUT YOUR PREDICTIONS ALWAYS MEAN REAL TROUBLE.
WE NEED TO BE CAREFUL--I'LL RUN THE PROG ONE MORE TIME.
STONE BOY...?
SERIOUSLY...
COMPUTO NEEDS AN UPGRADE. THIS IS GETTING RIDICULOUS.

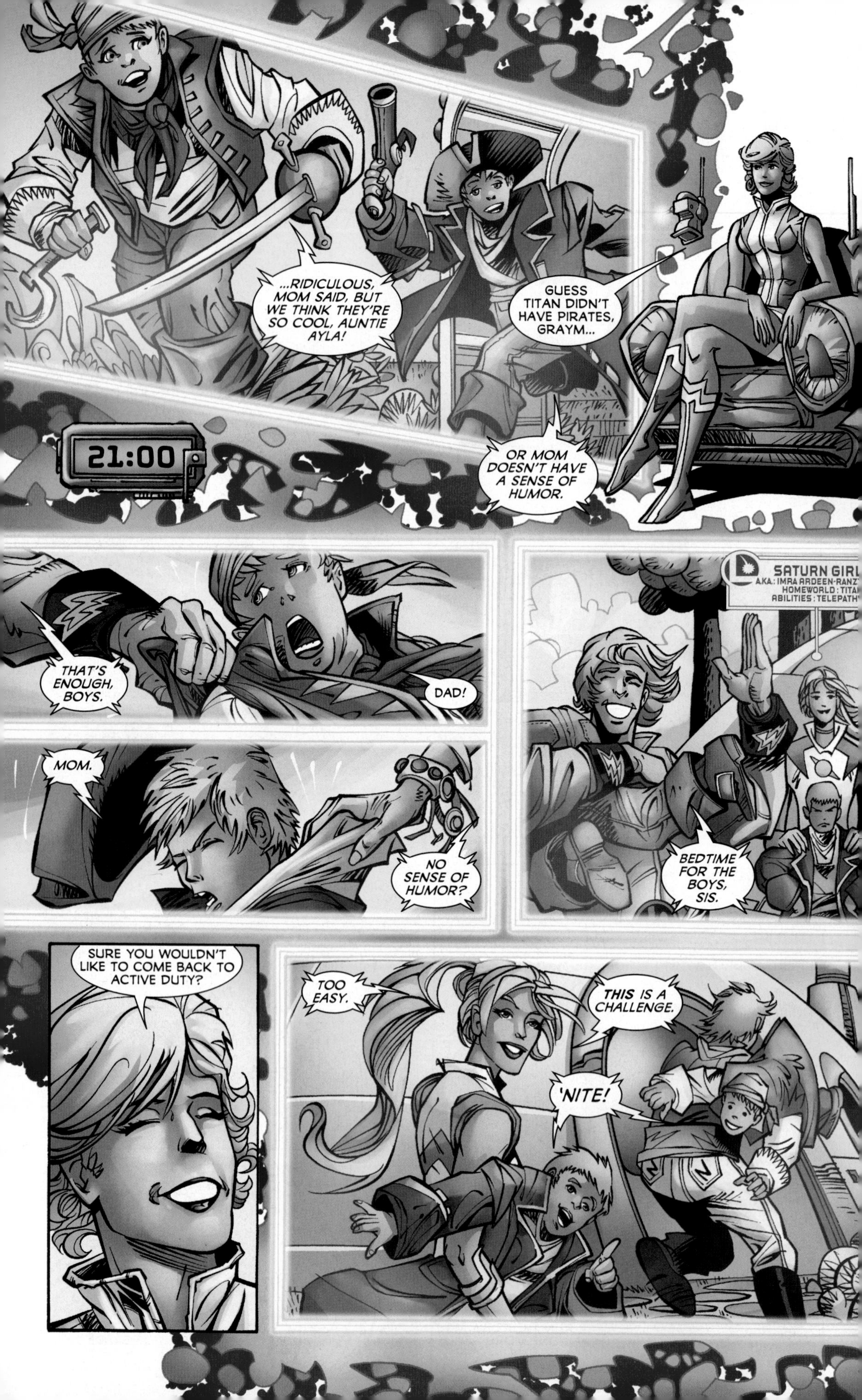
...RIDICULOUS, MOM SAID, BUT WE THINK THEY'RE SO COOL, AUNTIE AYLA!
GUESS TITAN DIDN'T HAVE PIRATES, GRAYM...
21:00
OR MOM DOESN'T HAVE A SENSE OF HUMOR.
THAT'S ENOUGH, BOYS.
DAD!
MOM.
NO SENSE OF HUMOR?
SATURN GIRL
A.K.A.: IMRA ARDEEN-RANZ
HOMEWORLD: TITA
ABILITIES: TELEPATH
BEDTIME FOR THE BOYS, SIS.
SURE YOU WOULDN'T LIKE TO COME BACK TO ACTIVE DUTY?
TOO EASY.
THIS IS A CHALLENGE.
'NITE!

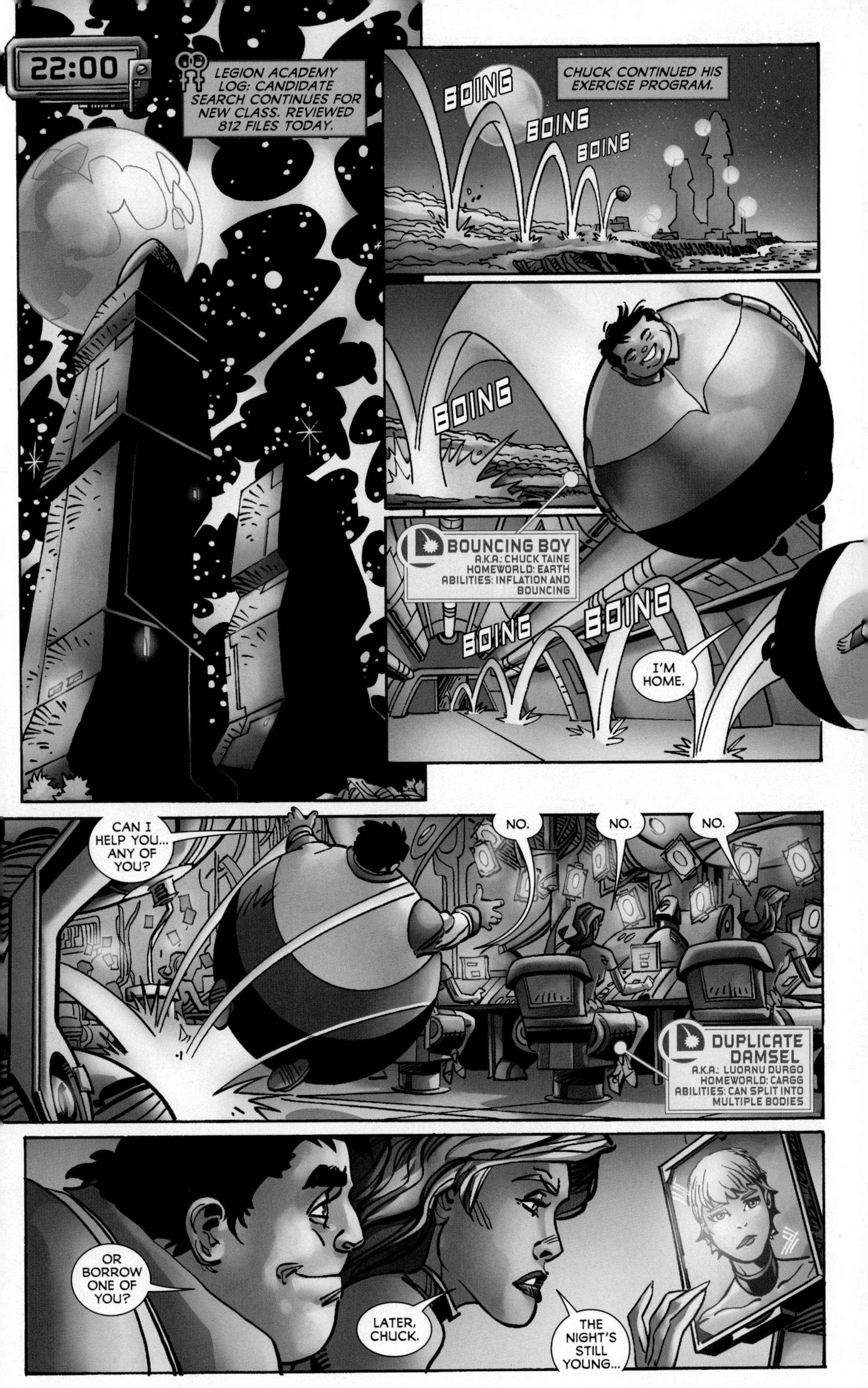
22:00
LEGION ACADEMY LOG: CANDIDATE SEARCH CONTINUES FOR NEW CLASS. REVIEWED 812 FILES TODAY.
CHUCK CONTINUED HIS EXERCISE PROGRAM.
BOING
BOING
BOING
BOING
BOUNCING BOY
A.K.A.: CHUCK TAINE
HOMEWORLD: EARTH
ABILITIES: INFLATION AND BOUNCING
BOING
BOING
I'M HOME.
CAN I HELP YOU... ANY OF YOU?
NO.
NO.
NO.
DUPLICATE DAMSEL
A.K.A.: LUORNU DURGO
HOMEWORLD: CARGG
ABILITIES: CAN SPLIT INTO MULTIPLE BODIES
OR BORROW ONE OF YOU?
LATER, CHUCK.
THE NIGHT'S STILL YOUNG...

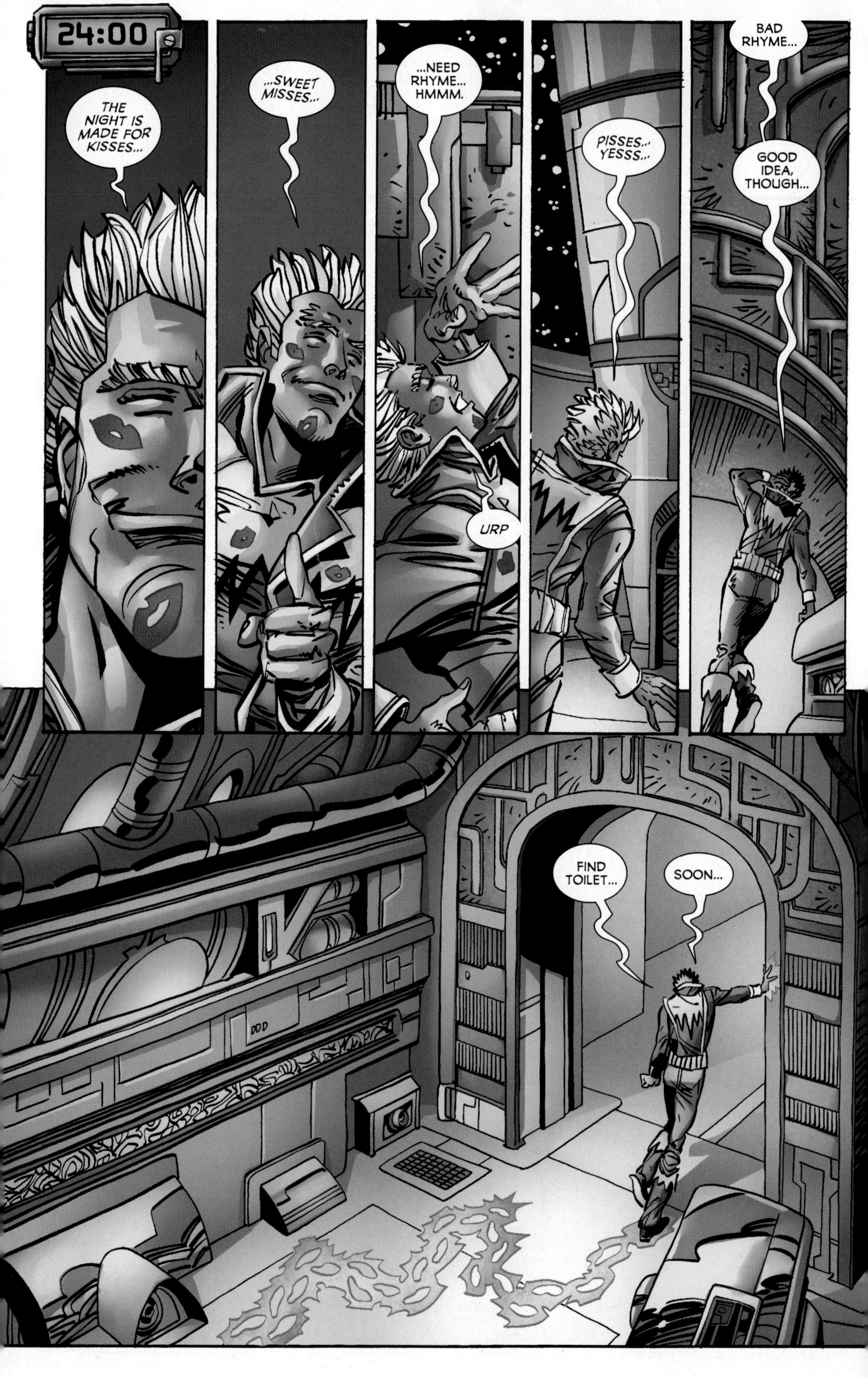
24:00
THE NIGHT IS MADE FOR KISSES...
...SWEET MISSES...
...NEED RHYME... HMMM.
URP
PISSES... YESSS...
BAD RHYME...
GOOD IDEA, THOUGH...
FIND TOILET...
SOON...

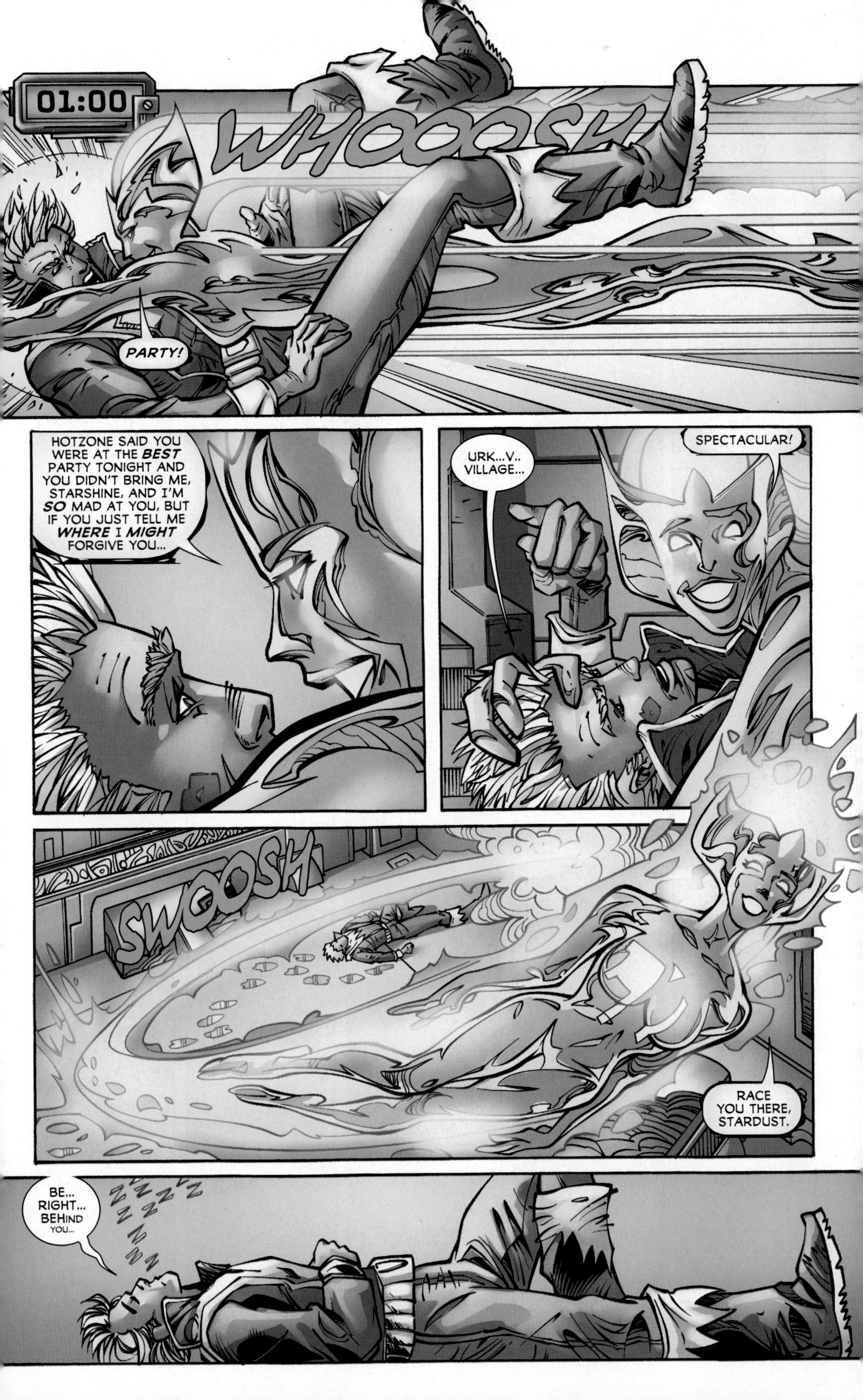
01:00
WHOOOSH
PARTY!
HOTZONE SAID YOU WERE AT THE BEST PARTY TONIGHT AND YOU DIDN'T BRING ME, STARSHINE, AND I'M SO MAD AT YOU, BUT IF YOU JUST TELL ME WHERE I MIGHT FORGIVE YOU...
SPECTACULAR!
URK... V.. VILLAGE...
SWOOSH
RACE YOU THERE, STARDUST.
BE... RIGHT... BEHIND YOU...

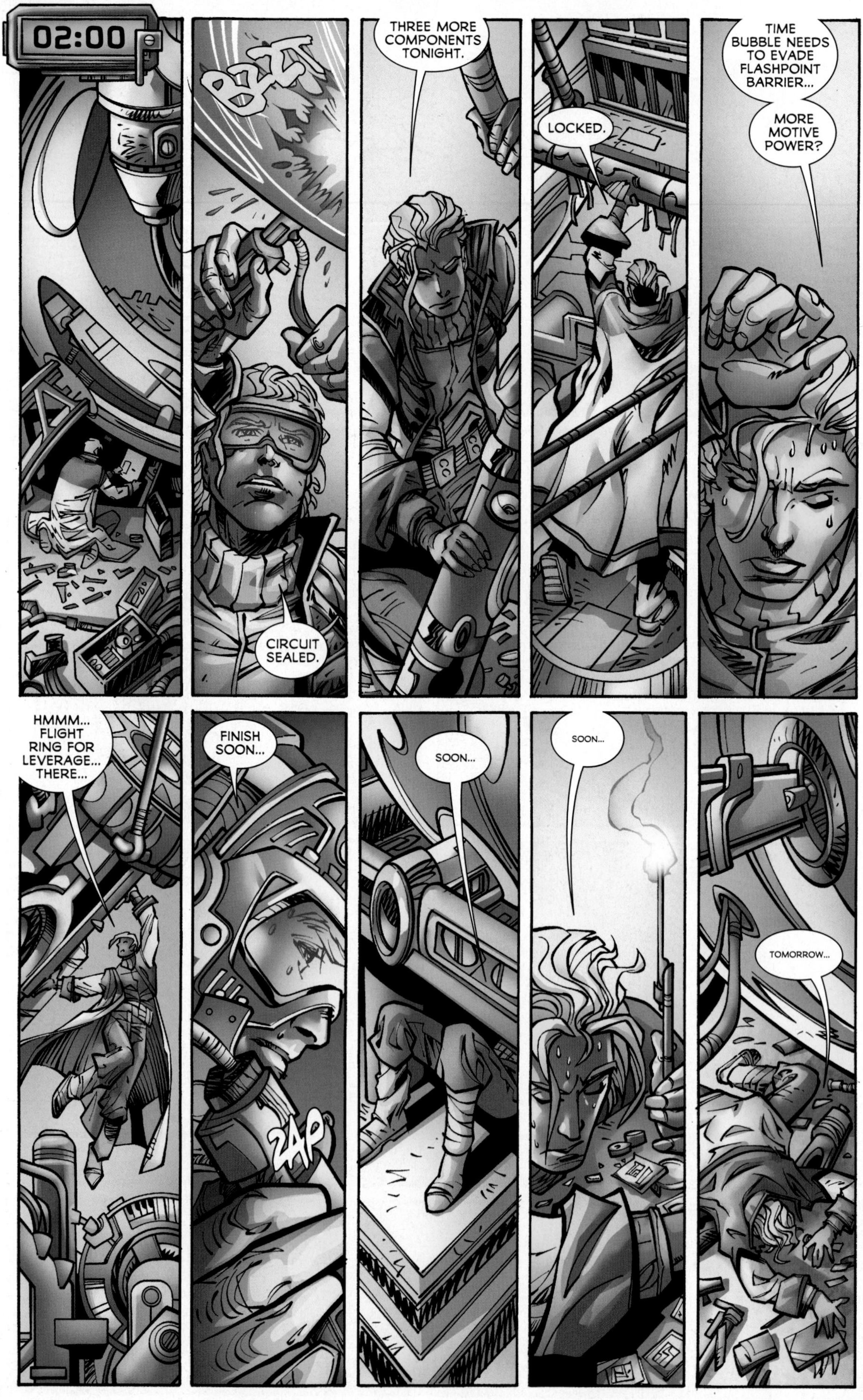
02:00
BZZT
CIRCUIT SEALED.
THREE MORE COMPONENTS TONIGHT.
LOCKED.
TIME BUBBLE NEEDS TO EVADE FLASHPOINT BARRIER...
MORE MOTIVE POWER?
HMMM... FLIGHT RING FOR LEVERAGE... THERE...
FINISH SOON...
ZAP
SOON...
SOON...
TOMORROW...

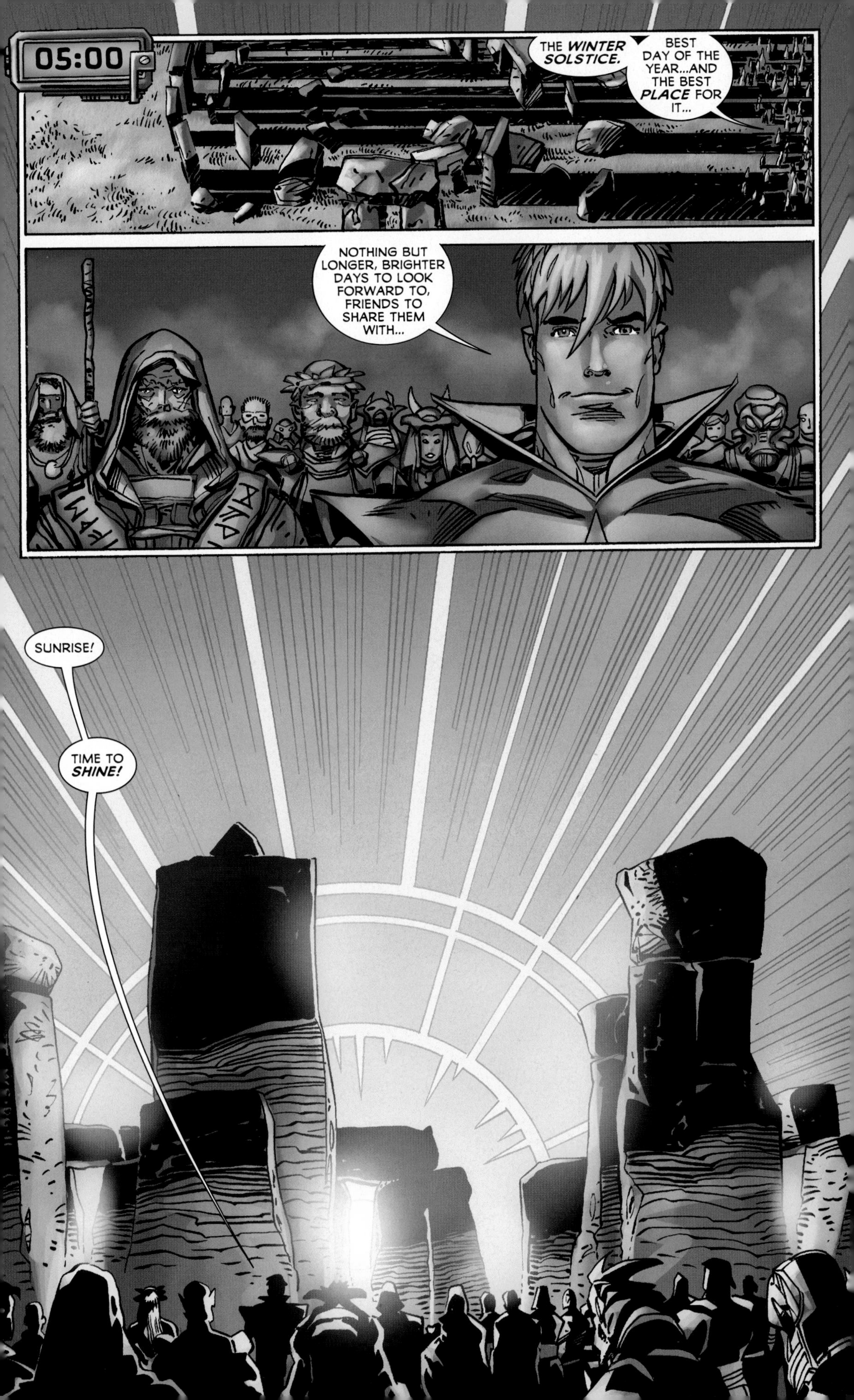
05:00
THE WINTER SOLSTICE.
BEST DAY OF THE YEAR...AND THE BEST PLACE FOR IT...
NOTHING BUT LONGER, BRIGHTER DAYS TO LOOK FORWARD TO, FRIENDS TO SHARE THEM WITH...
SUNRISE!
TIME TO SHINE!

cover art by
CHRIS SPROUSE, KARL STORY & GUY MAJOR

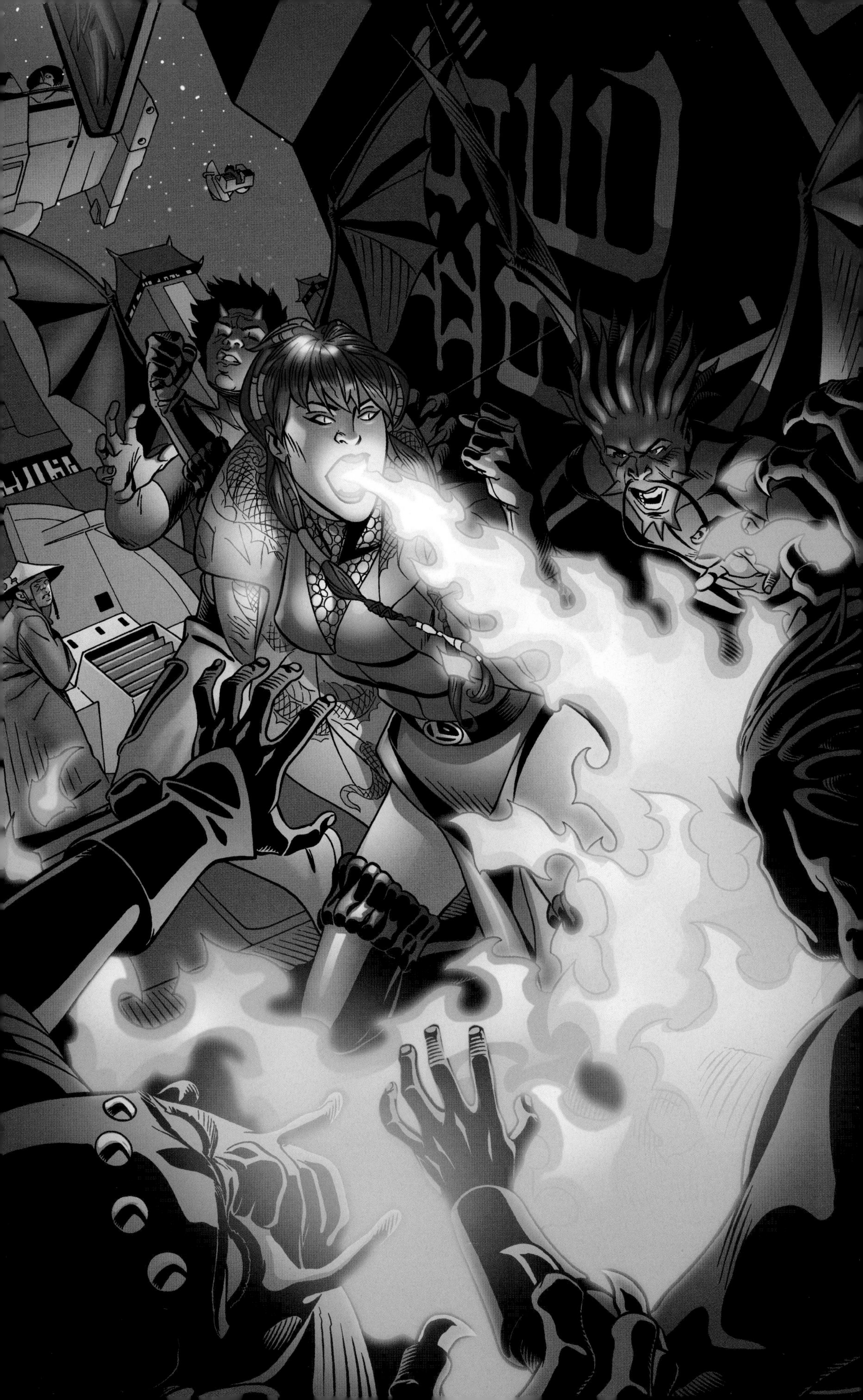

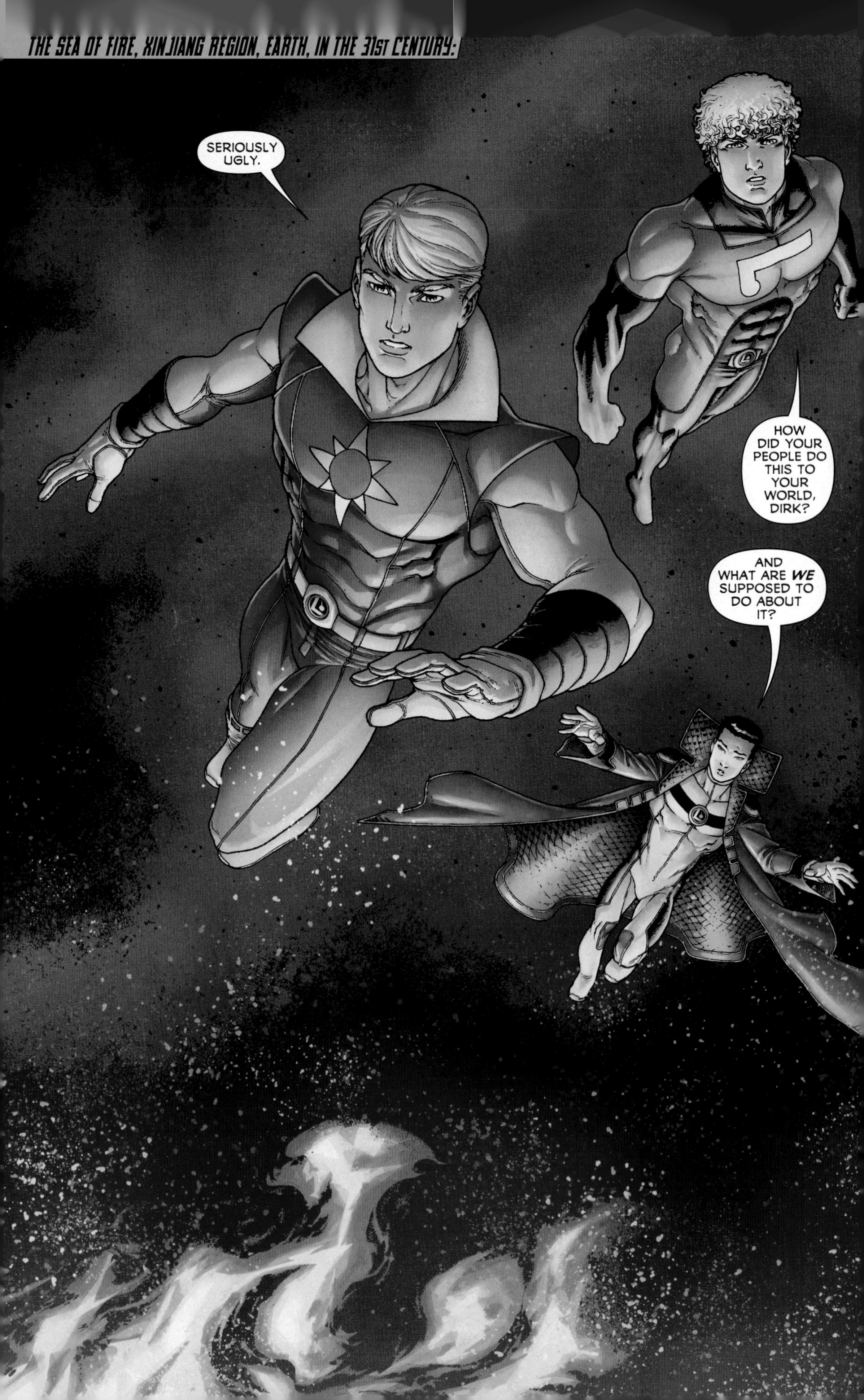
THE SEA OF FIRE, XINJIANG REGION, EARTH, IN THE 31st CENTURY:
SERIOUSLY UGLY.
HOW DID YOUR PEOPLE DO THIS TO YOUR WORLD, DIRK?
AND WHAT ARE *WE* SUPPOSED TO DO ABOUT IT?

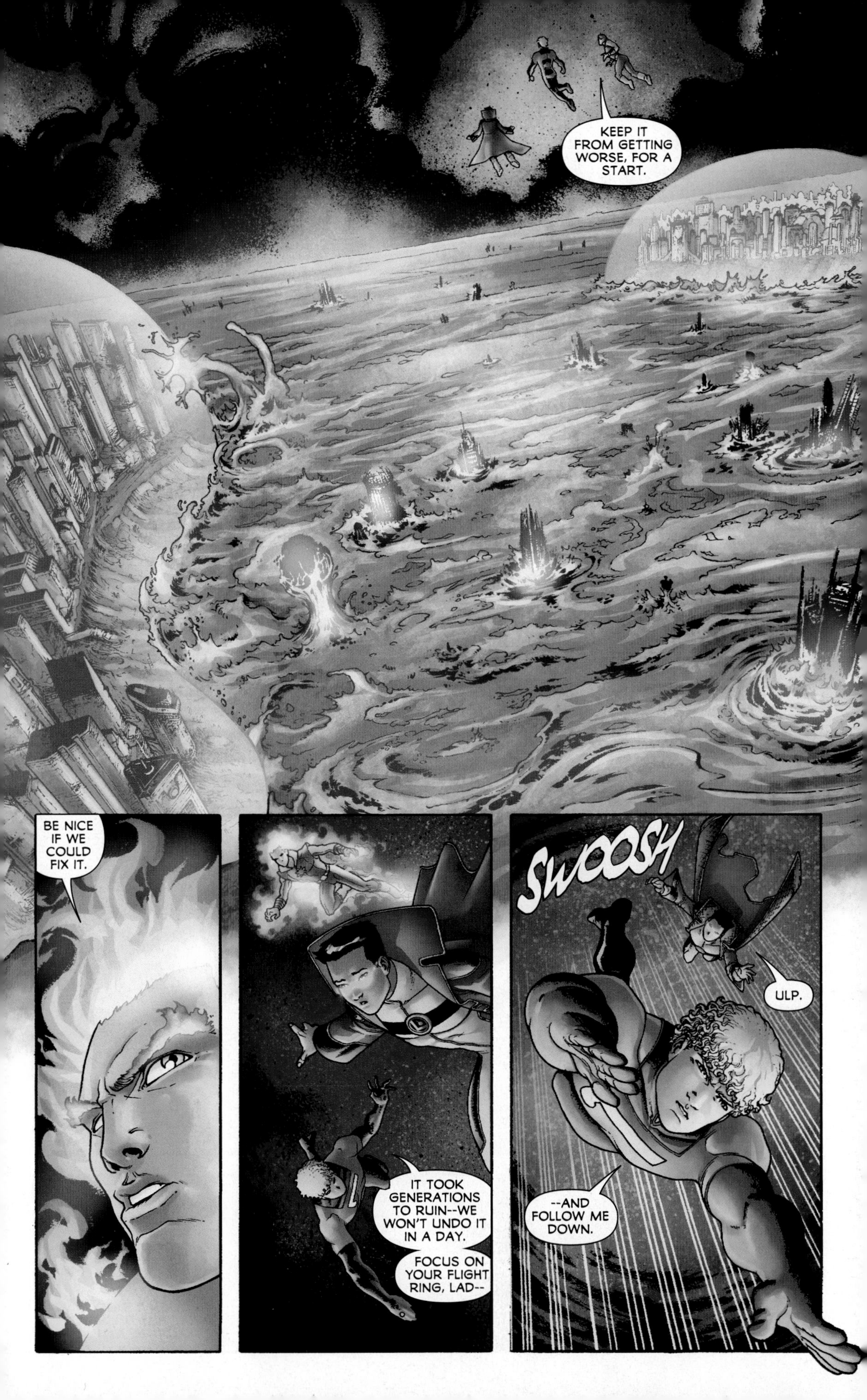
KEEP IT FROM GETTING WORSE, FOR A START.
BE NICE IF WE COULD FIX IT.
IT TOOK GENERATIONS TO RUIN--WE WON'T UNDO IT IN A DAY.
FOCUS ON YOUR FLIGHT RING, LAD--
SWOOSH
ULP.
--AND FOLLOW ME DOWN.

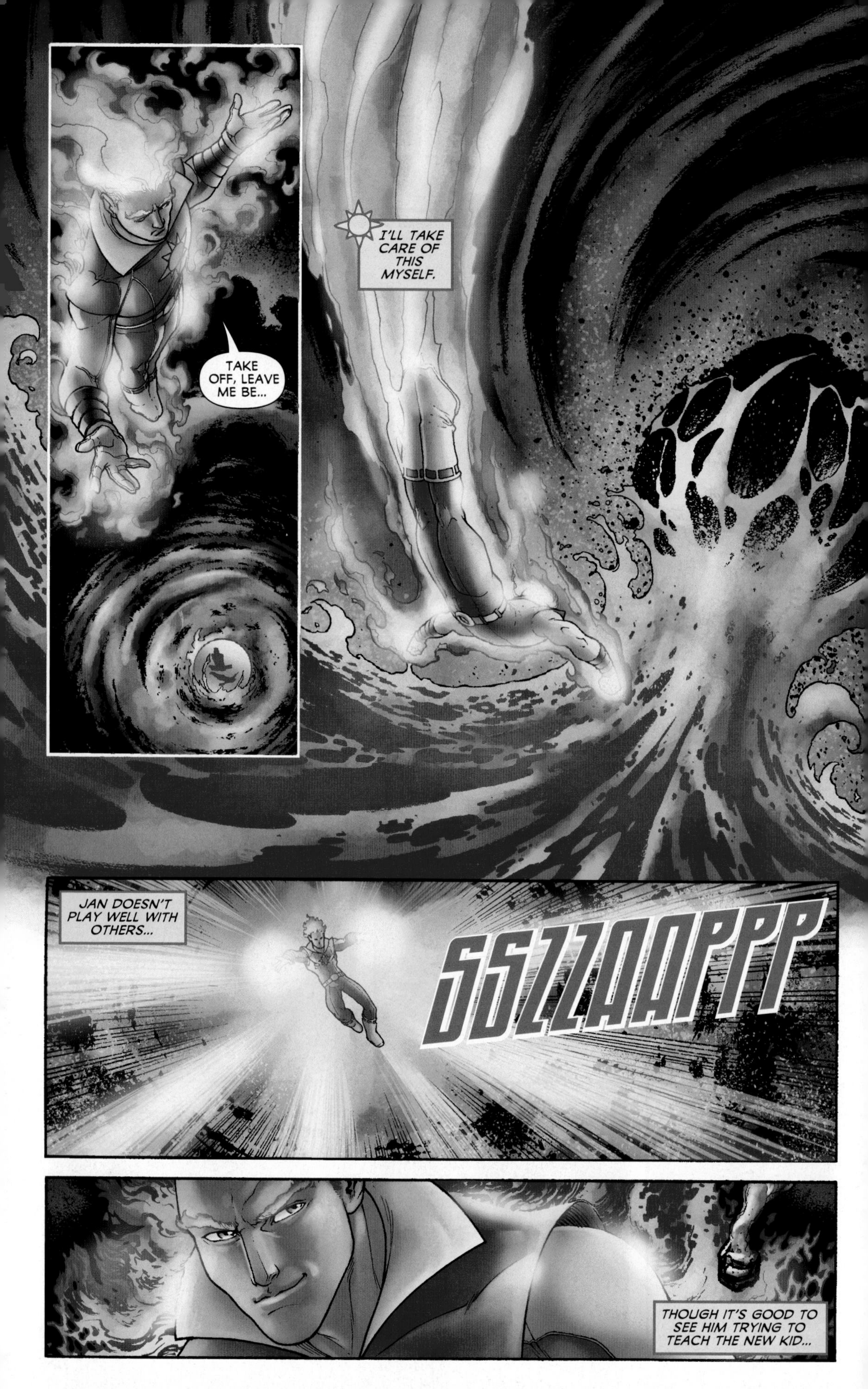
TAKE OFF, LEAVE ME BE...
I'LL TAKE CARE OF THIS MYSELF.
JAN DOESN'T PLAY WELL WITH OTHERS...
SSZZAAPPP
THOUGH IT'S GOOD TO SEE HIM TRYING TO TEACH THE NEW KID...

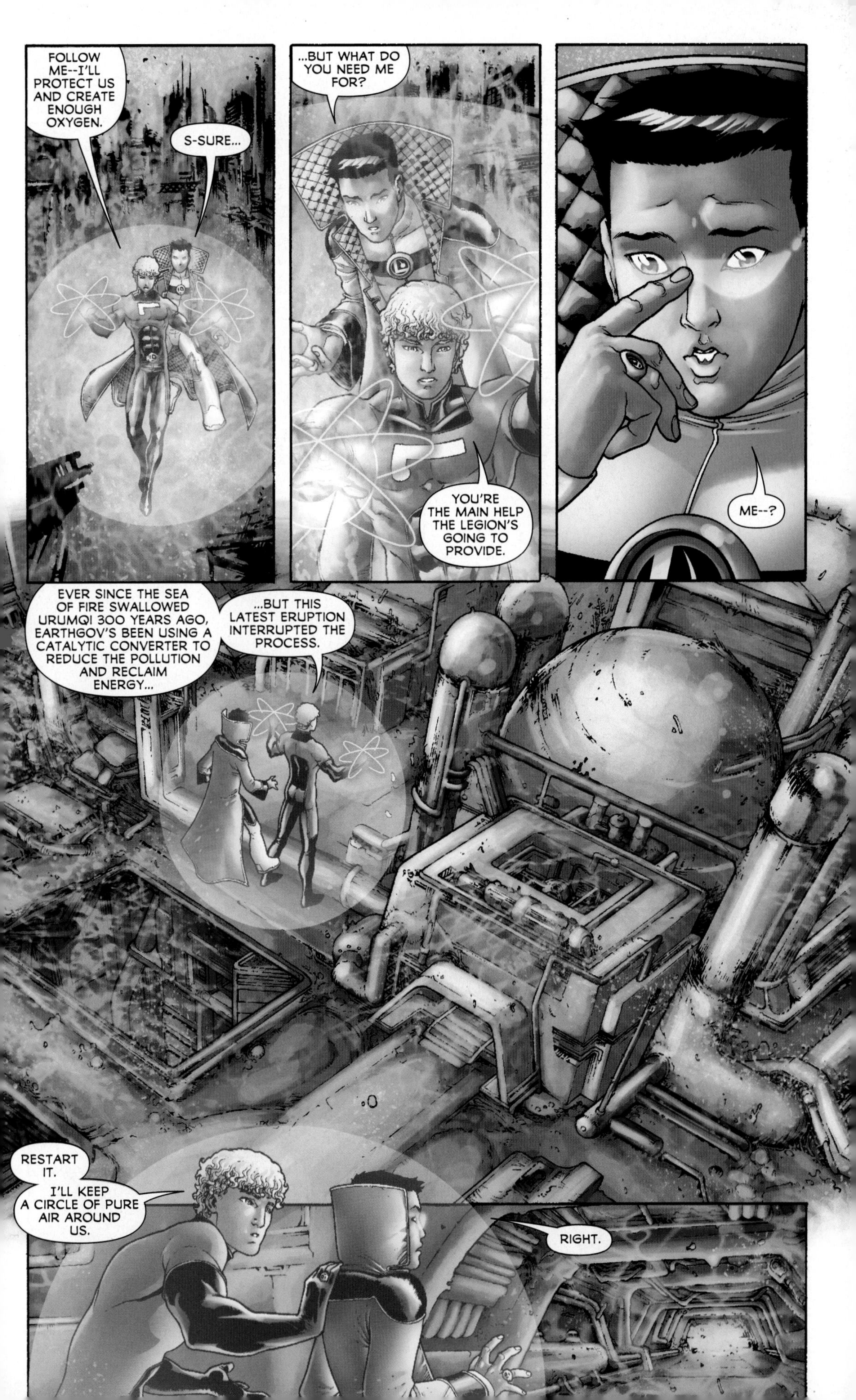
FOLLOW ME--I'LL PROTECT US AND CREATE ENOUGH OXYGEN.
S-SURE...
...BUT WHAT DO YOU NEED ME FOR?
YOU'RE THE MAIN HELP THE LEGION'S GOING TO PROVIDE.
ME--?
EVER SINCE THE SEA OF FIRE SWALLOWED URUMQI 300 YEARS AGO, EARTHGOV'S BEEN USING A CATALYTIC CONVERTER TO REDUCE THE POLLUTION AND RECLAIM ENERGY...
...BUT THIS LATEST ERUPTION INTERRUPTED THE PROCESS.
RESTART IT.
I'LL KEEP A CIRCLE OF PURE AIR AROUND US.
RIGHT.

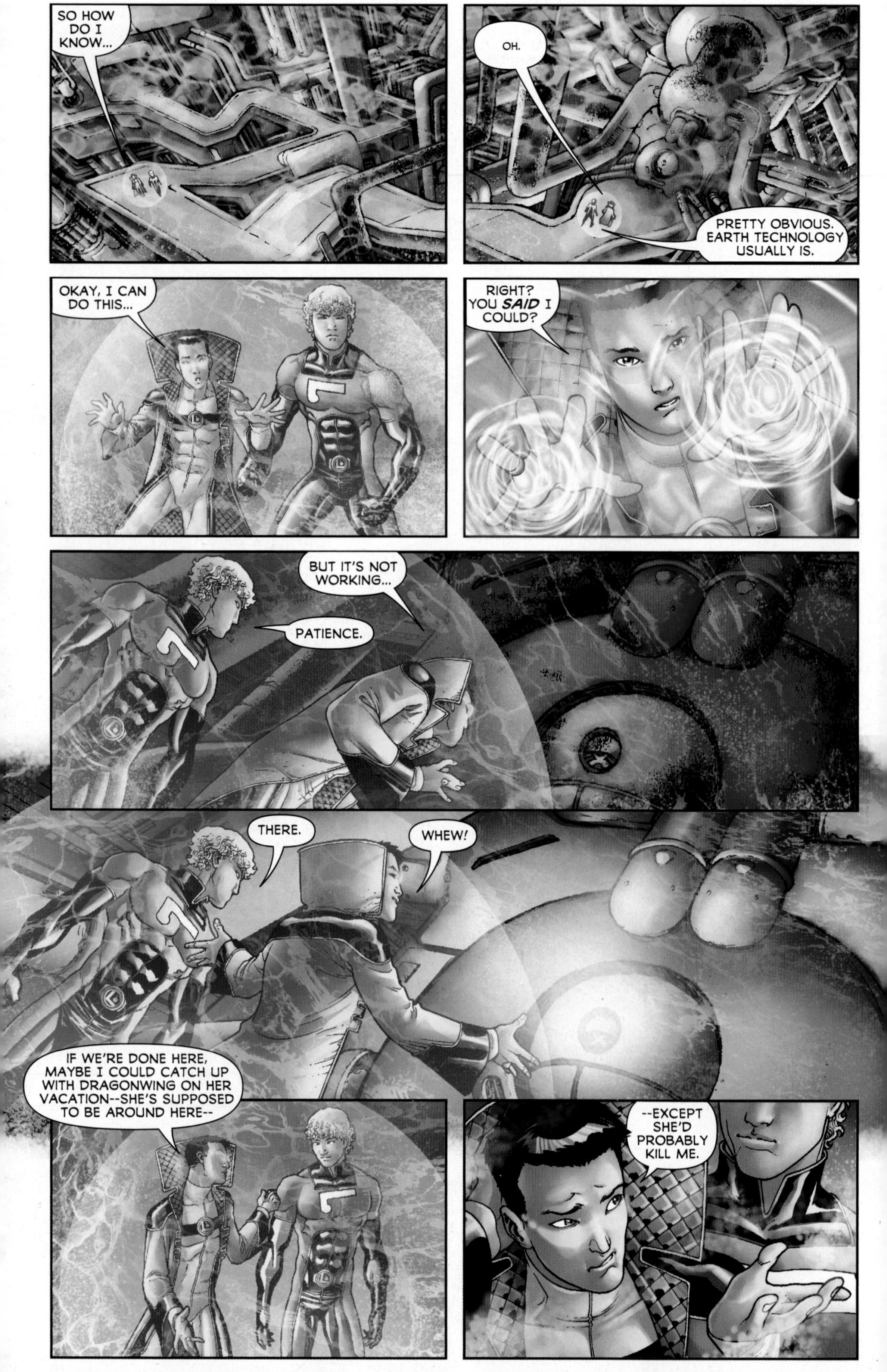
SO HOW DO I KNOW...
OH.
PRETTY OBVIOUS. EARTH TECHNOLOGY USUALLY IS.
OKAY, I CAN DO THIS...
RIGHT? YOU SAID I COULD?
BUT IT'S NOT WORKING...
PATIENCE.
THERE.
WHEW!
IF WE'RE DONE HERE, MAYBE I COULD CATCH UP WITH DRAGONWING ON HER VACATION--SHE'S SUPPOSED TO BE AROUND HERE--
--EXCEPT SHE'D PROBABLY KILL ME.

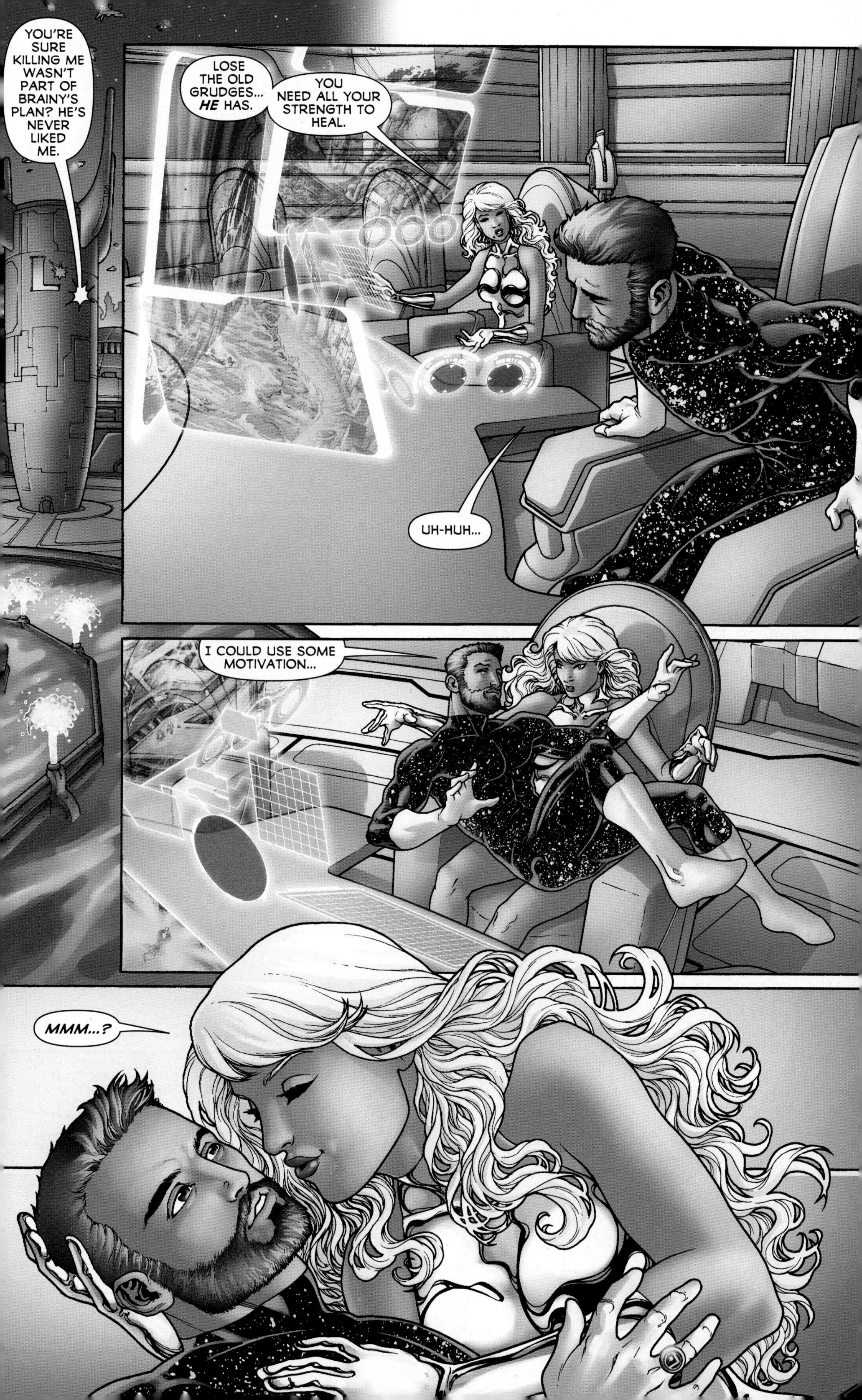
YOU'RE SURE KILLING ME WASN'T PART OF BRAINY'S PLAN? HE'S NEVER LIKED ME.
LOSE THE OLD GRUDGES... ***HE*** HAS.
YOU NEED ALL YOUR STRENGTH TO HEAL.
UH-HUH...
I COULD USE SOME MOTIVATION...
MMM...?

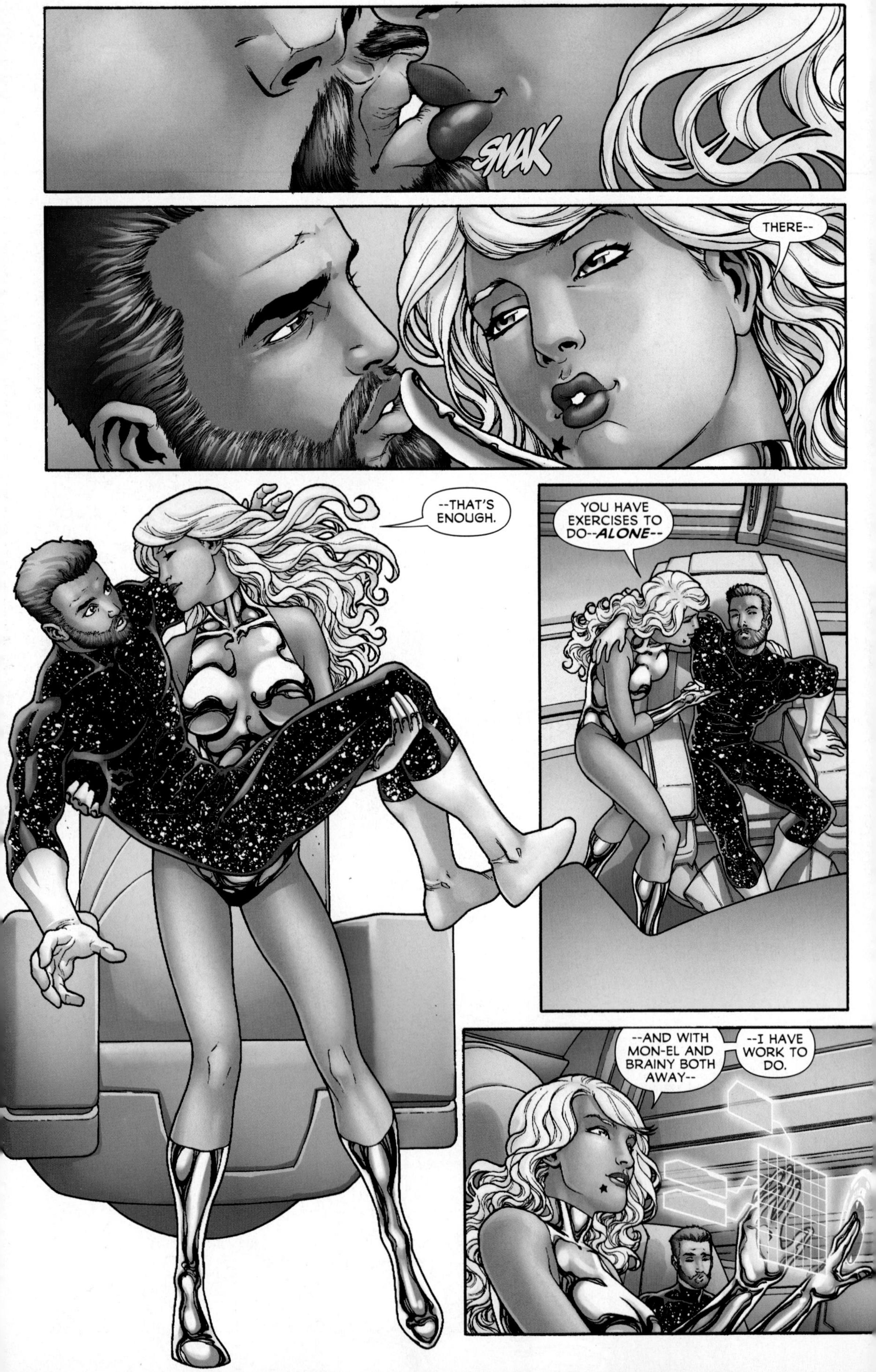
SMAK
THERE--
--THAT'S ENOUGH.
YOU HAVE EXERCISES TO DO--ALONE--
--AND WITH MON-EL AND BRAINY BOTH AWAY--
--I HAVE WORK TO DO.

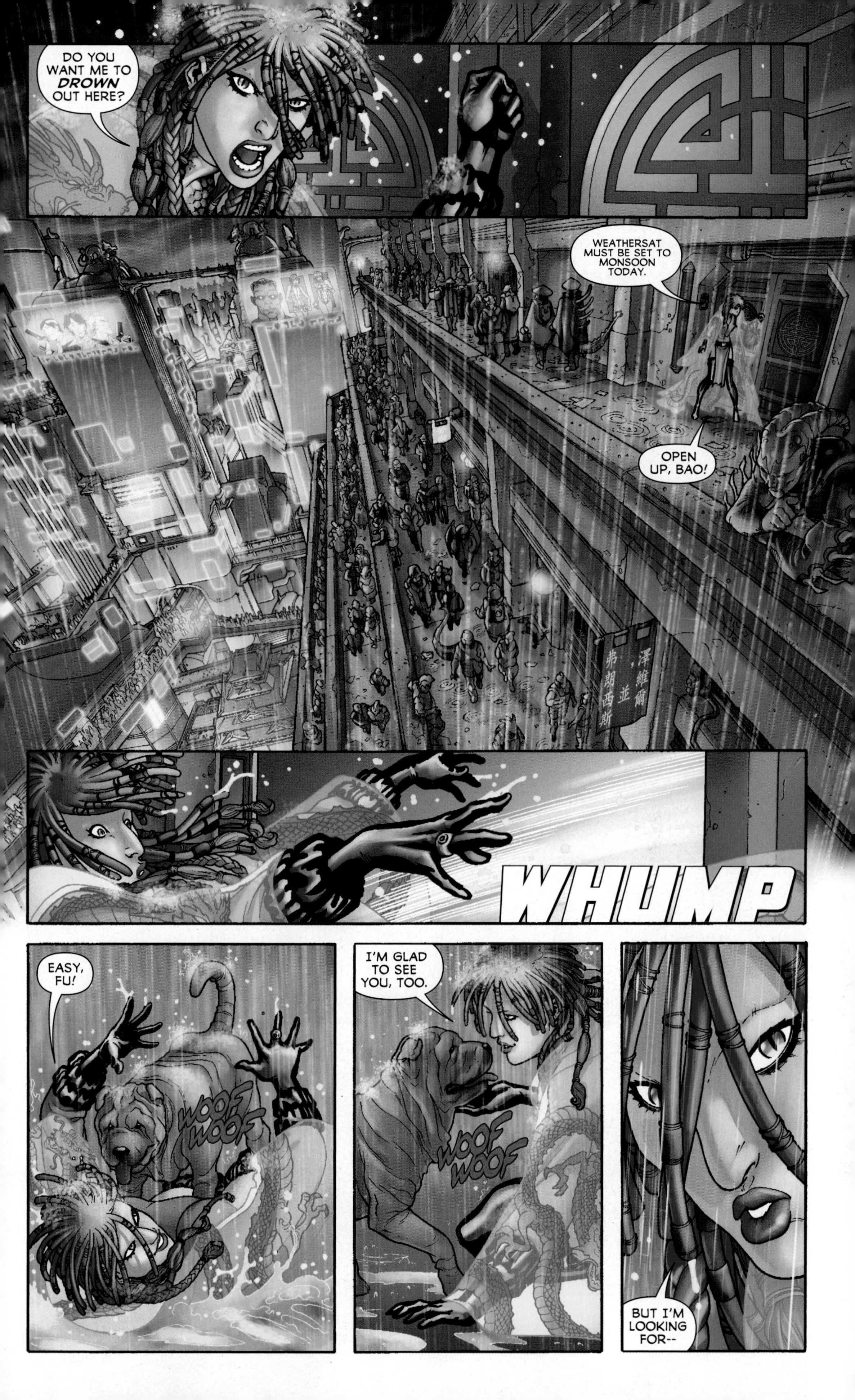
DO YOU WANT ME TO *DROWN* OUT HERE?
WEATHERSAT MUST BE SET TO MONSOON TODAY.
OPEN UP, BAO!
澤維爾並弗朗西斯
WHUMP
EASY, FU!
WOOF WOOF
I'M GLAD TO SEE YOU, TOO.
WOOF WOOF
BUT I'M LOOKING FOR--

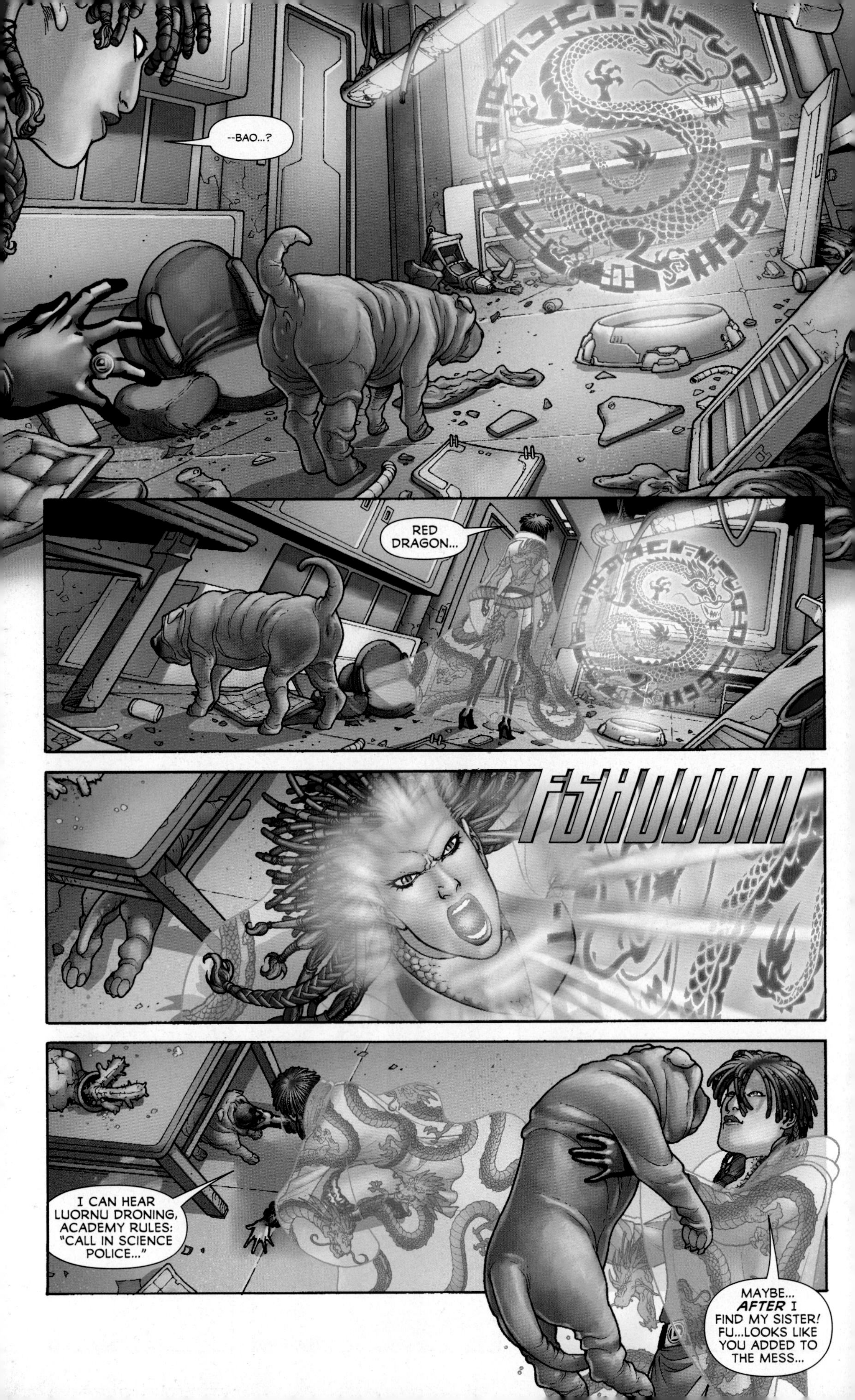
--BAO...?
RED DRAGON...
FSHOOOOM
I CAN HEAR LUORNU DRONING, ACADEMY RULES: "CALL IN SCIENCE POLICE..."
MAYBE... AFTER I FIND MY SISTER! FU...LOOKS LIKE YOU ADDED TO THE MESS...

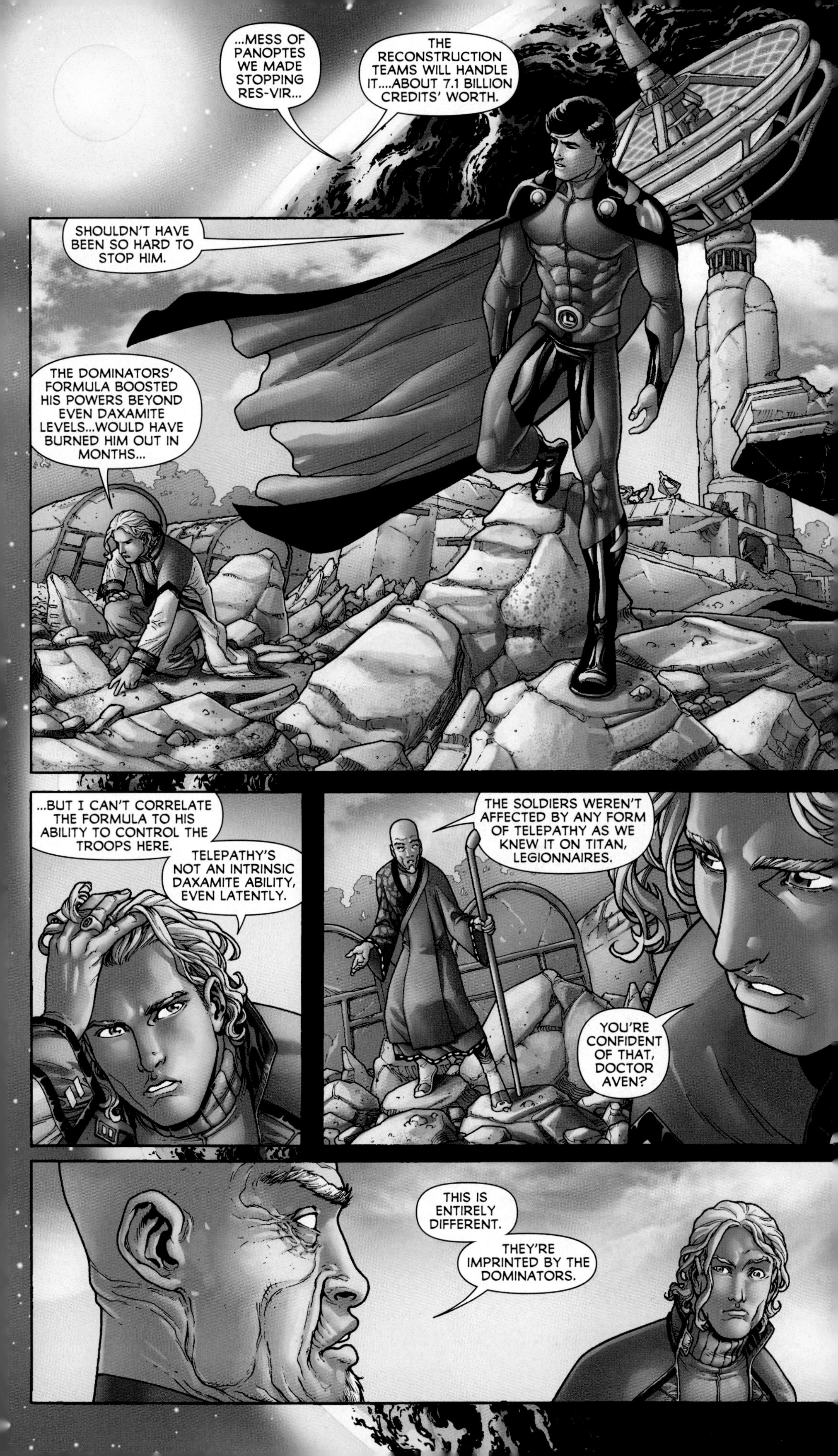
...MESS OF PANOPTES WE MADE STOPPING RES-VIR...
THE RECONSTRUCTION TEAMS WILL HANDLE IT....ABOUT 7.1 BILLION CREDITS' WORTH.
SHOULDN'T HAVE BEEN SO HARD TO STOP HIM.
THE DOMINATORS' FORMULA BOOSTED HIS POWERS BEYOND EVEN DAXAMITE LEVELS...WOULD HAVE BURNED HIM OUT IN MONTHS...
...BUT I CAN'T CORRELATE THE FORMULA TO HIS ABILITY TO CONTROL THE TROOPS HERE.
TELEPATHY'S NOT AN INTRINSIC DAXAMITE ABILITY, EVEN LATENTLY.
THE SOLDIERS WEREN'T AFFECTED BY ANY FORM OF TELEPATHY AS WE KNEW IT ON TITAN, LEGIONNAIRES.
YOU'RE CONFIDENT OF THAT, DOCTOR AVEN?
THIS IS ENTIRELY DIFFERENT.
THEY'RE IMPRINTED BY THE DOMINATORS.

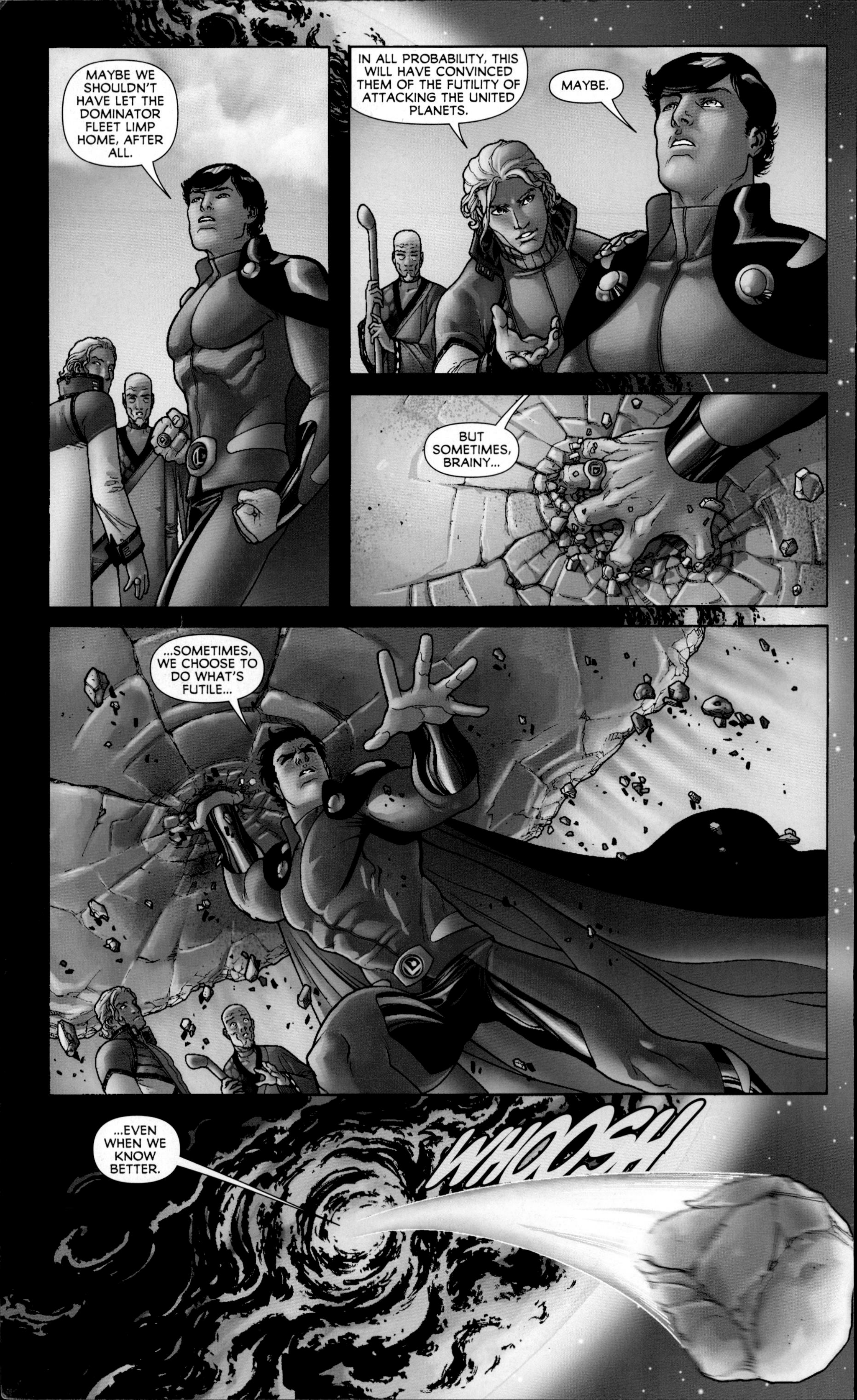
MAYBE WE SHOULDN'T HAVE LET THE DOMINATOR FLEET LIMP HOME, AFTER ALL.
IN ALL PROBABILITY, THIS WILL HAVE CONVINCED THEM OF THE FUTILITY OF ATTACKING THE UNITED PLANETS.
MAYBE.
BUT SOMETIMES, BRAINY...
...SOMETIMES, WE CHOOSE TO DO WHAT'S FUTILE...
...EVEN WHEN WE KNOW BETTER.
WHOOSH

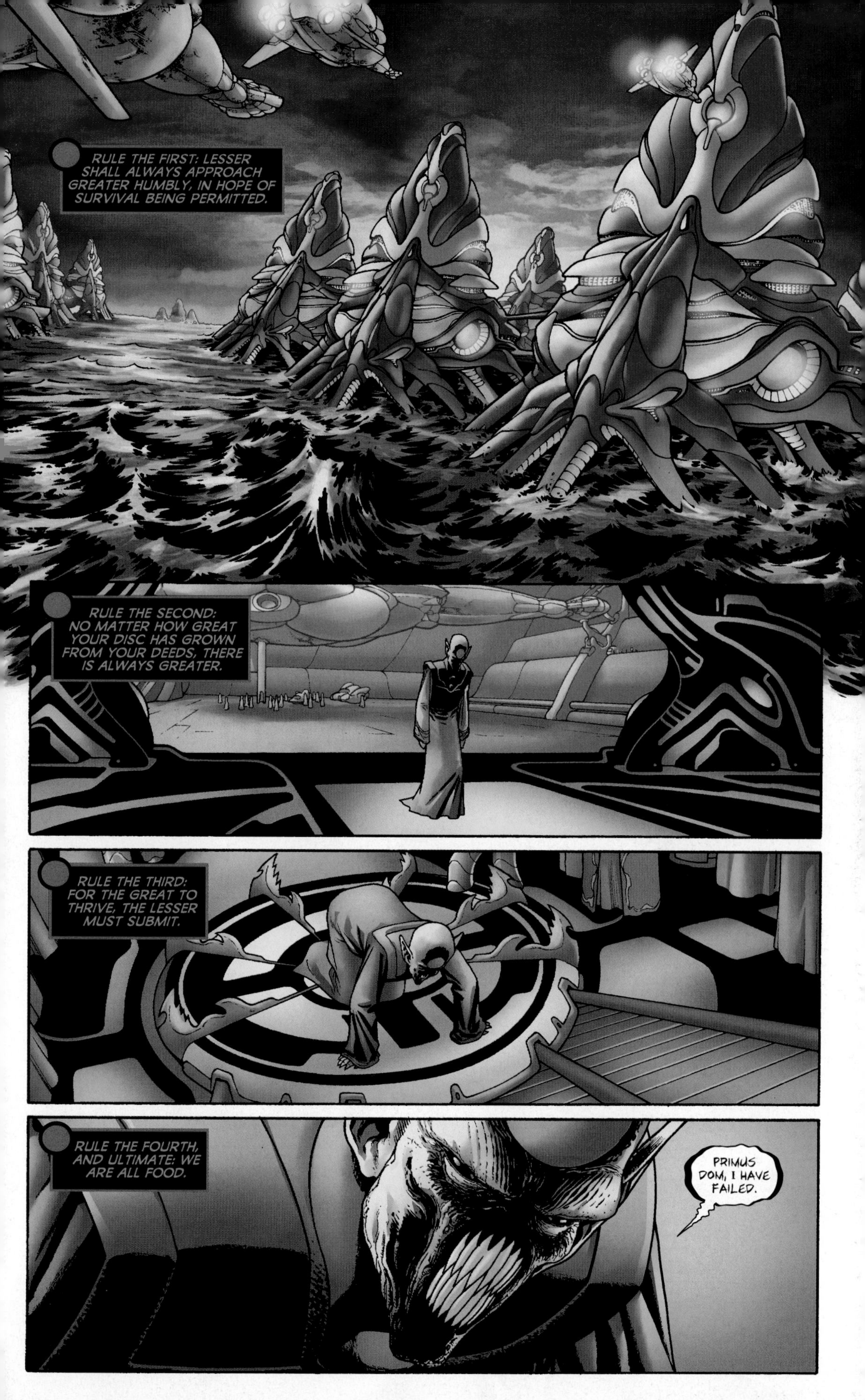
RULE THE FIRST: LESSER SHALL ALWAYS APPROACH GREATER HUMBLY, IN HOPE OF SURVIVAL BEING PERMITTED.
RULE THE SECOND: NO MATTER HOW GREAT YOUR DISC HAS GROWN FROM YOUR DEEDS, THERE IS ALWAYS GREATER.
RULE THE THIRD: FOR THE GREAT TO THRIVE, THE LESSER MUST SUBMIT.
RULE THE FOURTH, AND ULTIMATE: WE ARE ALL FOOD.
PRIMUS DOM, I HAVE FAILED.

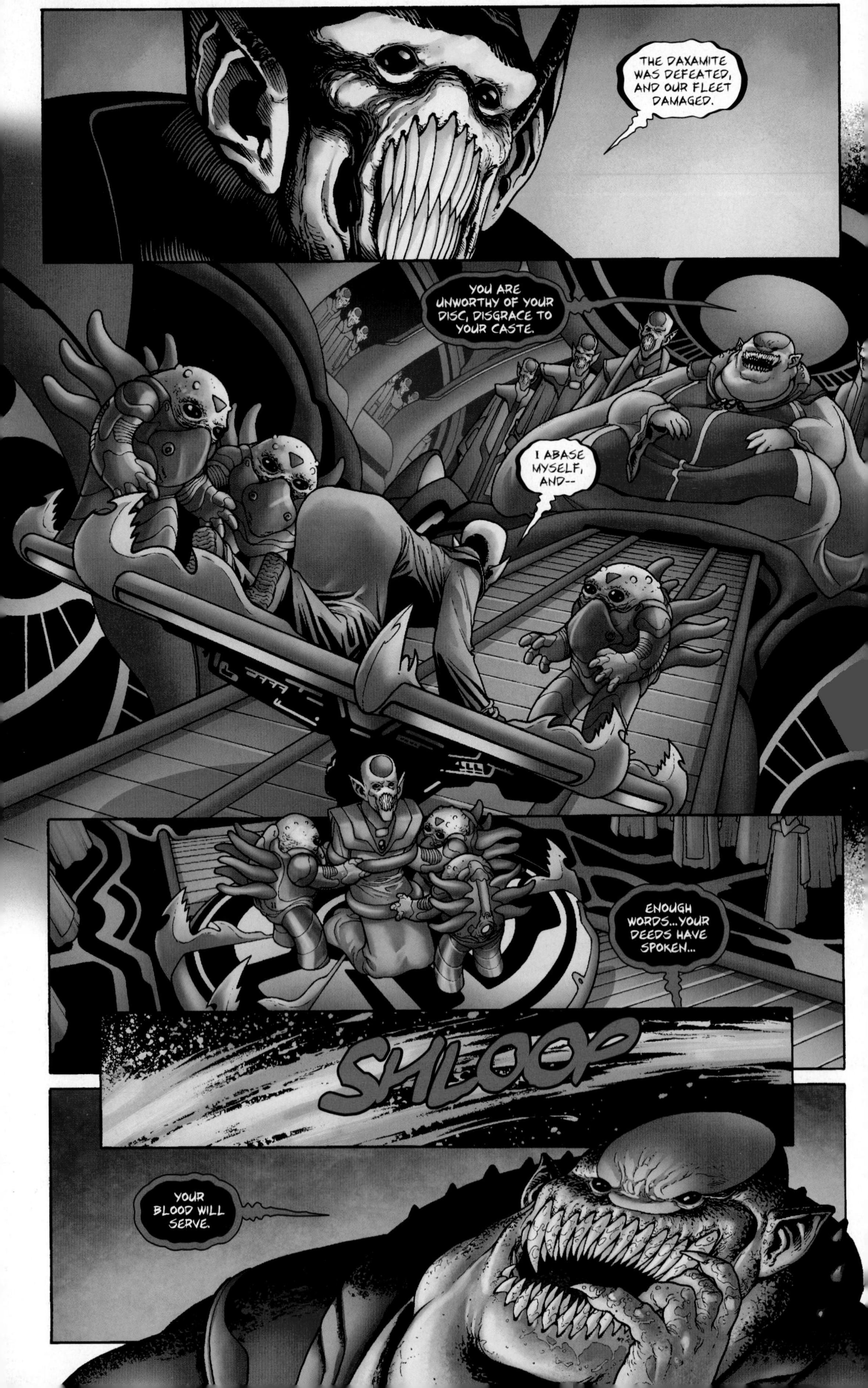
THE DAXAMITE WAS DEFEATED, AND OUR FLEET DAMAGED.
YOU ARE UNWORTHY OF YOUR DISC, DISGRACE TO YOUR CASTE.
I ABASE MYSELF, AND--
ENOUGH WORDS...YOUR DEEDS HAVE SPOKEN...
SHLOOP
YOUR BLOOD WILL SERVE.

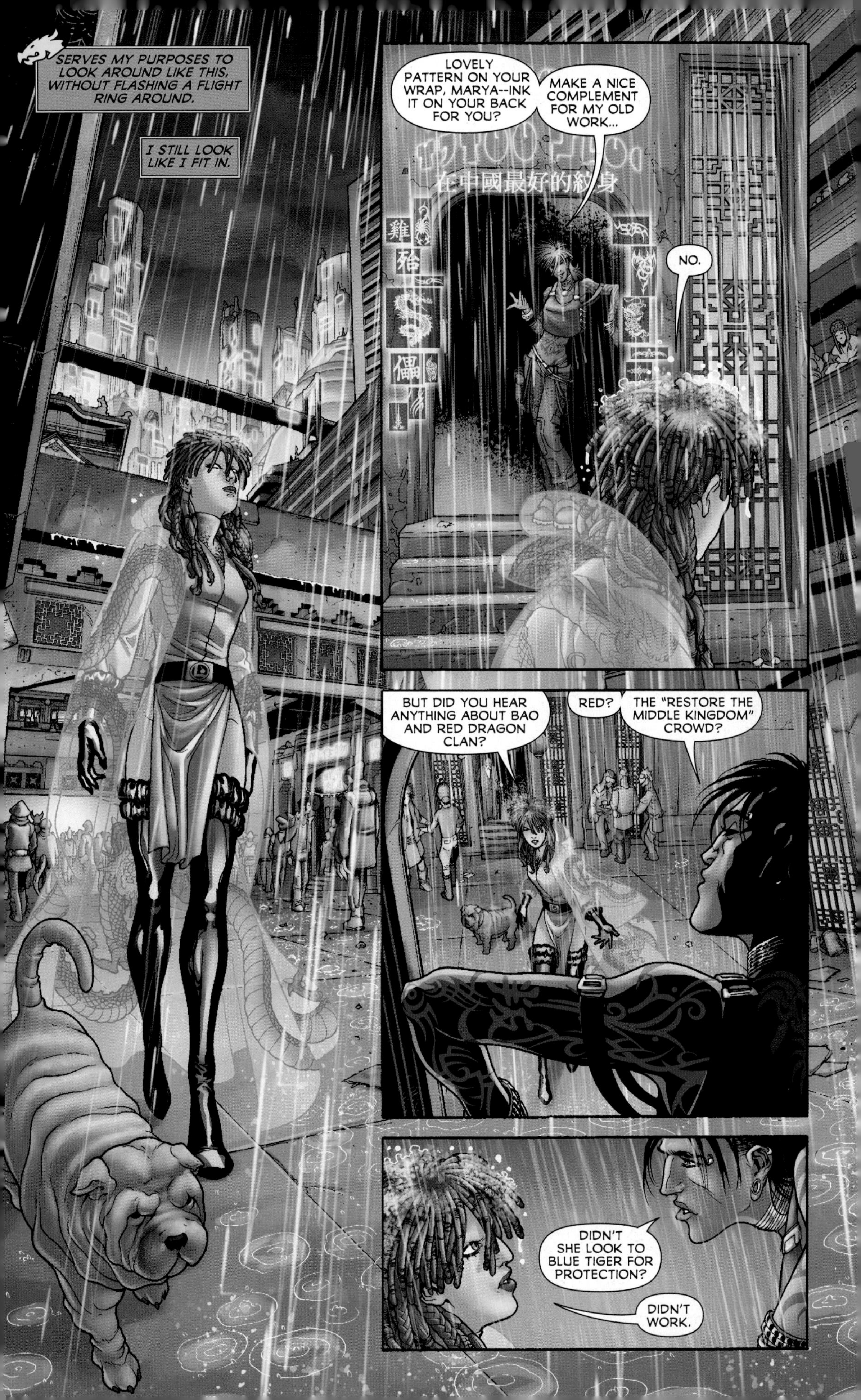
SERVES MY PURPOSES TO LOOK AROUND LIKE THIS, WITHOUT FLASHING A FLIGHT RING AROUND.
I STILL LOOK LIKE I FIT IN.
LOVELY PATTERN ON YOUR WRAP, MARYA--INK IT ON YOUR BACK FOR YOU?
MAKE A NICE COMPLEMENT FOR MY OLD WORK...
在中國最好的紋身
NO.
BUT DID YOU HEAR ANYTHING ABOUT BAO AND RED DRAGON CLAN?
RED?
THE "RESTORE THE MIDDLE KINGDOM" CROWD?
DIDN'T SHE LOOK TO BLUE TIGER FOR PROTECTION?
DIDN'T WORK.

YOUR LITTLE BEAST HAS YOU ON A LEASH, MARYA?

GUESS SO...

GOTTA GO.

HA HA HA

WAS THAT REALLY NECESSARY?

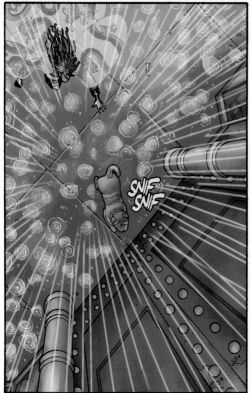

SNIF SNIF

WOOF WOOF

FWHIP

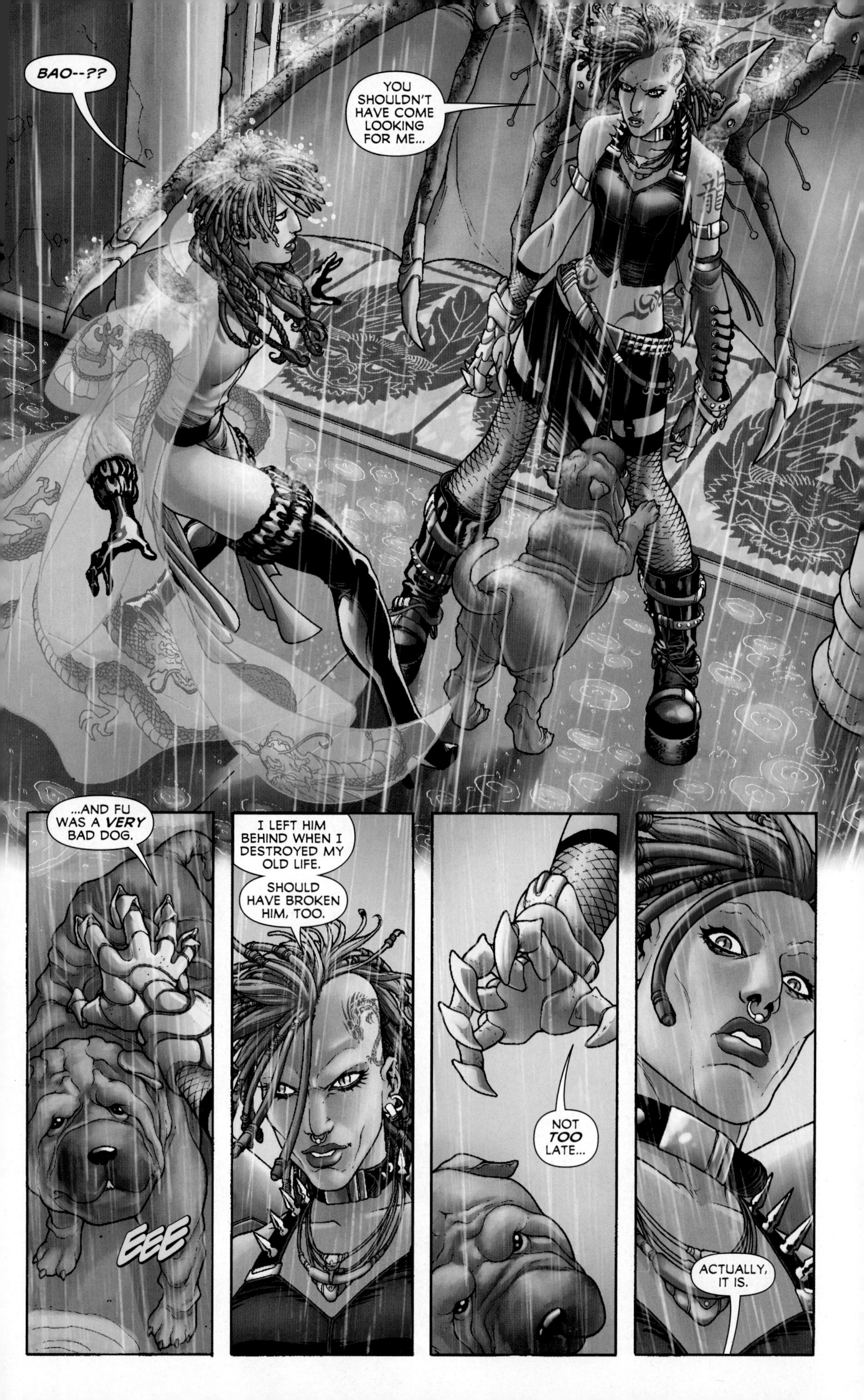
BAO--??
YOU SHOULDN'T HAVE COME LOOKING FOR ME...
...AND FU WAS A *VERY* BAD DOG.
EEE
I LEFT HIM BEHIND WHEN I DESTROYED MY OLD LIFE.
SHOULD HAVE BROKEN HIM, TOO.
NOT *TOO* LATE...
ACTUALLY, IT IS.

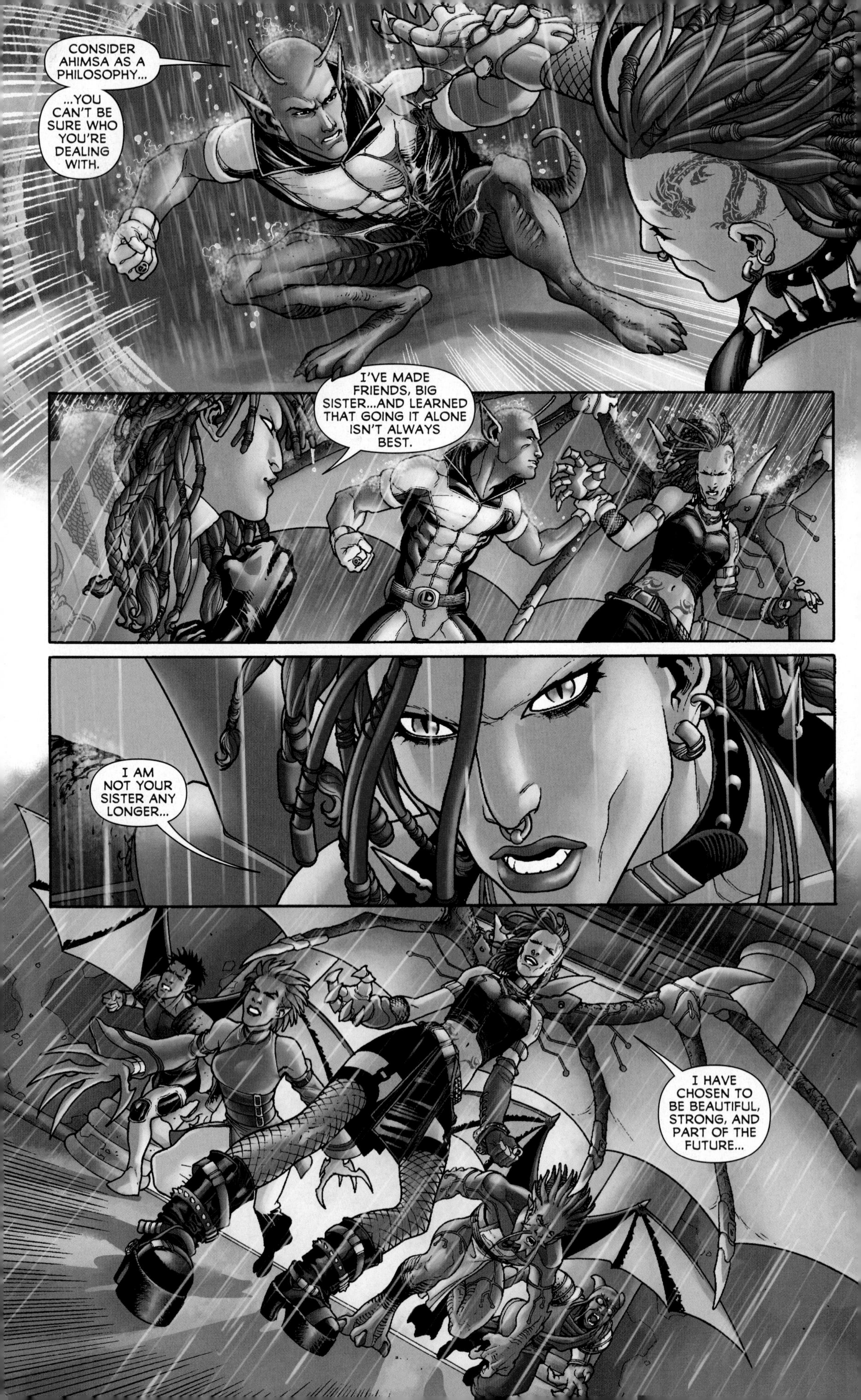
CONSIDER AHIMSA AS A PHILOSOPHY...
...YOU CAN'T BE SURE WHO YOU'RE DEALING WITH.
I'VE MADE FRIENDS, BIG SISTER...AND LEARNED THAT GOING IT ALONE ISN'T ALWAYS BEST.
I AM NOT YOUR SISTER ANY LONGER...
I HAVE CHOSEN TO BE BEAUTIFUL, STRONG, AND PART OF THE FUTURE...

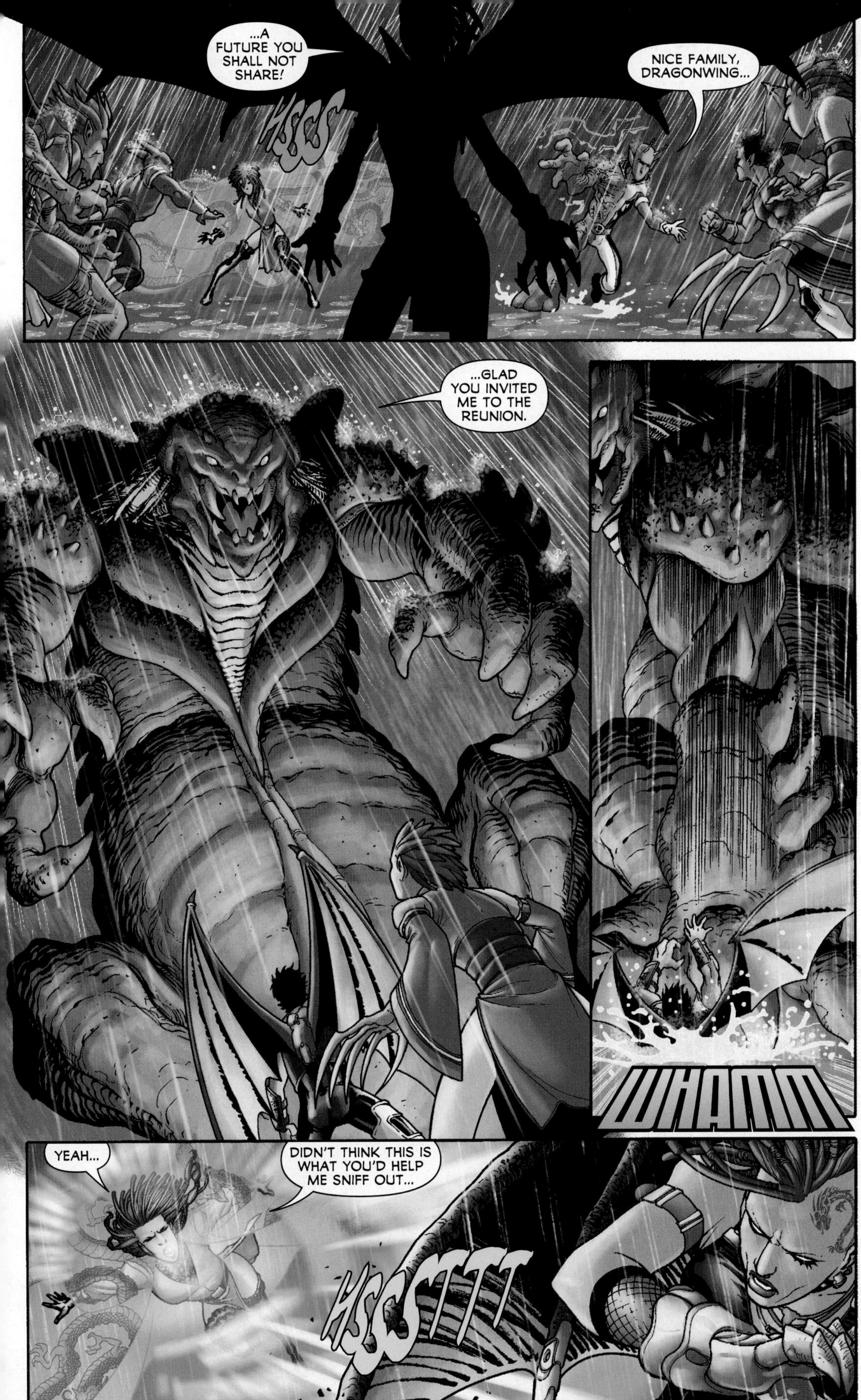
...A FUTURE YOU SHALL NOT SHARE!
HSCS
NICE FAMILY, DRAGONWING...
...GLAD YOU INVITED ME TO THE REUNION.
WHAMM
YEAH...
DIDN'T THINK THIS IS WHAT YOU'D HELP ME SNIFF OUT...
HSCSTTT

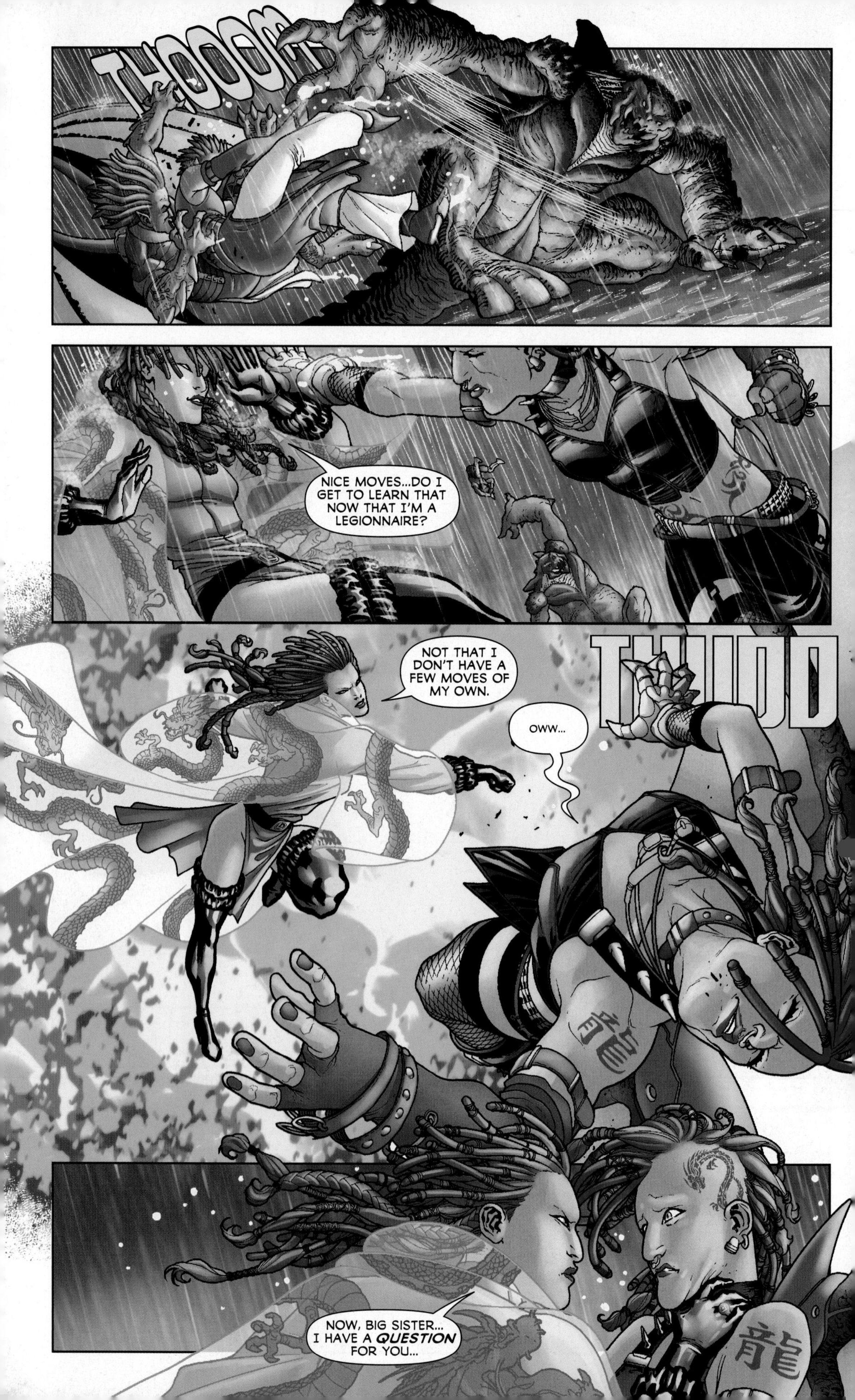
THOOOM
NICE MOVES...DO I GET TO LEARN THAT NOW THAT I'M A LEGIONNAIRE?
NOT THAT I DON'T HAVE A FEW MOVES OF MY OWN.
THUDD
OWW...
NOW, BIG SISTER... I HAVE A *QUESTION* FOR YOU...

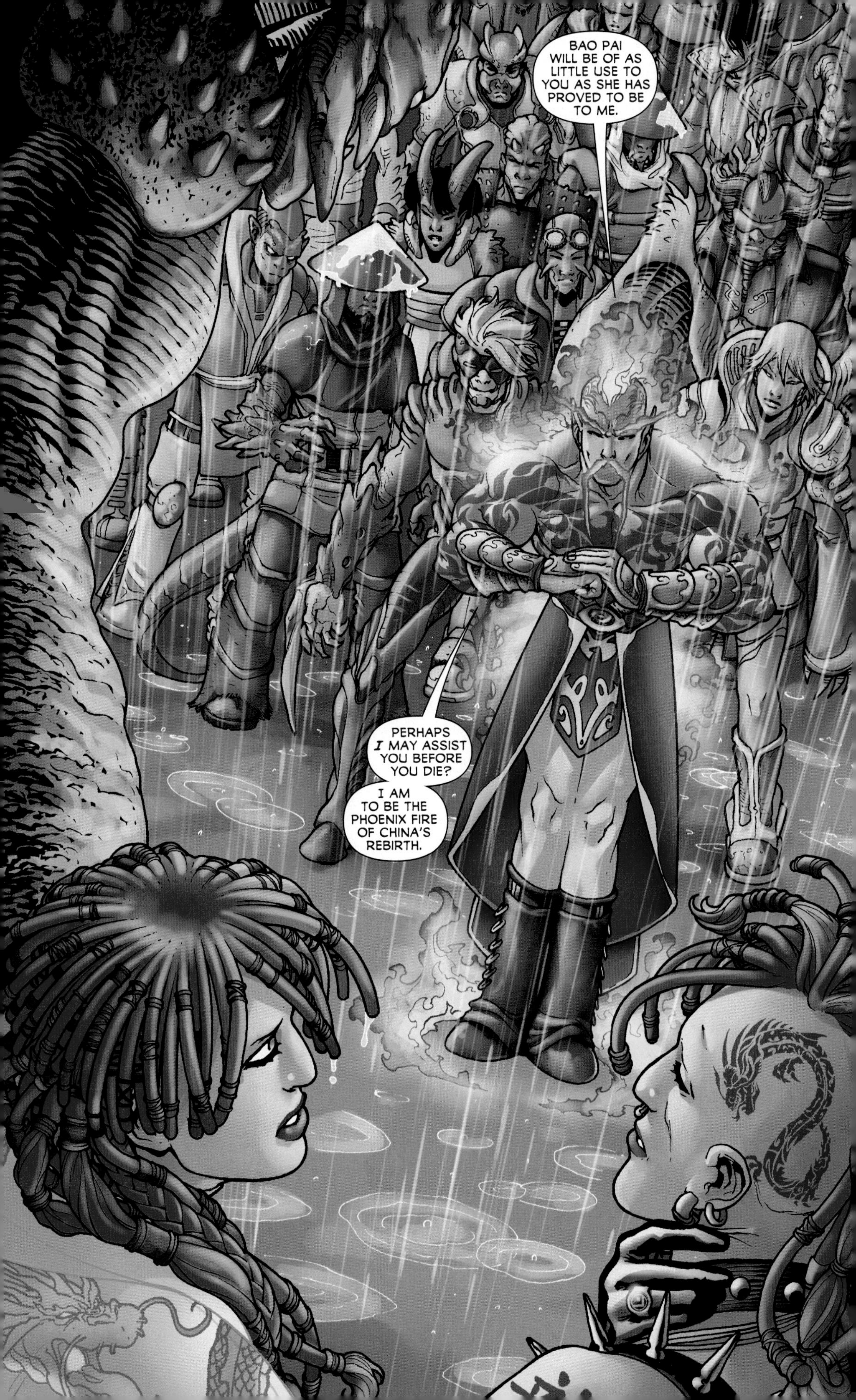
BAO PAI WILL BE OF AS LITTLE USE TO YOU AS SHE HAS PROVED TO BE TO ME.
PERHAPS I MAY ASSIST YOU BEFORE YOU DIE?
I AM TO BE THE PHOENIX FIRE OF CHINA'S REBIRTH.

cover art by
CHRIS SPROUSE, KARL STORY & GUY MAJOR

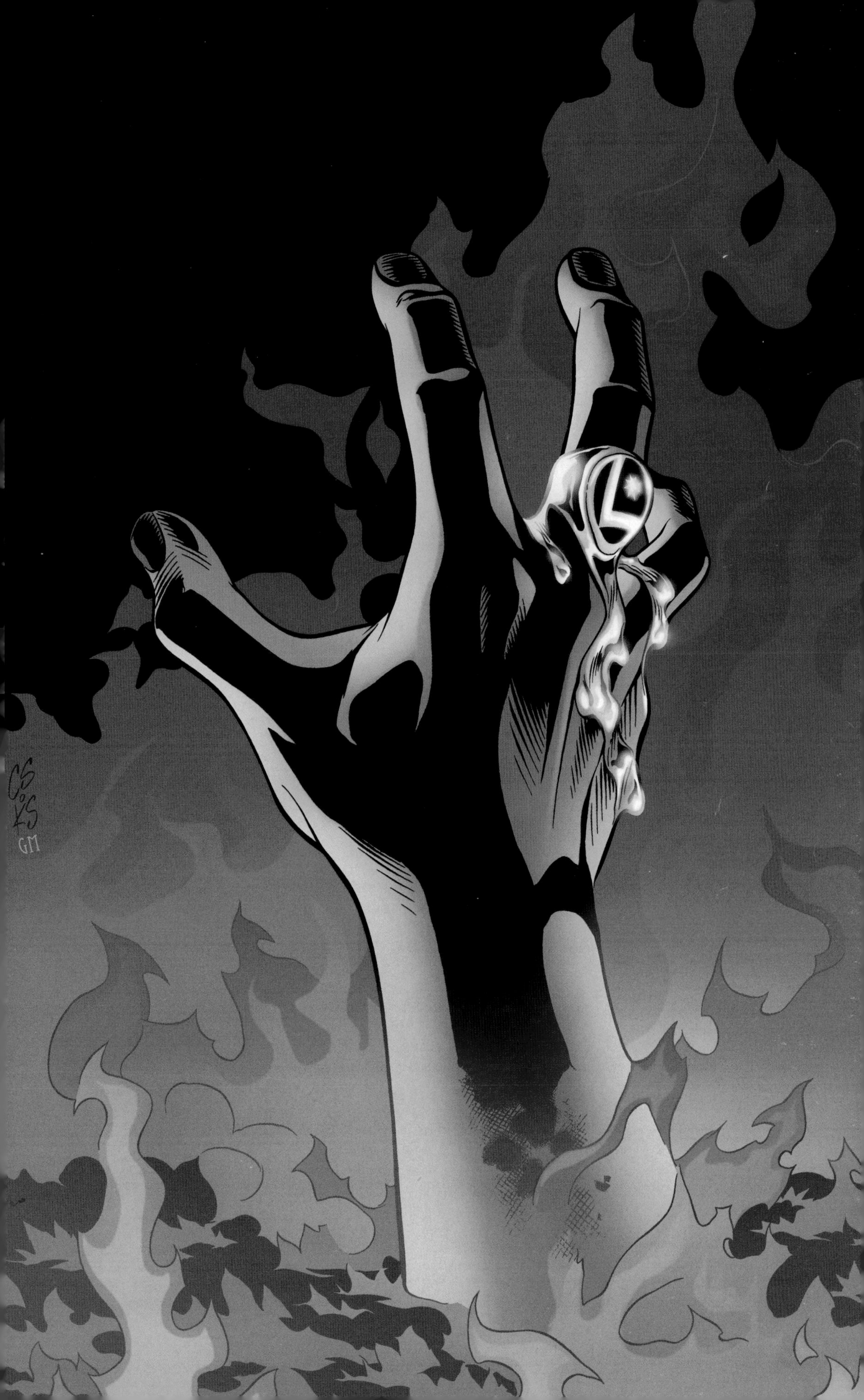

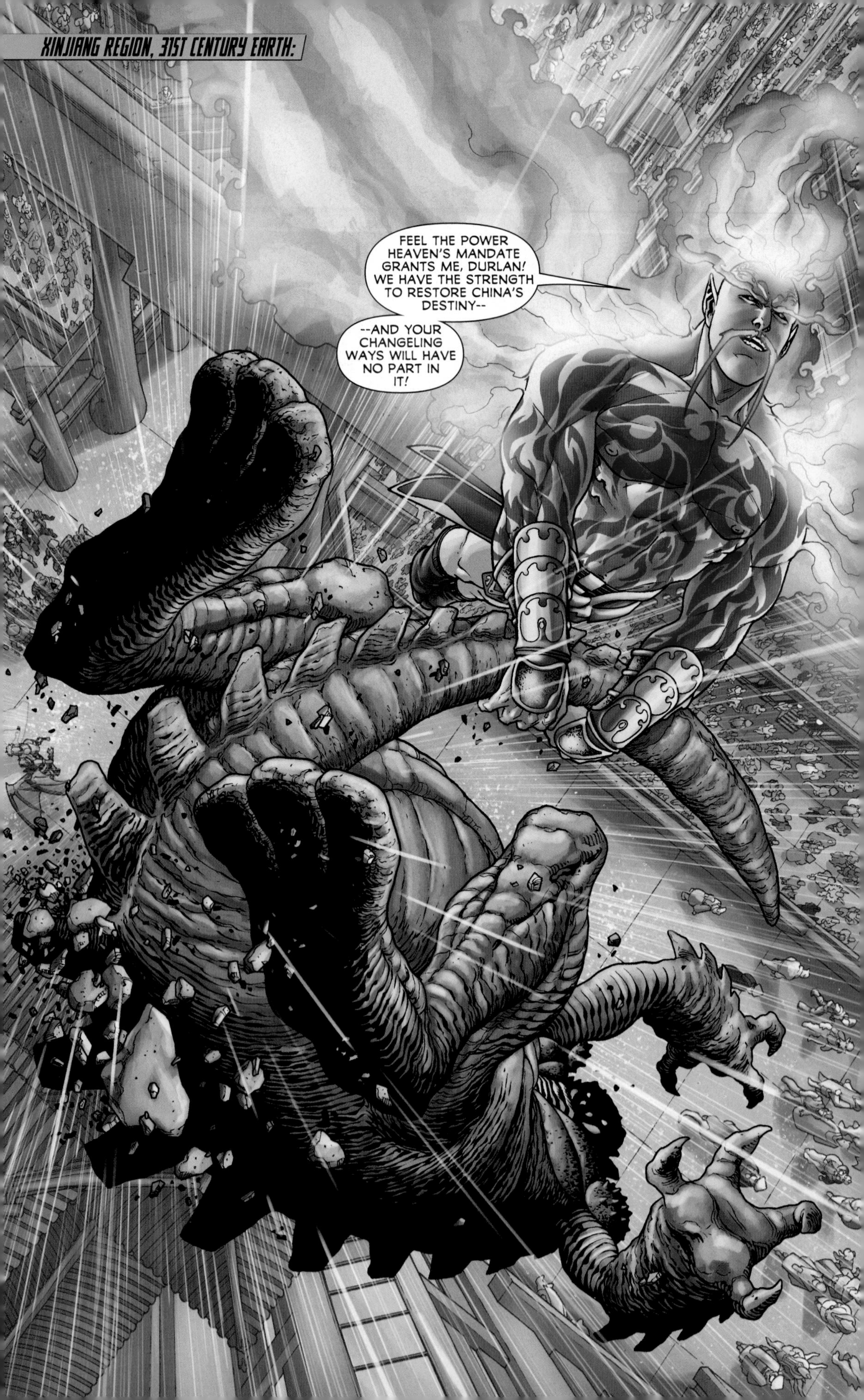
XINJIANG REGION, 31ST CENTURY EARTH:
FEEL THE POWER HEAVEN'S MANDATE GRANTS ME, DURLAN! WE HAVE THE STRENGTH TO RESTORE CHINA'S DESTINY--
--AND YOUR CHANGELING WAYS WILL HAVE NO PART IN IT!

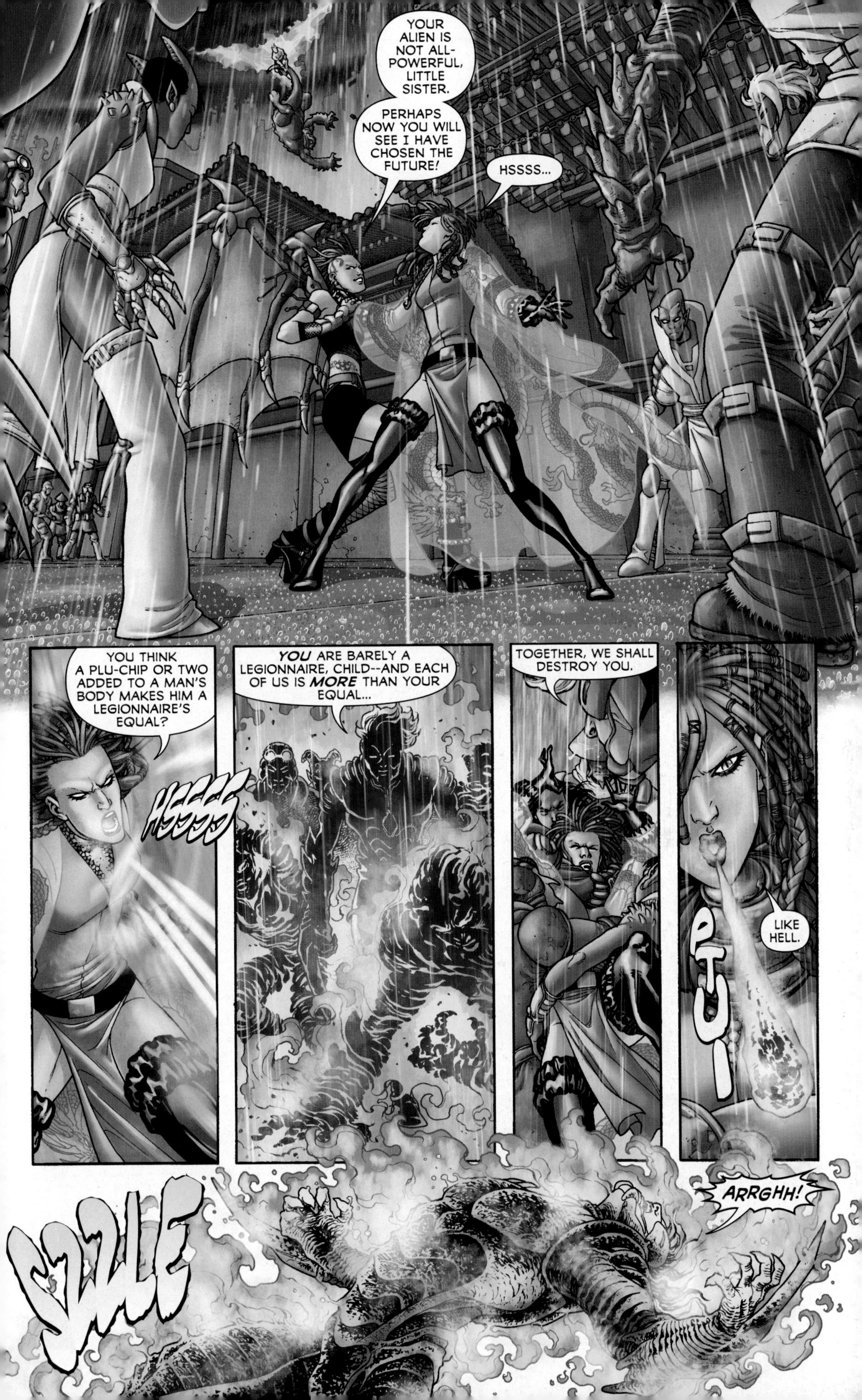

YOUR ALIEN IS NOT ALL-POWERFUL, LITTLE SISTER.
PERHAPS NOW YOU WILL SEE I HAVE CHOSEN THE FUTURE!
HSSSS...
YOU THINK A PLU-CHIP OR TWO ADDED TO A MAN'S BODY MAKES HIM A LEGIONNAIRE'S EQUAL?
HSSSS
YOU ARE BARELY A LEGIONNAIRE, CHILD--AND EACH OF US IS *MORE* THAN YOUR EQUAL...
TOGETHER, WE SHALL DESTROY YOU.
PTUI
LIKE HELL.
ARRGHH!
SIZZLE

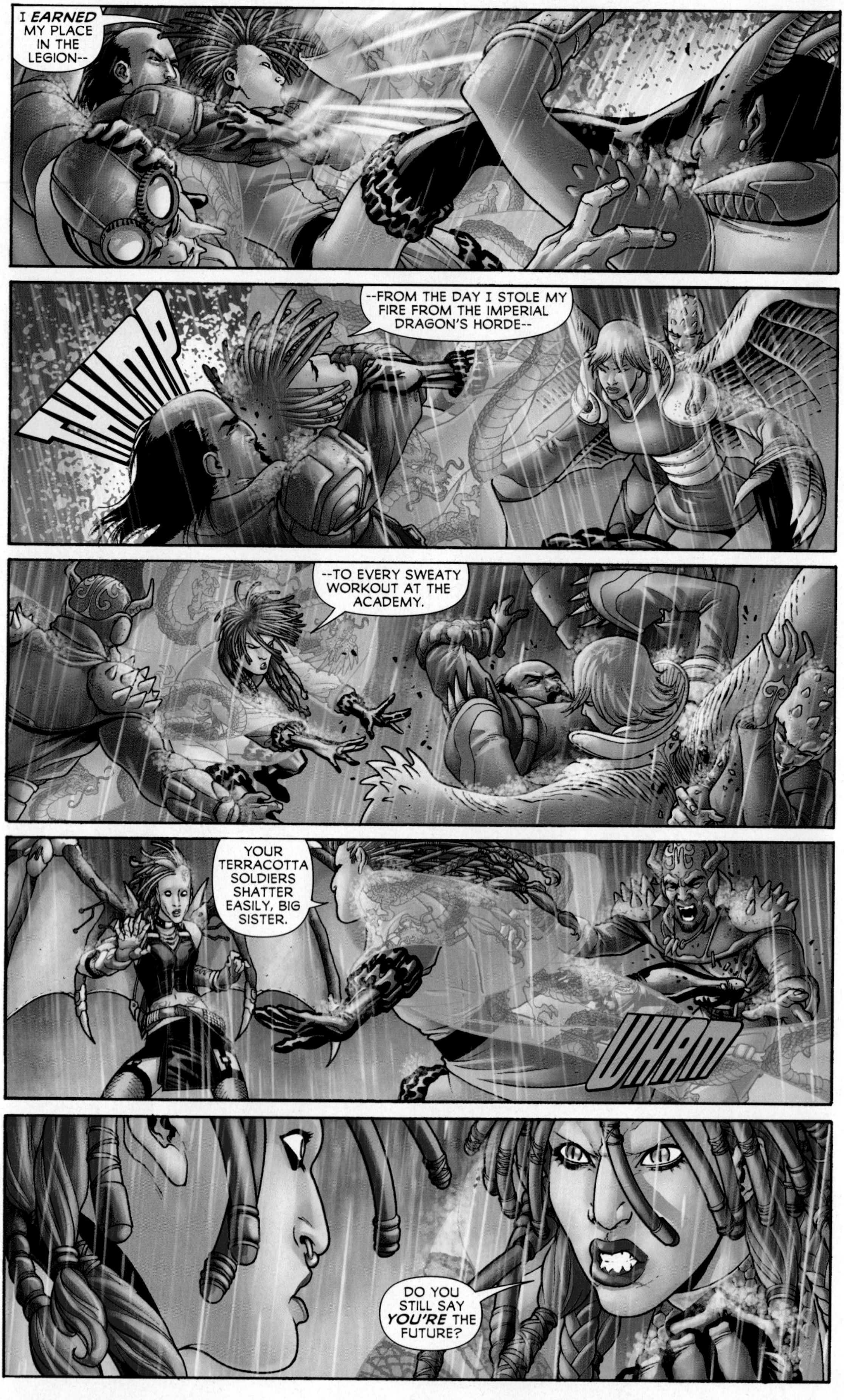
I EARNED MY PLACE IN THE LEGION--
--FROM THE DAY I STOLE MY FIRE FROM THE IMPERIAL DRAGON'S HORDE--
THUMP
--TO EVERY SWEATY WORKOUT AT THE ACADEMY.
YOUR TERRACOTTA SOLDIERS SHATTER EASILY, BIG SISTER.
WHAM
DO YOU STILL SAY YOU'RE THE FUTURE?

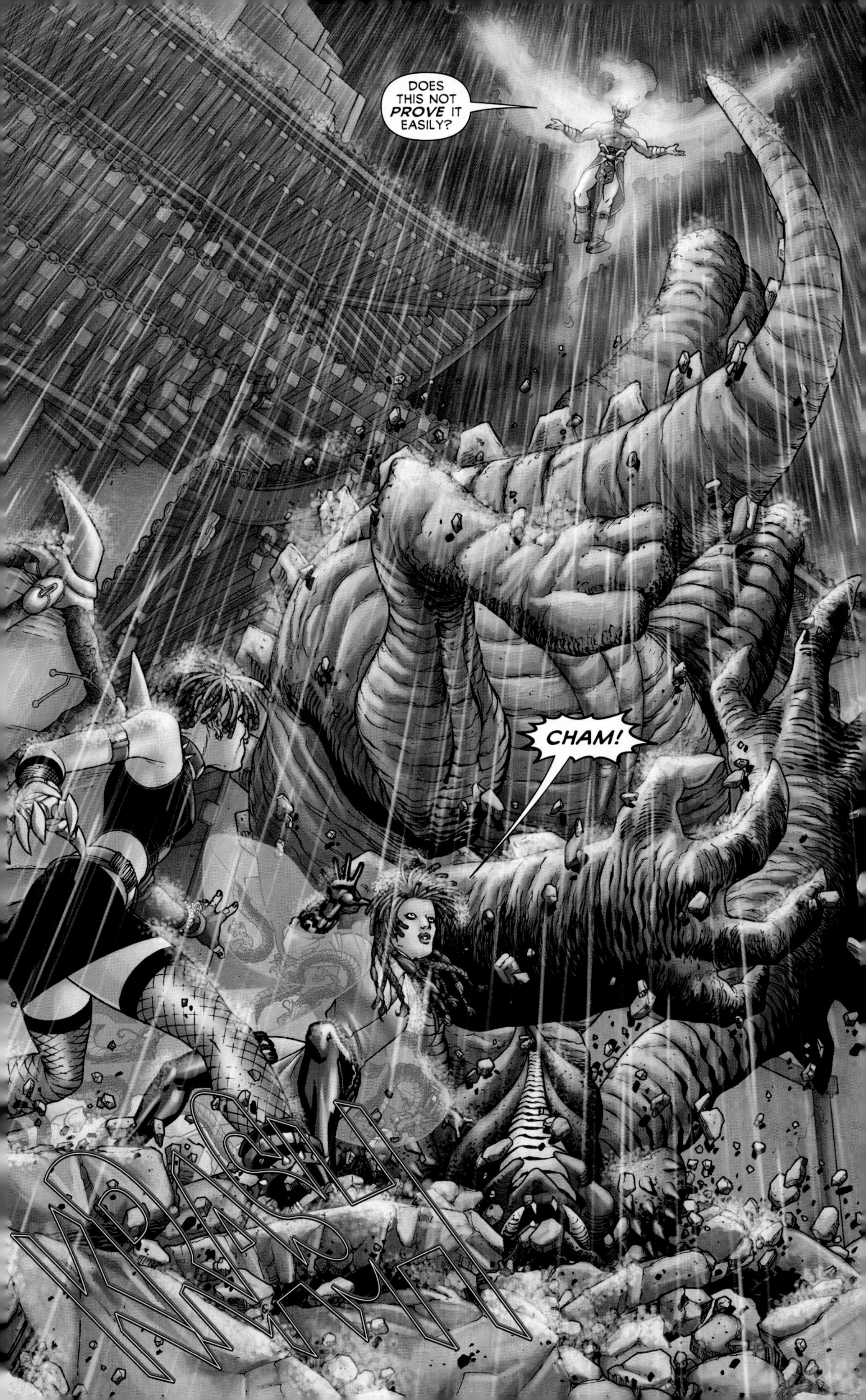
DOES THIS NOT *PROVE* IT EASILY?
CHAM!

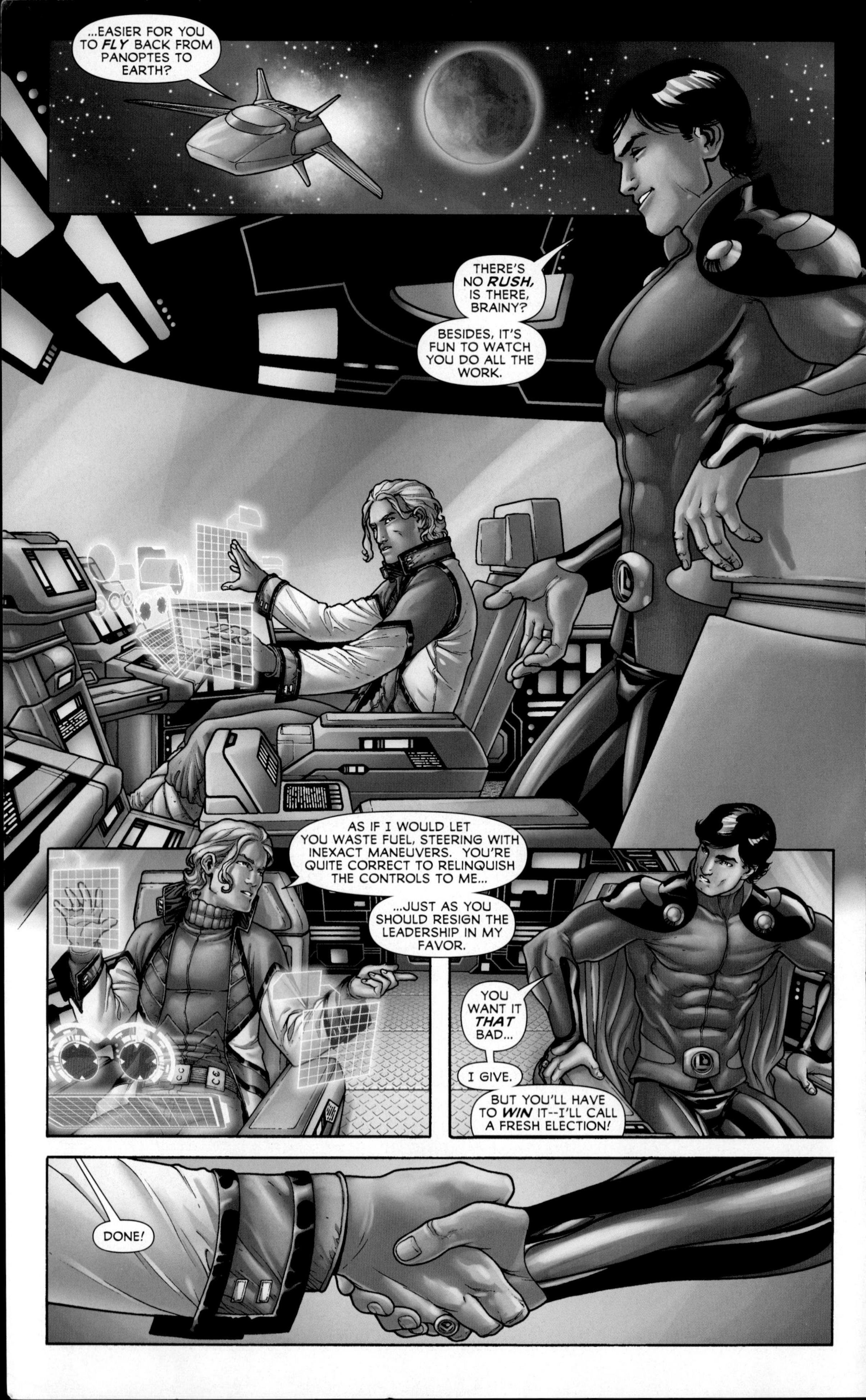
...EASIER FOR YOU TO FLY BACK FROM PANOPTES TO EARTH?
THERE'S NO RUSH, IS THERE, BRAINY?
BESIDES, IT'S FUN TO WATCH YOU DO ALL THE WORK.
AS IF I WOULD LET YOU WASTE FUEL, STEERING WITH INEXACT MANEUVERS. YOU'RE QUITE CORRECT TO RELINQUISH THE CONTROLS TO ME...
...JUST AS YOU SHOULD RESIGN THE LEADERSHIP IN MY FAVOR.
YOU WANT IT THAT BAD...
I GIVE.
BUT YOU'LL HAVE TO WIN IT--I'LL CALL A FRESH ELECTION!
DONE!

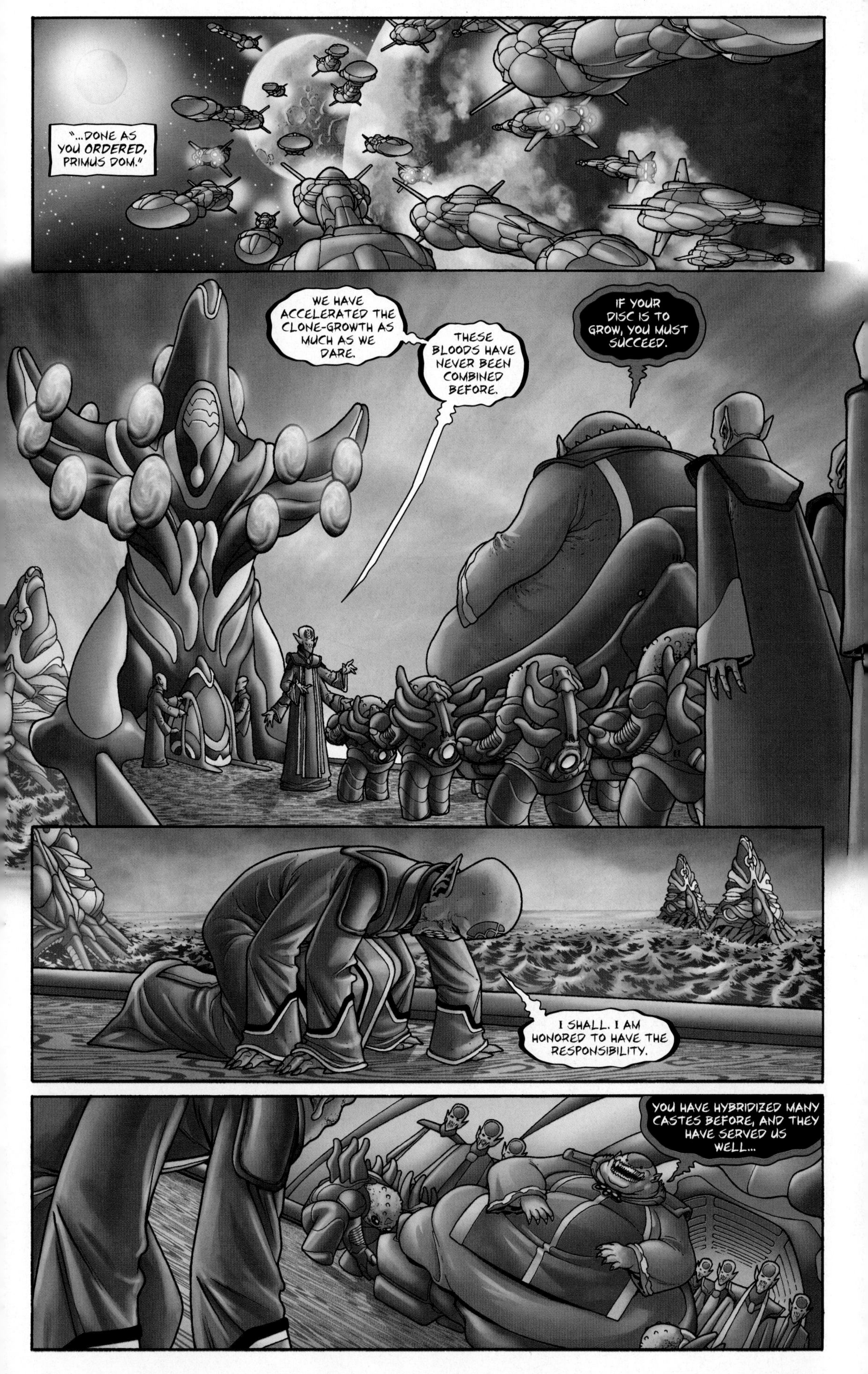
"...DONE AS YOU ORDERED, PRIMUS DOM."
WE HAVE ACCELERATED THE CLONE-GROWTH AS MUCH AS WE DARE.
THESE BLOODS HAVE NEVER BEEN COMBINED BEFORE.
IF YOUR DISC IS TO GROW, YOU MUST SUCCEED.
I SHALL. I AM HONORED TO HAVE THE RESPONSIBILITY.
YOU HAVE HYBRIDIZED MANY CASTES BEFORE, AND THEY HAVE SERVED US WELL...

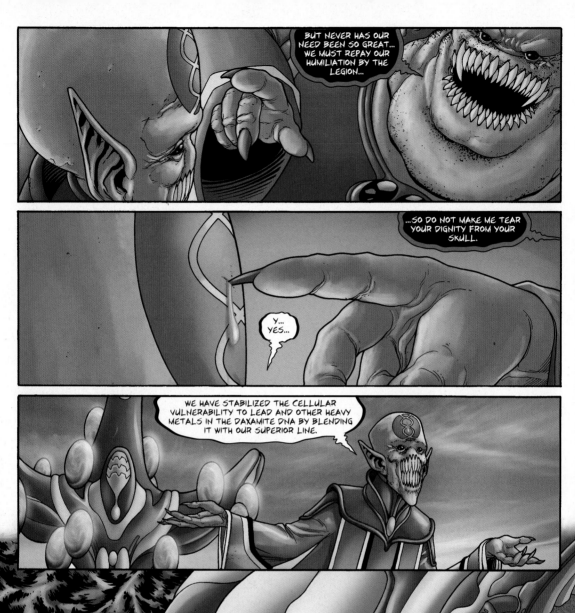

BUT NEVER HAS OUR NEED BEEN SO GREAT... WE MUST REPAY OUR HUMILIATION BY THE LEGION...

...SO DO NOT MAKE ME TEAR YOUR DIGNITY FROM YOUR SKULL.

Y... YES...

WE HAVE STABILIZED THE CELLULAR VULNERABILITY TO LEAD AND OTHER HEAVY METALS IN THE DAXAMITE DNA BY BLENDING IT WITH OUR SUPERIOR LINE.

YOU SHALL HAVE YOUR STAR-SPANNING ARMY....

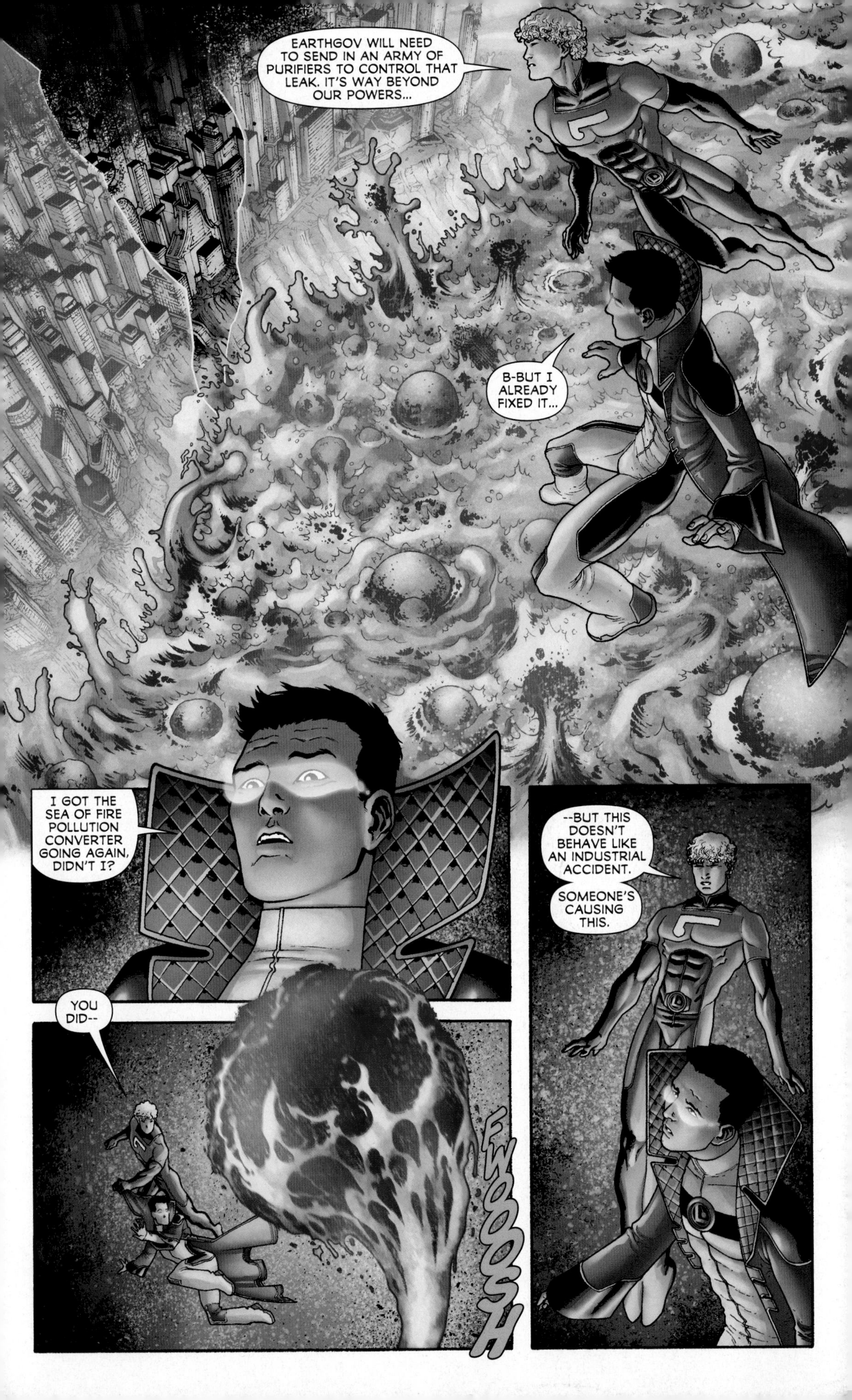
EARTHGOV WILL NEED TO SEND IN AN ARMY OF PURIFIERS TO CONTROL THAT LEAK. IT'S WAY BEYOND OUR POWERS...
B-BUT I ALREADY FIXED IT...
I GOT THE SEA OF FIRE POLLUTION CONVERTER GOING AGAIN, DIDN'T I?
YOU DID--
FWOOOSH
--BUT THIS DOESN'T BEHAVE LIKE AN INDUSTRIAL ACCIDENT.
SOMEONE'S CAUSING THIS.

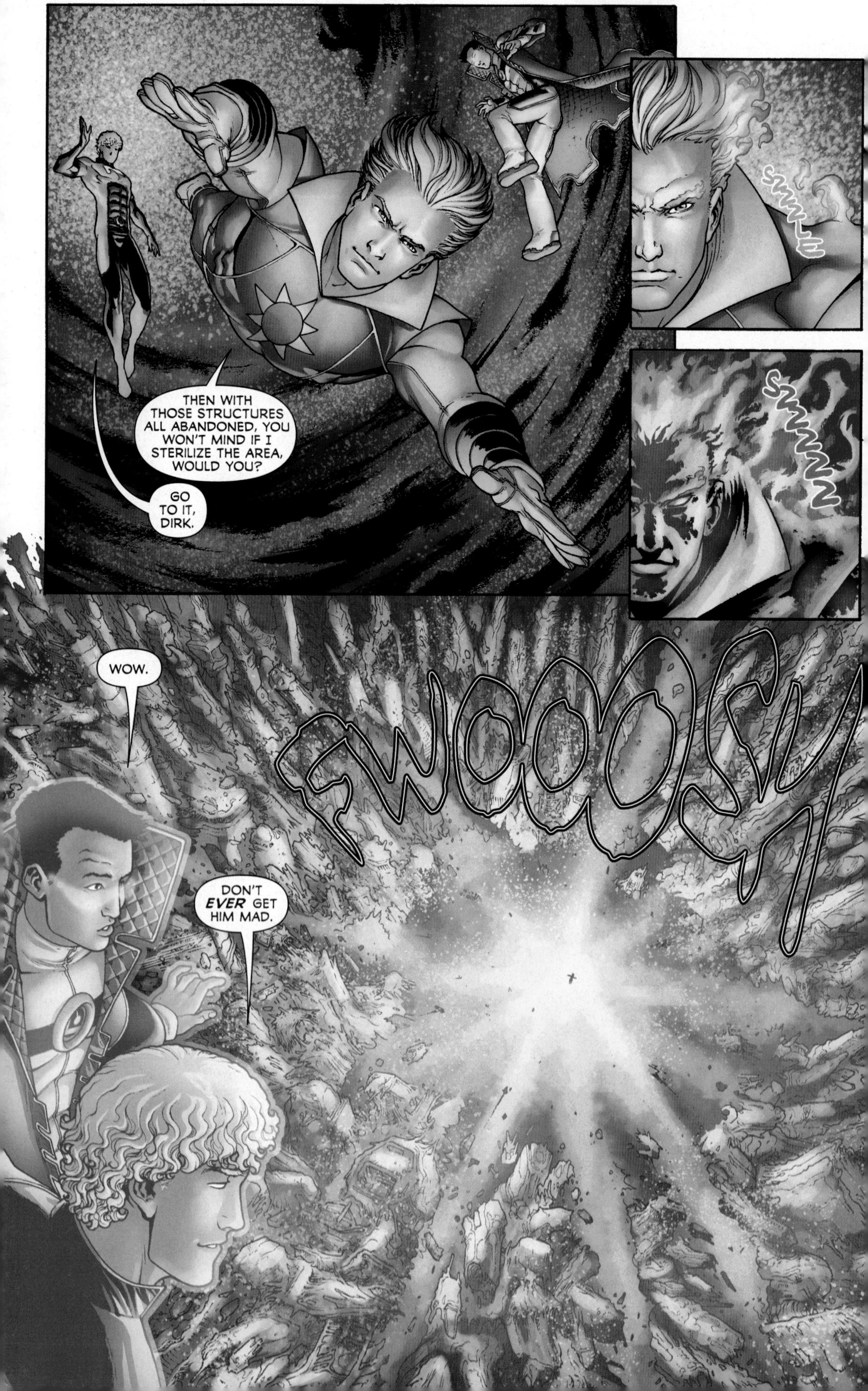
THEN WITH THOSE STRUCTURES ALL ABANDONED, YOU WON'T MIND IF I STERILIZE THE AREA, WOULD YOU?
GO TO IT, DIRK.
SMMLE
SZZZZZZ
WOW.
FWOOOSH
DON'T *EVER* GET HIM MAD.

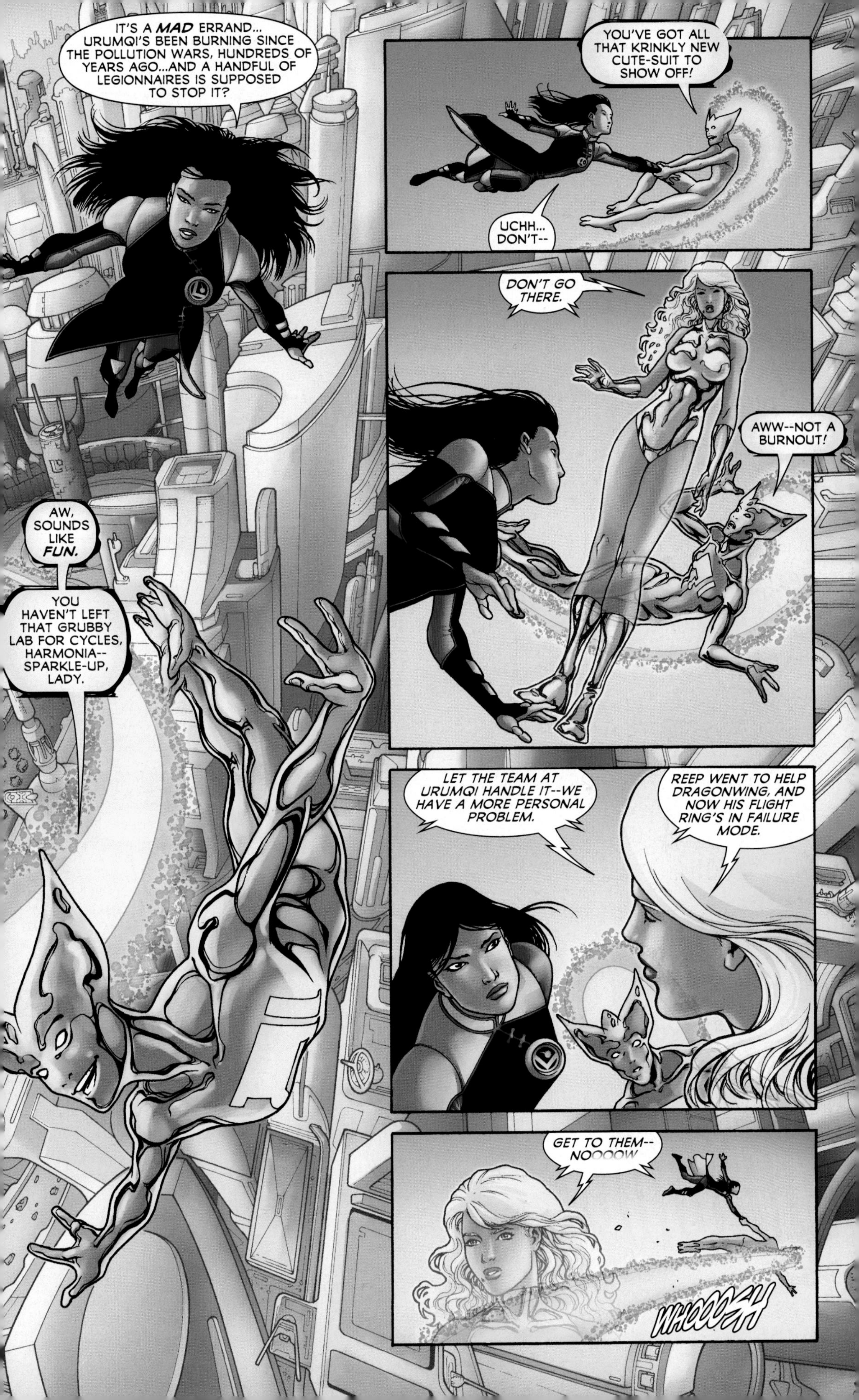
IT'S A MAD ERRAND... URUMQI'S BEEN BURNING SINCE THE POLLUTION WARS, HUNDREDS OF YEARS AGO...AND A HANDFUL OF LEGIONNAIRES IS SUPPOSED TO STOP IT?
AW, SOUNDS LIKE FUN.
YOU HAVEN'T LEFT THAT GRUBBY LAB FOR CYCLES, HARMONIA-- SPARKLE-UP, LADY.
YOU'VE GOT ALL THAT KRINKLY NEW CUTE-SUIT TO SHOW OFF!
UCHH... DON'T--
DON'T GO THERE.
AWW--NOT A BURNOUT!
LET THE TEAM AT URUMQI HANDLE IT--WE HAVE A MORE PERSONAL PROBLEM.
REEP WENT TO HELP DRAGONWING, AND NOW HIS FLIGHT RING'S IN FAILURE MODE.
GET TO THEM-- NOOOOW
WHOOOSH

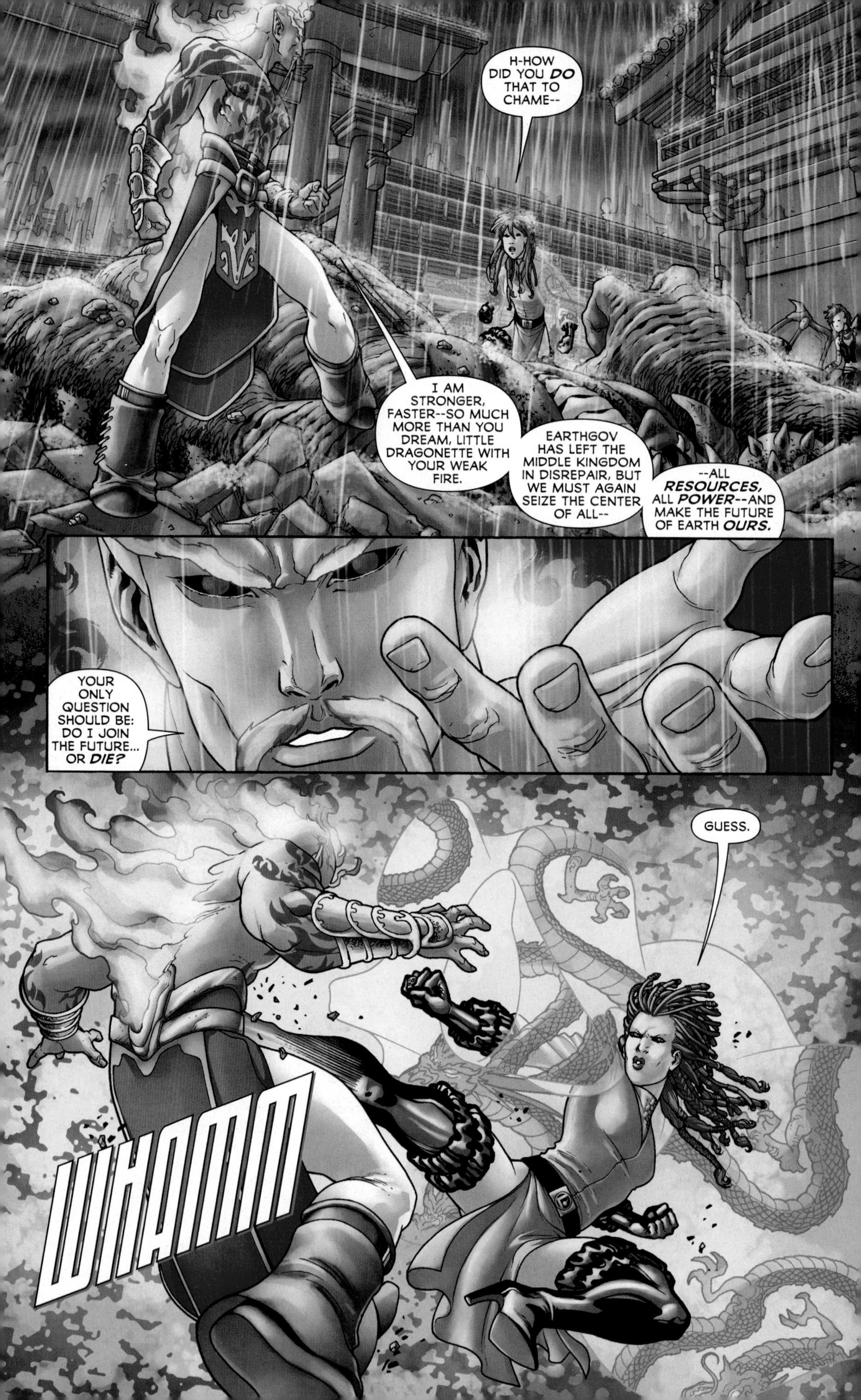

H-HOW DID YOU *DO* THAT TO CHAME--
I AM STRONGER, FASTER--SO MUCH MORE THAN YOU DREAM, LITTLE DRAGONETTE WITH YOUR WEAK FIRE.
EARTHGOV HAS LEFT THE MIDDLE KINGDOM IN DISREPAIR, BUT WE MUST AGAIN SEIZE THE CENTER OF ALL--
--ALL ***RESOURCES,*** ALL ***POWER***--AND MAKE THE FUTURE OF EARTH ***OURS.***
YOUR ONLY QUESTION SHOULD BE: DO I JOIN THE FUTURE... OR ***DIE?***
GUESS.
WHAMM

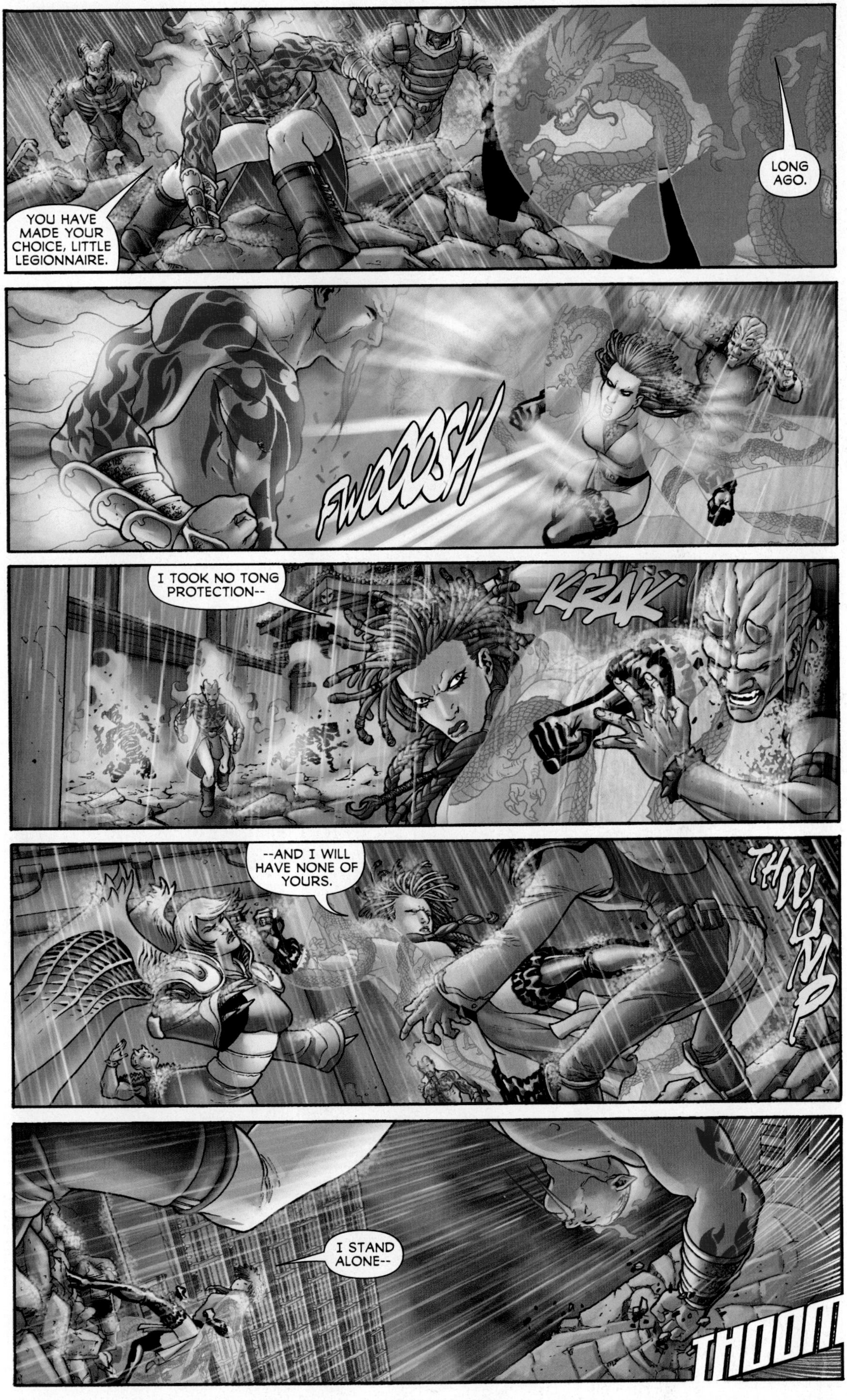
YOU HAVE MADE YOUR CHOICE, LITTLE LEGIONNAIRE.
LONG AGO.
FWOOOSH
I TOOK NO TONG PROTECTION--
KRAK
--AND I WILL HAVE NONE OF YOURS.
THWUMP
I STAND ALONE--
THOOM

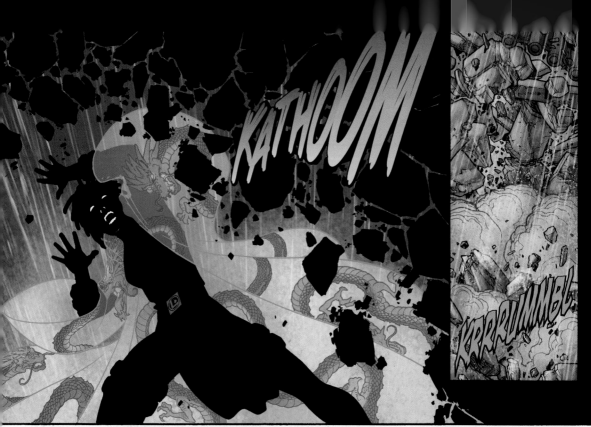

YOU WILL DIE WITH THE PAST, THEN.

NO.

MY SISTER...

...MY BLOOD.

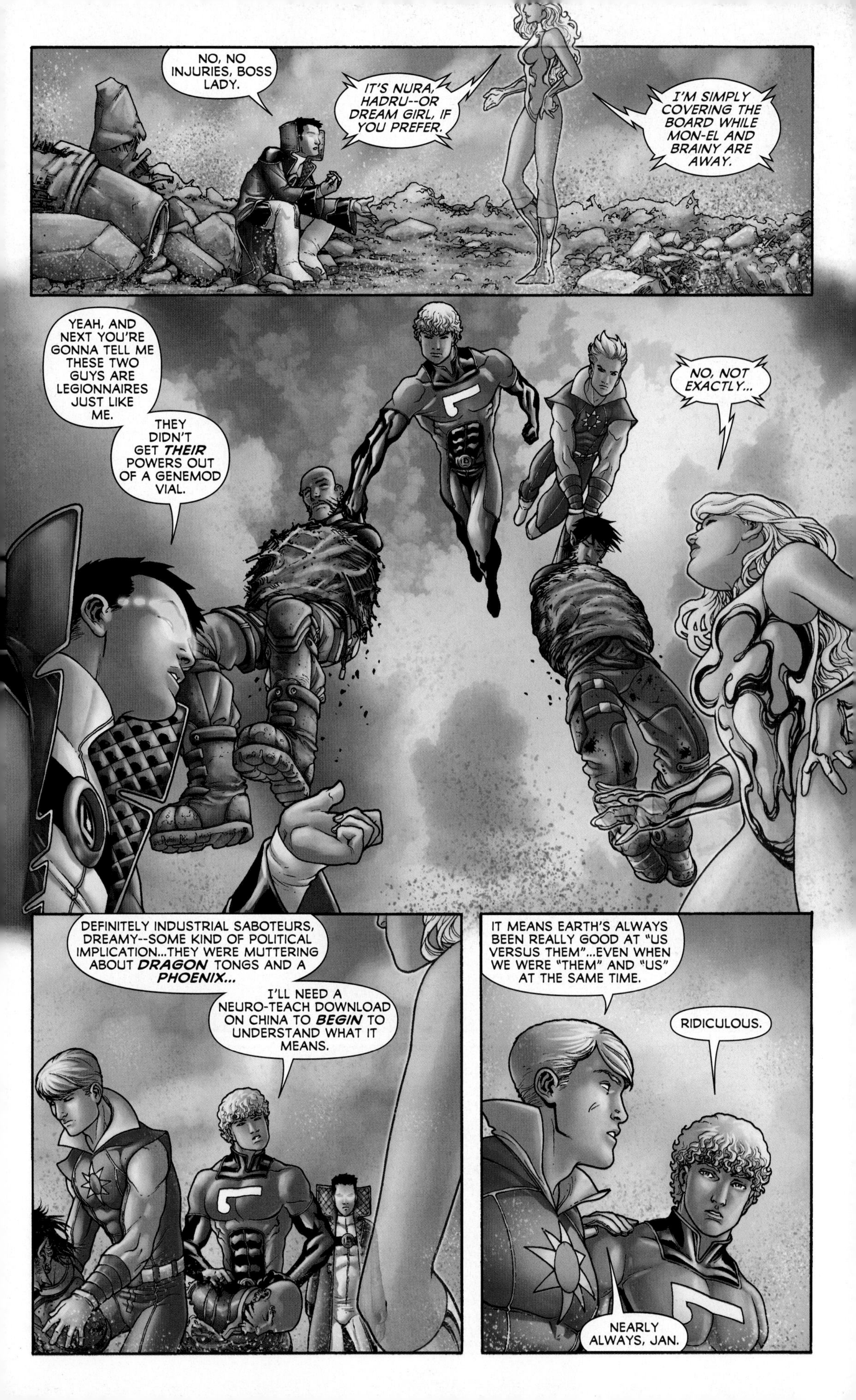
NO, NO INJURIES, BOSS LADY.
IT'S NURA, HADRU--OR DREAM GIRL, IF YOU PREFER.
I'M SIMPLY COVERING THE BOARD WHILE MON-EL AND BRAINY ARE AWAY.
YEAH, AND NEXT YOU'RE GONNA TELL ME THESE TWO GUYS ARE LEGIONNAIRES JUST LIKE ME.
NO, NOT EXACTLY...
THEY DIDN'T GET **THEIR** POWERS OUT OF A GENEMOD VIAL.
DEFINITELY INDUSTRIAL SABOTEURS, DREAMY--SOME KIND OF POLITICAL IMPLICATION...THEY WERE MUTTERING ABOUT **DRAGON** TONGS AND A **PHOENIX...**
I'LL NEED A NEURO-TEACH DOWNLOAD ON CHINA TO **BEGIN** TO UNDERSTAND WHAT IT MEANS.
IT MEANS EARTH'S ALWAYS BEEN REALLY GOOD AT "US VERSUS THEM"...EVEN WHEN WE WERE "THEM" AND "US" AT THE SAME TIME.
RIDICULOUS.
NEARLY ALWAYS, JAN.

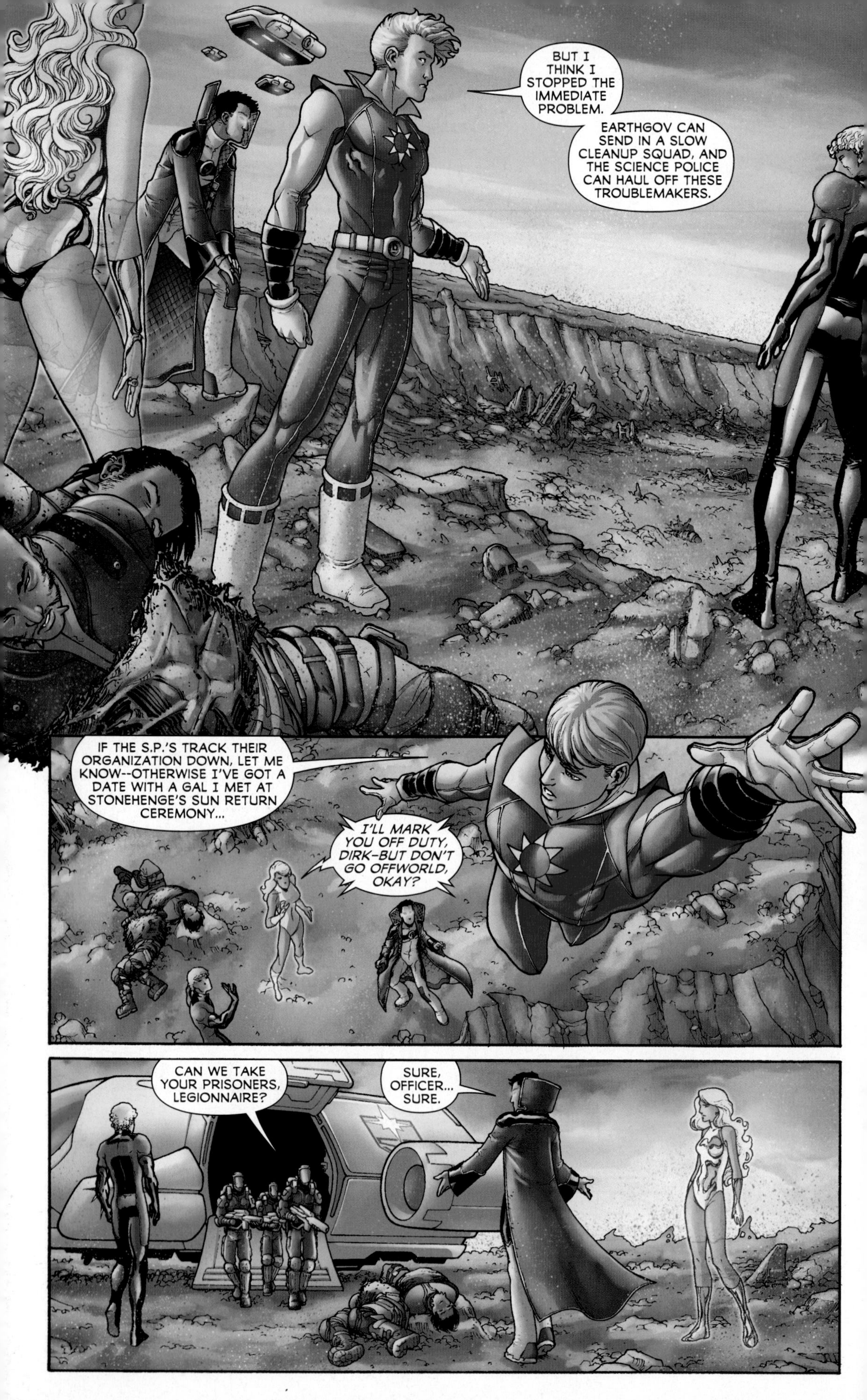
BUT I THINK I STOPPED THE IMMEDIATE PROBLEM.
EARTHGOV CAN SEND IN A SLOW CLEANUP SQUAD, AND THE SCIENCE POLICE CAN HAUL OFF THESE TROUBLEMAKERS.
IF THE S.P.'S TRACK THEIR ORGANIZATION DOWN, LET ME KNOW--OTHERWISE I'VE GOT A DATE WITH A GAL I MET AT STONEHENGE'S SUN RETURN CEREMONY...
I'LL MARK YOU OFF DUTY, DIRK--BUT DON'T GO OFFWORLD, OKAY?
CAN WE TAKE YOUR PRISONERS, LEGIONNAIRE?
SURE, OFFICER... SURE.

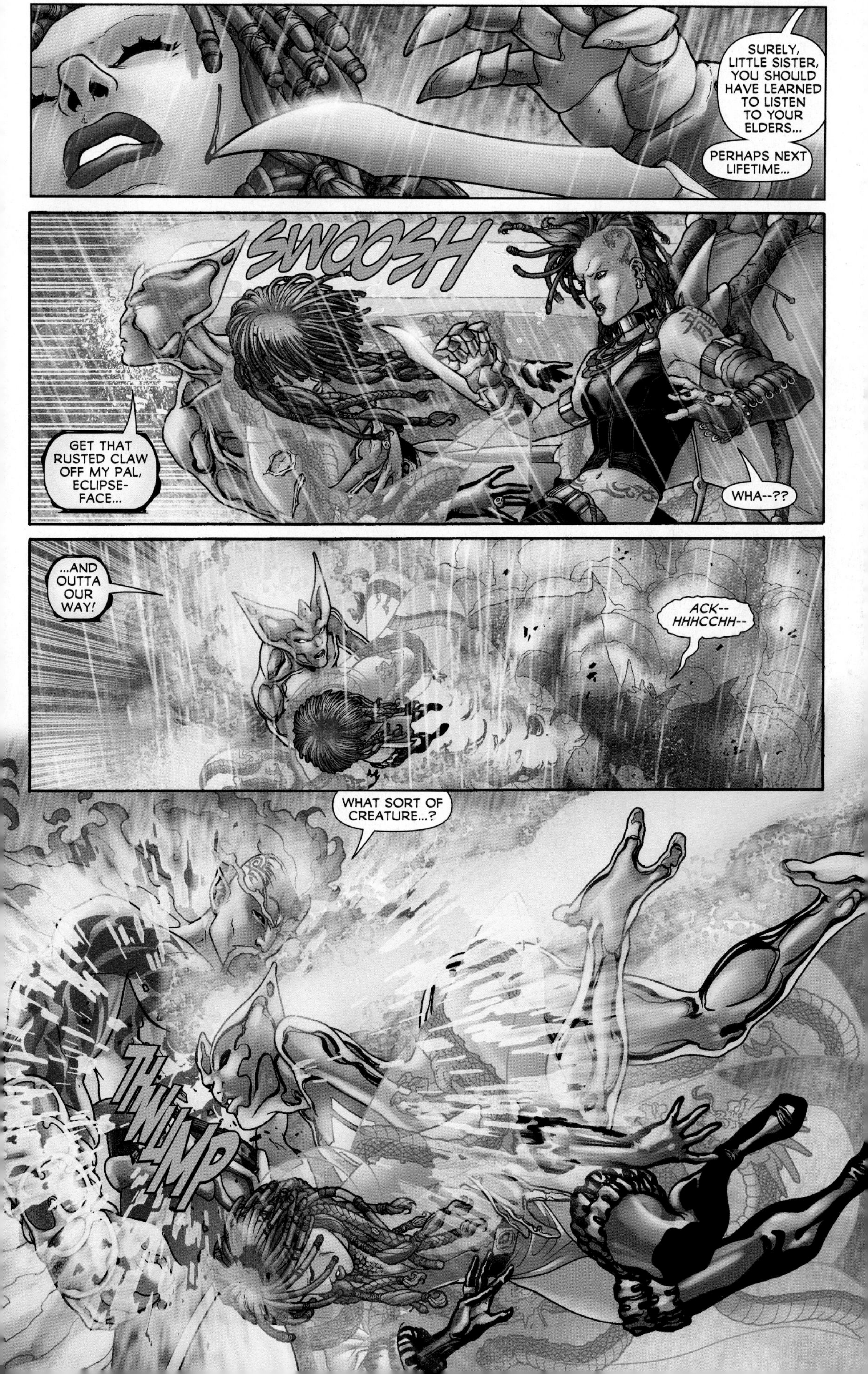
SURELY, LITTLE SISTER, YOU SHOULD HAVE LEARNED TO LISTEN TO YOUR ELDERS...
PERHAPS NEXT LIFETIME...
SWOOSH
GET THAT RUSTED CLAW OFF MY PAL, ECLIPSE-FACE...
WHA--??
...AND OUTTA OUR WAY!
ACK-- HHHCCHH--
WHAT SORT OF CREATURE...?
THWUMP

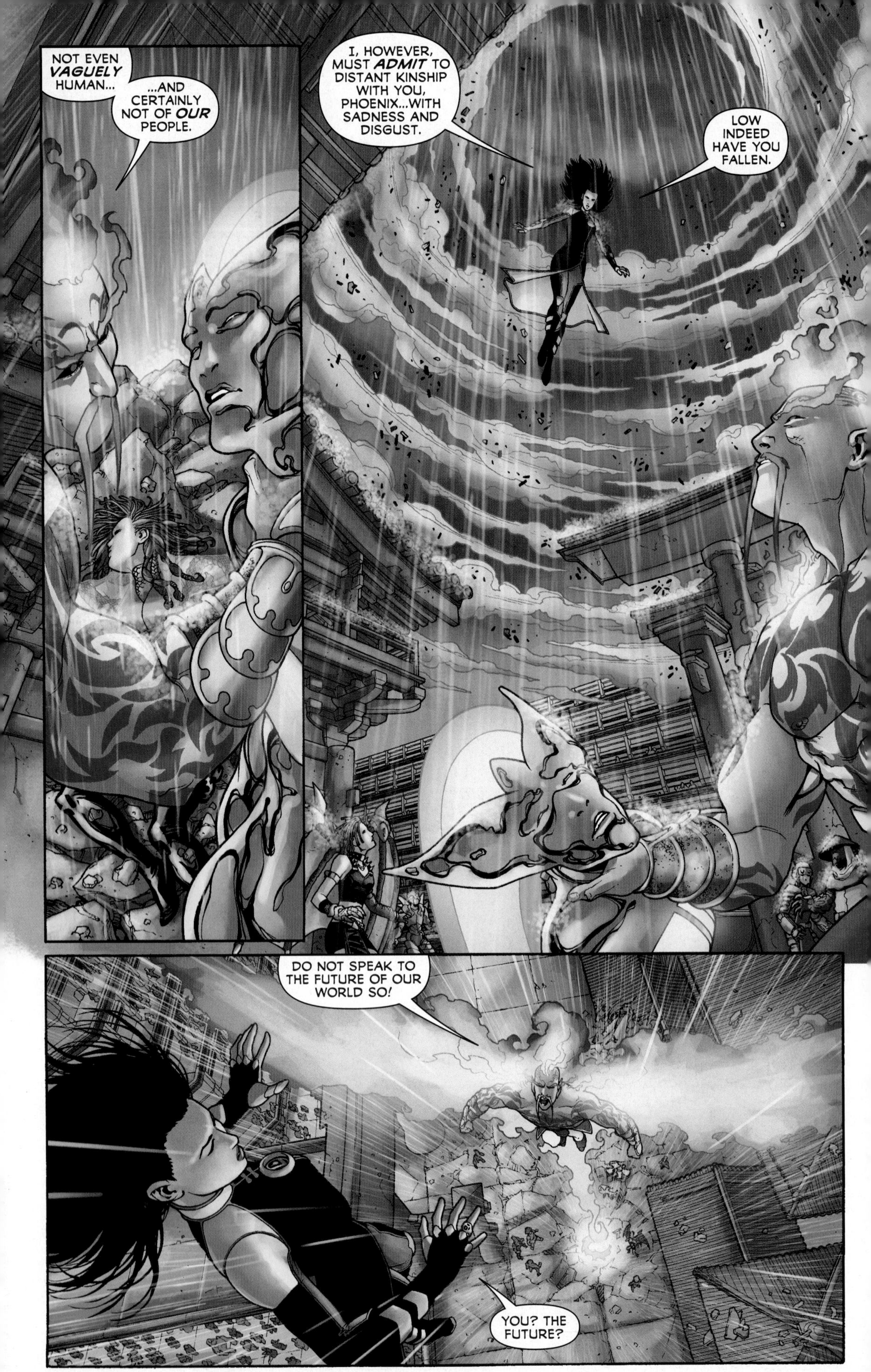
NOT EVEN *VAGUELY* HUMAN...
...AND CERTAINLY NOT OF *OUR* PEOPLE.
I, HOWEVER, MUST *ADMIT* TO DISTANT KINSHIP WITH YOU, PHOENIX...WITH SADNESS AND DISGUST.
LOW INDEED HAVE YOU FALLEN.
DO NOT SPEAK TO THE FUTURE OF OUR WORLD SO!
YOU? THE FUTURE?

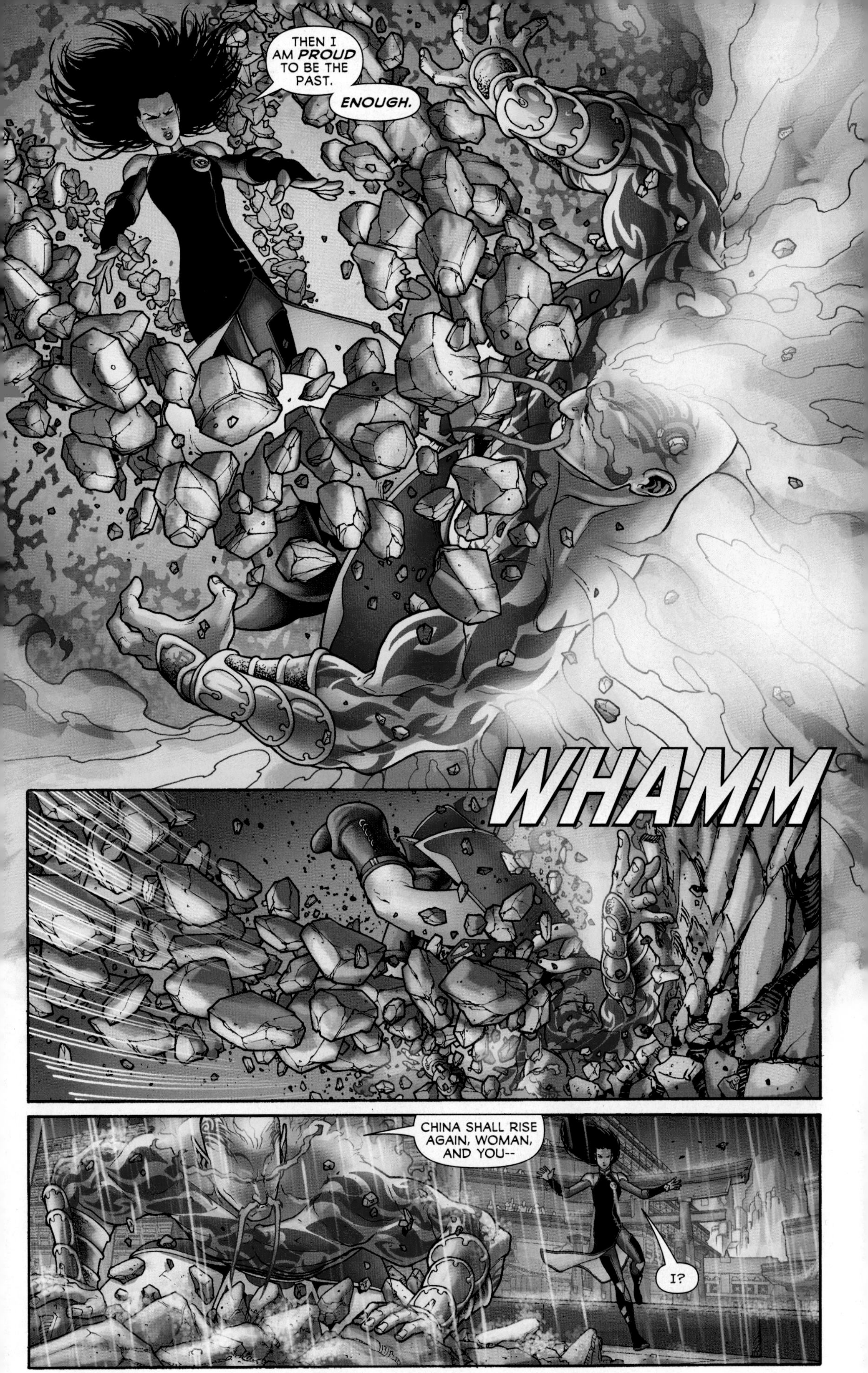

THEN I AM *PROUD* TO BE THE PAST.
ENOUGH.
WHAMM
CHINA SHALL RISE AGAIN, WOMAN, AND YOU--
I?

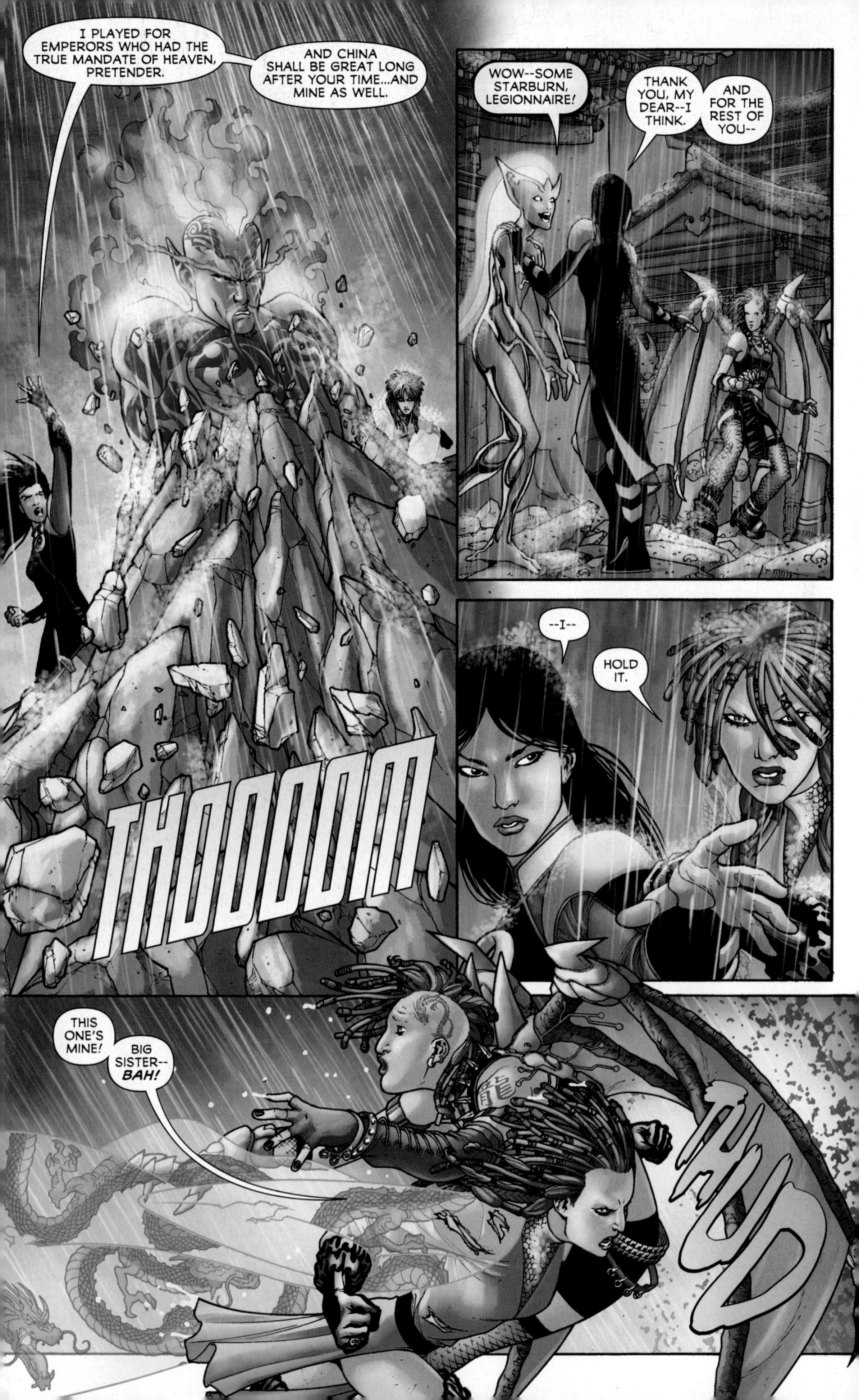
I PLAYED FOR EMPERORS WHO HAD THE TRUE MANDATE OF HEAVEN, PRETENDER.
AND CHINA SHALL BE GREAT LONG AFTER YOUR TIME...AND MINE AS WELL.
THOOOOM
WOW--SOME STARBURN, LEGIONNAIRE!
THANK YOU, MY DEAR--I THINK.
AND FOR THE REST OF YOU--
--I--
HOLD IT.
THIS ONE'S MINE!
BIG SISTER-- BAH!
THUD

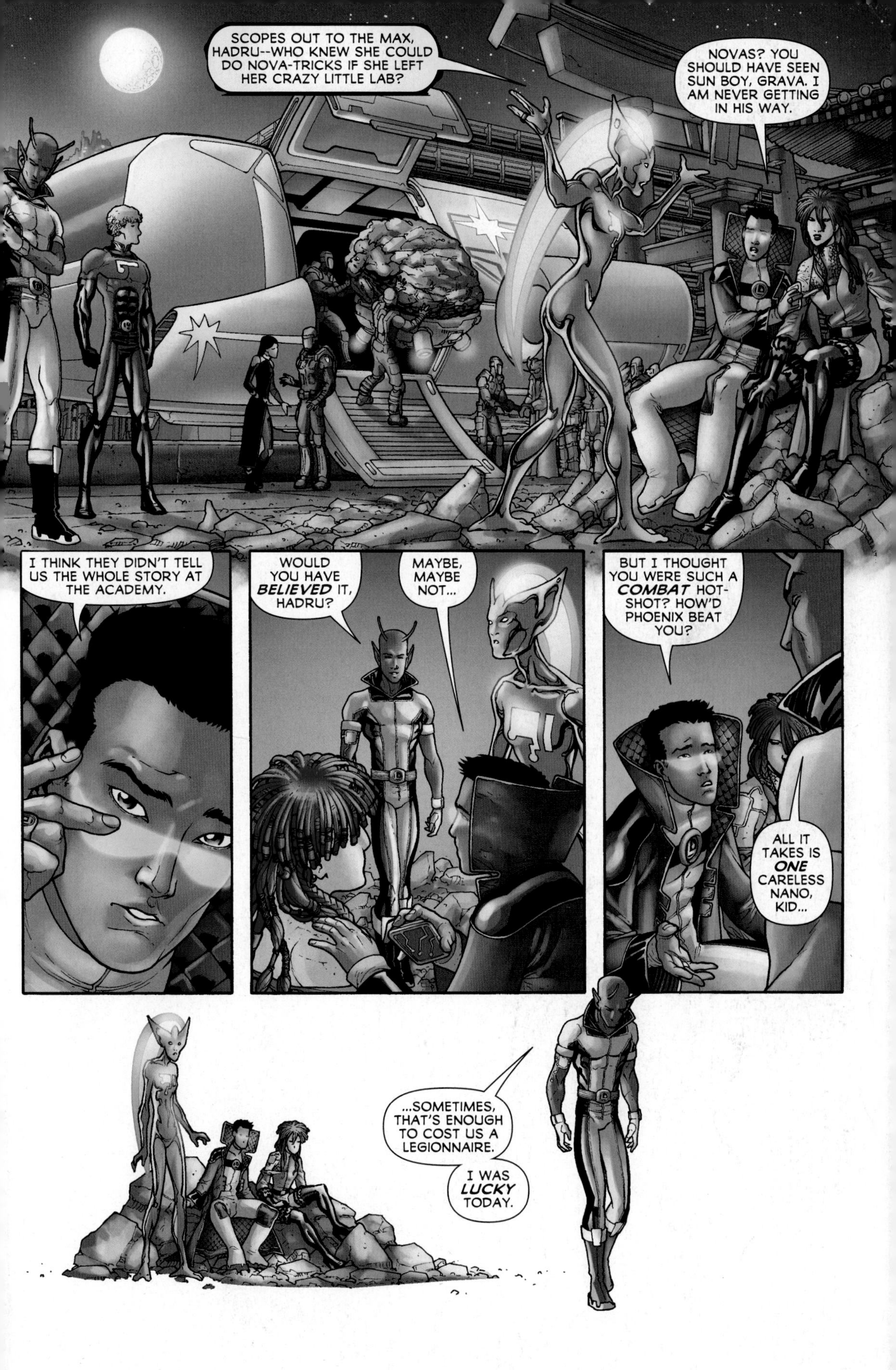
SCOPES OUT TO THE MAX, HADRU--WHO KNEW SHE COULD DO NOVA-TRICKS IF SHE LEFT HER CRAZY LITTLE LAB?
NOVAS? YOU SHOULD HAVE SEEN SUN BOY, GRAVA. I AM NEVER GETTING IN HIS WAY.
I THINK THEY DIDN'T TELL US THE WHOLE STORY AT THE ACADEMY.
WOULD YOU HAVE BELIEVED IT, HADRU?
MAYBE, MAYBE NOT...
BUT I THOUGHT YOU WERE SUCH A COMBAT HOT-SHOT? HOW'D PHOENIX BEAT YOU?
ALL IT TAKES IS ONE CARELESS NANO, KID...
...SOMETIMES, THAT'S ENOUGH TO COST US A LEGIONNAIRE.
I WAS LUCKY TODAY.

CHEMICAL KID AND ULTRA BOY SKETCHES BY JIM LEE

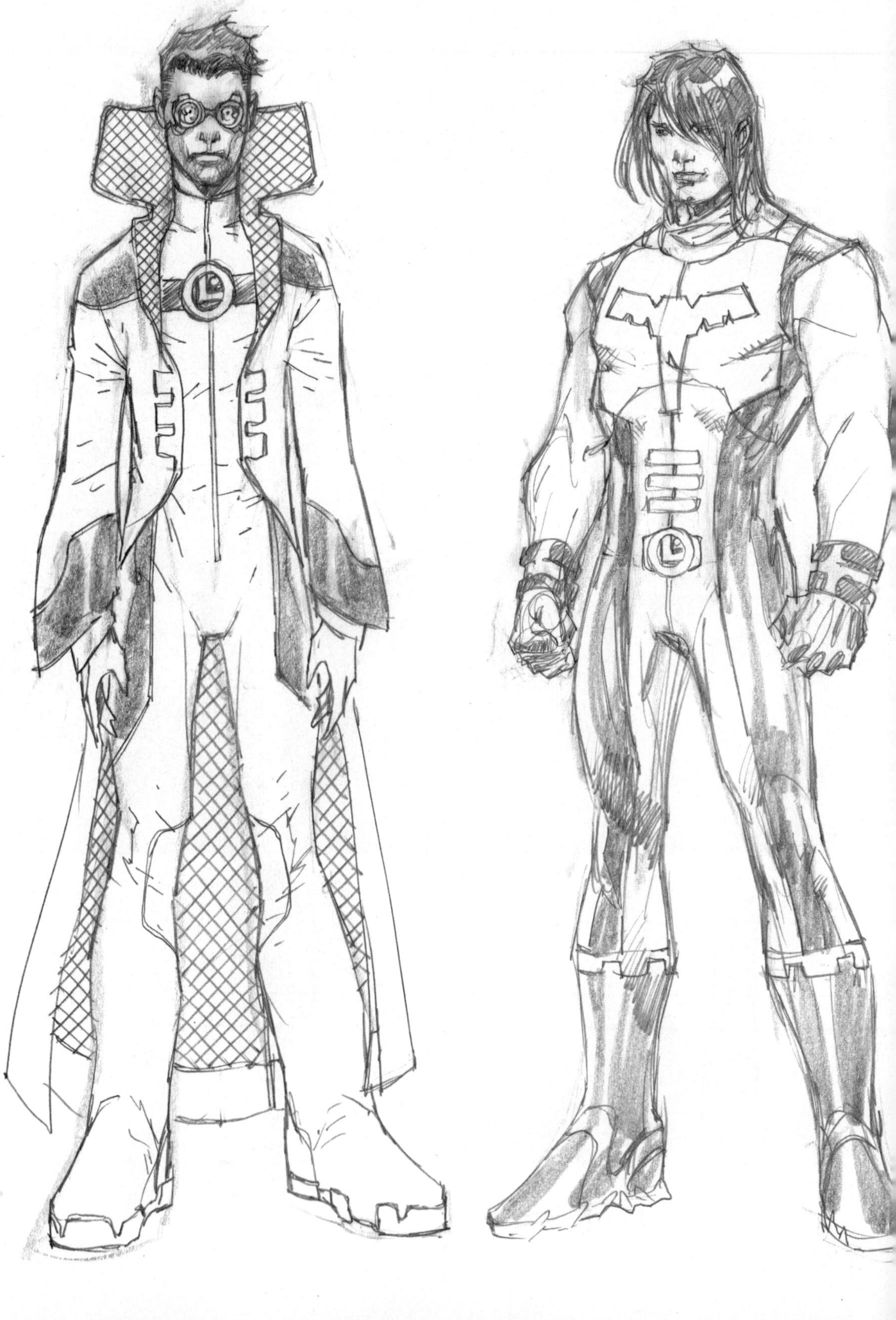

LEGION OF SUPER-HEROES PART 5
PAGES 1, 6, 14, 19 PENCILS BY WALTER SIMONSON

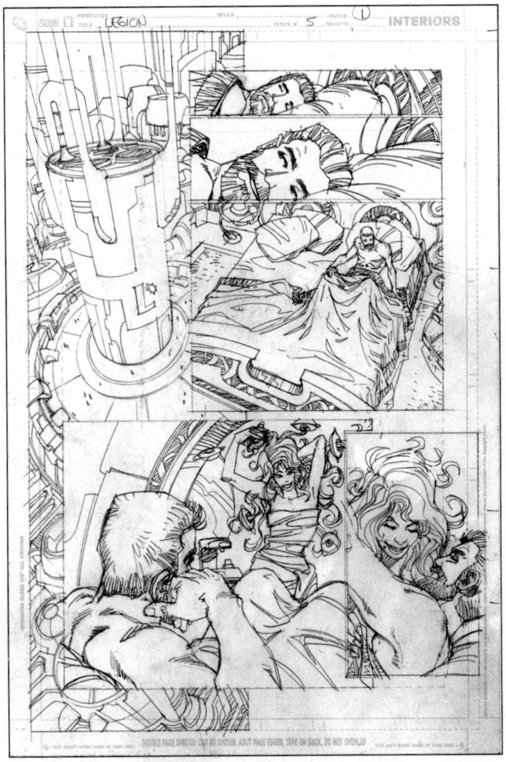
LEGION
INTERIORS
DOUBLE PAGE SPREAD: CUT AS SHOWN, ABUT PAGE EDGES, TAPE ON BACK, DO NOT OVERLAP

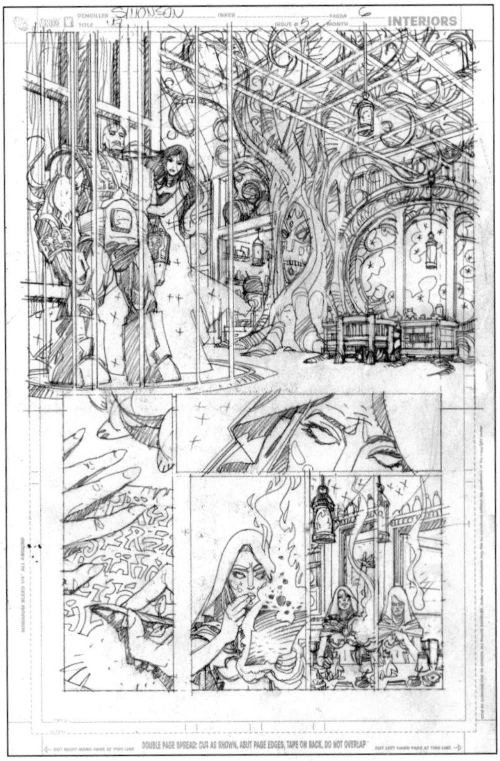
SIMONSON
INTERIORS
DOUBLE PAGE SPREAD: CUT AS SHOWN, ABUT PAGE EDGES, TAPE ON BACK, DO NOT OVERLAP

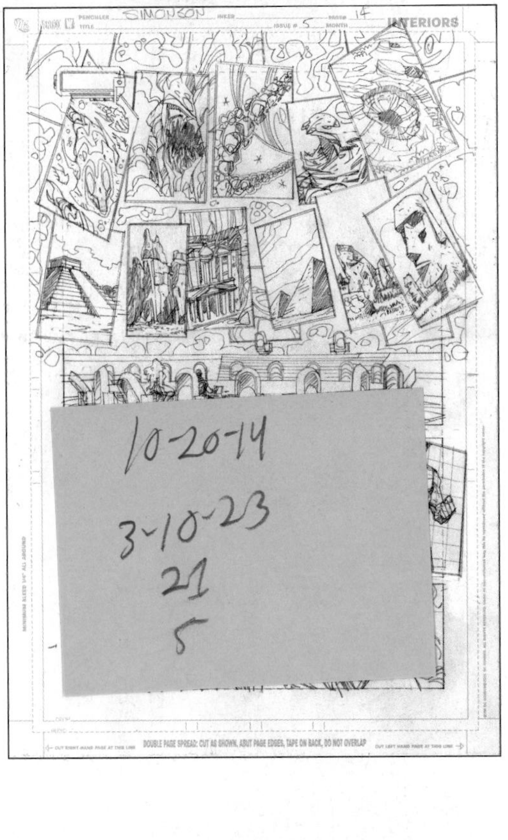
SIMONSON
INTERIORS
10-20-14
3-10-23
21
5
DOUBLE PAGE SPREAD: CUT AS SHOWN, ABUT PAGE EDGES, TAPE ON BACK, DO NOT OVERLAP

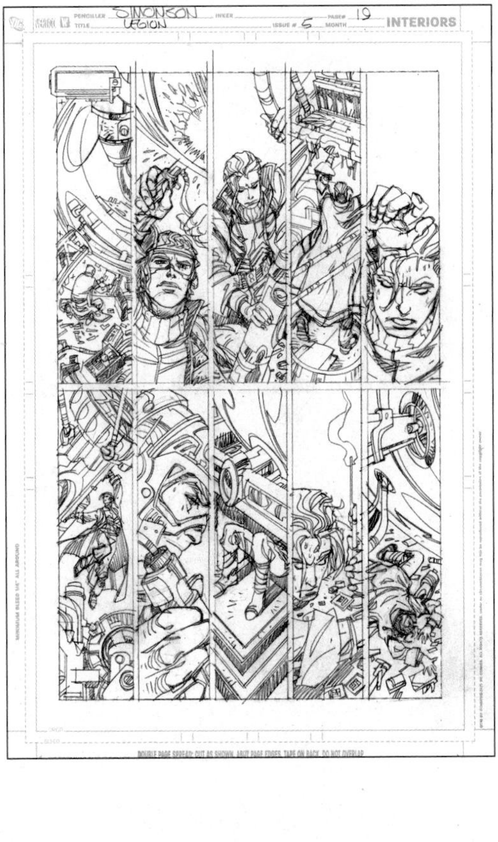
SIMONSON
LEGION
INTERIORS
DOUBLE PAGE SPREAD: CUT AS SHOWN, ABUT PAGE EDGES, TAPE ON BACK, DO NOT OVERLAP

MON-EL AND GLORITH SKETCHES BY JIM LEE HARMONIA COLOR SKETCH BY FRANCIS PORTELA

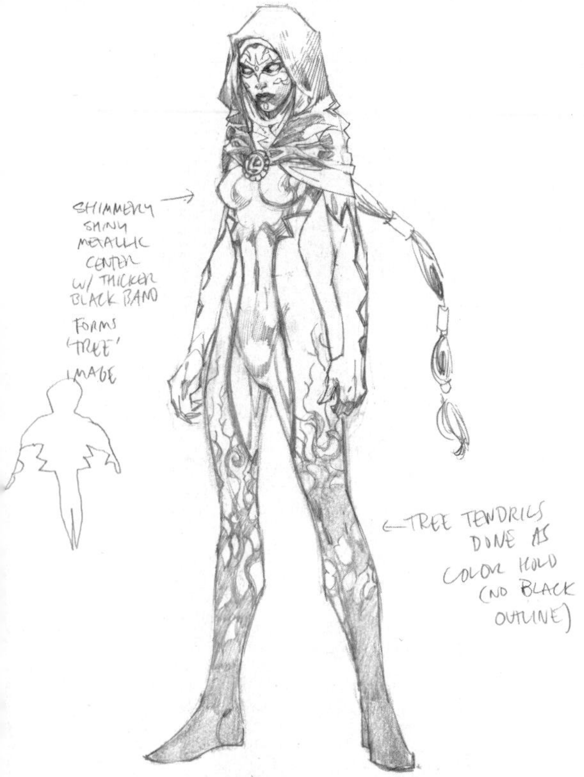
SHIMMERY
SHINY
METALLIC
CENTER
W/ THICKER
BLACK BAND
FORMS
'TREE'
IMAGE
TREE TENDRILS
DONE AS
COLOR HOLD
(NO BLACK
OUTLINE)

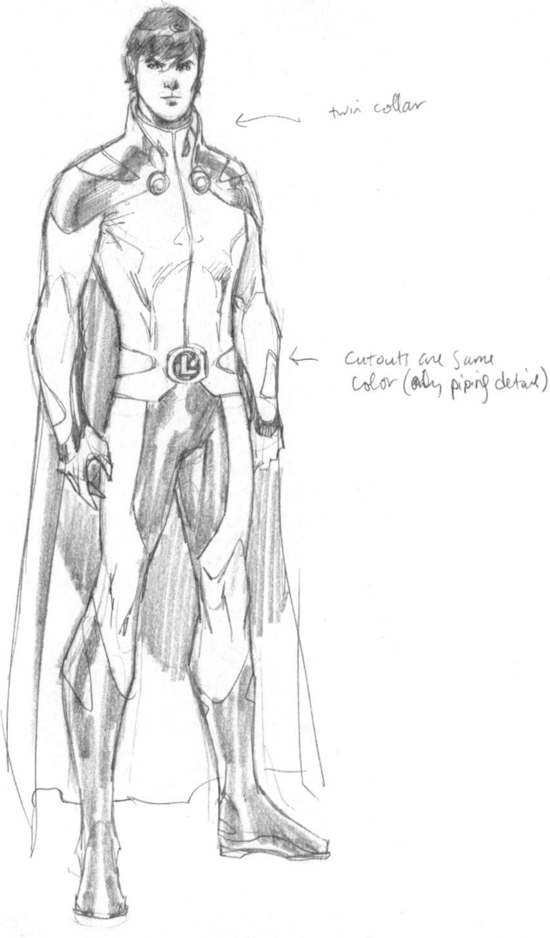
twin collar
cutouts are same
color (only piping detail)

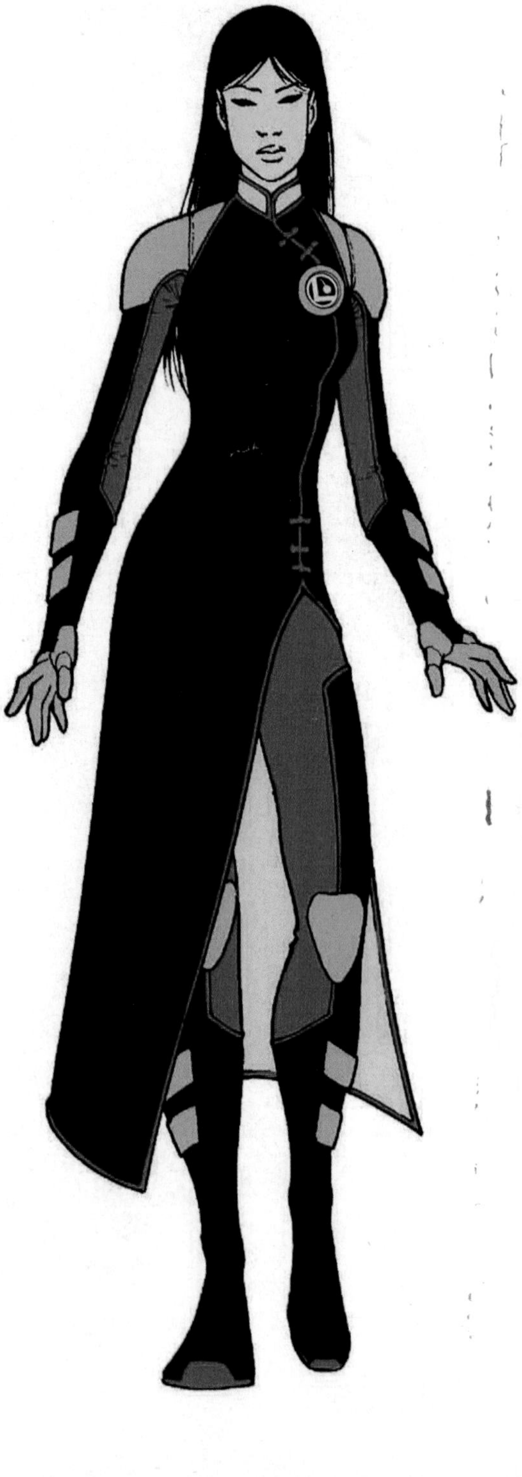

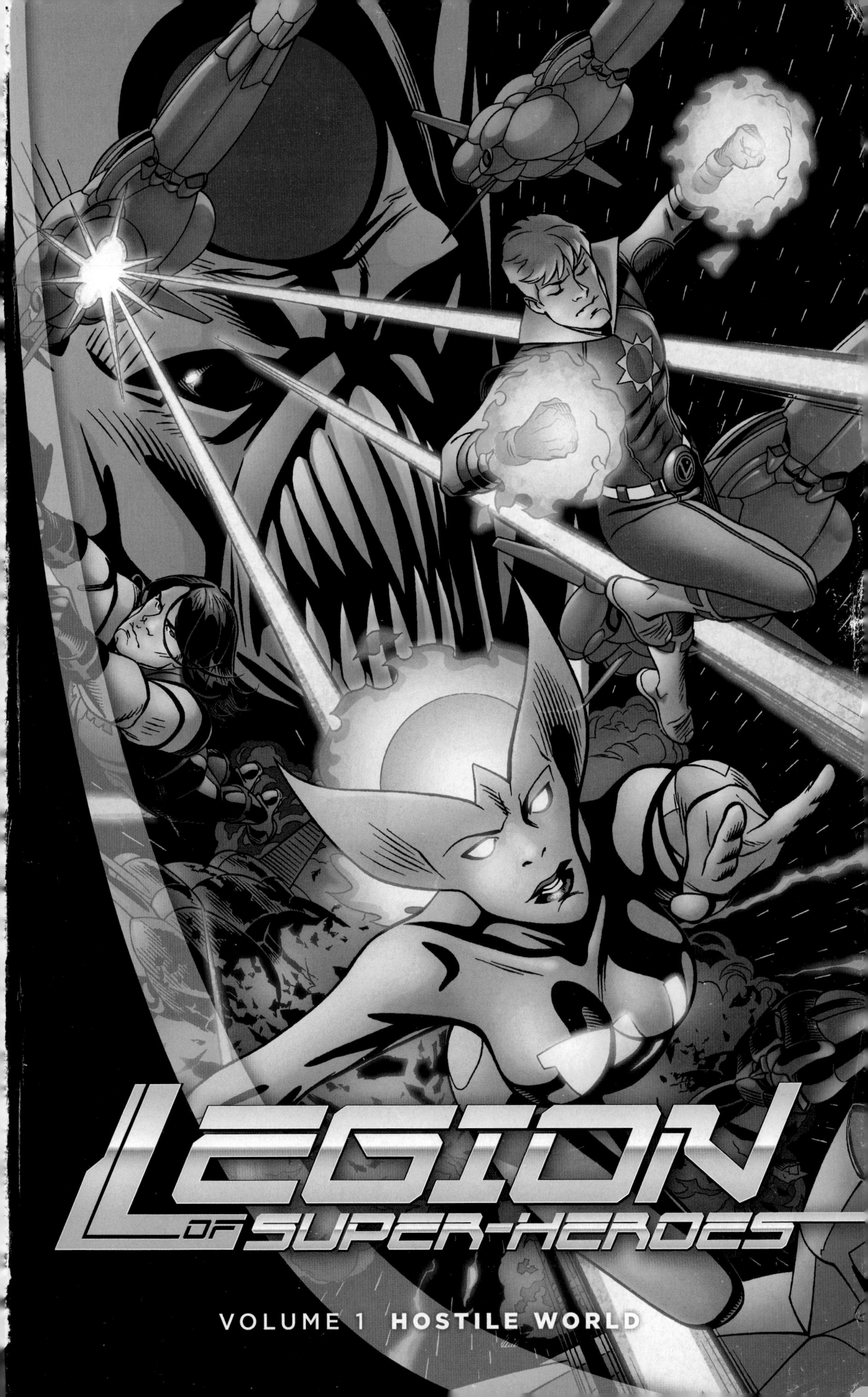
LEGION OF SUPER-HEROES
VOLUME 1 HOSTILE WORLD

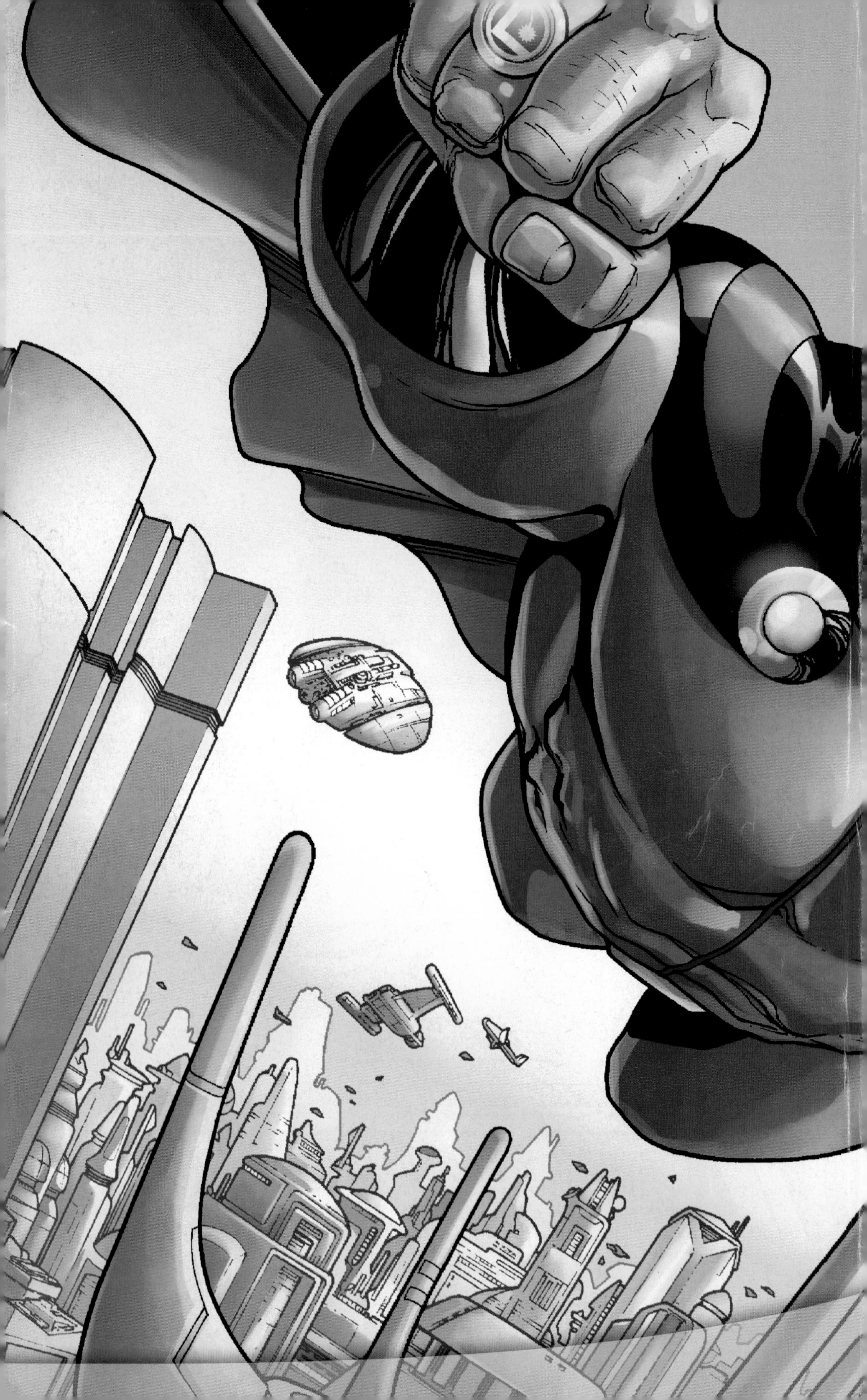